D1012935

BRITISH SOCIAL POLICY, 1914-1939

BRITISH SOCIAL POLICY
1914-1939

Bentley B. Gilbert

CORNELL UNIVERSITY PRESS

ITHACA, NEW YORK

First published 1970

International Standard Book Number 0-8014-0578-5
Library of Congress Catalog Card Number 78-119702

Printed in Great Britain

Contents

Preface

This book is not precisely a second volume of the *Evolution of National Insurance in Great Britain*. Rather it is a following study of somewhat different scope upon the same general topic—the development of welfare policy. Over long periods the politics of social reform do not lend themselves to neat, encapsulated, uniform description. There are times of action and of talk, of innovation and reaction. A history of legislation, for example, appropriate for the decade before the First World War would miss much that was of political significance in the twenties and thirties when the nation's leaders were struggling to come to terms not with the political question of how to supersede the Poor Law, but with a single overpowering economic fact, massive unemployment. The inter-war decades were not a period of legislative innovation but a time of adjustment, with to be sure some extension, of legislation worked out in another era for a different set of circumstances. Furthermore, the major political parties were no longer drawn essentially from the same economic and social classes, nor dominated by men holding similar beliefs about the fundamental nature of the society in which they lived. The homogeneity of British politics had disappeared and with it had gone the certainty that whichever party was in power things would not change very much.

This study, then, is about the search for a new political consensus on what had become a central issue of parliamentary contest, social policy. Essentially, its argument is that in the two decades between the wars, while labouring under a singular and huge economic handicap, Britain's political leaders finally agreed, almost unconsciously, that society in some way or another would have to find a means to support all its citizens at a decent level of civilized life—in effect the national minimum. This understanding, whether or not publicly accepted, was a private political consensus by the end of the 1930s.

Hence, 1939 provides a reasonable terminal date. The social planning that occurred during the Second World War was not the out-growth of national attempts to find a social policy. Rather it was the reflection of the conviction at which the nation had already arrived. The Beveridge Report and the White Papers on National Insurance and the National Health Service, children's allowances, and the announcement of a policy for full employment were all products of wartime experience. But, more important, they represented attempts to find solutions to problems of peace. The questions they raised turned on matters of administration, not on matters of principle. The principle had already been agreed upon. Out of the twenties and thirties a commitment had evolved. The destruction of wealth between 1939 and 1945 made action more immediately necessary, but the war itself did not bring the welfare state.

There are many issues which could be defined as social politics that are left out of this book—local authority activity on behalf of maternity and child welfare for instance, the whole field of public health, in the sense of preventative medicine, and the story of educational policy. These topics, and others, have been omitted not because they were unimportant for public welfare, but simply, as in the case of maternity and child welfare, they were not a matter of high politics, or, as in education after the evisceration of the Fisher Act, there is little to write about. When the political leaders of both major parties are unable to redeem a 20-year-old promise to increase the school leaving age beyond 14, a nation can hardly be said to have a deep concern with public education.

In any case the political focus was elsewhere. Public men, who before the First World War might have thought that the promotion of the health of children and the maintenance of the aged were useful, if narrow, avenues to social justice, were faced after the conflict not with the request for charity for the helpless, but with an intractable demand for work or maintenance from society's most dangerous and volatile element, the unemployed adult male. Beside the threat of revolution, nothing else was important.

I have been helped in the writing of the book by a number of people whose names should appear here ahead of my own. For information and personal experiences in the Ministry of Labour and the Ministry of Health, I must thank Sir John Hawton and Mr Henry W. Stockman. Particularly I must name Sir John Walley, not only for much helpful and otherwise unobtainable information about the Ministry of Labour, but for his suggestions on lines of investigation. Lastly I should express my obligation again to Mr Ernest Wybrow of the Ministry of Social Security library whose expert bibliographical knowledge and understanding of the business of industrial insurance from his own work in the industry has provided this historian with the rare privilege of a glimpse of what things were really like.

For this book, as for the previous one in the series, I must acknowledge the financial support over the past eight years of The National Library of Medicine which has made possible extended stays in the United Kingdom, travel in this country, and perhaps most valuable of all, secretarial and research assistance.

This volume never would have appeared without the editorial and research assistance of Ellen MacVeagh, Barbara Farr and Fredrica Harris, and the help of Doris Racich who did much of the typing. Finally, for continual reminders to get on with it, I thank my editor at B. T. Batsford, Peter Kemmis Betty, whose criticism and patience, cajolery and threats, have been an unvarying source of inspiration.

Bentley B. Gilbert

The University of Illinois at Chicago Circle   9 January, 1970

1 The war and the peace

Perhaps historians ought not to attempt to describe the effect of the First World War upon the people of Great Britain. The magnitude of the struggle, its appalling cost in lives and wealth, and, most important, its incalculable disruption of the careers and aspirations of 40 million individuals, the British nation, confound both language and scholarship. What happened to the United Kingdom between 5 August 1914 and 11 November 1918 can scarcely be reported let alone assessed and explained. A world died and a new one was born in slightly more than four years. The most surprising thing was not that so much was lost but that anyone had anything left worth keeping.

Yet after having admitted the difficulty of the task, after having asserted the near-impossibility of making sense of it, the historian obviously can not ignore the war. Although he might feel that British history would have been simpler to explain had it not occurred, the great war remains a central fact of the twentieth century and he must deal with it as best he can. Fortunately, even though the total impact of the war may be incomprehensible, certain results of the conflict are easy enough to identify. For the historian of social and economic institutions, the war appears to be at once a catalyst for reform and an obstacle to change. On one hand the war demonstrated the utility of government activity in the fields of social and economic control and hence of the feasibility of other experiments in this direction in peace. On the other hand, the huge personal and economic wastage occasioned by the conflict made dearer to many of the nation's leaders the remaining institutions and usages of the prewar world, and so reinforced conservatism. Thus there was no unanimity in England about how the nation should be rebuilt. In the twenties nostalgia for Edwardianism tended to obscure the grievous social injustice of those days, while the political insecurity of the times made demands for moderate social reform seem revolutionary.

Hence war does not inevitably produce social change. War destroys, and necessitates rebuilding. But the shape that reconstruction should take, certainly after the First World War, may have been determined more by what was remembered of the past than by what was hoped for in the future. The reconstruction plans of Lloyd George's Coalition Government were mostly continuations and expansions of welfare institutions established, or projected, before the war. In this sense his reform programme was itself essentially traditional and nostalgic; in this sense also, as this study intends to show, it was inappropriate for the nation that emerged from the conflict. Lloyd George was a conservative reformer and the postwar solutions of his administration were answers to prewar questions.

The war and the fall of Asquith

Of all the things to be said about Britain's lack of preparation for the First World War perhaps the most important is the total lack of comprehension on the part of both the leaders of the Government and the population at large of the effect that the struggle would have upon the nation. Much of this was the result of the century of relative peace Britain had enjoyed since the Napoleonic Wars and of the security and sense of isolation provided by the navy. No less important were the popular assumptions, again shared by the best-informed, that the very factors that made Britain great and powerful, her financial strength and pre-eminence in world trade, precluded a long conflict. More than ever, it was assumed, war would be a matter of the collision of professional armies. The very complexities of military science and technology would make impossible the use of amateur soldiers. Modern developments in transportation and the skill of military planners would ensure rapid mobilization of forces and the quick carrying out of previously planned operations. The victor in the first great battles would win the war. The nation whose armies were defeated would have to surrender immediately. These speculations all seemed to be confirmed by the precedent of the Franco-Prussian War. Finally, should military victory somehow elude either side, the vast cost of modern weapons and the interlocking and interdependent nature of finance and commerce would soon force a peace through the disruption of domestic economies and national bankruptcy.[1]

Britain therefore entered the First World War with the expectation that the conflict would be short. The first great change in the public mood lay in the transition from the expectation that the war would come to an end any minute to the feeling that it would never end. The excitement of 1914 gave way to confusion and exasperation in 1915 and finally to despair and anger in 1916.

If there is a discernible trend, perhaps it can be defined as a gradual disintegration of confidence in the Government. In August 1914, the British expeditionary force—'man for man the best trained and

---

[1] An example of this point of view was the unemployment relief fund established under the patronage of the Queen and the Prince of Wales immediately after the outbreak of the war to aid those who were expected to be economically distressed shortly. Little of the £3 million quickly collected was ever used of course, and most of the sum eventually went to the Red Cross.

equipped army in the world'—had crossed the channel without incident, as one expected of the Royal Navy, and had fought with notable gallantry on the left of the French Army before the Battle of the Marne. The appointment of Lord Kitchener as Secretary of State for War reinforced the seriousness of Britain's determination. The nation had given what it could. It had fulfilled its commitments. As the reports of German atrocities in Belgium reassured Englishmen of the righteousness of their decision to enter the war, so the stopping of the German drive on the Marne seemed to assure that the right would triumph. Although Kitchener himself had warned that the war would be a long one and had announced that Britain ought to raise an army of 70 divisions enlisted for at least three years' service, many in the first month expected the war to be over by Christmas. However, well before the end of the year it had become clear that this would not be the case and by early 1915, with multiplying reports flowing in from abroad of mismanagement, lack of planning and postponed decisions, criticism of the national leadership began to mount. The result on 25 May 1915 was the end of the last independent Liberal administration in British history and the formation of a coalition of the Liberal, Conservative and Labour parties, still headed, to be sure, by Prime Minister Herbert Asquith, but with a number of the more conspicuous and powerful Government posts now in the hands of the Conservatives. One of the most important changes at this time was the creation of a Ministry of Munitions of War which was put in the charge of the man who was at this time perhaps the most controversial figure in British politics—David Lloyd George.

In many ways his appointment at the Ministry of Munitions marks the opening of a new phase in Lloyd George's career. Although for nearly a decade he had been one of the most powerful men in the Government, he had been regarded principally as a leader of the radical wing of the Liberal party. There was always something of the partisan or the insurgent about him. Even though he had been Chancellor of the Exchequer he had not been a member of the real inner circle of the Liberal leadership. But between May 1915 and December 1916, with the Government posts divided among other major parties, with Asquith's confidante R. B. Haldane excluded from the Government by the Conservatives and Edward Grey failing in health, with a number of junior Liberals discontented as a result of enforced resignations to make way for men of other parties, and with continuing charges of indecisiveness and lack of leadership, Asquith's administration grew continually weaker. But, even though the prestige of the Government as a whole declined, Lloyd George's position improved. At the Ministry of Munitions he was able to keep himself highly visible and to build a personal position even though politics were officially adjourned.

Lloyd George made the Ministry of Munitions into a species of general department for domestic industrial affairs. In the name of producing munitions for war, he concerned himself not only with industrial arbitration but with the health, feeding, and housing of munitions workers and with problems of entertainment, morale, and indeed with the restriction of the hours of sale of alcoholic beverages. More important, at the Munitions Lloyd George made himself respectable. Here he and the English business and financial community became acquainted. He came to appreciate imagination and energy of businessmen, qualities he often felt were lacking in the civil service. And they, on the other hand, came to realize that the reputed destroyer of the British economic system might well yet become the saviour of the nation and the organizer of victory.[1]

For Britain 1916 was a year of disillusion and disaster. The spring saw the Easter Rebellion in Dublin and the passage of the Conscription Act after months of halfhearted experiments by which the Government had hoped to avert this final conclusion. Finally in July came the supreme trial when Kitchener's new army was thrown into battle on the Somme, an effort which tailed off in November after hideous losses. The end of the Somme offensive brought the nadir of Britain's will to fight, the time when the Government at last lost its power of command, when executive authority appeared to be no longer able to deflect the course of events and when the war itself seemed to acquire an aimless but irresistible momentum of its own so that men could neither guide it nor bring it to an end.[2] In the midst of this crisis, to a large extent as the result of it, David Lloyd George became Prime Minister. His task was to revive flagging national energies by giving the war a meaning and peace some significance other than the end of fighting. The old exaltation of 1914 was dead as were the original reasons for entering the conflict—the integrity of Belgium and the promises to France. Lloyd George understood intuitively, as he understood many things, that the revival of national energy which victory demanded would have to be purchased. The cry for peace at any price could be countered only by the argument that the rewards for sacrifice were greater.

Thus in the two years between December 1916 and December 1918

[1] Lord Beaverbrook suggests that Lloyd George's attempts to induce the Government to nationalize the liquor trade during 1915 led to conversations with Conservatives that helped heal the old wounds of the 1909 budget and Home Rule and so 'smoothed the way towards Coalition'. Lord Beaverbrook, *Politicians and the War, 1914–16* (London, 1928), 69–70.

[2] For a classic description of the wartime destruction of social values see: C. F. G. Masterman, *England After War* (London, 1922).

Lloyd George presided over a national revival. But while lending his energy, imagination and enthusiasm to spur the strictly military effort, the new Prime Minister began building for the British nation a framework of promises for peace. This programme of national reconstruction included much that inevitably could be counted simply as extensions of the prewar New Liberalism. But it implied more: there was also a promise to the ordinary citizen that peace would bring not only a return of the old ways, but a new more spacious and more rewarding life in a nation fit for heroes to live in. The men who had bought national security at the risk of their lives in war were given to understand that they would receive personal security in peace.

Reconstruction or revolution

Programmes and promises of programmes for reconstruction were, as has already been asserted, a central theme of Coalition ministry propaganda in its two years' tenure before the General Election of 1918. For the immediate future, Lloyd George assured the nation, nothing would be left undone for the welfare of the returning soldier. Again and again in speeches, he compared the situation after the Napoleonic Wars with what would be done after the present conflict. 'Reaction versus reconstruction' appeared as a continuing jingle in his speeches. To this end, a Ministry of Pensions and a Ministry of Labour were created at the time of the formation of the Lloyd George Coalition, both under Labour party ministers. On a broader scale Lloyd George took time in March 1917 to promise a group of Labour party leaders, in a widely quoted but informal speech, that while nothing would be done to detract from Labour's progress before the war, the goal of peace was the rebuilding of the nation. 'There is no doubt at all,' he said,

> that the present war ... presents an opportunity for reconstruction of industrial and economic conditions of this country such as has never been presented in the life of, probably, the world. The whole state of society is more or less molten and you can stamp upon that molten mass almost anything so long as you do it with firmness and determination. ... I firmly believe that what is known as the after the war settlement is the settlement that will direct the destinies of all classes for some generations to come. The country will be prepared for bigger things immediately after the war than it will be when it begins to resume the normal sort of clash of self-interests which always comes with the ordinary work-a-day business affairs and concerns of the world. I believe the country will be in a more enthusiastic mood, in a more exalted mood for the time being—in a

greater mood for doing big things; and unless the opportunity is seized immediately after the war, I believe it will pass away. . . .

I hope that every class will not be hankering back to prewar conditions. I just drop that as a hint but I hope the working class will not be the class that will set such an example, because if every class insists upon getting back to prewar conditions, then God help this country! I say so in all solemnity.[1]

In many ways the speech of 6 March, although it contained little in the way of concrete proposals, marked the beginning of the campaign for postwar reconstruction. The nation, particularly the working class, was invited to think in large terms, to forget past injuries and past wrongs, even past victories, and to plan for a better world for all. Nevertheless, even before his speech to the Labour party deputation, Lloyd George had established what might have been the most significant agency in his programme of rebuilding the nation. On 15 February 1917 a War Cabinet minute established again the Reconstruction Committee first appointed by Asquith on 18 March 1916 with himself as chairman. As with many other plans of the Asquith government, the first Reconstruction Committee had done little; in the nine months of its existence it held only six meetings. Nor did the second committee, under the chairmanship of Edwin Montagu, accomplish much more. But, on the other hand, it became the permanent or sponsoring agency of seven subcommittees which were more active. Most important of these, coming into existence in the summer of 1917 just at the time the Reconstruction Committee evolved into the Ministry of Reconstruction, was the Local Government Committee under Donald MacLean (usually styled the 'MacLean Committee').[2]

The creation of a Ministry of Reconstruction, and appointment to it of Christopher Addison, Lloyd George's most loyal, but perhaps not his most valuable, lieutenant, on 17 July 1917 demonstrates perfectly both the power and weakness of the Prime Minister's position in the two years after he took office and before the election of December 1918. On one hand, Addison was one of the few Liberal office-holders, certainly almost the only radical, who had remained consistently loyal to the Welshman after the departure of Asquith and his followers. Many junior Liberals had been dropped in the formation of the first coalition in May 1915 and the most important senior Liberals, Grey, McKenna and Simon, who had survived this reconstruction, had remained loyal to Asquith. Thus Addison, who himself had succeeded

[1] M. B. Hammond, *British Labour Conditions and Legislation During the War* (London, 1919), 270–1. See also: *The Times*, 7 March 1917.

[2] The MacLean Committee signed its report on 19 December 1917. Specifically it was charged with considering 'the steps to be taken to secure the better co-ordination of Public Assistance in England and Wales'. See Chapter 3.

to the Ministry of Munitions on 10 December 1916 received the patronage of the few domestic offices available to the Liberals and accordingly presided over the rather unconventional, but successful, appointments of David Alfred Thomas, Baron Rhondda, to the Local Government Board and H. A. L. Fisher to the Presidency of the Board of Education.[1]

Then, in the summer of 1917, with British domestic politics and social affairs moving steadily toward a new period of crisis, Lloyd George proposed to remove Addison from the Ministry of Munitions and place him in a conspicuous yet weak position, the newly created Ministry of Reconstruction. The Prime Minister's motives for this are unclear. However, because Addison would become a central figure in much of the social planning of the Lloyd George period and because the Ministry of Reconstruction, whatever its prestige among politicians and civil servants, was supposed to provide public evidence of Government optimism and foresightedness about the conditions of peace, the evidence surrounding the Prime Minister's decision deserves some examination. Certainly for a national leader with the essentially experimental or empirical mind of Lloyd George, a Ministry of Reconstruction could do no harm. As a part of the general programme for building a better Britain, it would presumably improve the Government's stature with social reformers, working class or intellectual. Lloyd George, even in the midst of a desperate war, was never willing to admit that any man cared more than he for the welfare of the people.

In addition even a slightly bogus ministry, in the summer of 1917, would solve several practical, and important, political problems. The Labour establishment that had for so long, if unenthusiastically, supported Lloyd George was discontented with Christopher Addison as Minister of Munitions. Addison had antagonized several powerful trade unions, notably the Amalgamated Society of Engineers.[2] Thus removing Addison from the Ministry of Munitions may have been necessary. But there was a more pressing political reason. Lloyd George desired to bring Winston Churchill into the Government. Churchill was one of the few prewar Liberal frontbenchers still loyal to the Welshman.

---

[1] For a discussion of the circumstances surrounding these appointments see: Newman Diaries, III, MS entry, 9 December 1916. See also: Christopher Addison, *Four and a Half Years* (London, 1934), I, 278.

[2] A number of civil servants, interviewed after the Second World War, who had personal experience in the Ministry of Reconstruction, agreed that Addison was 'not a good administrator', Paul Barton Johnson, 'Post-war Planning in Britain, 1916–19, The Committees and Ministry of Reconstruction' (unpublished Ph.D. dissertation), University of Chicago (August 1964), 115–16. Beatrice Webb noted in her diary on 18 July 1917, the day after Addison's appointment, that 'Addison had failed at Munitions'. Margaret I. Cole, ed., *Beatrice Webb's Diaries, 1912–24* (London, 1952), 91.

Churchill disliked Asquith whom he felt had inadequately supported him in 1915. He had still, although would not for long, a reputation as a radical. He was, as the world knew, a dynamic speaker and a first-class administrator. And yet he had been in the political wilderness since the autumn of 1915.

Unfortunately, he was hated by the Tories—who indeed had made his removal from the Admiralty a precondition of the coalition of May 1915—and the Tories held nearly every major ministry of state. The displacement of a member of that party for a Liberal, particularly Churchill, would have caused an uproar. The Ministry of Munitions was nearly the only office of adequate importance held by a Liberal. Hence, on 16 July 1917, Churchill was offered the Ministry of Munitions. Addison does not appear to have known that a change was in store for him until afterwards.[1]

Addison commented on the circumstances of his appointment to Re-construction slightly over three years later, on 3 March 1920, when the Prime Minister asked him to give up the Ministry of Health and become a political adviser 'to help strengthen the Government'. Addison replied that he had done this kind of thing at the Ministry of Reconstruction. That Ministry had been weak, practically without portfolio, as was now proposed. This, said Addison, was 'one of the bitterest experiences a man could have'. It was put about and believed, said Addison, that he had only been given the job because 'it enabled you to find a job for a friend who had been a failure elsewhere'. He would rather sweep crossings, said Addison, than repeat such an experience.[2]

The creation of the Ministry of Reconstruction and Addison's appointment as its head may have deserved the parliamentary criticism it received. But the ideal of a national agency for postwar planning was more than 'sheer window dressing' as it had been termed.[3]

---

[1] Addison's correspondence with Lloyd George shows that he was reluctant to leave Munitions and that he did not yet know the circumstances of his replacement. Addison to Lloyd George, 17 July 1917, L.G. Papers, F/1/3/27. Addison, *Four and a Half Years*, II, 411–15. Addison's diary is untrustworthy on this point as occasionally it is elsewhere. Strangely, Addison says that Lloyd George asked him secretly on 17 July to leave Munitions although in fact both Churchill's and Addison's appointments appeared in *The Times* on that day, presumably in the morning. R. J. Minney, with customary shoddy craftsmanship, repeats this story uncritically. R. F. Minney, *Viscount Addison: Leader of the Lords* (London, 1958), 161.
[2] Addison to Lloyd George, 3 March 1920, L.G. Papers, F/1/6/4.
[3] Johnson, 'Reconstruction', 115–16. Report of a personal interview with Sir Horace Wilson in March 1953. Characteristically Lloyd George forgot to abolish the old Reconstruction Committee, which remained in existence until Addison reminded him that it was no longer necessary now that a Minister of Reconstruction had been appointed. Addison to Lloyd George, 7 August 1917, L.G. Papers, F/1/4/2.

Clearly the Prime Minister hoped to provide a job for an important and necessary political friend and to acquire Winston Churchill's unquestionable debating power on the Government front bench, but the Ministry of Reconstruction was intended also to write the constitution of the new Liberal party (a better style might have been the 'Party of the New Liberalism'). The Ministry was to be a species of government-supported idea-factory for a postwar party that would evolve under the leadership of Lloyd George. Addison, with his unimpeachable radical credentials and his intense loyalty to the Prime Minister, was the ideal person to be its chief. Each Monday, he breakfasted with the Prime Minister and regularly attended meetings in the Whip's office at 12 Downing Street. Only a fully fledged radical programme, the Prime Minister believed, such as he and Winston Churchill had been pressing on the Liberal party since 1908, could recover the working-class voter from the Labour party. Liberalism would restore itself as the spokesman of the underprivileged, and would seek to establish social and economic equality as so long it had fought for political equality.[1]

The need personally to recapture and revive the Liberal party represented only one of Lloyd George's goals. A second, of perhaps more immediate importance in 1917, was the aim of sweeping away the residue of pacifism and war weariness that threatened to suffocate Britain's military effort. The causes of the unrest were many and derived from various sources, by no means all domestic, nor was the discontent confined to Britain alone. Basic in all nations were the military disasters of 1916 and the subsequent disillusionment about the war. Abroad this unhappiness had its most obvious result in the mutinies that broke out in the French army in the first days of May 1917 and spread rapidly so that a month later, according to Paul Panlevé, the French Minister of War, there were only two divisions between Soissons and Paris that were absolutely reliable.[2] Although the British were not told of the mutinies officially until 2 June, the Government had received unofficial reports of instances of indiscipline as early as 12 May, and fear that similar outbreaks could occur in the British army were understandable.

Particularly frightening was the fact that the discontent both at home and abroad had not only pacifist but socialist and revolutionary overtones. The same month that brought mutinies in France saw a widespread series of unofficial strikes in Britain, principally against the

---

[1] On Addison's political activity while at the Ministry of Reconstruction see: Addison, *Four and a Half Years*, II, 459, 553.
[2] On the mutinies see: Bentley B. Gilbert and Paul Bernard, 'The French Army Mutinies of 1917', *The Historian*, XXII (November 1959), 24–41.

dilution of labour but also against the growing economic dislocation and hardship caused by the war.[1]

Coupled with industrial violence and anger was the growth of socialist pacifism within Labour party ranks. This erupted in June in a large working-man's conference at Leeds, addressed by both Arthur Henderson and Ramsey MacDonald (Henderson at that time was a member of the War Cabinet), which demanded the formation of soldiers' and workers' councils in Britain. Meanwhile, earlier in the year, the Dutch and Scandinavian sections of the old International Socialist Bureau had issued a call for an international socialist conference to meet in Stockholm to make possible direct communication among representatives of the warring powers. This was followed on 10 August 1917 by a Labour party resolution endorsing British representation at the conference. Although the effect of this resolution was considerably weakened by widespread attacks on pacifist party leaders from within the trade union movement itself, by the declaration of the Sailors' and Firemen's Union to the effect that seamen would decline to transport representatives to Stockholm, and finally, when the resolution came up a second time on 21 August, by its repassage with a much reduced majority, the Government was seriously concerned. Matters became worse when Arthur Henderson returned from Russia where he had been sent in June soon after the Leeds meeting to infuse some vigour into that country's declining war effort. Instead he returned convinced himself that a compromise peace was necessary immediately and had addressed the Labour party conference in support of the Stockholm resolution. He was formally rebuked by the Cabinet without being allowed to state his case and thus virtually ordered to resign, which he did on 11 August. Meanwhile, the Government itself, apparently under pressure from France which since the first announcements of the conference in the spring had declined to allow its citizens to attend, refused to issue passports to any prospective British delegates.[2]

It is, of course, important to note that British unrest owed little to the example of Russia. The abdication of Czar Nicholas II on 15 March 1917 had been welcomed in Allied countries who looked forward to a resurgence of Russian national enthusiasm for the war in the tradition of the declaration of the French Republic in 1792. Indeed the Western Powers made special efforts in the next few months to rush military equipment to the newly formed Provisional Govern-

---

[1] On the causes of industrial unrest in spring 1917, see: Hammond, *British Labour Conditions*, 243–62.

[2] The French decision to refuse passports for the Stockholm conference figured repeatedly in the manifestos of the military units engaged in the mutinies during May and June.

ment (which supplies would become a considerable embarrassment with the Russian surrender) and it was not until the clear failure of the Brusiloff offensive in July that the British public became aware of the failing strength of their eastern ally. In effect, Britain's leaders regarded, no doubt rightly, the demands for peace by certain groups in Russia as symptoms of a general malaise in which Britain shared. Hence when the general unhealthiness developed into the fever of Bolshevism the lesson for Britain was frightening. The preliminary symptoms were present at home. Might not the result be the same?

Clearly the Government took seriously the outbreak of strikes in Britain in the spring of 1917 and the general growing discontent among the British working class—unfocussed distrust manifesting lack of confidence in Government promises or in the promises of trade union officials. On 12 June 1917 Lloyd George appointed eight commissions to 'enquire into and report upon industrial unrest and to make recommendations to the Government at the earliest practicable date ...'. The commissions worked rapidly and provided the Cabinet with advance copies of their reports within five weeks, by 17 July. These documents gave endless detailed examples of the widespread working-class unhappiness that was becoming all too familiar. Particularly important were high prices, especially of food, restrictions of personal freedom, lack of housing, restrictions on liquor and dilution of labour. Most resentful of all were highly skilled workers, tool- and die-makers or gauge-makers, who had been well established before the war with permanent employment and high wage rates. These aristocrats of labour now found themselves falling behind less skilled workers frequently working at piece rates who had entered employment since the war.[1]

The Labour party resolutions on the Stockholm conference, resulting in Arthur Henderson's expulsion from the Cabinet, the pressure from the armed services for 250,000 more men which caused serious resistance in the skilled trades, the growing appearance, although not the reality, of food shortages, and above all, by September, the obvious decline in Russian fighting power, reinforced the nervousness that had been apparent among the upper classes since the beginning of the year. On 25 September *The Times* began a series entitled 'A Ferment of Revolution' and accompanied the first articles with a leader warning Englishmen of the danger of revolution: 'The central fact is that behind the meaningless and stupid terms "labour unrest" lies a conscious revolutionary movement which aims at the complete overthrow of the existing economic and social order not in some uncertain future but here and now.'

[1] For a discussion of this investigation see: Hammond, *British Labour Conditions*, 243–62.

Generally the articles attempted to define the two new classes into which Britain had become divided—the 'two nations' of the twentieth century. One class included the propertied classes, the professions, the agricultural interests and unorganized wage earners. The second included organized labour and everyone connected with it; there were about four million families in each class. One nation represented 'old England'. The other had pretty nearly cast off Government authority.[1]

Less than a month later on 7 November 1917 came the Bolshevik seizure of power in Petrograd, which the Lenin Government followed immediately by a series of peace offers to the Central Powers, and on 29 November the *Daily Telegraph* published Lord Lansdowne's famous letter proposing a compromise peace. None of these events could be safely ignored. They brought to a climax, as it were, the readjustment of the British attitude toward the war which had begun the year before with Lloyd George's assumption of power.[2]

Yet, on the other hand, the situation was not without advantages. If the defection of Russia represented a military loss, it also freed the Allies from embarrassing diplomatic obligations (which the Bolsheviks announced to the world by the publication in December of a number of secret treaties with the Western Allies). Lord Lansdowne's letter, calling as it did for a restatement of Allied war aims, gave the Government an excuse for exactly the kind of statement which could counteract the Russian diplomacy and provide the idealism that the military effort needed. There were other motives also for such a statement. The Cabinet had been in touch, secretly, with Austrian envoys who were attempting to elicit some kind of terms upon which the Dual Monarchy could leave the war. At almost the same time, at the end of December, a conference called jointly by the Labour party and the Trades Union Congress executive agreed by an overwhelming majority

[1] *The Times*, 25, 26 September 1917. The articles were by Edward Vernon Arnold, Professor of Latin, University College, Bangor, who sent the Cabinet a most alarmist memorandum denouncing the Central Labour College and the Workers' Educational Association, among others. Thomas Jones, Deputy Secretary to the War Cabinet, had told the Webbs at lunch on 4 October that the Cabinet was much perturbed at 'rumours of revolutionary feeling among the working class'. Cole, ed., *Webb Diaries, 1912–24*, 26–97, diary entry 5 October 1917.

[2] Typical of the communications the Cabinet was receiving in December a memorandum from George Young who had organized the Admiralty intelligence in 1915, telling of a long talk the previous night with the Labour intellectual who was very gloomy. 'He thought the general outlook, social and industrial after the war was very dark.' The working class was getting power but was not yet capable of exercising it. There was too much apathy. The Government had handled the Russian revolution badly. George Young to Lloyd George, n.d. (covering letter by Christopher Addison dated 15 December 1917), L. G. Papers, F/1/4/5.

to press for a humanitarian and just, rather than a victor's, peace with Germany.

The proceedings of the Labour Conference attracted widespread attention, particularly among the Liberals, and the Government took action almost immediately. On 29 December, the evening that the resolutions were adopted, Lloyd George agreed to make a statement on war aims. A week later, on 5 January 1918, at a Labour meeting at Caxton Hall, he announced the British programme for peace, which not only had been confirmed by the United Kingdom and Dominion Cabinets but discussed also with the Asquith Liberals. The Prime Minister's statement on war aims generally laid down the line that would be taken by American President Woodrow Wilson's fourteen points three days later. But whereas Wilson addressed himself to the world at large, and cast himself perhaps too selfconsciously in the role of a leader of humanity, the British Prime Minister dealt with practical political problems at home. He called for compromise, for justice, for the sanctity of treaties, for self-determination, and for international organization to prevent war. He stood for the rehabilitation of Belgium and the rectification of the wrong done France in 1871. But generally he was wary of specific promises. By mingling emotion and caution while specifically repudiating punishment of Germany, the speech struck precisely the right note and so undermined the programmes of British pacifists without doing anything to discourage enthusiasts for a complete victory. Its importance for this study lies in the fact that it matched in external affairs the Government's reconstruction promises in domestic affairs. Together the two programmes constituted Lloyd George's intended platform for the election of December 1918 — reconciliation and reconstruction. The tragedy for the future was that in December 1918 Lloyd George would allow popular pressure to drive him from a compromise peace precisely as popular pressure had forced him to that position a year earlier. In both cases the force to which he yielded was the fear of working-class unrest.

The politics of the Coupon Election

During the next seven or eight months, evidences of working-class discontent diminished. No doubt part of this was the result of the endless promises of reconstruction at home and compromise abroad. Unquestionably also, the enormous intensification of the war that began on 21 March 1918 with the great German peace offensive diverted everyone's attention away from home affairs. Finally, perhaps most important of all, was the fact that the Office of Food Controls, under

Lord Rhondda, at last became effective in slowing the rise in the price of food.[1]

During the winter and spring of 1917–18, even while the crisis over pacifism was at its height, Lloyd George had been reflecting upon and discussing his political prospects and the future of the Liberal party. Early in the year he had considered the possibility of a wartime election and had discussed seriously with Lord Riddell and others—in anticipation of attempts at what was later referred to as 'fusion'—the formation of a 'National Party' made up of moderate elements among the Conservatives and Liberals. The great German offensive beginning in the third week of March interrupted, for a time, such speculations about the future, but by the end of July with the initiative clearly in Allied hands an election became again a possibility even though the war might continue into 1919.[2]

In the first week of August the Prime Minister began to plan for an election within the next few months without setting a date. Early in August he retired to Criccieth with Dr Bertrand Dawson (who in 1920 would become upon Lloyd George's recommendation Lord Dawson of Penn) and Christopher Addison, upon whom he depended heavily for advice on domestic social politics. Addison was at this time deeply involved in preparations for a Ministry of Health and also attempting to promote the planning of a large-scale Government housing programme. Inevitably the conversations turned to the welfare of the people—particularly upon the continuation of prewar programmes for improving the condition of the city, and above all the country, labourer.[3]

At Criccieth the Prime Minister developed his plans, maturing from the unspecific reconstruction promises of 1917, for carrying the energy of war into the battle for a better nation in peace. He would wrest initiative from the other parties and use the power of the State to improve the condition of the people. '... the physique of the people of this country is far from what it should be,' he told Lord Riddell, 'particularly in the agricultural districts where the inhabitants should be the strongest.'

That is due to low wages, malnutrition, and bad housing. It will have to be put right after the war. I have always stood during the

[1] Between November 1917 and July 1918 the index for the price of food increased only four points from 206 to 210. In the previous nine months it had risen 14 points. In this scale, prices of July 1914 equalled 100. *Cmd. 2849*, 'Statistical Abstract for the United Kingdom', 1927, 91.
[2] See, for instance, *Lord Riddell's War Diary* (London, 1933), 309, 317, 337, diary entries 27 January, 2 March, 30 June 1918.
[3] For details of the Criccieth conference see: Addison, *Four and a Half Years*, II, 564.

whole of my life for the under-dog. I have not changed and I am going still to fight his battle. Both parties will have to understand that. We have set a Committee to consider a programme, and I shall make a strong point, a very strong point, of what I have just said to you.[1]

By this time the opening speech of the electoral campaign had already been set for Manchester on 12 September. This was the city, Lloyd George told his audience, in which he had been born. The Manchester speech was made in anticipation of an election that would be held in wartime although the Prime Minister reminded the listeners in the Hippodrome that the war was nearly over and that 'Prussian military power must not only be beaten, but that Germany herself must know it'. Nevertheless the Allies had no intention of arming Germany 'with a real wrong'. They would neither 'accept nor impose a Brest-Litovsk Treaty'.

But beyond these few remarks, Lloyd George said little about external affairs. Generally the Manchester speech followed the line of, and amplified, the promises for a better world that he had been making since he assumed the Prime Ministership. The State, he said, should take a more intelligent interest in the health of the people. More than a million men who might have been in the fighting line, it was estimated by the National Service Department, had been lost through neglect of public health, 'You can not maintain an A-1 empire with a C-3 population', he reminded the audience, reiterating precisely the point of view health reformers had been maintaining since the first concerns about national physical deterioration had appeared during the Boer War.

The two great responsibilities of the nation were housing and health. The Government must see that houses actually were built and not held up by regulation and red tape. The other thing to be dealt with was

a more intelligent organization of forces which have special charge of the health of the nation—national, municipal and medical. In this respect I doubt if there is a first-rate country in the world where less has been done. We have enormous losses to make up, the fallen, the crippled, the mutilated. Their case must be particularly thought out but we must also think of the generations who are to come to fill up the gaps in the present generation and the State must see that they are built up into a fine, healthy, strong, vigorous people. There is no surer way of strengthening the country than that. (Cheers)

The Prime Minister concluded his address with oblique reference

[1] *Riddell Diary*, 346, diary entries 13, 14 August 1918.

to the fears of popular discontent that were again beginning to occupy the minds of Government leaders. The nation needed neither reaction nor revolution but steadiness and bold reconstruction, he said. Although there must be no diversion of energy from the prosecution and winning of the war, peace should not take the nation unawares.

There is a great deal of talk about preparing for war in time of peace, but it is equally important to prepare for peace during war. Delay will be disastrous. ... There are disturbing symptoms all over Europe which we at home would be wise to take note of and to provide against. In my Welsh home we have a method of ascertaining when a storm is coming. There is a lighthouse beyond the western hills and when the weather is fair or settled you never see its light, but now and again it illuminates the darkness, and then you know a storm is coming. I have been scanning the horizon and I can see flashes on the sky which indicate to me there are grave atmospheric disturbances in the social and economic world. In the natural world you can not avert a storm by thinking. In the more artificial world of human society you can, if you take things in time, avert the hurricane. I have one word of advice to my countrymen, and I say it solemnly to them: Take heed in time, and if you do we shall enjoy settled weather for the great harvest which is to come when the fierce heat of the summer which is beating upon us in this great war will be over and past. (Loud cheers)[1]

That evening, after a speech principally concerned with health, Lloyd George was struck down by a severe attack of influenza which kept him in bed in Manchester for nearly two weeks, until 21 September. During this time the collapse of the Central Powers began, and although the Germans continued to fight vigorously on the western front, Austria, Turkey and Bulgaria were disintegrating. Peace might steal up upon the nation, Churchill remarked to Lord Riddell, 'like a thief in the night'.[2]

The possibility of a sudden end to the war confused the schedule for an election and upset seriously the planning of the legislative programme of social reconstruction upon which the Government's platform was based.[3] Perhaps most seriously and even calling into question the expediency of any election for the present, the prospect of an imminent end of the fighting stimulated an unhealthy, indeed markedly vicious, change in British public opinion about the treatment of the collapsing enemy nations. The hopefulness and idealism that the Government had sought to stimulate in the previous two years, and

[1] *The Times*, 13 September 1918.
[2] *Riddell Diary*, 258, diary entry 24 September 1918.
[3] *Ibid.*, 361, diary entry 27, 28 September 1918.

indeed the widespread working-class socialist-pacifism which the Government pronouncements themselves had been designed to counteract, began to evaporate. In its place appeared, within a few weeks of Lloyd George's Manchester speech promising justice abroad and reconstruction at home, a popular undercurrent demanding heedless revenge upon Germany.

The sources for this revolution in feeling are obscure although within a few months its impact on the contending parties in the general election would be disastrous. It did not stem from the well-known newspaper campaigns of the Northcliffe press for a harsh peace because these had not yet begun and would not appear until the very end of November, about two weeks before the date of the election, while most of the Labour papers, notably the *Herald* (a weekly, not a daily at this time) remained uniformly conciliatory. Until the end of November the journal most vigorous in demanding a peace of revenge was Horatio Bottomley's *John Bull* which, although not without influence, rarely affected the view of any of the political parties.[1]

The best evidence available to the Government of the subtle but profound change in the mood of the British working man toward his nation's expiring enemy came from a highly secret organization established early in the war to keep an eye on industrial unrest and subversion for the Ministry of Munitions—the Directorate of Intelligence. This organization, which would in the next two years have perhaps too much influence on political decisions concerning the working class, had been set up by Lloyd George to keep himself informed about labour attitudes that were likely to interfere with the output of war material. When the Welshman became Prime Minister, the intelligence activities of the Ministry of Munitions were transferred to Scotland Yard and the so-called 'Special Branch' of the Criminal Investigation Department of the metropolitan police was formed under an Assistant Commissioner, Sir Basil Home Thomson, who henceforth reported directly to the Home Secretary. The title of 'Directorate of Intelligence' finally came into existence early in 1919 when Thomson, whose connections with the highest centres of political influence were by now intimate, was able to remove himself and about 150 special police officers altogether from the jurisdiction of the Yard and place his office directly under the Home Secretary within the immediate supervision of the Cabinet. In this position, until his disastrous eclipse in the autumn of 1921 when the Directorate of Intelligence returned to Scotland Yard (where it now remains as the Special Branch), he appears to have enjoyed much prosperity and influence. He had the responsibility not only of spying upon the more obvious subversive radical and Irish organizations within the United Kingdom, but also

[1] See: Caroline E. Playne, *Britain Holds On* (London, 1933), 378–80.

of keeping the Cabinet informed about the private activity of the most respectable trade union and Labour party leaders besides maintaining the security of the person of the Prime Minister.[1]

By early October, Thomson was repeatedly warning the War Cabinet that the mood of the country about the impending defeat of Germany was changing. Although the present wave of strikes was annoying, he wrote on 21 October, the old discontent had disappeared and high morale among the workers was the rule. Even the shop stewards, former pacifists, now were enthusiastic about victory and for making Germany pay the cost of the war 'even if it takes them a thousand years to do it'. 'If the Government does not make Germany pay for the War,' his correspondents reported workers saying, 'we will have to find the money and we don't see why we should.' Germany, the argument went, had made France pay in 1870, and even those who formerly had found excuses for Germany now demanded indemnities. 'After all,' Thomson reported a correspondent as saying, 'this war has been more for the Democracy of Germany than for anyone else. It will result in their emancipation; instead of being ruled by a Military class, they will rule themselves. . . .' 'As we are going to bestow benefits upon the Germans, they ought to pay the market value for them.' All peace organizations were despondent.[2]

During October, the Prime Minister was almost continually occupied with problems of external affairs, spending nearly half the month in France. As a result, and also perhaps trusting his own knowledge of the British electorate above the warnings of his secret service, he, as well as all other party leaders, continued to neglect almost completely in public utterances any discussion of the problems of treatment of Germany. If, as may be imagined, the Prime Minister wished to keep electoral politics free from the problems of peace-making and to focus his campaign beyond the settlement with Germany and upon the reconstruction of Britain, it was certain that an election must come soon. The programme which Addison had been building for many months was ready. Tentative arrangements had been made with the Conservatives for the continuance of the Coalition. So on 2 November he wrote to Andrew Bonar Law proposing that the Coalition Liberals and the Conservatives fight the election together on a platform of

---

[1] The best source on the short and obscure history of the independent Directorate of Intelligence is a memorandum by Brigadier-General Sir William T. F. Horwood, Commissioner of the Metropolitan Police from 1920 to 1928, holder of a post that Thomson had hoped to obtain for himself. Understandably Horwood was no friend of Thomson's whom he felt was running a rival police organization. 'Memorandum on the Special Branch of the Metropolitan Police', 26 October 1921, Lloyd George Papers, F/28/1/6.

[2] 'Fortnightly Report on Pacifism and Revolutionary Organizations in the United Kingdom and Morale in France and Italy', 21 October 1918, Cab. 24/67, GT 6079.

domestic reconstruction, imperial preference, home rule for Ireland and disestablishment of the Welsh Church. Neither treatment of Germany nor any other matter of foreign policy was mentioned.[1]

The long-projected election was publicly announced at party meetings on 12 November, the day after the armistice. Lloyd George's speech to somewhat more than 150 Liberals at 10 Downing Street set the tone in which he hoped the campaign would be conducted. Most of his speech was devoted to home politics. In the short mention of foreign policy he referred to the peace imposed by Germany upon France in 1871 which had outraged all principles of justice and fair play and which set an example that the Allies must be careful not to follow.

> Vigorous attempts will be made to hector and bully the Government in the endeavour to make them depart from the strict principles of right and to satisfy some base, sordid, squalid idea of vengeance and avarice. We must relentlessly set our faces against that. The mandate of this Government at the forthcoming election will mean that the British Delegation to the peace conference will be in favour of a just peace.

Concerning domestic politics, the Prime Minister cited the 'fatal example' of 1815 when 'advantage was taken of victory to deny reform. In fact, the prestige of victory was actually used to create a barrier against reform.' Again and again he spoke of health, of the recruiting statistics which showed that British soldiers were of poorer physique than Australians and Canadians, and of the need for a great housing programme that would bring 'light and beauty into the lives of the people. ... we must have habitations fit for the heroes who have won the war.' But again he warned of the revolutionary spirit that was in the air. Needed to combat it was national unity, cooperation and sacrifice. On one hand, this spirit could be dangerous; on the other it could help press the nation forward to greater things. 'If that spirit can be preserved for five years,' he concluded, 'the face of this country will be transformed. Revolution I am not afraid of. Bolshevism I am not afraid of. It is reaction that I am afraid of. Yes, reaction and disunion!'[2]

Yet while the Prime Minister described his England of the future inhabited by happy, physically fit, well-housed urban workers and a new countryside populated as of old by merry, sturdy farmers tilling their

---

[1] *The Times*, 18 November 1919. See also: Trevor Wilson, *The Downfall of the Liberal Party, 1914–35* (London, 1966), 142–3.
[2] *The Times*, 13 November 1918. *The Times* gave this speech much attention referring to it several times, clearly regarding it as the platform of the Coalition. See also: *The Times*, 16 November 1918.

own land,[1] English public opinion was growing still more revengeful and ferocious. 'A very strong demand', wrote Basil Thomson in his report for the last two weeks of November, 'on the part of working men particularly in Newcastle and the North that Germany should be made to pay an indemnity is making itself felt, and the people who used to advocate Peace by negotiation have become very unpopular.' On the other hand, continued the report, talk of revolutionary violence had reappeared.

> During the past fortnight, the idea of direct action by the workers has certainly gained ground, particularly in London. Among the advanced people there appears to be a quiet certainty that Revolution is coming.... There is, for instance, one persistent story in London that two regiments stationed in England have made known their intention of siding with the people in the event of any important strike.

Thomson admitted that the rumours of disaffection in the army were probably untrue but he reiterated that English radical leaders, whose letters he regularly opened, all looked forward to a working-class uprising.[2]

The decline in responsible politics began in the last week of November. All at the same time British Government leaders, the national newspapers, and individual parliamentary candidates began to drop the note of idealism, the emphasis on justice for Germany and reconstruction at home, and to concentrate instead almost solely upon the punishment of Germany and German leaders, mentioning domestic reform only to imply that Germany would pay for it. Until nearly the end of the month *The Times* had supported Lloyd George and the Coalition leaders in their emphasis on domestic reconstruction as the sole electoral issue.[3] The change in emphasis took only a few days.

To begin with a large part of the cause was clearly the realization by both Government spokesmen and parliamentary candidates that their golden promises of a reconstructed Britain were, as Basil Thomson had been reiterating for a month, out of tune with the

---

[1] Repopulation of the countryside was a matter that had long interested Lloyd George and which would preoccupy him for the rest of his life. He returned to it at length in a speech in Westminster on 16 November.
[2] 'Fortnightly Report on Revolutionary Organizations in the United Kingdom and Morale Abroad', 2 December 1918, P.R.O. Cab. 24/71, G.T. 6425. Alfred Mond had written to the Cabinet on 12 November deploring the spread of Bolshevik ideas in Britain and saying that only the Defence of the Realm Act prevented more overt manifestations of this feeling. Particularly Mond was disturbed by the clear resentment of the 'war profiteers'. Alfred Mond, 'Suggestions to Prevent the Spread of Revolutionary Ideas in the U.K.', P.R.O. Cab. 24/69, G.T. 6270.
[3] See *The Times*' leader on the dangers of nostalgia, 27 November 1918.

national mood. The nation was not, in fact, looking to the future. The horrors of war were still with it. The dead were still dead, the soldiers were still abroad, the rule of life was still the dull greyness of wartime shortages, while the future, instead of bringing hope, brought uncertainty. Germany would have to take the blame.

Secondly, growing from the first point, was the fact that the Labour party had irrevocably committed itself to what might be termed a 'soft' peace. At the same time there was no possibility that the Coalition could outpromise Labour in social reform. Hence a realistic electoral position, given the clear mood of the nation, suggested an attack on the Labour party programme where it had no room for manoeuvre.[1]

Finally, the vehicle for the transition that carried the tone from idealism to ferocity was provided by the pitiable physical condition of the returned British prisoners who began to arrive in England just at this time. The release of Allied prisoners had been among the stipulations in the Armistice and had begun immediately. On 20 November, the British Government had officially protested to Berlin about their condition and treatment in German prison camps. The following day, 21 November, the first shipload of released prisoners had left Hamburg in a Danish liner. By this time, British newspapers had published of course extended accounts of the ill treatment and privation that war captives had suffered without, it should be noted, suggesting any political retribution. But by 26 November with the leadership of the 'Government Committee on the Treatment by the Enemy of British Prisoners of War' under Robert Younger, brother of George Younger, chairman of the Conservative party organization, condemnation of Germany was widespread.[2] On that day *The Times* in a survey of election addresses remarked:

> One note is common to all. Emphasis is universally placed on the need of providing for the men whose endurance and bravery have made victory possible—some are broken by wounds, others by barbarities practised in German prison camps—and for the dependants who have fallen.[3]

At this stage only two election addresses, those of Lord Robert Cecil, not running as a Coalition candidate, and Donald MacMaster, Coalition Unionist candidate, spoke of general reparations. Both stated, in almost identical terms, that Germany should be required to 'pay

[1] On the Labour platform, see: *Why Labour Left the Coalition*, November 1918 (paperback pamphlet published by the *Herald*, 8 pp.).
[2] *The Times*, 26 November 1918.
[3] *Ibid.*

indemnities as well as make reparations for damages and those guilty of murder and other brutalities should be punished'.[1]

Within two weeks the trickle of well-deserved sympathy for the undeniable hardships suffered by British prisoners in German camps had become a torrent of abuse demanding not only that Germany pay pensions for war prisoners and wounded, but large unspecified reparations as well, and culminating with the requirement that the Kaiser himself be given a fair trial and then hanged.[2]

By this time, the new emphasis was apparent everywhere else. At Dundee on 26 November Winston Churchill, after briefly referring to the war as a triumph of political ideals and Liberalism, launched into a violent attack on Germany. The whole German nation was guilty of the crime of aggressive war conducted by brutal and bestial means. It was no use pretending that only the Government was to blame. Everyone was in it and all must suffer for it.

> In particular individuals against whom breaches of the law of war on land or sea can be proved, or who can be proved to have treated prisoners with cruelty should be brought to trial and punished as criminals. . . . Reparations must be made by Germany to the utmost limit possible for the damage she has done. I cordially sympathize with those who say, 'make them pay the expenses of the war.'

The next day, still in Dundee, Churchill estimated that German reparation ought not to be less than £2,000 million.[3]

Within the next three days, by 29 November, the transition in the Coalition campaign was complete. At Newcastle, the Prime Minister, who was almost the last of the members of the Government to adopt the new style and who clearly approached the entire subject of the peace negotiations only with the greatest reluctance, spoke at length on the German treatment of prisoners, the submarine warfare and invasion of neutral countries. He emphasized that there would be great difficulty in the collection of indemnities from Germany but said that it would be done.[4]

---

[1] *Ibid.* The quotation is from MacMaster's address.
[2] The leaders of the two parties were among the last to change the emphasis of their speeches from reconstruction to revenge. Lloyd George asked his famous rhetorical question, 'What is our task? To make Britain a fit country for heroes to live in', at Wolverhampton on 23 November. *The Times*, 25 November 1918. Two days later, Bonar Law in Glasgow dismissed the coming peace conference with a simple plea that the people ought not to ask that the hands of their leaders be tied, while devoting, like Lloyd George, the bulk of his speech to social reform, land for soldiers, housing and improved transport. *The Times*, 26 November 1916.
[3] *The Times*, 27, 28 November 1918.
[4] Not until 11 December at Bristol did the Prime Minister agree publicly that Germany ought to pay the cost of the war. *The Times*, 12 December 1918.

In an article on 29 November, the day of Lloyd George's Newcastle speech, *The Times* noted the changing mood of the election and remarked that new issues were

> gradually emerging from the apparent confusion of the moment and by no means all are concerned with the problem of reconstruction. The nature of the peace which is about to be made is a very burning question to the great mass of men and women in this country and candidates are finding it necessary to give more and more attention to it. The test for the simple elector is simply the position of the Kaiser. One of our Special Correspondents dealing with the contest at Shoreditch yesterday quoted Dr Addison as saying that he had been struck with the absolute determination of the people that the Kaiser and others responsible for the war must be brought to trial. Shoreditch is a typical London working class constituency, and many a candidate elsewhere would confirm Dr Addison's impression from his own experience.[1]

By this time also the papers reported daily pledges given by individual candidates to insist that Germany pay the entire cost of the war and to vote against the Government if they failed to require her to do so.

Thus the character of the Coupon Election altered entirely in the last two weeks before the voting on Saturday, 14 December 1918. The detailed promises of reconstruction, which had been so much a feature of earlier speeches, virtually disappeared from the utterances of Coalition candidates. In their place was the simple assertion that Germany must be made to pay for the war and above all that the Kaiser must be brought to trial. As a reflection of popular sentiment of the moment, this was certainly good politics. Punishment of Germany was an issue that the Labour party with its pacifist tradition could not, or would not, debate. As a result the Coalition won an overwhelming victory while Labour, although they fielded 388 candidates, succeeded in electing only 63 and lost some of their most important leaders in the process.

Excluding from consideration here the disastrous European consequences of the peace to which Britain was forced to commit herself, perhaps the most unfortunate domestic political result of the Coupon Election and its great importance for this study, lies in the fact that, despite all the preparations to the contrary, the Lloyd George victory had not been won on a platform of reconstruction of Britain and improvement of working conditions for the people. The Parliament that assembled on 4 February 1919 was, to be sure, much concerned with the threat of popular unrest and revolution and while the danger

[1] *The Times*, 29 November 1918.

seemed imminent it was willing to support the Government in whatever measures were necessary to buy off the discontent. But the men
elected on 14 December were not social reformers, nor were they Tory
Democrats, nor, indeed, were they even politicians. In the much-
overworked phrase they were 'hard-faced businessmen' who saw
membership in the House of Commons as a useful way to protect or
promote their private affairs. Men such as A. R. Barrand of the
Prudential Assurance Company, H. Kingsley Wood, insurance company lobbyist, and A. H. Warren of the Manchester Unity of Odd
Fellows—to mention three who will appear prominently in this study—
had been given the coupon as a reward for supporting the Government
in the struggle over plans for the Ministry of Health. Their concern
for politics lay in the defence of interests they represented, in this case
the approved societies, which were the administrators of national
health insurance. The tragedy of 1918 was not so much that the new
Parliament was made up of men concerned with the protection of the
traditional capitalist classes of Great Britain, but that there was nothing
in the circumstances of the election to suggest that they should be
concerned with anything else. In many ways the men of the Coupon
Parliament and indeed the Ministry resembled less their immediate
predecessors of Victorian and Edwardian days, who served public or
party welfare as they conceived it, than men of eighteenth-century
parliaments who took it for granted that they served the interest which
had put them there—the East India Company, the West Indian sugar
planters, or the Crown. A seat in Parliament was not an end in itself
or even a stepping stone to higher office but a shield for the protection or promotion of extra-political affairs.[1]

They were, indeed, aware of the exceptional circumstances that had
brought them into the House of Commons. As will be seen, the fear,
particularly among the Conservatives, that many of them would not
return should Lloyd George dissolve the sitting Parliament and break
his connection with their party maintained for a long time a reluctant
obedience to the Liberal Prime Minister. But the only obligation they
felt to the electors was the one manifest in the pledge that many of
them had signed: to seek the largest possible reparations from
Germany. There never was any comparable interest in social reform
even though the original, and presumably the basic, Coalition electoral
programme had been based precisely on this promise. And so in 1919

---

[1] Namier's description of the goals of men in Parliament in the *Structure of Politics*
could apply to the Coupon Parliament with scarcely the change of a word. Sir
Lewis Namier, *The Structure of Politics at the Accession of George III*, 2nd ed.
(London, 1957), 2–3. On this characteristic of the Coupon Parliament see also:
Viscount Norwich, *Old Men Forget: The Autobiography of Duff Cooper* (London,
1953), 141.

the Coalition backbenchers brought pressure on Lloyd George for doing too little in regard to German indemnities; by 1920 they resisted him on reform, particularly housing and unemployment insurance, for trying to do too much. Quite possibly it would have been to his advantage to go to the country without the Conservatives. In any case a more vigorous opposition would have served to discipline the Government benches, and, in a way, to protect the Prime Minister from his own followers and from the enthusiasm of his own electoral success. Even though a number of his most experienced advisers on working-class matters urged him until the very end to maintain the emphasis on reconstruction in his speeches, he appears, characteristically, to have adapted himself easily to the new mood of punishment for Germany.[1]

But eventually the Parliament that had demanded revenge upon Germany took its revenge upon the Prime Minister for the injustices which it had forced him to commit, first by driving from office his most trusted radical ministers, then by destroying the radical programme and the party, and finally by overthrowing Lloyd George himself.

The decline of the Coalition

The returns of the general election of 14 December, when they were announced two weeks later, threw for the moment the leaders of working-class discontent and revolution into despair. Correspondingly they briefly raised hopes among the leaders of the Government that the danger of revolution had passed.[2]

'The shadow of the general election has been weighing heavily upon the spirit of the revolutionaries', wrote Basil Thomson on 31 December,

> and since the Albert Hall Meeting revolutionary meetings have been few.[3] My correspondent in Leeds says that the defeatist-revolutionaries in the West Riding had a distinct set back during the period of canvassing. In the public houses and working men's clubs there was satisfaction in the belief that the Coalition Government would secure a new lease on life.

Thomson, whose political intelligence was usually excellent, noted in closing a fact that would become a weakness in Labour party elec-

[1] T. J. Macnamara to Lloyd George, 10, 15 December 1918, L.G. Papers, F/36/1/9–10; Lord Riddell, *Intimate Diary of the Peace Conference and After, 1918–1923* (London, 1933), 3, 48. Diary entries 30 November 1918, 9 April 1919.
[2] Officially 478 candidates holding the coupon were elected. In fact, however, the government was supported by 48 other non-coupon Conservatives and Irish Unionist Members.
[3] See *Daily Herald*, 23, 30 November 1918.

C

toral politics for many decades in the future: Labour men were admitting sadly that their personal votes frequently had been cancelled by the contrary vote of their wives.[1]

Almost as this report was being written, its optimistic anticipations of the end of unrest and working-class discontent were contradicted. Between 3 and 7 January occurred a series of outbreaks among troops in England demanding swifter demobilization of the army and resisting the rotation of some soldiers back to France.[2] The Government quieted the discontent among the soldiers by publishing, on 29 January, a revised scheme of demobilization based on the simple principle of 'first in—first out'. But in doing so it cast aside a well-thought-out programme, the results of many months' work, which attempted to prevent large-scale unemployment among servicemen by releasing soldiers only as rapidly as industry could absorb them. By the end of the month serious disorders had broken out among civilian workers particularly in the north and centering in Glasgow. On 27 January that northern city was virtually immobilized by a general strike called technically to enforce demands for a 40-hour week aimed at the creation of jobs for returning servicemen. Four days later, on the 31st, police had to fight a pitched battle with a mob of men attempting to take over the city hall. These disorders, lasting for about two weeks and spreading briefly to other Scottish and north England cities, were not particularly the result of revolutionary leadership, although Thomson emphasized Bolshevik agitators were active in attempting to focus and channel discontent. Rather they were the outcome of genuine grievances against wartime restrictions, the slowness of demobilization of men, the continuation of wartime controls, particularly on liquor, the shortage of housing and clearly rising prices. Above all, however, they represented a general unspecified but profound distrust of the Government, of Government promises and intentions, and of Government personnel.[3]

The predictions of a growing disenchantment with the Government were strikingly confirmed in March, at the beginning and at the end of the month, with two humiliating and unexpected Coalition defeats in by-elections, at Leyton West on 1 March and more seriously in Central Hull on 29 March. Although both seats were technically defeats of Coalition Unionists by Asquithian Liberals, the election at Central

[1] PRO, Cab. 24/73, GT 6603, 'Fortnightly Report on Revolutionary Organizations in the United Kingdom and Morale Abroad', 31 December 1918.

[2] In his report of 31 December, three days before the first outbreak, Thomson had warned of rising unhappiness on this score in the forces and had noted that Bolshevik agitators were busy. *Ibid.*, 112.

[3] PRO Cab. 24/74, GT 6713; Cab. 24/75, GT 6876, 'Fortnightly Report on Revolutionary Organizations in the United Kingdom and Morale Abroad', 28 January, 10 February 1919.

Hull caused by the death of Mark Sykes was the more shocking. Here the victorious candidate was Commander J. M. Kenworthy, the son and heir of Lord Strabolgi, who, although technically a Liberal, was in fact a well-known Labour sympathiser (he eventually joined the Labour party in 1926). He had campaigned on a platform of relaxation of wartime restrictions, abolition of conscription, free trade and negotiation with Russia. In his speeches Kenworthy talked freely about the coming revolution in Britain and had said that the Navy was ripe for revolt. The last assertion had resulted in his arrest by the Directorate of Intelligence and an interrogation on 12 March by Basil Thomson and the Director of Naval Intelligence.[1] Nevertheless Kenworthy succeeded in overturning what had been a Coalition majority of over 10,000 in a total poll of only 17,000 three months before, causing serious disquiet in ministerial circles and joy for the opposition.[2]

The popular discontent already manifest by the spring of 1919 would undermine and eventually destroy the Lloyd George Coalition. It had among its causes, to be sure, the deliberate provocations of revolutionary agitators who sought to overthrow British capitalism and the hardly less violent denunciations of ministerial honesty and civil service integrity—similar in both bad taste and inaccuracy—from the Northcliffe press. Yet, after all, after examining the reports of secret investigators for the Government, working-class newspapers and pamphlets, and even the sober reports of Labour politicians themselves attempting to explain the position of their followers, the historian cannot avoid gaining the impression that the British workman's discontent with his Government, and indeed with the social, economic and political establishment of his nation, proceeded from genuine, and not manufactured, grievances. The trauma of war had changed the nation in many ways. On one hand it had instilled in the soldier the feeling that British society owed him a debt, a feeling that politicians did much to articulate. As he had served the nation so the nation henceforth must serve him. But to this commonplace should be added the less familiar but perhaps the more important observations that, in addition to the $5\frac{1}{2}$ million soldiers who assumed that Britain bore them an obligation, the war had brought to perhaps 15 million civilian workers better wages and more security, and indeed paradoxically, perhaps a better life than many had ever known before. Beatrice Webb's acute observations of late January 1916, upon the increasing affluence of the British

---

[1] PRO Cab. 24/78, GT 7196, 'Report on Revolutionary Organizations in the United Kingdom', No. 1, 30 April 1919. From this date on the fortnightly reports became weekly reports and grew in size from approximately 10–12 to about 20 pages.

[2] For Labour comment on the by-election see: *New Statesman*, 19 April 1919. The journal called it an 'indictment against Parliament'.

civilian war workers, were echoed after the war by commentators disparate as Basil Thomson, G. D. H. Cole and Auckland Geddes.

The British working man, his wife and daughters are making good money—more than ever before—and they are working longer hours and have no time to be discontented. So long as full employment and bigger incomes continue, there will be nothing more serious than revolutionary talk, and occasional local outbreaks of disorder. And as no one will be allowed to report either the talk or the disorder, the world will be assured that there is industrial peace in Great Britain.[1]

But whereas Mrs Webb had assumed during the war that job security and high wages would maintain industrial calm, both men writing after the war saw the same conditions as causes of unrest. 'It must be remembered', wrote Basil Thomson at the end of 1920.

that as a result of the war, the working classes generally have become accustomed to better conditions of life than in former times when unemployment has been acute, and consequently they resent it more, they are, moreover, accustomed to act under discipline.

The problem, unfortunately, is insoluble, for it is brought about by world-wide conditions over which we have no control, but naturally to the mind of the unemployed this fact is unknown and the Government alone is to blame.[2]

Similarly Arthur Henderson and G. D. H. Cole in a memorandum for the National Industrial Conference in February 1919 dwelt upon Labour's fear that the gains during the war would be lost.

It must be remembered that throughout the war the workers had been led to expect that the conclusion of hostilities would be followed by a profound revolution in the economic structure of society. Not only social theorists but also the most prominent spokesman of the Government, and not a few employers have consistently told the workers that we should never revert to the old conditions of industry, that an altogether higher standard of life and altogether superior status toward the man and his industry would be secured as soon as the immediate burden of hostilities was removed.

The workman had discovered during the war, Henderson and Cole concluded, that 'private profit is not an equitable basis on which to

[1] Cole, ed., *Webb Diaries 1912–1924*, 55, diary entry 31 January 1916.
[2] PRO Cab. 24/116, CP 2273, 'Report on Revolutionary Organizations', No. 84, 9 December 1920, 3.

build'. Democratic control was necessary. Labour could no longer be coerced; it had grown too strong.[1]

Finally in one of the many confidential surveys of working-class feeling that the Cabinet received in the months after the Armistice, Auckland Geddes reminded his colleagues they were responsible for the present difficulties. 'Uncertainty' about conditions of the peace-time economy was by itself a disturbing element, Geddes believed,

> coupled with a sense of impending change. We have heard so much of the new and better Britain that the people await a sign. Employers do not know whether it is to be heralded by confiscation of capital, by nationalization of great industries, by a marked increase in the income tax.... The workers expect that it will be inaugurated by new houses, less work, higher wages or a combination of all three.

The housing scheme, he concluded his long memorandum, 'is the most conspicuous as well as the most urgent item in the Government pro-gramme, and it is of the greatest importance ...' that there should be no delays in acquiring sites or materials.[2]

Strangely the transition from war to peace generated fear. In a way the war represented security, and peace uncertainty. So long as the fighting continued the British working man knew the extent of his power and the strength of his economic position. And notwithstand-ing the growing austerity of civilian conditions during the last months of 1917 and through 1918, the workmen, no less than the soldier, had the glowing promises of a safe and democratic world and a better Britain to look forward to. But somehow all of this evaporated with the election of the Coupon Parliament and the appearance in power everywhere of unnamed, but potent and malevolent, 'war profiteers', men who had grown rich on rising prices, who attempted to dilute union work with unskilled and unorganized labour in order to increase their earnings, who threatened unemployment in order to make labour more tractable, who used influence to secure building materials for moving picture theatres and hotels while workers' housing lagged, who opposed the reconstruction of the Poor Law and the creation of the Ministry of Health, who supported continuing military conscription and intervention in Russia, whose presence seemed to mock the war-

---

[1] *Cmd.*, *501*, 'Report of the Provisional Joint Committee presented to a meeting of industrial conference, Central Hall, Westminster, 4 April 1919', 1920, Appendix I, 'Memorandum on the causes of and remedies for labour unrest', 27 February 1919, ii.

[2] PRO Cab. 27/58, G 237, Ad Hoc Committee on Unemployment, 'Unemploy-ment and the State of Trade', 14 March 1919.

time hope by reviving Edwardian opulence and privilege without any vestige of aristocratic sense of duty.[1]

Consequently the reaction against nearly all forms of political and economic authority was immediate and unprecedented. That the Coupon Parliament had not been chosen on the basis of enthusiasm for social reform, but on promises of revenge upon Germany, was almost forgotten. Pacifism and socialism, so much a part of the British working man's creed since 1916, reasserted itself. The most visible political result was the crippling series of Coalition by-election defeats.[2]

But more serious was the residue of antagonism left by the events of the years immediately after the Armistice that poisoned British politics of the interwar period. Although the Coupon Parliament ironically was the first to be elected under genuine universal manhood franchise, the years of its tenure saw a near breakdown of communication between the working and governing classes of Britain and an unprecedented readiness by the British workman to take the law and affairs of state into his own hands, characterized best perhaps by the current phrase 'direct action'. Behind, or underlying all this, was of course the threat of revolution. There was always a fear that the British working man would find the ordinary channels of political activity inadequate or useless. With some justification it was assumed that he distrusted his own leaders, and that a Labour government if it ever came to power would fail, not succeed in office. Hence a Labour Government must not be allowed to come to power lest by its own ineptitude it discredit itself and drive the working class to more radical leaders. The failure of Labour could be a greater danger than its success. The history of the 'fusion' movement was as much a story of attempts to keep Labour out as to keep Lloyd George in.

Looking at the political climate immediately after the war from the workers' point of view, one is struck most forcibly by the fact that so far as a large part of the British wage-earning class was concerned Bagehot's prime requisite for stable Cabinet Government had disappeared: the English were no longer a 'deferential people'. This applied not only to politics but to social and economic structure as well. If a hierarchical class structure is to be maintained in a functioning democracy, the structure must be believed in by the lower as well as the upper classes. The workman as well as the lord must believe

[1] In 1920 Harold Laski calculated that the House of Commons included 61 insurance directors, 138 general manufacturers, 115 land owners, 28 bank directors, 17 coal directors, and 102 lawyers. 'Mr George and the Constitution', Nation, 9 October 1920.
[2] There were 20 between March 1919 when the first one occurred and October 1922. The Lloyd George Government suffered more defeats than any other administration in the present century.

in the legitimacy of his place. Arguably this orthodoxy had begun to crumble before the First World War. But the relatively slow growth of the Labour party, the willingness of the enfranchised working man to vote for the traditional governing parties and, more significant, for individual parliamentary candidates of the traditional governing classes even in working-class constituencies suggests that the erosion had not gone very far before 1914.

After the First World War the new form of radicalism and the new working-class attitude toward the Government would become a factor in all subsequent politics. Without attempting to delineate too clearly the indefinable, British labour presented the rest of the nation with two distinct challenges, each in a way connected, in a way contradictory. On one hand was the growth of a class-conscious but peaceful socialism most explicit in the Labour Party Charter of 1918. However, behind this constitutional facade lay the threat of extra-legal force, of direct action—of economic coercion for political ends.[1]

Possibly this class antagonism would have become more violent were it not for the debilitating influence of the chronic unemployment of the interwar period, the weakness of the Labour party's own leadership and, probably above all, of the soothing and pacifying personality of Stanley Baldwin, who was somehow able to play the role of a national leader standing above faction while operating at the same time as a shrewd and deeply committed Tory party politician.

On the other hand a second working-class demand upon the society and Government of the nation, partly complementary, partly inconsistent with the first, appeared in the assumption that the State had an obligation to underwrite the economic welfare of its citizens. The Labour party's slogan 'Work and Maintenance' was its most succinct statement. Patently, this new attitude was a product of the war, of the participation by the mass of Englishmen for the first time in a national enterprise, of Lloyd George's promises for a better Britain, and, no doubt, of the extension of the franchise in 1918, which gave the working class far more political leverage than it had possessed before. (However, one may argue—and clearly the Conservatives assumed—that the extension of votes to women would benefit the right wing rather than the left wing of British politics.)

But all of this does little to explain the extent of the revolution in popular attitudes towards State activity that have been manifest in

[1] One example of protest appearing in every Labour party history was the dockers' refusal on 10 May 1920 to load coal on the *Jolly George*, a vessel carrying munitions to Poland in support of that nation's war with Russia. This incident is almost invariably blown out of context. The vessel was the *Jolly George*, not, as it frequently appears, the *Jolly Roger:* a better name, but the wrong one. See for instance: Henry Pelling, *A Short History of the Labour Party* (London, 1961), 47.

British politics since the First World War and which are in a large measure the core of this study. To say simply that the Unemployment Insurance Act of 1920, for instance, was an extension of Part Two of the National Insurance Act of 1911 is true in the formal sense that the second act reproduced many of the clauses and phrases of the first and gave unemployment insurance on approximately the same terms to virtually all of the urban working class. But here the similarity ended. Between 1911 and 1920 the attitude of the Government toward the unemployed workman had changed completely and no less profoundly altered were the expectations of the workman about the obligations of society toward him. In 1911 William Beveridge and H. Llewellyn Smith could build into their measure an elaborate framework of safeguards and restrictions designed to protect the solvency of the insurance fund and, most important, could feel no responsibility whatever toward a workman who exhausted his benefits—in effect, being no more concerned over the fate of a man unable to take advantage of the unemployment service than was the postmaster general about an individual unable to afford a stamp to mail a letter. But after the Armistice this official detachment was impossible and the act of 1920 became only another Government instrument, inadequate and inefficient to be sure, for dealing with the problem of unemployment itself. The Government could no longer leave the unemployed man to shift for himself once his statutory benefits were exhausted. The preemptory demand for 'Work or Maintenance' had to be heeded and its legitimacy respected. The core of this central truth was not so much that the working man felt society owed him at least a bare living but the nation's leaders had come unquestioningly to accept this obligation. There was no use any longer arguing that the Poor Law offered a reasonable alternative or, indeed, of suggesting, except hesitantly and half-heartedly, the imposition of a means test. In this way unemployment insurance was transformed into nothing more than a vast system of working-class relief. So came the endless ramshackle extensions of the scheme—the uncovenanted benefits, the extended benefits, the transitional benefits, and finally the transitional payments —all of which were lumped with the standard benefit itself into the common term 'the dole'. The safeguards to the unemployment fund virtually were forgotten and the cost of unemployment relief came close to bankrupting the State by 1931. In essence what had been given in 1911 as a narrowly restricted and carefully guarded privilege to well-established workers in a few select industries was in 1920 accepted by both the governors and the governed as a perquisite of citizenship, a right to a national minimum that had been arrived at in an unspoken compromise between British politicians and the citizens who elected them.

Fusion and after

The story of Lloyd George's attempts to broaden his political base by the construction of a 'fusion' party is in many ways the story of the Prime Minister's political decline after the 1918 election and of his increasing isolation in British politics even while remaining formally the King's First Minister. The failure of fusion meant finally his eclipse.

The significance of these events for the history of social reform lies in the fact that they demonstrated the Prime Minister's realization that the welfare programme he had in mind would be impossible to accomplish with the Parliament he had at his back. He was sure that the New Liberalism he intended to revive would be better for the nation than the alternative of an inexperienced Labour party even, as he may have considered, under himself. But finally, perhaps most important, he feared that, unless a true reform programme were completed, or to put the same thing in reverse if the Tories were permitted to slip back and become a party of pure reaction, the Labour party would come to power, inevitably fail in its task, and be replaced by some new group dedicated to revolutionary communism. A combination of all non-socialist progressive forces therefore was the answer. In the process the New Liberalism would be revived albeit under another name and Lloyd George himself could look forward to long years of power as the head of a stable organization made up of all progressive and right-thinking Englishmen.

As has been seen, Lloyd George had been troubled by the lack of institutionalized party support almost from the time he became Prime Minister and had discussed with Lord Riddell and others the possibility of making the Coalition into a permanent political organization. No doubt he realized before the Coupon Election, as *The Times* pointed out in a long article on 4 December 1918, that his chances were good for winning a general election alone, purely on the strength of his reputation. But he hesitated to drive the Conservatives into opposition. Fighting the 1918 election as a Coalition, dividing the available seats between himself and Bonar Law and then using his oratorical magic on behalf of Conservative candidates, which would force from the Parliament an acknowledgement of his leadership, clearly seemed a better course. The loyalty of Bonar Law ensured the continued obedience of the Conservatives. The device of the coupon would secure the election of enough Liberals to keep Liberalism respectable.

In purely electoral terms the plan worked perfectly. The Coalition as a whole won an overwhelming victory. The parties seated almost precisely equal percentages of their candidates and the Coupon Liberals received, in fact, about 500 more votes per candidate elected than did the Conservatives. But there the happiness ended. Chiefly because Coupon Liberals were reluctant to face Asquithian Liberals in constituency fights George Younger had been able to field more than twice as many Coalition Conservatives as were the Coalition Liberals. As a result, Lloyd George elected only 133 of his own followers to 335 of Bonar Law's. Again, the Coupon Parliament was not elected on the Lloyd George programme of advanced New Liberalism, but upon promises concerning foreign affairs that the Prime Minister had tried to exclude from the electoral campaign. Then, more seriously, came the reaction in the spring of 1919 to the political aberrations of the last months of the previous year. The working-class discontent with the leaders they had so recently put in office was manifest in both reports of revolutionary conspiracy and in outbreaks of domestic unrest, and, beginning in March, by a series of sharp and unexpected Coalition defeats in by-elections.

All of this was the more disturbing because as yet, from the Government's point of view at least, the working class had little to be discontented about. The peace treaty with Germany was unsigned, the promises for a better Britain had not been dishonoured, indeed the Government was working hard toward their fulfilment. More objective reasons for complaint would appear later, to be sure, but in the spring of 1919, and indeed well into 1920, even the most meticulous investigations of working-class attitudes, both public and confidential, could uncover few specific complaints that were not either the result of wartime shortages and dislocations—lack of housing, high prices, remnants of wartime controls upon liquor, fears, until the summer of 1920 virtually groundless, of unemployment—or the result of instructions given the Government in foreign affairs by the voting population itself—punishment of Germany or the pressure upon European Bolshevism which always carried with it the possibility of continued military conscription.

A last factor not to be discounted in Lloyd George's interest in fusion, but difficult properly to assess, can be said to lie in the 'political style' of the Prime Minister. He was by nature a negotiator, a compromiser, a smoother, a fixer. Although a superb parliamentary orator when the need arose, he appears always to have had—and certainly he clearly showed by the end of the war—a basic distrust of traditional parliamentary action where each decision had to be recorded in terms of aye and nay, where compromises were clearly delineated, and where victory left discontent for the minority and defeat could not be hidden. Almost as soon as he attained his first office in December 1905, he displayed perhaps his most effective political talent in private negotiation among small groups of men. Whether he was simply a mediator attempting to arbitrate differences between workers and employers, or a party to the dispute harmonizing conflicting vested interests in national health insurance, his incredible charm, the quickness of his mind and the fluency of his tongue, his ability to listen and to learn from what he heard—not perhaps about the facts at issue but about the mental processes and prejudices of the speaker—gave him an immense advantage in a committee room. He had sought Coalition in 1910 in order to outflank the immense political power of the industrial insurance companies and to trade compromise with the Conservatives on tariff reform, reform of the House of Lords, military conscription and Irish union for his own broad programme of social reform.[1] He had failed at that time, but now, since December 1916, England had had a Coalition under his leadership. As he saw it, however, it was endangered on the right by the reactionary and irresponsible elements within the Tory party and on the left by newly militant, but badly led, Labour, who in fact used the reactionary fraction of Coalition supporters—the so-called 'war profiteers', the 'hard-faced men'—as a weapon with which to discredit the Government as a whole.

The most potent argument for fusion, certainly the one most likely to appeal to Tories of any persuasion, either moderate or reactionary, was the danger from the left. If Lloyd George saw the formation of a new party as a means of keeping himself in power and exercising the direct political control that only a recognized party leader can exercise, the Conservatives were more interested in keeping Labour out and saw the disarray of existing political organizations as a grave danger. The increasing threat of a revolution was a continuing theme in Basil Thomson's reports through the late months of 1919 and into 1920. It was reinforced, publicly and obviously, by the accession of more and more radical leaders to positions of power in local Labour party organizations and by the continuing success of Labour in by-elections.

> The most serious factor of the moment is unemployment, which is driving many more moderately minded ex-Servicemen into the revolutionary camp.
>
> There is abundant evidence that the great mass of Labour is drifting steadily to the Left. One sign is the increased membership of the Independent Labour Party which, in Scotland, is becoming more extreme in its programme. A serious factor is the inclination of the lower middle class toward Labour.
>
> In my mind is not the least doubt that during the coming winter

[1] See: Bentley B. Gilbert, *The Evolution of National Insurance in Great Britain* (London, 1966), 326–32.

there will be practically an upheaval if not revolution engineered by
... hotheads, and many otherwise harmless men may be drawn into
it by the specious arguments I have heard repeatedly used, 'we have
got nothing at present, so we can't lose anything and we may get
some, they can't take anything away from us.' This is dangerous
doctrine but it appeals to men respectable and loyal to King and
Country who are out of work and brooding over the sight of wealthy
people going shopping in their cars and they see big displays in all
the shop windows, clothing, food and toys they would love to purchase for their wives and children but have not the means.

No words could adequately convey the seriousness of this situation to you.[1]

Essentially then, the elements of this danger as it appeared toward
the end of 1919 were, first, that the Coalition Government as it was
then constituted was prevented from the accomplishment of effective
reform by the large and vocal reactionary wing of the Conservative
Party. Second, the Government's failure in making good on wartime
promises were compounded by the weaknesses of the Coalition Liberals
in constituency organization. This made it difficult for Lloyd George
to maintain a loyal following at his back with which to stand up to the
Conservatives and resulted also in far too many three-cornered constituency fights with Liberals facing each other and allowing, as a
result, the election of a Labourite. (The by-election at Spen Valley
on 20 December 1919 which brought the fusion movement to a head
was an occurrence of precisely this kind.) Third, despite the almost
uniform Labour successes in by-elections, the fatness of the Coalition
Government's majority seemed to make the possibility of a Labour
Government remote and compounded the cynicism with which working
men regarded promises of reform. The result was the terrifying threat
of 'direct action'.[2]

Finally on all sides, among working men as well as Conservatives,
always apparent but rarely articulated, was the assumption that
the Labour party, as then constituted in Parliament, could not govern
if it came to power. Lloyd George put this feeling most forcibly in a

---

[1] Letter from a correspondent in Birmingham, PRO Cab. 24/96, CP 429, 'Report
on Revolutionary Organizations in the United Kingdom', No. 36, 9 January
1920, 1–2, 9. For the effect of these warnings on the Cabinet see: Keith Middlemas,
ed., *Thomas Jones, Whitehall Diary, 1916–1925* (London, 1969), 99–103.
[2] Robert Horne, at that time Minister of Labour, wrote the Prime Minister on
14 December warning that the miners were building stocks of food in cooperative
stores and preparing generally plans for a concerted seizure of the pits, waiting
only until their plans were complete and until the further demobilization of the
army occurred in March 1920. (Horne to Lloyd George, 14 December 1919,
LG Papers, F/24/6/27.) Basil Thomson had long been saying the same thing.

conversation with Philip Lloyd Greame in January 1920 when fusion negotiations were at their height. After explaining that the 'National Party' he proposed would be neither Tory nor Liberal but would include parts of both while dropping people 'at both ends' he explained the necessity of such a combination. 'A Labour Government', he said, 'would land the country in revolution because it would resist direct action by talk and not force. It would be Kerenski over again. I want strong government. I want private enterprise. But private interprise must give the workers a change and a *certainty*.'[1]

No less frightening, and more colourful, were the conclusions of an American investigator of British labour conditions who spent the summer of 1920 among Welsh miners and steel workers posing as an itinerant American working man. Among his questions was always one trying to elicit attitudes toward the Labour party. What did they expect, he would ask, of a Labour Government? 'In such a case I can hear my friends saying over their beer: "A fair wash-out they are —like all the rest of 'um. Speakin' us fine words til they got their canes and their fine clothes and all, and then forgettin' of us." "True enough", will then come the answer of the extremists and revolutionists. "They've let you down, all right. Now give *us* the chance".'[2]

C. F. G. Masterman, whose knowledge of the tangled underbrush of Liberal party leadership was unrivalled and who indeed knew the Prime Minister better than any man except Harold Spender and Lord Riddell, gave in the *Contemporary Review* for February 1920 perhaps the fullest delineation of the Prime Minister's intentions with the new party.[3]

The main promise of the new party, said Masterman, would be the 'removal of poverty and the elimination of all injustice without doing injury to any class'. In effect it would be the Labour party programme without the doctrine of class struggle. Quoting a speech by Churchill the previous summer the new party would combine the 'patriotism

[1] Earl of Swinton, *Sixty Years of Power* (London, 1966), 47–8. Swinton added that he committed this conversation to paper in a letter to his father immediately afterwards.

[2] Whiting Williams, *Full Up and Fed Up, The Workers' Mind in Crowded Britain* (New York, 1921), 298–9. Williams was no sensationalist journalist, but a vice-president of the Hydraulic Steel Company of Cleveland, Ohio, a writer on labour problems, and a lecturer at the Harvard School of Business Administration and at the Wharton School of Finance.

[3] C. F. G. Masterman, 'The New Democratic Party', *Contemporary Review*, CXVII (February 1920), 153–62. Lord Beaverbrook thought Masterman one of the two best journalists in England. The other was Winston Churchill. Kenneth Young, *Churchill and Beaverbrook, A Study in Friendship and Politics* (London, 1966), 94.

and stability of the Conservative Party with the broad humanity and tolerance of Liberalism'.[1]

Most important in Masterman's article, which was the first of a series on the fusion negotiations, was his clear analysis of the almost universal assumption that Labour inevitably would fail in office should it come to power. The business of Government, he felt, would be too complicated for the inexperienced leaders of the party, even granting as he did the traditional loyalty of the Civil Service. They had made far greater promises than the Coalition in the 1918 election and would be unable to fulfil them. The glad confident morning of British Socialism would soon fade; their followers would become discontented and revolutionary agitators would appear demanding their turn. It was necessary therefore to have a strong alternative party free of the elements of Tory reaction, an 'advanced' but non-socialist party which could step forward offering both reform and order.[2]

Masterman suggested that the decision to begin the formation of a new party came after the railway strike of September 1919, when Lloyd George realized he was faced with the alternatives either of extending the lines of his party to the left, which he could not do satisfactorily with the hampering influence of the reactionary Tories on the right, or of making open war upon Labour, which he did not care to do after the unfriendly public reaction to the Government's attacks upon the railway workers who had been denounced as anarchists. (The railway strike lasted from 26 September to 5 October.) By standing forth as the champion of social reform, he would recover his reputation as a leading radical and leave stranded both the extreme right and the extreme left.[3]

Even before the strike Lloyd George had been considering with intimates, as indeed he had for several years, the need for stabilizing the political situation. During the middle weeks of September, he discussed with Lord Riddell on several occasions the proposition that the right wing of the Conservatives hurt him more than it helped him. On 12 September, Riddell recorded that the Prime Minister had remarked that he 'thought the time had come for him to strike out on his own account, and that the present situation was very artificial. He said, "Then those who are for me will declare themselves, and I shall know who are against me and will do the same. Then I shall know where I am." ' The House of Commons, Lloyd George

[1] *Ibid.*, 158. Although demonstrating the level of appeal of the new group, Masterman thought this phrase meaningless.

[2] *Ibid.*, 159–60.

[3] *Ibid.*, 153–5. Masterman noted that Lloyd George's name by now was 'an anathema' to the lower ranks of the Labour party although the party's leaders, particularly those who had worked with him personally, were still vulnerable to his charm.

and Riddell agreed eight days later, on 20 September, would eventually resolve itself into two groups. One with a forward policy, and the other a Labour party with a still more advanced policy. His own policy, Lloyd George insisted, would be neither for the 'haves' nor for the 'have-nots'.

> My policy is to endeavour to hold an even balance between the two. I intend to advocate reforms which will remove gross inequalities and grave abuses. On the other hand, I am convinced that the work can not be carried on without the aid of a skilled managerial class. You must have leaders and captains of industry if you are to have any progress. You can not have adequate production unless you invoke the aid of clever manufacturers and businessmen working for their own profit. But you must see that they do not get too much and that they do not grind the other classes under their heel.[1]

After the railway strike popular discontent with the Government appeared to reach a new peak and the possibility that the Coalition would be overthrown was generally discussed in working-class circles. 'I have alluded to the general belief that a Labour Government will shortly be returned to power', wrote Basil Thomson on 20 November.

> No doubt the high prices and housing difficulties have much to do with the discontent among working men, who regard the Government as a patron of trusts and profiteers. My Newcastle correspondent says there is a very marked feeling against the present Coalition, which is generally believed to have had its day.
>   The men in the Liverpool area are stating openly that they will not starve while the Government allows others to make huge profits.[2]

Thus, in the last months of 1919 the position of the Coalition Government deteriorated. Several sitting Coalition Liberal Members of Parliament deliberately gave up the Government whip and returned to Asquith's party. More serious was the secession of some of the few constituency organizations controlled by the Coalition Liberals, particularly as the result of the introduction of the Safeguarding of Industries or 'Anti-Dumping' Bill, which seemed to many old-fashioned Liberals as another evidence of the Government's captivity by Tory big business.

'The plight of the Coalition Liberals, indeed, is a terrible one', wrote *The Times* on 4 December, 'and members of that party are at last beginning to realize the tragedy of their position.'

[1] Riddell, *Diary of Peace Conference*, 127, diary entries 12, 20 September 1919.
[2] PRO Cab. 24/93, CP 168, 'Report on Revolutionary Organizations', No. 30, 20 November 1919, 3, 5.

Resolutions are continually reaching them from Liberal friends in the country on Free Trade, Ireland, and other public questions, which prove conclusively the way the wind is blowing. The Coalition is clearly not popular with their constituents, and, where it is tolerated, it is only as a buffer to Labour. The Coalition Unionists are a separate party; the Coalition Liberals are not.

The alternatives for the Coalition Liberals are a reunited Party or a fusion with the Unionists into a permanent Coalition party. There are many who think the first desirable and who flatly reject the second. The problem for Mr Lloyd George to solve is fundamental. He had declared he could not go on without Liberal support, and it is to be expected that he will make a fresh bid for it at Manchester on Saturday. If he fails to enlist it he will be at a parting of the ways, and the new Coalition will sooner or later have to find a new basis.[1]

The Manchester speech of 6 December 1919, which *The Times* had referred to, technically marked the third anniversary of Lloyd George's accession to the Prime Ministership. In fact it turned out to be, in contradiction to what the paper had expected, not an appeal to the old Liberals, but a trial balloon for fusion. Briefly Lloyd George made an appeal for popular support of the Coalition, reminding the nation of his previous Manchester speech in September 1918 and insisting that he had not abandoned the promises made at that time.[2] Most important he dwelt, as had Winston Churchill in his famous 'untrodden fields' letter to the *Nation* in March 1908, on the broad meadows of reform yet untilled: '... there is a wide field of activity, administrative and legislative, which is common ground to all parties, and it is in that field you have got now to plough, to harrow, to sow and to reap.' His party could do it, the Coalition could do it; the Labour party could not. There were many moderate men in the Labour party: 'But there are also Socialists, there are Syndicalists, there are Direct Actionists, there are Sovietists, there are Bolshevists.' One could not separate the bad from the good. The Coalition must be kept in office, lest England be brought to revolution not reform.[3]

In the months following the Manchester speech the Prime Minister worked to assemble a consensus that would support him in the leadership he hoped to give Great Britain. He knew, as most of his public did not, that national finances were deep in crises, that the Cabinet was receiving daily pressure from the Bank of England to reduce its spending and end Government raids into the City capital market, and

[1] *The Times*, 4 December 1919.
[2] *Ibid.*, 8 December 1919.
[3] *Ibid.*

that the Government, at least as presently constituted, would be unable
to resist pressure from these traditional sources of economic power.[1]

The move toward fusion appears to have reached a final stage with
the Spen Valley by-election of 20 December 1919. Here one of the
new constituency associations controlled by the Coalition Liberals at
the time of the Coupon Election had seceded and had adopted Sir
John Simon as its candidate. Contrary to their practice the year before
the Lloyd George Liberals put up a candidate of their own with the
consequence that Labour won the seat T. P. Whittaker had held since
1892.[2]

Spen Valley seems to have driven Lloyd George into the uncharacteristic state of near panic. Liberalism, he told Lord Riddell, on
1 February 1920, was facing a serious crisis and he had informed
'Bonar Law that I am not going to go on like this'.

> We are losing by-election after by-election. There is no proper
> political organization in the country and no enthusiasm. A great
> deal can be done by working with constituencies. I know this from
> my experience in connexion with the 1919 Budget and the Insurance
> Bill.

The Prime Minister then reviewed the courses open to him. He could
retire; he could resign and organize the Coalition Liberals into a
stronger party leading them in the House of Commons. His third course
could be fusion in which he had already the support of the Conservative party leaders. After Riddell had suggested to him that the election
defeats would continue unless the 'constitutional forces' of the country
joined together, the Prime Minister admitted that his proper course was
to weld his present followers into some kind of a permanent organization.

> They have treated me well. They gave me a chance to win the war,
> and, as you say, they supported me loyally in the House of Commons.
> From that point of view I am quite with you, and I agree about
> the programme. It might be necessary for us to shed some of the
> more reactionary members of our party—some of the hard com-
> mercial men who have no bowels of compassion for the mass of the
> people—men who look upon the workers as nothing more than

---

[1] For a discussion of the influence of the City on the most expensive and most
contentious of all reform programmes, housing, see Chapter 3. Writing in February
of 1920 Masterman announced sadly that Lloyd George had allowed the chance
to make war on wealth to slip away. The financial debate of October 1919 announcing
the policy of deflation was the 'crucial moment'. Masterman, *Contemporary Review*,
February 1920, 154. *Official Report, House of Commons Debates*, CXX (October
29–30), cols. 738–816, 939–1052.

[2] Viscount Simon in his almost useless memoirs gives the date of the Spen Valley
by-election as 'December 1920'. Viscount Simon, *Retrospect* (London, 1952), 123.

D

producers of goods. I will never stand for that. I told Bonar Law and, to do the Conservatives justice, I don't believe they care for these people any more than I do.[1]

Later Riddell recorded that Lloyd George had seriously been discussing fusion with his chief Liberal advisers and that Addison and Macnamara, 'who know much more about electioneering' than the others, had urged him toward fusion.[2]

During January, February and March 1920, while British national finances were going through a crisis that would eventually bring all thought of social reform to an end, the Coalition Government seemed to be in danger of breaking up. Lloyd George himself continued to negotiate with both his own Liberal following and with the Conservative leaders. In this he was supported by most of the Liberal radical leaders, but opposed by the Liberal rank and file in the House of Commons, who were fearful of their own very tenuous base in the constituencies, and by Captain Frederick Guest, the Coalition Liberal Whip (whom Lloyd George replaced with Charles McCurdy the next year, although making Guest Secretary of State for Air).[3] Among the Conservatives he appeared for a time to have more success. A number of senior parliamentary leaders of the party, Bonar Law, Balfour and Birkenhead, attempted for a time to promote the idea of permanent coalition among the rank and file Members of Parliament. But generally members of the party hierarchy outside the Government and Conservative leaders in the country—with the exception of Archibald Salvidge of Liverpool—were wary.[4] Many party leaders, for instance Lord Derby and Lord Salisbury, were strongly against fusion even while acknowledging the Prime Minister's great electoral power.[5] At the by-election at Stockport on 27 March 1920 Salisbury obtained defeat of the official Coalition candidate and succeeded in electing a Unionist by publicly advising the voters there not to support the official candidate.[6]

---

[1] Riddell, *Diary of the Peace Conference*, 164–6, diary entry 1 February 1920.
[2] Addison to Lloyd George, 3 March 1920, LG Papers, F/1/6/4. On 7 February, at Wrekin, the Coalition Liberals lost yet another seat.
[3] Wilson, *Downfall*, 200. A few of the Liberal party leaders, Churchill and Macnamara notably, had already been repudiated by their own constituency organizations.
[4] On the growing split between the Conservative party leadership at Westminster and the constituency organizations over fusion see also: Almeric Fitzroy, *Memoirs* (London, n.d.), II, 726, diary entry 22 March 1920. Stanley Salvidge, *Salvidge of Liverpool, Behind the Political Scene, 1890–1928* (London, 1934), 180, 184. See also Salvidge to Churchill, 21 February 1920, LG Papers, F/9/2/9.
[5] See a letter from Derby to Philip Sassoon, 23 December 1920, quoted in Randolph S. Churchill, *Lord Derby, King of Lancashire* (London, 1959), 387–8.
[6] Salisbury's open letter made Lloyd George extremely angry. Riddell, *Diary of the Peace Conference*, 175, diary entry 7 March 1920.

But, in the last analysis, the man who upset the attempts at fusion or, more specifically, frustrated Lloyd George's attempt to split the Tory party and gather its moderate wing with the Coalition Liberals around himself as a new party and who finally may be credited for the destruction of the Prime Minister himself by absorbing many of Lloyd George's own party into the Conservatives rather than the other way round, was Sir George Younger. Younger does not appear to have opposed fusion directly.[1] Rather he took the line that if Lloyd George and the Coalition Liberals were to fuse with the Unionists and to gain the advantages of the efficient Unionist constituency organizations, Lloyd George would have to give up his personal campaign war chest, 'the Lloyd George Fund'.[2] His most important service to the Conservatives lay in forestalling a general election until the Coalition Liberals had thoroughly discredited themselves. At the same time he supported the courage of his own party's rank and file by reiterating, in contradiction to most of the other leaders, that Lloyd George needed the Tories more than they needed him.[3]

Younger was helped by the return of Asquith for Paisley at the end of February 1920 after 15 months' absence from Parliament, which event may have marked the end of any possibility of real fusion between the Coalition Liberals and the Tories. With an impeccably respectable alternative leader on the Opposition front bench, Lloyd George's claims as the only national spokesman for Liberalism were substantially diminished and his dependence upon the Tories became greater. At the same time, although the likelihood that Asquith would emerge as the leader of a revolutionary Labour party appears remote in perspective,[4] many Tories seem to have regarded this as a possibility increasing the danger of radicalism so bringing to an end the first proposals for fusion.[5] So long as Bonar Law remained loyal, the

---

[1] Churchill, *Derby*, 386–7.

[2] Max Aitken, Lord Beaverbrook, *The Decline and Fall of Lloyd George* (New York, 1963), 9n., 10, 14. Beaverbrook reiterates what is clear from many other sources: that the basis of Lloyd George's power over the Conservatives was the belief of many backbenchers that they owed their seats to the Prime Minister.

[3] He 'was much closer to the rank and file of his party in the country . . . ' than the other leaders, emphasized Leo Amery, and he knew the extent of the disaffection in the constituencies. Leopold S. Amery, *My Political Life* (London, 1953), II, 231–2, 235.

[4] Reports of a possible electoral arrangement between the independent Liberals and the Labour party continued throughout the year, growing proportionately more serious as the popular disenchantment with the Coalition increased. C. F. G. Masterman, 'The Policy of an Electoral Arrangement', *Nation*, 23 October 1920. See also: C. F. G. Masterman, 'Fusion: The First Phase', *Contemporary Review*, CXVIII (August 1920), 182.

[5] *Ibid.*, 185–6.

Prime Minister was probably in little immediate danger, but his prospects for a continuing political base were sensibly lessened.

The Prime Minister's first thought was to risk all in a general election, which he considered some time in March 1920. Lloyd George had spoken frequently perhaps insincerely of hoping to clear the air in this way, but he was dissuaded by the pleas of his own Liberal followers and apparently also by Younger who is reported to have firmly opposed the idea. The resurgence of the independent Liberals had now strengthened the position of the Conservatives who argued there was a real need to avoid three-cornered constituency fights in which candidates from two of the constitutional parties opposed each other and threw the seat to Labour.[1]

Then, briefly, in the late spring the Prime Minister attempted to form a full-fledged party independent of Asquith's Liberals. An organizational meeting was held at Leamington. Guest and McCurdy were sent around the country to attempt to organize what were to be called 'National Liberal' constituency organizations and a new magazine, the *Lloyd George Liberal Magazine,* was established.[2] But all was in vain. By the middle of June supporters of fusion in both sections of the Coalition had virtually disappeared. Instead of the likelihood that there would be a new party made up of the rump of Liberals and a majority of the Conservatives, remarked the *New Statesman,* whose estimates of the future at this period were remarkably accurate:

> Powerful, wealthy and well organized forces of Conservatism intend to absorb rather than fuse with the Coalition Liberals.... Despite every effort made by the Prime Minister to equip himself and his personal following with a rival organization the entourage must know in their hearts that it is a choice between absorption and disruption that they must come to in the end.

The final crisis, felt the journal, might come on a matter vital to Lloyd George: 'that of a redistribution of the seats so amazingly cornered at the last election by Sir George Younger.'[3] How far the historian may be justified in deducing a changed point of view from uncharacteristic decisions made by a man in a position of power — or how much those decisions may reflect only the force of circumstance — would involve a larger excursion into the philosophy of causation than could be justified in this study. In any case, in the spring of

[1] *New Statesman,* 8 May 1920.
[2] Wilson, *Downfall,* 200; *New Statesman,* 5, 19 June 1920; also: Charles Mallett, 'Liberalism and Mr Lloyd George', *Contemporary Review,* CXVII (June 1920), 774–82.
[3] *New Statesman,* 19 June 1920. See also: C. F. G. Masterman, 'The Coalition, Liberalism and Labour', *Contemporary Review,* CXIX (May 1921), 606–17.

1920, Britain's economic prospects were changing rapidly and Lloyd George's opinions about what was desirable, or possible, in the way of social reform began to change with them. In March, the Cabinet received warning that the fiscal exuberance so evident since the end of the war would have to stop. In the long run financial restriction spelled the end of housing and of expanded welfare legislation on behalf of national health programmes. Arguably it played a major role in the great postwar depression which had settled upon England by the end of 1920, which itself saddled the nation with the chronic problem of unemployment and made critical support of the unemployed whose demands obscured nearly every other social problem. But for whatever reason, politics or economics, the new situation had its effect upon a Prime Minister, whose outlook was essentially empirical and whose opinions tended to be taken from men from whom he could learn. 'I notice that L.G. is steadily veering over to the Tory point of view', wrote Lord Riddell on 27 March 1920.

> He consistently refers to the great services rendered by captains of industry and defends the propriety of a large share of profits they take. He says one Leverhulme or Ellerman is worth more to the world than 10,000 sea captains or 20,000 engine drivers, and should be remunerated accordingly. He wants to improve the world and the condition of the people, but he wants to do it in his own way.
>
> He seems convinced that socialism is a mistaken policy. I observed this conviction growing upon him during the past four years. His point of view has entirely changed.[1]

The evolving attitudes which Lord Riddell had noted in the spring of 1920 were reflected in the increasing difficulties encountered in the Cabinet by particularly Christopher Addison, in attempting to secure support for advanced projects of social reform. (At this time Lloyd George even tried to replace Addison at the Ministry of Health with Alfred Mond, a businessman, a man of great wealth and one of the most determined opponents of fusion among the Coalition Liberals. He would succeed in doing this precisely one year later.)

By mid-summer, just as the impossibility either of fusion with the Conservatives or the creation of a genuinely permanent and independent National Liberal party had become clear, the sensitive indicators available to the British Cabinet began to show that the postwar boom was coming to an end, even though unemployment was at an unprecedented postwar low and the inflation of retail prices went on unabated and would do so until December. In June a slow decline in wholesale prices began and Basil Thomson, whose economic intel-

[1] Riddell, *Diary of the Peace Conference*, 179.

ligence was usually excellent, began his summary for the third week of the month with:

It now seems certain that we are on the eve of a new industrial crisis which must take place during the next two or three months. The feeling of the employers seems to be that at the present rate in the increase of wages they must either fight or close down their works, and if the fight has got to come they had better have it now while they are full of orders. Their great hope is that the Government will stand out a bit and let them settle the matter with their employees.[1]

In early August T. J. Macnamara, since March Minister of Labour, presented the Cabinet with a frightening report on the certainty of coming unemployment and labour unrest, noting particularly that about 150,000 ex-servicemen were unemployed of whom between 15,000 and 20,000 were in London. The situation, Macnamara concluded, was dangerous. *'I wish the Cabinet clearly to understand that from November onwards—if not earlier—particularly in any locality where civil unemployment may increase, these men will lead unemployment processions and will not stick at trifles.'*[2]

By December 1920 unemployment was three times the figure of June 1920 and approaching one million people (although before the payment of unemployment insurance accurate statistics are rare) and by the end of 1920 slightly more than two million insured working people were registered at employment exchanges representing 17.9 per cent of the insured work force. The Government's response—except for the Unemployment Insurance Act of 1920, which was the last piece of major welfare legislation that can be reasonably ascribed to the Lloyd George reform programme—was a virtual shelving of any plans to do anything about the Poor Law, some encouragement for emigration, training for the unemployed, public works by local authorities, and certain credit facilities guaranteed by the Government to both purchasers of British goods abroad and British exporters.

Finally, in autumn 1921, came a major scheme of Government credit facilities to promote the modernization and extension of British industry. The Trade Facilities Act of 1921 (subsequently extended by similar acts in the next five years but eventually dropped in 1927) was characteristic of the new orientation in the Prime Minister's thinking: that business initiative and efficient private enterprise held the best cure for unemployment. The importance of these measures lay not so much in their effect on the total amount of unemployment, which although

[1] PRO Cab. 24/107, CP 1490, 'Report on Revolutionary Organizations', No. 59, 17 June 1920.
[2] T. J. Macnamara, 'Unemployment', 4 August 1920, LG Papers, F/ 36/1/25.

incalculable was probably slight, but in the fact that they provided a precedent for tackling the problem of the distress of the jobless, not through the provision of relief but through deliberate attempts by the Government working within the capitalist system to provide jobs. This principle, unacknowledged and probably unrecognized, which would be adopted in the United States with the Reconstruction Finance Corporation and the Public Works Administration, appeared as assumption 'C' in William Beveridge's *Report on Social Insurance and Allied Services* and finally became basic policy for all British governments since the Second World War. Whether or not it is good for national productive efficiency, it has been accepted that the Government must assume the responsibility for ensuring the maintenance of a relatively high level of economic activity. Otherwise the problem of the support of the unemployed becomes unmanageable.[1]

The Trade Facilities Act of 1921 had its origin in a series of Cabinet conferences at Gairloch on the west coast of Scotland to which the Prime Minister had retired early in September to recover from an illness caused by an infected tooth. There in a speech Lloyd George questioned briefly whether British finances had not been deflated too much and noted that some members of the Cabinet, Churchill particularly, were saying that 'the country was being sacrificed upon the altar of banks'. In view of the fact that the 'state of the exchanges was the most serious question of the day', the Prime Minister asked generally for an expression of opinion on whether there was not some way to bring increasingly scarce British capital to the aid of manufacturing industry as well as financial institutions.[2] The upshot of the conference was a report submitted on 2 October by Hilton Young, at that time a Financial Secretary to the Treasury, proposing the establishment of a national committee of about five representatives from industry to decide on capital schemes that would expand industry, stimulate exports, and most of all help unemployment. The Government would borrow a national development fund to finance programmes. Eventually the proposed sum to be raised was set at £50,000,000.

The City reacted almost immediately. Through the Chancellor of the

---

[1] Because of their short life the Trade Facilities Acts have received little attention from economic historians although the Webbs, with their usual insight, realized their significance even in 1929, shortly after the scheme was allowed to lapse. See: Sidney and Beatrice Webb, *English Poor Law History: Part II: The Last Hundred Years* (London, 1929), II, 697–8, 707–9. For William Beveridge's discussion of the Government's importance as a regulator in the maintenance of employment see: *Cmd. 6406*, 'Social Insurance and Allied Services, Report by Sir William Beveridge', 163–5.

[2] For part, although not all, of the discussions at Gairloch see: Riddell, *Diary of the Peace Conference*, 325–6, diary entry 15 September 1921. See also: CP 3371, 'Memorandum of the Cabinet Committee on Unemployment', in PRO Cab. 23/27, Cabinet 76 of 1921, meeting 6 October. Appendix I, II.

Exchequer, Robert Horne, the Governor of the Bank of England, Montagu Norman, informed the Cabinet bluntly that he

> was aware of schemes to be placed on the market sufficient to absorb all the money available during the next six months, [and] any further demands would have to be fitted in as circumstances permitted. He was not prepared to advise that the Government guarantee should extend beyond a maximum capital sum of £25,000,000. The Governor ... also expressed himself as strongly opposed to any proposal to finance the Gairloch guarantee ... by any form of short term borrowing for at least six months. Finally the Governor of the Bank was quoted as being 'strongly of the opinion that the backing of the Government would not make the difference anticipated in the initiation of new enterprises.'[1]

Thus the first hesitant step towards a regular partnership between government and private enterprise which could have refurbished Lloyd George's tarnished reputation as a radical reformer in the guise of an enlightened Tory Democrat was nearly stifled at birth by traditional finance. The measure that finally was passed in November offered loan guarantees for a year (applications were to be accepted during the next year, the loan was not required to be of a single year's duration) to a maximum of £25 million.[2] During the period of the various extensions of the act down to 1927 there was little that the most prudent economist could charge against its administration. Requests for loans were carefully examined and little money was wasted. The chief result was to help those who needed help least. Businessmen efficient enough to qualify for Government assistance simply were enabled to borrow at five per cent funds that they had planned to borrow in any case at nearly twice the rate. The effect on employment was not discernible. Of the £25 million authorized by the first act, less than 20 million were actually issued during the remaining years of the Lloyd George administration. In contrast during approximately the same period, the financial year ending 31 March 1922, nearly £58 million was spent on unemployment insurance benefits and another £45 million on poor law relief in England, Wales and Scotland.[3]

Lloyd George and reform

Lloyd George's final dismissal from political power came as a result of events that have little to do with the story of British social policy.

[1] PRO Cab. 23/27, Cabinets 79 and 80 of 1921, 14, 17 October 1921.
[2] For the second reading see: *H of C Deb.*, CXLVII (25 October 1921), cols. 655–784.
[3] *Cmd. 2849*, 'Statistical Abstract for the United Kingdom', 68, 82, 124–5.

Yet it seems possible to say that barring some dramatic reversal in domestic economic conditions the fate that overtook him in October 1922 was inevitable after the winter of 1919–20. His political base had been that of an advanced radical, a non-socialistic social reformer. Before the war, he and perhaps Winston Churchill had been the Liberals' answer to the threat of the Labour party. His credentials in all this were certified by the detestation he received from nearly all Conservatives. The circumstances of his accession during the war to the Ministry of Munitions and the Prime Ministership, and particularly his clear association and camaraderie with English businessmen, although doubtless necessary for the prosecution of the conflict, inevitably began to dilute his radical reputation. There can be no question that he realized this was happening and that he intended, at least after 1916, to begin rebuilding his contacts with Labour and resuming his position as the head of reform or 'advanced' British politics. But at the same time he was disturbed, in common with nearly every other member of the British Government, by the apparent growth of revolutionary sentiment among the working class. To be sure, it was reasonable to think that at bottom the ordinary English working man really believed in established institutions but the Prime Minister knew as well as anyone that the working man also had genuine grievances upon which agitators could fix and unless these grievances were somehow allayed revolution could break out. Thus he felt the country needed his leadership for reconstruction after the war precisely as it had needed his organizational abilities for military victory during the conflict. He promised to overcome poverty and distress and the Bolshevism that fed upon them as he had defeated the Germans. To do this he would ask, as he had demanded during the war, the support of all Englishmen of goodwill, and so he looked forward to a reorganization of parties that would have included his own Liberal followers and all but the most unredeemable Tories.

A barrier to his plans appeared in the Parliament elected by the Coalition victory of December 1918. Despite the intentions of both parties the election had not been fought over promises of peace but over promises to continue pressure through diplomatic channels toward the complete punishment and humiliation of Germany. Whether or not this was feasible in international and diplomatic terms, or indeed desirable in domestic British terms, it proved to be disastrous for Lloyd George and the National Liberals politically. The danger, certainly at first, was not so much that they were in fact prisoners of the 'hard-faced men and war profiteers', but that to the average English working man they appeared to be. New houses, new schools, secure employment and lower prices could not be legislated into existence. Indeed in many cases, as Christopher Addison well knew, reforms demanded by workmen were held up by the irresponsibility of workmen themselves. As the Prime Minister's alienation from his former radical and Labour supporters increased he became in fact what had only been apparent before: a prisoner of the Tories. To be sure, Bonar Law's supporters feared him for his electoral power; many of them owed, or believed they owed, their seats to him. But on the other hand if the Coalition were ever to win an electoral victory, it would have to be managed by the Conservative constituency organizations. Lloyd George himself had no such local bases and seemed unable to build any. Thus the last two years of the Coalition tenure were a period of sham arrangement. The Coalition rank and file distrusted but needed their leader; the leader despised but needed his following. The arrangement ended on 19 October 1922 when the Conservative back bench rose in what must have seemed to many a hopeless rebellion not only against the Prime Minister but against those of their own leaders who remained faithful to him. They had already destroyed David Lloyd George's dreams for a better England. In the end they destroyed his career as well.

2 Britain out of work

Of all the social problems that Britain faced between the wars, none was more intractable, more persistent, more dangerous to the economic system, nor indeed to the maintenance of law and of the King's Government, than unemployment. The notion that unemployment of adult males was in any way a matter with which politicians should concern themselves did not appear until the last 15 years of the nineteenth century.[1] It derived from a growing awareness among the established political parties of the power both of revolutionary socialism and, more immediately, of household franchise guided by a Labour movement growing increasingly political. At the core of the difficulty was the uncomfortable fact that the assumptions underlying the only existing State provision for the unemployed, the Poor Law of 1834, clearly were no longer valid. Classical, or 'Manchester', economic theory had assumed that at some wage level jobs were available for all and that a man's idleness therefore was caused by his own laziness. The Poor Law, hence, treated an applicant for relief as a quasi-criminal and sought to force him by the pressure of humiliation and discipline back into the labour market.

So long as the men who made the laws were not elected by people who were likely to become clients of the Poor Law such a system could work. But after the enactment of household franchise in 1885 the punishment of the idle man became politically dangerous. Whatever the cause of his condition, he was now a man with a vote. For the next 20 years, from 1885 to 1905, British political leadership took the line that the treatment for unemployment would be found in the provision of work. Through a series of acts and departmental orders, various public and private agencies were encouraged in times of depression to provide jobs to worthy men who applied for them. These experiments culminated in the Unemployed Workmen Act of 1905 in which, briefly, the national Government, through a network of statutory 'Distress Committees' established by each major local authority, attempted to supervise the administration of relief work and other activities for

[1] The word 'unemployed' did not appear in its modern meaning in the *Oxford English Dictionary* until the late 1880s, and 'unemployment' was not a separate heading in *Hansard* until after the Boer War. When Bagehot in *The British Constitution* referred to the Prince of Wales as being 'unemployed' he was not suggesting that Albert was a potential member of the English labour force but rather that he had nothing of any importance to do.

the aid of the respectable unemployed. The most that can be said about the Unemployed Workmen Act is that it showed what was *not* possible in the way of help for the jobless and although the act lingered on until 1929, after only a very few months of operation—certainly by the middle of 1906—most advanced social planners had come to the conclusion that artificially stimulated employment was impracticable within a capitalist system.[1]

Barring the overthrow of capitalism the best way to deal with unemployment after 1906 appeared to lie in help for the unemployed man himself—the organization of the labour market, training in new skills, the regularization of employment in industries using casual labour such as the docks and railways, better attention to health to prevent unemployment through sickness, and most important of all, the widespread establishment of labour exchanges to give all working men access to all situations available throughout the country. Labour exchanges became the special project of William Henry Beveridge as a result of his experiences in administering the Unemployed Workmen Act in London. In articles in the *Morning Post* and other journals, Beveridge advocated labour exchanges as a way of introducing some measure of real competition into the most imperfectly competitive labour market. In the summer of 1908, he entered the civil service at the Board of Trade under Winston Churchill, who had offered him a post at the behest of Sidney and Beatrice Webb. Here he began work upon a measure which became the Labour Exchanges Act of 1909. On 1 February 1910 the Labour Exchange Department of the Board of Trade came into existence with William Beveridge as its first director. By the end of 1913 there were 430 exchanges in existence in the United Kingdom in addition to 1,066 small branch agencies set up to handle unemployment insurance.

Unemployment insurance, Part II of the National Insurance Act of 1911, represented probably the boldest experiment in social legislation of the entire period of the New Liberalism. Churchill had originally intended to couple labour exchanges with some provision for the insurance of the unemployed. The political explosion caused by the 1909 budget and the subsequent Parliament Act forced the postponement of this plan until 1911. The programme of insurance that went into effect on 15 July 1912 was narrowly limited both in coverage and in benefit. To the trades eligible for it—principally building and engineering—Part II offered an unemployment benefit of 7s. per week for a maximum of 15 weeks in any 12-month period. In 1911, this sum amounted to perhaps one-third of the average weekly wage of the

---

[1] On the early experiments to care for the unemployed see: Bentley B. Gilbert, *The Evolution of National Insurance in Great Britain* (London, 1966), 38–9, 253–6, 259–65.

lowest regularly paid city worker. (Agricultural wages were still lower, but workers on the land were not covered.) For this small support the worker and his employer each paid a weekly contribution of 2½d. The Government added a subsidy of about 1⅔d., making a total contribution of 6⅔d., of which a net of 6d. went toward insurance. Of great importance for the future, the scheme assumed an average unemployment of 8·46 per cent among eligible workers.

It should be emphasized that the trades covered by Part II of the National Insurance Act of 1911 numbered, as it turned out, only about 2¼ million men in a total male labour force of slightly over 10 million. By design they included almost no women, were skilled and well-organized providing stability of personnel, did not, by custom, put their employees on short-time during a depression and, it was hoped, were subject only to reasonable and predictable seasonal economic fluctuations. In effect the planners of the world's first compulsory state unemployment insurance programme loaded their actuarial calculations and narrowed their risk in every possible way. Deliberately they did not choose for insurance a representative sample of British industrial society and while this sensible policy protected a highly experimental programme, it also made the programme less useful as a guide in the years ahead.

A fact of importance for the future was the decision, during the framing of the act, not to build a permanent insurance reserve, but to create, instead, a revolving fund to be supported by current premiums and depleted through current benefits. The men at work at any one time would maintain those unemployed. In cases of general unemployment the fund was given the right to borrow from the Treasury to a maximum of £3 million, and correspondingly the Treasury could require reductions in benefit and increases in premiums if the borrowing grew too heavy. The assumption was that the income and expenditure of the fund would balance at the unemployment rate of about 8½ per cent.[1] But significantly the original act established the principle that in the last analysis the Treasury furnished the reserve for paying unemployment insurance claims. The £3 million limit was only as firm as the determination of Members of Parliament to resist the political pressures to increase it.

Unemployment insurance exemplified the prevailing attitude about the proper areas of State action held in the years before the war. In every way the programme was tentative, narrow and carefully guarded. No contributor had any right to expect benefits beyond the stipulated

[1] For discussion of the financial and actuarial considerations of Part II of the National Insurance Act see: Gilbert, *Evolution of National Insurance*, 276–87. See also: A. F. Comyns Carr, W. H. Stuart Garnett and J. H. Taylor, *National Insurance* (London, 1912), 106–10, 441–2.

15 weeks per year. An eligible contributor did, to be sure, receive his benefits as of right, within the terms of the act, but there was no implication that the State had any obligation to support any unemployed workman. The waiting period of six working days, the requirement of six months' contributions before eligibility, the limitation of the allowable period of unemployment, and, overriding all else, the rule that no worker at any time could claim more than one week of benefit for each five weeks of contributions, all underlined this assumption.

The difficulty was that these rules, like the limitation on Treasury advances, were only as strong as the political will to enforce them. In any elective society the Government's attitude toward a large group in the population needing help is likely to be a reflection of the expectations of the voters. It follows that so long as economic conditions were good and contributions were high in proportion to benefits the limitations on the unemployment insurance scheme of 1911 were reasonably safe. But with the uncertainty that came with the end of the war, with the extravagant promises for a better Britain on the one hand and the growing threat of communist revolution on the other, the nation began to question whether economic security was only for a few and to believe that every returned soldier, and indeed every worker, deserved a measure of economic security as a matter of right.

Such a consensus undermined the defence of the limitations on the borrowing power of the unemployment fund and of the limitations on the right to benefit. The relaxation of any rule, passed in haste by a frightened Parliament, came immediately to be regarded as a vested right by the working class, leading to further relaxations. Actuarial safeguards disappeared and unemployment insurance became simply an awkward and expensive agency for the payment of general welfare benefits basically financed by ordinary taxation.[1]

Unemployment insurance and war: the coming of the dole

Thanks to the prosperity Britain had enjoyed in the years between 1912 and 1914, when the First World War broke out the unemployment insurance fund had a balance of more than £3 million. Although unemployment rose briefly after the declaration of war, from 2·8 per cent in July 1914 to 7·1 per cent by the end of August, it soon fell to the irreducible minimum of between 0·4 per cent and 0·8 per

---

[1] The question of whether unemployment insurance deserved any longer the name 'insurance' became the topic of wide debate during the crisis of 1931 although Sidney and Beatrice Webb wrote an excellent definition of the problem two years before that time. Sidney and Beatrice Webb, *English Poor Law History: Part II: The Last Hundred Years* (London, 1929), II, 834.

cent where it remained throughout the war. (These figures represent the percentages of trade union unemployment only. There are no exact statistics for overall unemployment until the beginning of the 1920s.) A most important result of the high wartime employment was that from £3,211,000 the fund had increased by the end of 1918 to £15,200,000, with the important effect of encouraging what may have been imprudent extensions of insurance.

One reason for the rapid growth of the fund was the National Insurance (Part II) (Munitions Workers) Act of 1916, which extended unemployment insurance to all workmen engaged 'on, or in connection with, munitions work' and to all workmen in certain trades—ammunition, explosives, chemicals, metals, rubber, leather and bricks—whether or not these trades were themselves engaged in munitions work. Perhaps more important, the 1916 legislation made possible the extension of insurance by departmental order to any trade or branch of an industry in which substantial amounts of munitions work or any other work for war purposes was being conducted. The bill was set to expire five years from 4 December 1916 or three years after the end of the war, whichever date was later. It passed both Houses of Parliament without opposition, and virtually without comment, becoming law on 4 September 1916.

The act of 1916 demonstrated in its operation the rather low esteem in which unemployment insurance was generally held by the workers. For practical purposes the act made possible the extension of unemployment insurance to nearly every industry in the United Kingdom, for no enterprise was without some war work. But in fact extensions of insurance everywhere met with great resistance. The woollen and cotton industries, both of which could have become completely insured, insisted upon being excluded. The boot and shoe trade was specifically included in the statute and could not be left out by administrative order. Here, reported William Beveridge,

the employers and work-people went into passive resistance; they refused to work the Act or to pay the contributions and were retrospectively excluded by an Amending Act in 1917. In these and in other cases the line was taken that the trade had unfilled orders to keep them busy for years after the war, and that if they did have unemployment, they could provide for it better by themselves than under a State scheme. None of the trades in fact made any serious attempts to frame schemes of their own; employers and work-people were content to unite in purely negative opposition to officials and the State. The net result of the new Act was to bring into insurance 1,100,000 persons, of whom about three-quarters were women and girls. They were brought in at the old rate of contribution and benefit. In spite of the manifest and growing change in the value of money and the rise in money wages, proposals by officials to increase insurance contributions in order to give better benefits found no favour.[1]

The failure to make unemployment insurance universal during the war or at least to extend it widely, when the evil to be guarded against was virtually non-existent and when regular contributions from large numbers of workers would have made possible the building of a substantial reserve fund, possibly may be viewed as the most serious single mistake in all the planning for reconstruction. Whatever workers may have thought during the war about the likelihood of unemployment, their attitude was markedly changed when the conflict was over. The popular fears and uncertainty that derived from the prospect of economic adjustment to the peacetime world, which gave so fertile a field for revolutionary agitators—and which offered so marked a contrast to the jubilation at the end of the fighting itself—dictated some form of action. But nothing was ready. The result was the 'unemployment donation', the original dole.

The story of unemployment insurance is inextricably bound up with the emergency 'out-of-work donation' which came into existence with the 1918 Armistice. In fact unemployment donation made universal unemployment insurance inevitable. The Government did not proceed to unemployment insurance in deliberate and calculated steps, but was driven to it at the end of 1920 by the fear of what would happen when the unemployment donation ended. Moreover, exactly as the universal unemployment donation forced unemployment insurance, the civilian part of the donation was itself consequence of the military donation, which was indeed the only portion of the entire apparatus for the care of unemployed to which the Government had given any mature consideration. The vast and intractable problems which proceeded from the make-shift nature of unemployment insurance in the interwar period were less the result of bad planning than of no planning. The Unemployment Insurance Act of 1920 was the product of a series of expedients, of political concessions made necessary by previous concessions.

Consideration for the care of the unemployed after the war, like reflection about many other postwar problems, began in the expansive —one might almost say 'heroic'—period of Lloyd George's tenure at the Ministry of Munitions, between the spring of 1915 and the summer of 1916. Among other obligations the Ministry had the duty of super-

[1] William H. Beveridge, 'Unemployment Insurance in the War and After', in James T. Shotwell, ed. *War and Insurance* (London, 1927), Carnegie Endowment Series, 232,

vising plans for demobilization of the military forces which had already been drafted by other departments. It took upon itself, however, the task of considering arrangements to be made for workers in the national munitions factories, who would become unemployed at the termination of hostilities. In 1917 the planning functions within Munitions on this subject were taken over by the newly created Ministry of Reconstruction under which a 'Civil War Workers Committee' received the task of considering and reporting 'upon arrangements which should be made for the demilitarization of workers engaged during the war in national factories ... in other firms engaged in the production of munitions of war, on Government contracts, or in firms where substitute labour has been employed for the duration of the war'.[1] The committee met for the first time on 25 July 1917. At the time of its appointment it became clear that there would be a need for an extension of unemployment insurance to ease the period of transition from war to peace. It therefore established a sub-committee headed by William Beveridge and including among others J. J. Mallon and C. F. Rey. The sub-committee reported on 12 February 1918. The main committee approved the report unanimously on 14 March and forwarded it to the Cabinet.[2] Taken together, these reports are of considerable importance even though they received absolutely no attention from the Government. The most important finding of the sub-committee was that it could discover no useful way to distinguish workers engaged in supporting the military effort from other workers. In one sense or another, the sub-committee reported, nearly every industrial worker in Britain would be affected by the end of the war and by the return of men from the forces. Hence the extension of unemployment insurance to any designated set of industries would do little to ease the economic problems of transition from war to peace. If insurance were to be used at all for the treatment of economic dislocation after the war, the scheme would have to be universal. Recalling how workers on the fringes of the munitions industry had fought to be excluded from unemployment insurance after the act of 1916, the report noted that a universal extension would be less unpopular politically than an extension to designated trades, each of which would feel itself discriminated against. 'On these grounds', concluded the report,

> we are satisfied that the only effective and adequate way of meeting the problem is by a scheme of general insurance designed to cover the whole area of employment. We think it probable that a general

---

[1] Beveridge, 'Unemployment Insurance in the War', 234–6.
[2] *Cd. 9192*, '2nd, 3rd, 4th and 5th Interim Reports on the Civil War Workers' Committee, Ministry of Reconstruction', 1918.

E

scheme, in spite of its magnitude, is likely to prove less controversial than any attempt to single out particular trades, while it makes certain, as no partial scheme would, of really covering all the ground and excluding the necessity for hastily improvised supplementary measures.[1]

The report urged that any plans for insurance should be implemented 'at the earliest possible date. Otherwise it may be impossible to avoid the disastrous chaos of unorganized and improvised methods of relieving distress.' Specifically the committee feared that, unless a scheme were in force for a considerable length of time before the war ended, many unemployed would not have made enough payments to draw benefits. Finally, and reluctantly, it suggested that, if this were the case, it might be possible for a worker to be paid benefits beyond those justified by the total of his contributions. Thus it anticipated the worse abuse of unemployment insurance after the war—the system of 'uncovenanted benefit' which within a decade would bring insurance close to bankruptcy.

The only action taken by the Government on the Civil War Workers' Committee report was to refer it to another committee, the Unemployment Insurance Sub-committee of the Labour Resettlement Committee of the Ministry of Labour, which also reported later in the year repeating the recommendation for general unemployment insurance. In extenuation of official neglect of the report it can only be said that the attitude prevailing with regard to unemployment insurance was the same as that toward all other reforms—health insurance, a Ministry of Health, reform of the Poor Law. In the spring of 1918 the war did not appear to be coming to an end but rather reaching a climax and the quick collapse of Germany in the autumn was totally unexpected. Lloyd George's interest in social reform was sincere. He needed, and intended to have, a programme of reconstruction which would become the platform of his new party. But he did not expect to be forced to produce it in 1918 and, as his neglect of the Ministry of Health would show, he was unwilling to devote time to it while even the question of a British victory seemed very much in doubt. To this consideration can be added the clear political unpopularity of contributory insurance as shown by the protest against the attempted extensions two years before and by the fact that no working-class or intellectual reform group in the country strongly supported the idea. Consequently, at the time of the Armistice, only one worker in four, or slightly fewer than four million in a total force of about 14 million, was covered by insurance. In 1914 approximately the same proportion had been insured in a considerably smaller labour force.

[1] *Cd. 9192*, 3, 7, Appendix B.

Suddenly, in early October, it became clear the war would soon come to an end. The first man at ministerial level to remember that the Government was unprepared with any plan to cope with the most important problem of peace for the ordinary individual citizen of the nation—the resumption of normal economic life—was Christopher Addison. As Minister of Reconstruction he had, in any case, the responsibility for keeping some part of the Cabinet's attention directed toward questions of social welfare and, particularly, for building a programme of reform on behalf of the Coalition Liberals. On 19 October 1918 Addison sent the Cabinet a long printed memorandum arguing in the strongest terms that something should be done immediately to prepare for the transition of civilian workers from war to peace. He noted that 2,433,000 men and women were covered by the act of 1911 and another 1,364,000 by the act of 1916, but that this left about 10 million workers without any support except the Poor Law in case of unemployment. It would be impossible now, he pointed out, to enact a comprehensive unemployment insurance scheme and to make the necessary administrative arrangements. Therefore he simply urged that the principle of the out-of-work donation for soldiers be adopted for civilians. The military out-of-work donation was one of the few programmes that had already been worked out as part of the general plan for demobilization. It provided what amounted to a paid-up unemployment insurance policy for all discharged servicemen. Addison proposed that for some period after the war all British civilian workers should be eligible for some kind of a payment to last perhaps six months in case they were unemployed. During this time all regular insurance schemes would be suspended.

In virtually the same terms put forward six months earlier by the Civil War Workers' Committee, Addison argued that the scheme could not be limited in practice to munitions workers and that if it were public opinion would oppose it. In addition, time was short. Questions of administration, the attendance at labour exchanges, availability for work, all other ordinary prerequisites of unemployment insurance, would be solved more quickly if the scheme were universal.

Towards the end of his memorandum, the Minister of Reconstruction made a suggestion of great importance for the future of unemployment insurance. If the scheme were to follow the precedent of the soldiers' out-of-work donation, which was in fact a separation allowance, it would have to give extra benefits for dependants. The programme, he insisted, would have to be attached to the cost of living if it were to do any good. In concluding he admitted that a universal civilian out-of-work donation would establish awkward precedents and put difficulties in the way of a contributory scheme later, as would the payment for dependants. Nevertheless, he argued, this was the way to proceed.[1]

Addison's universal civilian out-of-work donation—or perhaps the Government's acceptance of it a little over three weeks later—marks a new direction in the movement of postwar welfare history. Although the announcement of the scheme emphasized that it was a purely emergency measure, that contributions would continue to be collected under regular unemployment insurance and that 'in the meantime the Government are pressing forward with their scheme for general contributory insurance, which would be based on permanent considerations and must not be prejudiced by the non-contributory scheme here announced ...', somehow a new principle had been established.[2] In effect society was admitting that an adult working man unable to find employment had a *right* to make a claim upon it. This obligation, grudgingly admitted at first as a temporary dispensation, became fixed. When the first six months of the dole came to an end it had to be renewed until 24 November 1919. And when the civilian donation finally ended, even though unemployment at the time was virtually non-existent, the Government was forced to couple the disappearance of the dole with the announcement of a universal unemployment scheme which, in fact, it did not have ready. In spite of the widespread criticism that the civilian donation received for lax or even corrupt administration, wrote William Beveridge in 1931, the harm done by the programme lay not in its abuse, which was in fact minor, but in the principle of the programme itself, which damaged permanently the principle and credit of unemployment insurance. 'From the donation scheme dates the term "dole" indiscriminately applied to the later insurance benefit also; and from it dates the conception of largesse which all were entitled to share.'[3]

The damage effected by the civilian out-of-work dole lay in the fact that technically it offered far more than the contributory and strictly limited insurance programme which succeeded it. The rule in welfare programmes appears to be that, while expansion is easy, contraction is extraordinarily difficult. If the Government intended to proceed with the principle of universal contributory unemployment insurance, it should have had such a programme ready at the end of the war. But it did not have such a programme ready and was forced to fill in

[1] PRO, Cab. 24/67, GT 6047. C. Addison, 'Demobilization and Employment', 19 October 1918 (printed Memorandum, 10 pp.). Only now, on 31 October, did the Government publish the Report of the Civil War Workers' Committee recommending universal unemployment insurance.
[2] The civilian unemployment donation was announced in *The Times* on 13 November 1918.
[3] William H. Beveridge, *Unemployment: A Problem of Industry*, 2nd ed. (London, 1931), 274.

with a more generous, or 'better' programme. But once having offered a more generous programme, a return to the old, limited, prewar principle proved in the event to be impossible. It is not the purpose of this study to argue whether unconditional maintenance or limited contributory insurance is more desirable. Rather, the aim is to suggest that the Lloyd George Government, having decided upon a limited programme, took steps to make any reasonable fulfilment of its plan virtually impossible. It allowed the nation to become accustomed to the 'better' plan, unconditional maintenance, and then it offered a worse one, limited contributory insurance. The result, inevitably, was that it found itself unable to keep the new programme either limited or contributory and was forced to come forward with subsidies that not only made a mockery of the principle of insurance but appeared, briefly, to come close to bankrupting the nation. In addition, by adopting dependants' benefits, it virtually committed itself to a continuation of them under the contributory programme. As experience particularly in the 1930s would show, the payment of a benefit based on need, as of right and without a means test, not only made insurance open to abuse but frequently tended to give workers in the lowest-paid categories larger income in benefits than they were likely to receive in wages. The decisions made at the end of the war put the British Government into a trap from which it never succeeded in extricating itself until after the Second World War. It was caught between a limited programme it could afford but was not allowed by public political pressure to maintain and an unlimited one which the public seemed to want but which the leaders of the Government felt was beyond the nation's resources.

Universal unemployment insurance

Of the history of the out-of-work donation only a few things need be mentioned. First, as a part of the unspoken understanding that the dole was not simply a small addition to existing savings, but a subsidy to maintain a man at something approximating a respectable level, the amount of the donation became a matter of crucial importance. Addison had proposed in his memorandum of 19 October that the basic benefit for men be 20s. per week.[1] He records in his diary that at a meeting on 31 October, a representative from the Treasury had said that the Treasury might possibly concede 14s. (precisely twice the prewar level of benefit and exactly in line with the increased cost of living). Addison records he replied that if he told men returning from France that 14s. was enough for them to live on if they couldn't get a job

[1] GT 6047, 8.

upon demobilization he would probably be hung and he would deserve it.[1]

Eventually the Government accepted Addison's point of view that the unemployment donation ought not to be a mere gratuity in aid of savings but real maintenance.[2] The basic benefit for men was set not at 20s. but at 24s. per week for 13 weeks; women received 20s. There was an extra 6s. for the first dependent child under 15, and 3s. for all others. These rates of benefit were in effect less than a month. On 11 December, conveniently four days before the General Election, the Government announced increases of 5s. per week in both men's and women's benefits, and smaller increases for juvenile workers.[3]

Inevitably the out-of-work donation was charged with waste and laxity of administration, although the more thoughtful journals, even among those opposing the scheme, feared the precedent set by the dole rather than its administration.[4] These charges resulted in the appointment of a departmental committee of enquiry into the operation of the scheme. The committee, which reported on 25 July 1919, found, as was almost certainly the case, no widespread corruption but a good deal of inefficiency and lackadaisical administration. Besides recommending a general tightening up of procedures, it criticized the Government for laying upon employment exchanges an almost impossible burden with no preparation and very little warning.[5]

The restrictions on the civilian dole began even before the committee reported. At the beginning civilian workers had to prove simply that they had paid national health insurance contributions for at least three months previous to 25 November 1918. Early in the spring, this stipulation was increased to at least five months' employment at some time during 1918 and later, on 25 May, when the dole was extended for

[1] Christopher Addison, *Four and a Half Years* (London, 1934), II, 585. The fact that only two weeks before the programme was announced the basic question of amount of benefit had not been settled exemplifies the haste with which the Government attempted to put together a reform platform in the last days of the war.
[2] On the question of whether the Government in fact admitted an obligation to pay benefits at the maintenance level, in effect establishing a national minimum, it must be noted that official statements between the wars denied any such policy. See for instance: *Cmd. 3872*, 'First Report of the Royal Commission on Unemployment Insurance', 1931, 32.
[3] *The Times*, 11 December 1918. Five days earlier a special war bonus of 20 per cent had been added to the ordinary war pensions for disablement or death due to war service. *The Times*, 6 December 1918. Rates of benefit for military and civilian out-of-work donations were equal, although the military scheme was set to run for 12 months and gave 26 weeks' benefit while the civilian programme in the first instance was to run only for six months and give 13 weeks' benefit.
[4] See for instance: *Charity Organization Review*, XLV (March, 1919), 57–8.
[5] *Cmd. 305*, 'Final Report of the Committee of Inquiry into the Scheme of Out-of-Work Donations', 1919, 11–12. For William Beveridge's comments on the administration of the civilian schemes see: Beveridge, *Unemployment*, 273–4.

the second six months, the applicant was required to show to the satisfaction of the employment committee that he was 'normally in employment, genuinely seeking employment, and unable to obtain it'. In addition, the second 13 weeks of benefit were reduced to the rate of 20s. for men and 15s. for women.

Altogether the expenditure for both civilian and military schemes was about £67 million of which £44 million was spent for the military and £23 million for the civilian programmes. The far higher expenditure for the military dole may be accounted for by the fact that while the civilian scheme lasted only a year the military scheme, originally scheduled for a year, remained available for 30 months, until 31 March 1921 and payments under it went on into 1922.

The civilian dole had been extended for a second six months simply because the Government had not yet decided what to do about unemployment insurance. It possessed, to be sure, the recommendations of the Civil War Workers' Committee of the Ministry of Reconstruction, and of two subsequent committees, all of which had reported in virtually the same terms. But it had also any number of clear indications that the working class did not like contributory unemployment insurance and that workers in stable industries would seriously resist being forced to pay for the support of their less fortunate colleagues in other trades. Thus in the autumn of 1919 the Cabinet dithered, conscious that it was in a trap of its own making. By failing to have a contributory scheme ready at the end of the war it had been forced into an expensive alternative. It was aware of the unpopularity of contributory insurance. It was equally aware that the dole could not be continued indefinitely but that the programme could not be ended without something to put in its place. Driven by these irreconcilable forces, the Cabinet, on 14 August 1919, made the unheroic decision simply to avoid any public discussion of unemployment insurance while deploring unemployment generally.[1]

The man with the responsibility for seeing that the Cabinet finally did something about unemployment insurance was Sir Robert Horne, the Minister of Labour. Three weeks after the Cabinet decision of 14 August Horne circulated a memorandum among his colleagues noting that, although the Cabinet had decided not to proceed with unemployment insurance in the autumn session, it was vital to have something under way before the military and civilian out-of-work donations expired. This would be 24 November for the civilian dole and one year from the date of discharge for the military. Hence by the end of the year many destitute workers would have no alternative to the Poor Law. In the strongest terms he stated the dilemma in which the Government had put itself. 'In the face of the precedent of the donation scheme, I

[1] PRO Cab. 23/11, War Cabinet 615, meeting 13 August 1919.

think we must start from the assumption that to allow the donation scheme to expire and to put nothing in its place is impossible.' Insurance, whether it was popular or unpopular, must come, Horne asserted, and the sooner the Government understood this the better.[1] He went on to describe the unemployment insurance scheme he proposed. It would have to be contributory, although all trade unions wanted the opposite. It must permit, therefore, voluntary associations outside the scheme for those who wished to have it. Benefits, he suggested, should be 15s. for men and 12s. 6d. for women. There were two big questions that the Cabinet would have to settle. First of all was coverage: should it be coextensive with national health insurance or should it exclude agriculture and domestic service, both of which had little liability for unemployment? The second question concerned the State contribution. Horne feared that the State would have to contribute about one-third of the total cost of insurance, although he warned that this might cause a demand from the approved societies for an increase in the national health insurance subsidy which was at that time two-ninths of the cost of men's benefits. On the other hand, he thought, the Government would surely come under pressure from Labour to pay a large proportion of the cost of unemployment insurance on the precedent of the out-of-work donation. In addition there was the virtual certainty that unemployment insurance for women, although there were few statistics, would be far more expensive than for men.[2]

The question of including agricultural workers and domestic servants was a serious one touching the entire basis of unemployment insurance itself. The chief objection of contributory insurance came, naturally enough, from those trades least likely to be unemployed. Yet excluding all trades in which employment was low would force the contributions for insured trades impossibly high. In effect the Government insurance programme could not be made up of bad risks alone, while leaving the stable trades to cover themselves through separate schemes with infinitely smaller contributions. And yet this would be precisely what these trades would demand, particularly, as in the case of the agricultural workers, if they represented singularly ill-paid occupations.

Thus, in order to become actuarially sound, the scheme would have to incur a maximum of political unpopularity. If it touched only the trades that most needed insurance it might be politically more popular, but it would be either impossibly expensive for the Government or actuarially weak. The problem was not only administrative but political, wrote Austen Chamberlain to the Cabinet on 11 September, in a dis-

[1] PRO Cab. 24/88, GT 8123, R. Horne, 'Unemployment Insurance', 5 September 1919.
[2] GT 8123, 2.

cussion of Horne's memorandum of the previous week. As drawn the plans depended upon agricultural workers and domestic servants. But these two groups, secure in the affections of Conservative Members of Parliament, would almost certainly be excluded by the House of Commons. The plan, therefore, would need either more Treasury money or be insolvent. Horne ought to produce a scheme that was actuarially sound without these groups.[1] In the next few weeks there was extended correspondence on the subject from Lord Lee, President of the Board of Agriculture and Fisheries, denying that unemployment was low in agriculture and arguing that the labourers there should be included, and from Christopher Addison saying that they should be left out.[2]

In planning unemployment insurance during these crowded and frightened months toward the end of 1919, the chief difficulty for the Cabinet was the lack of solid information. Chamberlain, for instance, after having insisted that the Minister of Labour prepare an unemployment bill providing for the exclusion of agricultural labourers and domestic servants was demanding by November that these groups be covered by unemployment insurance. No one in the Cabinet was certain what the attitude of agriculture was on the subject, although Chamberlain argued that they would likely 'resent exclusion', while it was fairly certain that the 'agricultural interests', meaning the landlords, would demand coverage for their workers.[3] On the other hand it was generally agreed, following the unfortunate precedent of the anti-stamp-licking campaign against national health insurance, that the inclusion of domestic servants would be unpopular and could be driven through the House of Commons 'only with the greatest difficulty'.

Again, despite seven years' experience in the operation of a limited unemployment insurance scheme and nine years' experience with labour exchanges, statistics on unemployment were seriously deficient and many assumptions based upon data that did exist turned out to be disastrously incorrect. Most serious in this regard was the conclusion by the Chief Government Actuary, Sir Alfred Watson, that the rate of unemployment assumed for the 1911 act, about 8·5 per cent, had been too high and that the appropriate rate for all trades covered by that measure should have been 6·5 per cent. As the 1911 measure dealt chiefly with construction and engineering trades, which were especially liable to unemployment, it would have been considerably above average for all English industrial workers. Unemployment in

[1] PRO Cab. 24/88 GT 8155, Austen Chamberlain to Cabinet, 11 September 1919.
[2] PRO Cab. 24/89, GT 8205, 24 September 1919; *Ibid.*, GT 8247, 29 September 1919.
[3] PRO Cab. 23/18, Cabinet 7 of 1919 meeting, 14 November 1919.

coal-mining, for instance, Watson estimated to be only 1·5 per cent and in cotton textiles no more than 3 per cent. Therefore, by adding 10 per cent to the general estimates of unemployment statistics (and admitting that in some industries, transport except for docks and railroads, clerks, shop assistants and public utility services, he had no real statistical information whatever) he calculated that a 5·32 per cent unemployment rate would be adequate for British industry as a whole.[1]

At least as unfortunate was Watson's calculation that the £19,000,000 surplus in the insurance fund (of which £16,000,000 derived from the 1911 trades) would provide an income equivalent to 2,600,000 contributors, or put another way, would provide nearly a 10 per cent increase in income. This £900,000 per year would provide a substantial surplus of income over expenditure, Watson estimated, concluding, however, with the ominous words 'so long as the existing fund is kept intact. . .'.[2]

Behind all the hurried conferences, Cabinet meetings, and hastily drawn reports on what was perhaps the most important and certainly most expensive welfare institution of the interwar period was the fear of popular violence if something were not done to provide economic security for the British working man. The capitalist system would have to honour its promises or the system would be destroyed. Stimulating the unrest was the fact that the civilian unemployment donation would come to an end on 24 November and the new programme, which had only limited acceptance in any case, was unready. For months various labour unions had been passing resolutions demanding that the dole be made permanent or insisting, as did a committee of TUC leaders headed by J. H. Thomas in an interview with the Prime Minister on 10 December, that the Government should provide work or maintenance.[3] Meanwhile, outside the more responsible centre of the Labour movement, radical agitation to keep the dole grew rapidly in the early weeks of November. 'The most important event in the week has been the victory of Labour candidates in the Municipal Elections', wrote Basil Thomson on 6 November.

They appear to have gained their successes by effective organization and have profited by the apathy of other Parties. Many of the successful candidates are frankly revolutionary, and it is to be expected that

[1] Sir Alfred W. Watson, 'Report by the Government Actuary on the Financial Provisions of the Bill', *Journal of the Institute of Actuaries*, LII (April 1920), 72–80. This report was dated 23 December 1919, the date that the Unemployment Insurance Bill, still virtually a dummy, was introduced into the House of Commons. *House of Commons Debates*, CXXIII (23 December 1919), col. 1256.
[2] 'Report by the Government Actuary', *Journal of the Institute of Actuaries* (April 1920), 77. This report does not appear to have been published as a Command Paper.
[3] *The Times*, 11 December 1919.

they may use their position to attempt to smash the machine of Municipal Government as a step toward the abolition of the capitalistic system.

There is consternation at the announcement that unemployment doles may be discontinued this month. . . . In Liverpool they say that the Government would not dare drop it during the winter months at any rate.

A week later he began his report gloomily with the note that the agitation against the discontinuing of the unemployment donation had not subsided. 'My Liverpool correspondent even goes so far as to say that there will be serious trouble if the doles are withdrawn during the winter. . . . The discontent among ex-soldiers is not diminishing. There is a possibility of disturbances in the London district when the unemployment donation is stopped.'[1]

This unrest and the demands that the dole should be made permanent came up at nearly every Cabinet in the last two months of 1919 and, above all else, were responsible for the carelessness with which the Unemployment Insurance Bill of 1920 was conceived. At least until the measure was before Parliament labour would have to be placated in every possible way. Because of growing unemployment in port towns that depended on the Navy work, the Cabinet on 4 November had seriously considered continuing the dole at Government dockyards where massive lay-offs were in prospect. However, even this, it was considered, 'might not prevent trouble'. Eventually the Cabinet decided to approve an Admiralty scheme expected to cost £450,000 which would suspend discharges for four months. A week later—at the same meeting in which the draft unemployment scheme was finally approved in principle, although few of the details were worked out—the Cabinet agreed 'in order not to antagonize the trade unions and labour interests' to see whether it would not be possible to increase the rate of benefit to 20s. for men and 15s. for women. In the bill as finally introduced the rates were 15s. and 12s.[2]

When on 10 December the Prime Minister announced to the TUC delegation that the Government would introduce 'before Christmas a bill for a comprehensive national scheme of unemployment insurance', no measure was even nearly ready. Indeed, eight days later on 18 December when *The Times* carried the formal announcement that the

---

[1] PRO Cab. 24/92, CP 32, 'Report on Revolutionary Organizations', No. 28, 6 November 1919. Cab. 24/93, CP 125, 'Report on Revolutionary Organizations', No. 29, 13 November 1919.
[2] PRO Cab. 23/18, Cab. 1 of 1919, meeting 4 November 1919. PRO Cab. 23/18, Cab. 7 of 1919, meeting 14 November 1919. The new series of Cabinet numbers reflected the dissolution of the War Cabinet.

Unemployment Insurance Bill would be introduced the next Monday 22 December the Cabinet was only receiving its first informal explanation of the draft bill.[1]

Horne's short memorandum—only seven pages—of his still very tentative measure was devoted largely to changes from the 1911 scheme proposed for the new programme.[2] Trade unions, for instance, would still be invited by a 5 per cent subsidy to help administer the measure, but the larger subsidy to unions of one-sixth of the cost of benefit which had provided an inducement to extend insurance by fostering voluntary schemes was dropped as unnecessary now that insurance was universal. Most of Horne's memorandum was concerned with the discussion of the special industrial plans which were expected to relieve unemployment insurance of some of the unpopularity it seemed always to accumulate. Individual industries were to be invited under what eventually became Section 18 of the act to draw up special insurance programmes which would pay presumably larger benefits for smaller contributions or which might provide benefit payment on somewhat different terms than the Government programme. This latter stipulation was expected to appeal to such industries as coal and cotton which normally put employees on short-time rather than laying them off. The initiative for special plans would come from the joint industrial councils, the 'Whitley Councils', a product of reconstruction planning, which were supposed to be organized in each industry with a view to ending the strife and competition between employers and employees. As it turned out special schemes under Section 18—which during the debate in Parliament was one of the most contentious parts of the bill, and which had been expected by the actuary to cover about $3\frac{3}{4}$ million of the approximately 12 million insured—came into effect for only two industries, banking and insurance covering about 210,000 workers together.[3] Because of the onset of general unemployment at almost the same moment that unemployment insurance itself began, this part of the act was suspended in 1921 and finally repealed in 1927.

Perhaps most significant for the immediate future, Horne proposed

[1] *The Times*, 18 December 1919. Voting in the Spen Valley by-election was set for two days later, 20 December. In fact the measure was introduced one day late, on the last day of the session, Tuesday, 23 December 1919.

[2] PRO Cab. 24/95, CP 315, 325, Sir Robert Horne, 'Unemployment Insurance Bill', 20 December 1919. Only with the last memorandum did Horne include a proposed draft for the new Unemployment Insurance Bill which was supposed to be introduced two days later.

[3] Except in the Civil Service no Whitley Councils were ever established. For a full discussion see: Amy G. Maher, 'Some Experiments with Contribution Rate Differentials in British Unemployment Insurance', *Social Security Bulletin*, VI (December 1943), 34–40.

in his draft measure that although the six-month period of required payment stipulated by the act of 1911 would be retained, a special benefit of eight weeks' duration could be given during the initial six-month period after the insured had paid four contributions. He noted that as the insurance reserve fund had accumulated between £19 million and £20 million, Clause 13 of the bill stipulated that henceforth £10 million would be the minimum for the unemployment fund. As before the Treasury would be permitted to make advances to the fund and to require changes in contributions and benefit.

The Parliament which reassembled on 10 February 1920 gave a second reading to the Unemployment Insurance Bill 15 days later before a very thin House.[1] Except for the exclusion of domestic servants and agricultural labourers, the measure as introduced offered insurance generally to all groups covered by national health insurance, that is, to all manual workers and to all other workers earning less than £250 per year. The weekly benefit, paid for a maximum of 15 weeks after a week's waiting period, was 15s. for men and 12s. for women. For this the workman and his employer would contribute 3d. each and the State 2d. (Women and their employers would each pay 2½d.) In addition to the special programmes already mentioned, the bill provided that certain occupations not usually subject to unemployment—railway employees and public authority employees were specifically mentioned—could be totally exempted from unemployment insurance if the Minister was satisfied that the exemption was in the interests of the workers.

Besides a strenuous, but ineffective, complaint from the Irish members because unemployment insurance would not extend to the other island, criticism during the second reading centered on the question of the measure's effect on national health insurance. One facet of the argument concerned the size of benefits. There was strong support from both sides of the House for making women's benefit 15s. equal to men's. The objection to this change was that it would cause women's unemployment benefit to be higher than their national health insurance benefit. This would be likely to cause women to apply for unemployment insurance when sick, to the detriment of the unemployment fund. While it would have been relatively inexpensive to raise the women's unemployment benefit, the cost of women's sickness was already too high and increasing both benefits was thus most inadvisable.[2] Discussion about increasing benefits continued so long as the Unemployment Insurance Bill was before Parliament, but the women's benefit remained at 12s. However, the difficulties in adjusting health

---

[1] *H of C Deb.*, CXXV (25 February 1920), cols. 1739–1811, 1851–74.
[2] PRO Cab. 24/101, CP 906, R. S. Horne, 'Unemployment Insurance Bill', 20 March 1920; PRO Cab. 23/20, Cab. 15 of 1920, meeting 22 March 1920.

insurance and unemployment insurance would remain a potent source of trouble in the future.

A far more important problem in the competition between health and unemployment insurance appeared in the controversy between the national health insurance approved societies and the Labour party over the demand that the societies be allowed to administer unemployment insurance benefits. The possibility that unemployment insurance might prove more attractive than health insurance had been discussed in the *National Insurance Gazette* early in the autumn of 1919 well before the Government had made clear any intentions about a permanent unemployment programme.[1] Increasingly through the winter of 1919–20 the *Gazette* expressed concern over the effect unemployment insurance would have upon health insurance, or more particularly upon the approved societies. Soon the paper had begun to suggest that it might be desirable if the approved societies became the administrators of unemployment insurance as they were of health insurance.[2]

Although it became the main issue in the debate over the Unemployment Insurance Bill, the friendly society intervention could be disregarded if it did not bring up two important points. First, this strange proposal illustrates the general suspicion of the administrators of national health insurance toward all other forms of welfare.[3] This hostility, which had already boiled up over the creation of the Ministry of Health, had begun to break up the ancient alliance between the societies and the Labour movement and would be partially responsible for the continuing demands by Labour in the coming years for the abolition of the approved society system.

Secondly, and more immediately important, the Government's hand-

---

[1] *National Insurance Gazette*, 6 September 1919. The *National Insurance Gazette*, founded in the spring of 1912, regarded itself as the semi-official organ of the national health insurance programme. It spoke for both friendly societies and the industrial insurance companies although it was under the control of the industrial insurance industry.

[2] *National Insurance Gazette*, 6 September 1919, 14 February 1920, 23 March 1920, 3 April 1920. The so-called approved societies were the old friendly societies and the industrial insurance companies which after a complicated series of negotiations in 1911 had received from the government the task of administering the cash benefits paid under national health insurance. For their activity in connection with the establishment of the Ministry of Health see Chapter 3. For a description of the place of the friendly societies and the industrial insurance industry in national health insurance see: Gilbert, *Evolution of National Insurance*, 165–80, 318–26.

[3] This fear of the state among friendly societies was ancient, dating back to the first proposals by Joseph Chamberlain in the early 1890s for a national contributory old-age pension. In the present case the societies reasoned simply that if they did not take over the unemployment insurance benefits from the labour exchanges there was the possibility that the labour exchanges, or some other body, might take over sickness benefits. For discussion see: *National Insurance Gazette*, 6 September 1919.

ling of the friendly societies illustrates the weakness of the Cabinet's control of Parliament by this time. The spring and summer of 1920 saw the failure of the fusion movement, the beginning of Lloyd George's attempts to build an independent National Liberal party and, finally, rapidly increasing restiveness among the Conservative rank and file. As a result the chronic weakness of the Lloyd George administration reappeared. The Government was caught between the demands of Labour, on whose behalf unemployment insurance had been introduced in the first place and the powerful anti-Labour sentiments among many of its own supporters. If the Cabinet insisted upon admitting approved societies to unemployment insurance administration it would antagonize the trade unions and lose whatever credit the Unemployment Insurance Act might have brought. But if it tried to placate the trade unions by keeping friendly societies out, it risked a revolt on its own back benches who found in the approved societies a convenient way of attacking the Labour party without appearing to be anti-working class.

Basically, Labour opposed the intervention of the approved societies in the administration of unemployment insurance because of the traditional trade union requirement of control by the union over the engagement of its members. Labour's particular concern in this matter had been recognized in the 1911 act. Unions had been given the right to administer unemployment insurance to their own members and had received, in fact, a considerable subsidy to do so. This monopoly they intended to keep even though many of the small unions had found the privilege difficult to exercise. From the opposite point of view the societies argued that the administration of health insurance could easily be expanded to cover in addition the unemployment scheme, although in fact they were less concerned with efficiency than with guarding their existing membership against trade union, or State, competition.[1]

The lines of contention were clear by late spring and by this time also the Government had virtually given up trying to guide the complex and expensive measure it had introduced in the middle of February. After a long meeting on 16 June 1920, recognizing that friendly society claims 'commanded a large amount of support in the House of Commons', the Cabinet authorized T. J. Macnamara, Minister of Labour since 16 March, to accept an amendment authorizing society participation. At the same time, hoping to restore a little credit with the Labour movement, it agreed to cut the waiting period for unemployment benefits from six days to three and to raise the men's benefit from 15s. to 18s. and the women's to 15s. It attached, however,

[1] *H of C Deb.*, CXXV (25 February 1920), cols. 1774–81. It is important to note that only the friendly societies among the approved societies, not the industrial insurance companies, were involved in the battle over unemployment insurance.

the specifications that the extra cost of these concessions would be taken from the employed contributions and not from the Treasury.[1]

The decision to accept the amendment aroused a storm of opposition among Labour that was not placated by the announcement of the increased benefits. Indeed the trade unions were doubly angered by the fact that the increased benefits meant larger workers' contributions without a rise in the State contribution. Hence, on 30 June, the Cabinet reversed itself again and decided to leave the entry of the approved societies to a free vote in the House of Commons.[2] At the same time it decided to return to the original 15s. and 12s. benefit.[3]

During the debate on approved society administration, the chief spokesmen for the two sides were A. H. Warren, former Grand Master of the Manchester Unity of Odd Fellows, now Conservative Member of Parliament, and J. R. Clynes, the leader of the Labour party. Both men stressed the long friendship between the unions and the societies and regretted the present disagreement. Warren noted that at the time of the passage of the 1911 act it had been intended that friendly societies would be permitted to administer unemployment insurance but that this had been changed.[4] When the free vote on friendly society participation finally occurred on 9 July, the trade unions were defeated 226 to 44.[5]

The decisions of 9 July were unfortunate ones for the already tarnished reputation of the Government. The result might be to wreck the Unemployment Insurance Bill altogether, the *New Statesman* concluded in an article the following week.

> When it was first proposed that bodies other than trade unions should receive a share in the administration, the trade union movement at once announced its uncompromising opposition. Even the Parliamentary Committee of the Trades Union Congress decided to advise all Trade Unions to boycott the measure, if such a clause became law, and a number of the largest groups of organized workers, including the Miners' Federation and the National Federation of General Workers, announced their intention of acting on this

[1] PRO Cab. 23/21, Cabinet 36 of 1920, meeting 16 June 1920.
[2] Since the bill had gone into committee, the Government had been under continual pressure from friendly society forces to remove the whip on divisions concerning the societies. The societies had no doubt of the sympathy for their cause and the hatred of Labour among the Conservatives. Questions on whether this would be done were asked several times. *H of C Deb.*, CXXIX (12 May 1920), cols. 438–9. *Ibid.*, CXXX (21 June 1920), col. 1734. Spokesman for the Government, generally Andrew Bonar Law, declined to commit the Cabinet.
[3] PRO Cab. 23/21, Cab. 38 of 1920, meeting 30 June 1920.
[4] *H of C Deb.*, CXXXI (2 July 1920), cols. 959–67. Clynes referred to the two movements as 'twin brothers'. This sympathy Warren supported heartily.
[5] *H of C Deb.*, CXXXI (9 July 1920), cols. 1858–9.

advice. For some time it was regarded as likely that the Government would climb down in the face of this opposition; but the forces of the 'approved societies' were strongly mobilized both inside and outside the House, and, in last Friday's critical division, the Labour Party was heavily defeated. The present House is always ready to regard any stick as good enough for a thwack of Labour, and it found a convenient bludgeon in the hands of the 'friendly societies' amendment.[1]

After allowing Labour to be humiliated by the friendly societies, Government liberalizing concessions that appeared in the bill as finally passed seemed almost derisory. Benefits remained at 15s. for men and 12s. for women although the reduction in the waiting period for benefit from six working days to three was kept. The amount of the increase in the employed contribution was slightly smaller than had originally been proposed.[2]

The Unemployment Insurance Act became law on 9 August 1920. Its main provisions were due to go into effect on 8 November. As this measure generally established the apparatus which Britain would use for the next 20 years to deal with joblessness, several weaknesses inherent in the measure, compounded but not caused by economic depression, may be worth noting. First, the act deliberately penalized the insurance fund by leaving agricultural labourers and domestic servants outside its scope, by permitting the exclusion of railway workers and public employees, and by allowing the establishment of special funds with government subsidies for certain favoured classes of workers. Although every principle of insurance dictates that in order to achieve normal experience the group insured must present a normal risk, the planners of unemployment insurance allowed their programme to begin with a built-in disadvantage.

Secondly, the act assumed that the unemployment insurance fund would be kept above £10 million and that the income from the fund would be available for the payment of benefits. Once the act was in operation, however, the surplus in the fund began to be depleted. Its very existence became an excuse for the payment of uncovenanted benefits. By the summer of 1921 the profitable credit balance in the fund had been replaced by a costly debit balance. The mistake here lay less in the wasting of the surplus than in the unrealism of an insurance plan which presupposed the maintenance of a surplus untouched by politicians and in the preparation of a budget for a scheme

[1] *New Statesman*, 17 July 1920. After all the turmoil, the friendly societies found they were unable to induce any substantial number of their members to register for unemployment benefit at society offices and soon dropped attempts to administer the act.

[2] *H of C Deb.*, CXXXI (9 July 1920), col. 1907.

F

which depended upon interest from that surplus. While assuming, in effect, that a surplus would help maintain a surplus, the planners forgot that the cost of a deficit balance would help drive the scheme further into debt.

Third, perhaps most serious and almost unbelievable considering the size of the venture upon which they had embarked, the planners of unemployment insurance had almost no information after nearly a decade of labour exchanges about the incidence of unemployment in Great Britain as a whole nor about the prospects for growth or decay of various British industries.[1] As a consequence the Unemployment Insurance Act of 1920 assumed an unemployment rate of 5·32 per cent, nearly a third smaller than the rate assumed in the act of 1911, and only about one-third the rate that finally prevailed in the prewar period. The mistakes following upon this premise were apparent in the levels of contributions and benefits provided in the measure. For instance the act of 1920 gave benefits slightly more than twice the size of the act of 1911, 15s. for men versus 7s. in 1911, but the total contribution paid on behalf of men was only about 50 per cent larger, 10d. as opposed to 6⅔d. per week. In addition the waiting period, which in 1912 and 1913 had relieved the unemployment fund of about one-half the cost of the insurance benefit, was cut from six working days to three.

Not all these defects, to be sure, were the fault of the Minister of Labour and his advisers. Some were forced upon the Government by the extraordinary political situation in the Coupon Parliament or by the attempts of the Lloyd George administration to maintain its image as both a generous friend of the poor and a thrifty custodian of the funds of the middle-class tax-payer. Nevertheless, it must be said in summary that the Unemployment Insurance Act of 1920 was conceived and passed with very little consideration of the world in which it would have to operate. The lessons that the 1911 act might have provided were disregarded and small account was taken of the probable future development of the national industrial plant. Arguably, in the summer and autumn of 1920, no one could have foreseen the length and bitterness of the trade depression into which Britain was sliding, but more deliberate preparation might have given the Government a sturdier weapon for defence of the citizenry against the most serious of all economic problems in the interwar years.

[1] The largest single industry to be covered by unemployment insurance would be coal-mining. This involved nearly 1,200,000 workers, of whom over a million were men, nearly one-tenth of the British labour force. Unemployment here, Watson and his colleagues estimated on the basis of past performance, would be about 1·5 per cent. 'Report by the Government Actuary', *Journal of the Institute of Actuaries*, April 1920, 74.

The decay of unemployment insurance

In terms of its assigned function, the Unemployment Insurance Act came into effect six months too late. By 8 November 1920, when contributions under the measure were scheduled to begin, nearly 1,500,000 men, upon Basil Thomson's estimates, were unemployed.[1] As a result the act of 1920, even in its unsatisfactory original state, never received a fair trial. From the beginning it had to deal with a large group of men who were ineligible for standard benefit because they had never been employed long enough to qualify under the ordinary terms of the measure. From this fact flowed a river of troubles. In attempting to adjust the unemployment programme to care for the thousands who could not qualify for regular or 'standard' benefit, the Government threw the new scheme into chaos from which essentially it did not recover until the Second World War.

From the Cabinet's point of view, the most serious factor in the rising unemployment was its effect on the temper of ex-servicemen. Already in September these men were 'in an ugly mood', as Basil Thomson reported. '. . . unless something can be done to reduce unemployment it may become serious. It must be remembered that in the event of rioting, for the first time in history, the rioters will be better trained than the troops.'

> Marches of the unemployed are frequent and although they are often made up of men who do not want work, the Communist party are gaining many recruits, while the meetings of patriotic societies are continually broken up. I have received specimens of the kind of speeches delivered by Communist agitators. They are all directed toward exciting class hatred. 'When', they say, 'are you going to begin? This is going to be a black and terrible winter for the workers; millions now will be thrown out of work. You will be forced to take action before long, or starve. Why wait? Why not begin now? Use the power that is in your hands', etc., etc.[2]

In a report on 4 November 1920, four days before unemployment insurance was due to go into effect, T. J. Macnamara reminded his

---

[1] PRO Cab. 24/114, CP 2089, 'Report on Revolutionary Organizations', No. 80, 11 November 1920. Since the middle of summer his reports had grown increasingly lugubrious and certainly may be assigned as part of the reason for the ill-conceived and hastily drawn compromises embodied in the act, particularly those dealing with the friendly societies.

[2] PRO Cab. 24/111, CP 1830, 'Report on Revolutionary Organizations', No. 70, 2 September 1920; *Ibid.*, /112, CP 1908, 'Report on Revolutionary Organizations', No. 74, 30 September 1920.

colleagues that the military out-of-work donation was about to come
to an end but that many former servicemen now getting it would
not be eligible for unemployment insurance. They were specifically
excluded from unemployment insurance while receiving the dole, but
when the dole expired those depending upon it, having paid
no contributions, would not be eligible for unemployment insurance.
The Government alternatives, the Minister of Labour remarked, were
either to extend the dole or to amend the Unemployment Insurance
Act. Macnamara recommended that the act be changed, while admitting, rather miserably, that there 'would be a certain illogicality in
amending an act not yet in force in a way strongly resisted by the
Cabinet when it was proposed in the House of Commons only a few
months ago'. The Cabinet, on the other hand, had no difficulty in
choosing the easier alternative and decided on 31 December to prolong
the dole for another three months until 31 March 1921.[1]

Although the extension of the military out-of-work donation eased
at least temporarily the problem of unemployed former servicemen, as
the end of the year approached an even more potent source of trouble
appeared among the 8 million other working people, not eligible for
the military dole who now for the first time were covered by contributory insurance. Very many thousands of these people would not qualify
for unemployment insurance benefit because they had had no work
whatever since 8 November. On 20 December, 'as a matter of some
urgency', Macnamara raised in the Cabinet the possibility of revising
eligibility requirements to make possible the payment of benefit to
those who had been continually out of work in the past six weeks.
He suggested that the stipulation be changed to allow benefit for any
man who had had either at least ten weeks' work since 1 January 1920
or four weeks since 5 July 1920. Each of these options, he estimated,
would cost about £1 million but the large surplus in the unemployment fund could carry the charge, he pointed out, and therefore it
would not be necessary to apply to Parliament for money.[2]

From the Cabinet's point of view, the labour situation was becoming
desperate by the beginning of 1921. Coupled with reports from the
Directorate of Intelligence of increasing radical activity in the coal-
mining areas—an industry that, despite a tendency to strikes, had
enjoyed considerable prosperity since the Armistice—the Government
was now faced with growing evidence that extremism had begun to
take advantage of unemployment. 'As seems inevitable under conditions
of widespread distress and discontent', wrote Thomson on 6 January,

[1] PRO Cab. 23/23, Cabinet 82 of 1920, meeting 31 December 1920. Appendix,
'Report of Conference', 4 November 1920.
[2] PRO Cab. 23/23, Cabinet 74 of 1920, meeting 20 December 1920. He added
also that the new charge would not involve anything unprovided for by the actuaries.

the Communists are gaining converts: the facts relating to unemployment are indisputable and they form a powerful weapon for attacking the Capitalist system; the workless are only too ready to believe that their lot could not be worse under a different form of government and might conceivably be better. The right to work is one which is difficult to deny and Soviet Russia is held up as a Utopia where work is not only a right but a duty.

Class hatred is increasing; my Glasgow correspondents, for instance, report that they have never known such bitterness on the part of the workers against anyone who is even slightly better placed than themselves; the same thing applies in London, where the East is becoming increasingly familiar with the luxury and ostentation displayed in the West.

'The best that can be said this week is that matters are better than might have been expected considering the increasing unemployment and the great efforts of extremists to promote class hatred', continued Thomson at the end of the month.

The revolutionaries are having matters all their own way and there is a steady increase in the number of persons who believe that the Capitalist system is doomed and that 'over-production' is the cause of the present slump. Simple explanations of the economic situation are very urgently needed. . . .

Practically no improvement in the employment problem is reported from the provinces: the only trades in which the demand for work exceeds the supply appear to be brick-laying and coach building. The feeling of the unemployed is becoming very bitter: on January 21st a queue of men at Liverpool was a quarter of a mile long and at the women's exchanges thousands of women waited hours in the side street for their insurance money; indignation against what is termed 'inhuman treatment' is reported to be intense.[1]

The Government was floundering. On one hand, it was under serious pressure from the Bank of England, to reduce all Government spending and so to permit capital again to flow into productive enterprise which presumably would bring the return of prosperity. Two significant results of this pressure were the decisions finally to cut the housing programme and to return the coal mines to private industry which brought in April the most serious miners' strike that Britain had suffered until that time. But then there were the fierce and implacable claims of the unemployed. 300,000 soldiers were drawing the out-of-

[1] PRO Cab. 24/118, CP 2429; CP 2493, 'Report on Revolutionary Organizations', Nos. 87, 90; 6, 27 January 1921.

work donation which would come to an end on 1 April. Another 900,000 civilian unemployed were receiving the uncovenanted eight weeks' benefit which would terminate at the same time. Of these about 500,000 were completely without work and the rest were on short time and drawing partial unemployment benefits.

The group most feared by the Cabinet were the 300,000 ex-servicemen presently on the dole. As extended the military out-of-work donation amounted to 20s. a week. The standard unemployment benefit was only 15s. What would the soldiers do when they were transferred from the military donation to the unemployment scheme and found their benefits decreased by one quarter? Macnamara, whose proposal on every occasion was for increasing or broadening benefits, suggested an amendment to the act increasing the unemployment benefit from 15s. to 20s. His chief argument for this, in addition to the obvious one that the reduction of the benefit to former soldiers would be politically and socially dangerous, was that it would enable the Government, at a time when it was under heavy siege, to make a 'firm stand' against further concessions. Again, he called attention to the surplus of over £24 million in the insurance fund and suggested that after 3 July, when the standard benefit was officially to begin, the Government might increase the employee and employer contribution.[1]

Apparently to allow room for parliamentary manoeuvre, Macnamara's amending bill introduced 12 days later although providing 20s. unemployment benefits for servicemen, raised the standard benefit for ordinary civilian workers only to 18s. It proposed also to increase contributions from 4d. from the workman, 4d. from the employer and 2d. from the State to 5d., 6d., and 2¾d. respectively, with proportionate increases for women. However, while the increases in benefits would begin immediately, the increases in contributions would not take effect until the beginning of the third quarter of the insurance year 4 July. In addition the measure increased the duration of benefits by providing two periods of eligibility—16 weeks from the passing of the bill until the end of October 1921, and a second 16 weeks beginning at the end of October in the new insurance year until July 1922. After 1922 the insurance year would commence in July and the benefit in each year would be henceforth 26 weeks instead of 15. The increase in benefit, in the absence of continuing legislation, would extend only until 1 July 1923. If, on the other hand, the stability of the fund were

[1] PRO Cab. 23/24, Cabinets 4 and 6 of 1921, meetings 28 January, 11 February 1921. One aspect of the unemployment insurance problem that would increasingly occupy the Cabinet's time was the almost hopeless administrative tangle that the Cabinet was causing by continually altering a measure that had not yet fully gone into effect. The changes in benefits now being proposed meant for instance reprinting some 14 million insurance cards that even yet had not become fully valid.

established by that time new legislation could continue the higher benefit. Macnamara admitted that at the present unemployment rate of 9½ per cent the 18s. and 20s. benefit would reduce the unemployment fund from £21 million to between £4 million and £5 million by July 1922.[1]

The bill immediately came under attack, as Macnamara certainly must have anticipated it would, because of its distinction between the benefit rate for civilian and ex-service unemployed. J. R. Clynes, then leading the Labour party, moved an amendment in committee to raise benefits to 40s. for all heads of families and to provide dependency benefits for children. Macnamara induced the withdrawal of this amendment by making the concession he clearly had long been prepared to make, raising all men's benefits to 20s. a week, while extracting from the House at the same time a promise that no further concessions would be pressed and admitting that the increase to 20s. would 'destroy the insurance fund'.[2]

At the meeting of 11 February, the Cabinet had agreed that among the concessions to be resisted most firmly was one maintaining the unemployment benefit being paid to nearly half a million workers who were not in fact unemployed, but who were on short time. The failure to deal conclusively in this expensive matter symbolized the Government's indecisions elsewhere. The beginning of this practice is something of a mystery. Evidently it was the result of local pressure on labour exchanges.[3] In any case when it set out to end a system far too reminiscent of Speenhamland and one which was particularly expensive and liable to abuse, the Cabinet ran foul again of the old rule that welfare benefits were virtually irrevocable. On 16 February, Austen Chamberlain, who had been appointed the head of an ad hoc committee to look into the question, was forced to report that part-time benefits had begun with the decision of an insurance umpire 'to which unfortunately the attention of the Government had not been drawn at the time, and in view of the general practice now prevailing and the

---

[1] *H of C Deb.*, CXXXVIII (23 February 1921), cols. 993–1097.

[2] *Ibid.*, (24 February 1921), cols. 1011–12, cols. 1238–40. There is no evidence in the Cabinet minutes that Macnamara needed to refer this increase back to the Cabinet. Indeed after the meeting of 11 February unemployment insurance was not discussed again for over three months. In view of the Cabinet's original approval of the general 20s. increase the historian can only conclude that the difference in benefit between ex-soldiers and civilian workers, which would in fact do more than destroy the surplus in the insurance fund, was a parliamentary red herring. Macnamara, after agreeing to the increase, said simply that it was all 'a risk'.

[3] Basil Thomson reports that miners, on short time as a result of the world-wide collapse of coal prices, were demanding payment of the dole when their wages fell below subsistence level. CP 2429, 6 January 1921.

arguments which had been brought forward, he was impressed with the difficulty and inexpediency of now ceasing to pay for partial unemployment'.[1]

The concessions of the winter and early spring of 1921 quickly destroyed the unemployment plan as a programme of insurance. In less than eight months, between 8 November 1920 and 3 July 1921, the £21,875,000 inherited by the new act from the 1911 and 1916 schemes, the possession of which made every extension seem politically uncomplicated, had disappeared and the insurance fund began to accumulate the debt that it did not retire until after the Second World War.[2] The chief cause of the disastrous run on the unemployment fund was the commencement of the great coal strike on 1 April 1921. Incredibly, this event appears to have been entirely unexpected by the Government, and its effect was not considered in the discussions of the increase in benefits, although Basil Thomson had been warning since the middle of January of growing apprehension in the coalfields about a possible decrease in wages.[3]

Through the spring the Cabinet was preoccupied with the miners' strike and the threatened sympathetic strike of the general workers and the railwaymen which did in fact occur. It neglected entirely the problem of unemployment until after the middle of May. On 26 May, Macnamara announced the arrival of the beginning of the second stage of the destruction of unemployment insurance with frantic memorandum saying that at the present rate of dispersal the unemployment fund, which he had expected at least to remain solvent until July 1922

[1] PRO Cab. 27/135 (Ad Hoc Committees), 'Meeting of Unemployment Insurance Committee', 16 February 1921.
[2] Total income to the insurance fund between 8 November and 3 July 1921 was £13,030,446. Of this amount, almost exactly £10 million were ordinary workers', employers' and State contributions. Ordinary benefits in the same period cost £33,577,946 or more than three times the workers' contributions. The actual proportion of these expenditures that can be attributed to the increase in benefits and the unconvenanted benefits cannot be deduced from the available statistics, partly as a result of the chaos existing in insurance administration in these early months. But available evidence suggests that through the entire period of the uncovenanted benefit, that is up until August 1924, the cost of this benefit was more than half the total cost of insurance. For a discussion see: Eveline M. Burns, *British Unemployment Programs*, 1920–38 (Washington, 1941), 369–70.
[3] CP 2452, 13 January 1921, 11–12. Through 1920 the world-wide shortage of coal had largely insulated the British mining industry from the unemployment that was becoming the rule in other industries. But in 1921 with European mines back in production, and with Germany paying reparations in coal, which Britain herself helped to enforce, world prices for the mineral tumbled. In 1920 Britain exported 24,932,000 tons of coal which earned £99,627,000. In 1921 the nation exported almost exactly the same, 24,661,000 tons, but received £42,952,000. *Cmd. 2849*, 'Statistical Abstract for the United Kingdom', 334–5.

would be exhausted by the end of June 1921 and instead would have a £16 million deficit by July of the next year. In February unemployment claims had been running at slightly over a million per week but were now over two million, principally due to the coal strike. He recommended reducing men's benefit to 18s. and women's to 14s. and increasing contributions, which would in any case have gone to 5d. for a worker and 6d. for his employer on 4 July, to 6d. and 7d. respectively. He asked that the borrowing rights of the fund from the Treasury be raised to £20 million and that the waiting period be increased from the working days to six.[1]

Macnamara's proposal to increase the borrowing authority of the unemployment insurance fund was immediately attacked by Robert Horne, now Chancellor of the Exchequer. The consolidated fund did not have £20 million to lend the unemployment insurance fund, insisted Horne, and while the Unemployment Insurance Act did allow the Treasury to borrow money for this purpose, in view of local authority borrowing for housing, the Treasury would not be justified in going into the money market.[2] Horne recommended that men's and women's benefit be reduced to 15s. and 12s. rather than 15s. and 14s., as suggested by Macnamara, but he was dubious about extending the waiting period as this would require legislation, which he was anxious to avoid. The decrease in benefits could be accomplished within the terms of the act by Treasury order. He noted that in an earlier memorandum Macnamara had made a proposal to extend the period of benefits even beyond the terms of the February amending act but he had not repeated it in his most recent memorandum. Horne argued strongly against this, saying that it would cost an extra £6½ million. Caught again in the dilemma of trying to please both the middle-class taxpayer and the working-class voter, the Cabinet eventually compromised. After 'taking note of the Minister of Labour's warning of possible serious consequences of discontent which would be aroused among employers and employed at the substantial increase in contributions at the present time ...', it agreed to lower benefits to 15s. and 12s. for men and women but to give two new periods of extended benefit— six weeks between July and October 1921 and a second six weeks between February and June 1922. At the same time men's contributions

[1] PRO, Cab. 24/123, CP 2975, 'Unemployment Fund, Proposals for Avoiding Insolvency', 26 May 1921.
[2] PRO, Cab. 24/123, CP 2987, 'Unemployment Fund, Proposals for Avoiding Insolvency', R. S. Horne, 28 May 1921. Unquestionably, the competition for funds between the unemployment insurance programme and housing was a factor in the Government's determination to wind up at the end of June the Addison schemes. See Chapter 3.

were increased to 7d. for the workmen and 8d. for the employers, with slightly smaller increases for the women.[1]

In presenting his second amending bill to the House of Commons Macnamara spoke at length on the extreme gravity of the unemployment situation. Unemployment was running at nearly twice the rate expected in March. The fund was paying out in benefits over £2 million per week. Income was less than £350,000 per week. The £22½ million surplus that the fund had enjoyed in March was now £8½ million and at the present rate of expenditure would last about another month.[2]

The second Unemployment Insurance Act of 1921 signalized not only the financial crisis of unemployment insurance but also brought to a head the general problem of the conflicting philosophies about the relief of the unemployed. Was the unemployment insurance benefit intended only to be an aid to other savings or was it to provide at least minimal maintenance for the applicant? Put another way, was the amount of money that the guardians of the public purse felt the State could afford adequate in terms of human need? Would it satisfy the moral obligation that society had to those in distress? Or for that matter would it even prevent violence? In practical terms, if 15s. per week was all the State could afford, was 15s. enough to maintain the average unemployed worker and his family, now that many had been without work for nearly a year and had exhausted any savings and trade union benefits they might have possessed?

The fact was that 15s. was not enough, indeed 20s. was insufficient for a man with a family. But if the State could not afford what the working man demanded, the consequence might be revolution. Thus, as the winter of 1921 approached and the number of unemployed remained obstinately above a million and a half with many men now beginning their second year entirely without work and many more having either exhausted the inadequate 15s. benefit or about to do so, the Government began to cast about for new expedients. The problem of the widespread loss of unemployment benefit was becoming serious, wrote Macnamara on 3 September 1921 to Lloyd George. About 200,000 people used up the most recent extension and this figure would rapidly increase. As things presently stood, no new benefit could be

[1] The State contribution was at the same time raised to 3¾d., nearly double the amount envisioned by the act of 1920. This measure, designated as Unemployment Insurance (Amendment 2) Act of 1921, also re-established a six working-day waiting period for benefit and ended the special trade schemes. Finally, the borrowing power of the unemployment fund was increased from the £10 million set under the Unemployment Insurance Act No. 1 in March to £20 million.

[2] H of C Deb., CXLII (8 June 1921), col. 1876. By 28 June at the time of the third reading of the bill, the fund had lost another £5 million and was down to £3,250,000.

paid until 3 November when the new period of 22 weeks began (16 weeks standard and six 'uncovenanted'). Most serious was the fact that the unemployed with lapsed benefits were concentrated in a few centres. This was a 'real danger', thought Macnamara. For instance, 13,000 of 66,000 registered unemployed in Glasgow had exhausted their benefits and about 10,000 of 80,000 in London. Even these figures probably underestimated the situation, because many who had exhausted benefits no longer registered at the exchange.[1]

More serious was the inadequacy of the 15s. payment itself. Although the overall cost of living had declined by nearly one quarter since November 1920 when it reached a peak, the index was still well over twice what it had been in 1914 and stood approximately at the level of the Armistice when the out-of-work donation had given both ex-servicemen and civilian workers benefits substantially higher than those now offered.[2]

Although Macnamara continually stressed the critical nature of the problems with unemployment insurance he found it difficult to get a decision from the Government. In the autumn of 1921 the inner circle of the Cabinet—the Prime Minister, Chamberlain, Churchill and Birkenhead—were fully occupied with the crucial negotiation directed towards bringing the civil war in Ireland to an end. At the same time they were distracted towards Europe by Germany's inability, or refusal, to pay war reparations and by the large and expensive French rearmament programme which distressed that nation's former allies more than it frightened her recent enemy. Finally through most of September Lloyd George was at Gairloch absorbed with the idea that industrial production might be stimulated through generous government credits, an embryonic pre-Keynesian economic regulator.

Whether the contraction of the Gairloch scheme required by the Bank of England, which took much of the Cabinet's time in the middle of October 1921, was responsible for the introduction of dependants'

---

[1] T. J. Macnamara to Lloyd George, 3 September 1921. Lloyd George Papers F/36/1/43. Macnamara repeated his warning two weeks later. 380,000 had now exhausted the unemployment benefit and the number would be 500,000 before the new benefit began. Communists were exploiting the situation, concluded Macnamara, and no matter what were the financial conditions, the problem 'has to be faced if grave civil disorder is to be avoided'. PRO Cab. 24/128, CP 3217, 'The Unemployment Problem', 17 September 1921.

[2] On an index of 100 based on July 1914 the cost of living in the United Kingdom reached a peak of 276 in November 1920. By August 1921 it had declined to 222, by November to 210, and would sink eventually by 1923 to the neighbourhood of 170 where it remained throughout the rest of the decade. Although the opposite is frequently stated, wages declined proportionately. From about 170–180 per cent above 1914 at the end of 1920, they fell to 110–115 per cent by the end of 1921, and finally settled at about 70 per cent above 1914 by the end of 1923. *Cmd. 2849*, 'Statistical Abstract for the United Kingdom', 91, 93.

benefits on unemployment insurance is impossible to say. The coincidence of dates may be significant. The Cabinet was informed on 14 October 1921 of the Bank's objections to government guarantees for wholesale industrial borrowing.[1] Three days later, on 17 October, Macnamara was authorized to go forward with the preparation of the Unemployed Workers' Dependants (Temporary Provision) Bill which established dependants' benefits under the unemployment insurance scheme.[2]

On the other hand the reports of working-class violence in the past few weeks had increased to a level approaching that of the early months of 1919. 'It is useless to disguise the fact that profound unrest and bitter feeling are growing among the unemployed throughout the country', noted the Committee on Unemployment, of which the Prime Minister himself was Chairman, in a report to the Cabinet on 6 October.

> A very large proportion of the unemployed today are not the usual type of unskilled or work-shy men, but are very largely people who all their lives have been used to regular work at good wages and many of whom are still making every effort to avoid having to apply to the Poor Law Guardians for relief. A very large percentage of these men fought in the war and they are not prepared to see their families endure misery and want without a serious struggle and even disorder.[3]

The response to the deepening crisis of the autumn of 1921 was a change which in the long run was among the most significant modifications of insurance of the period of the early 1920s, the establishment of dependants' allowances. Benefits as of right according to need had long been a part of Labour party doctrine but had always been resisted by the Government as incompatible with contributory insurance. During the passage of the Unemployment Insurance (Amendment No. 1) Act the previous February, Macnamara had made a long speech resisting precisely the measure that appeared in the autumn of the same year. Essentially, he argued, dependants' benefits were unjust. Equal contributions ought to provide equal benefits and the

---

[1] See: Chapter 1.
[2] PRO Cab. 23/27, Cabinet 80 of 1921, meeting 17 October 1921.
[3] PRO Cab. 23/27, Cabinet 76 of 1921, meeting 6 October 1921, Appendix I. A 'Week of National Agitation' was to begin on 13 October with marchers in all cities to the local town hall demanding work. Private instructions to the leaders of the unemployed workers, transmitted to the Cabinet on 10 October, were threatening. 'Don't stand on ceremony with these people' (local authority officials), the workers were told, 'but cut for the main essential and definite object "WORK OR FULL MAINTENANCE".' PRO Cab. 24/128, CP 3387, 'Unemployed Demonstration', 10 October 1921.

precedent of the out-of-work donation did not apply because it was not insurance.[1] Nevertheless on 11 October 1921 the Cabinet accepted the recommendation of a quickly organized 'Relief of Distress Committee' under the chairmanship of the Secretary of State for Scotland, Robert Munro, and approved the setting up of a special 'Distress Fund', separate from the Unemployment Insurance fund, to provide for the payment of benefits to the dependants of unemployed working men and women. The Cabinet agreed that the precedents for dependants' allowances, at least on the experience of the out-of-work donation, were not encouraging, but the situation was different now. 15s. was simply too little for a man with a family to live upon. In essence the question was whether all benefits should be raised, or only the benefits of those in the greatest need. But most important, on the assumption that any man with a family with only 15s. per week income could be assumed to be in distress, there would be no investigation of need. The benefits were to be 5s. per week for a dependent wife or husband and 1s. per week for each child up to a total of four children. They were to be paid for by special levy of 2d. each from the workman and his employer and 3d. from the Government (1d. and 2d. for women).[2]

The Cabinet authorized the Minister of Labour to draw up a bill along these lines on 17 October and on 24 October, without further consideration, it was introduced in the House of Commons to go into effect on 7 November 1921, the first anniversary of Unemployment Insurance.[3]

Thus by the end of 1921 unemployment insurance had acquired the properties which would characterize it, and make it almost unmanage-

---

[1] H of C Deb., CXXXVIII (23 February 1921), col. 1002.

[2] PRO Cab. 24/128, CP 3391, 'Relief of Distress Committee Report', 11 October 1921.

[3] H of C Deb., CXLVII (24 October 1921), cols. 471–582. In the spring of 1923 the Special Distress Fund was amalgamated with the ordinary Unemployment Insurance Fund. For an unemployed family a few shillings made a considerable difference. Interviews in the next decade revealed this importance even at a small increase in benefits. One man would 'pay off my debts. You'd be surprised how much is owing to the shop-keepers.' Another said it would go 'for replacing things around the house. My wife doesn't say so but I can see that making the best of it after things wear out and dishes get broken is hard for her. It doesn't take a lot of silver to make homemaking a joy. But it does take more than we have.' Self-respect also controlled the expenditure of this small sum. 'Buy some clothes. That's the first thing we do when I get a spell of work. As long as we keep up an appearance you keep your self-respect. This worn sleeve here is making me wonder about myself.' Another telling reply, 'Why I'd probably raise hell with it for the first week, just to show myself that I was a man again and had some choice about things.' E. Wight Bakke, Insurance or Dole ? The Adjustment of Unemployment Insurance to Economic and Social Facts in Great Britain (New Haven 1935), 23.

able, for the next two decades. Within a period of ten months, the precedents had been established for the payment of benefits above those actually justified by the applicant's contributions, for the adjustment of benefits to the cost of living, and for the payment of benefits based on need. These innovations were not really attempts to rectify the many proven inadequacies in the insurance programme itself but derived rather from political pressures. The question of whether the money might be better spent some other way was not considered. Unemployed workmen would have to be supported if England were to avoid revolution, and unemployment insurance was assigned to do this job. Remarkably the rulers themselves believed in the justice of the workers' demands and accepted the contention, without admitting it, of the right to work or maintenance, the right of the citizen in need to call upon the society that had called upon him when it was itself in need.

Unfortunately to maintain those in need, the State had at its disposal only two inadequate instruments, both the products of a previous age. One, the Poor Law, had been made punitive and unpleasant by design. The other, unemployment insurance, was directed less towards the relief of distress than the enforcement of the now obsolete doctrine of self-help.

The stabilization of unemployment in the twenties

Unemployment reached a peak in the late summer, autumn and winter of 1921 with slightly more than two million insured work people, or about 18 per cent of the insured work force, registered as unemployed. In the early months of 1922 it began to decline slowly but steadily. By the end of 1923 it had reached what would become the stable, or 'normal', unemployment for the interwar period, about 1,200,000 or 10 per cent of the insured work force. For unemployment insurance the most immediate result of this improvement in the economic climate was a striking decrease in the rate of accumulation of the debt in the unemployment insurance fund. Whereas between July 1921 and July 1922 the fund spent about £15,486,000 more than it received in contributions and ended the insurance year about £15,000,000 in debt, in the year between July 1922 and July 1923 expenditure exceeded income by only about £1,207,000. In the following year between July 1923 and July 1924 the fund's income exceeded its expenditures by £9,039,000, reducing the debt to about £7,094,000.[1] But behind the rather hopeful crude figure of an absolute decline in total

[1] These statistics are taken chiefly from *Cmd. 2849*, 'Statistical Abstract from the United Kingdom', 77, and Burns, *Unemployment Programmes*, 69.

unemployment lay the fact of the chronic dislocation in the structure of British industry that was now beginning to appear. The frictional and cyclical unemployment with which the original insurance programme of 1911 had been designed to deal was now being replaced by permanent sickness in certain industries, which for practical purposes left the men engaged in them with virtually no prospect in the future for a call upon their services. Although the national unemployment rate was about 10 per cent, ship-building and ship-repairing, for instance, employing more than a quarter of a million men and women, suffered an unemployment rate of over 28 per cent in 1923–24. Cotton textiles employing nearly 800,000 normally had about 16 per cent unemployed. General engineering—iron and steel founding—with over 600,000 workers, had an unemployment rate of 14·5 per cent, while marine engineering had over 16 per cent unemployed. Public works contracting, with 150,000 men in the industry, had by July 1924, about 16 per cent unemployed, while even building construction with nearly 800,000 in the industry had 10 per cent out of work.

Opposed to this, in the huge and rapidly growing car industry with well over 200,000 employed by July 1924, only 8 per cent were unemployed, well under the national average. And in retail sales, the largest single employer in the nation having passed agriculture in the middle of the 1920s, only 5·7 per cent were unemployed by July 1924.

These figures make clear what would become the peculiar characteristic of British unemployment since the First World War, indeed until the present period: it was confined to certain industries which were concentrated in narrow geographical localities. Joblessness was a feature of life in the North of England, Ireland, Scotland, and Wales in industries of cotton textiles, coal-mining, ship-building, and of the firms dependent upon them. The other half of the nation, the Midlands, the South-East and the South-West, would after the early 1920s, enjoy an unemployment rate that was almost normal.[1] Concentrated unemployment meant long-term unemployment, a problem with which the acts of 1911 and 1920 were never intended to deal. A sample survey in 1935 of 220,221 of its own clients by the Unemployment Assistance Board (which appears to have been the first of its kind) showed that 30·6 per cent of all recipients of benefit on 27 May of that year had been unemployed for more than two years, and among these workers, over 10 per cent, 25,000, had been unemployed for more

---

[1] For a discussion see: *Planning*, PEP Broadsheet XLVII, 'Inquest on the Unemployment Act', 26 March 1935, 12–13. See also: *Cmd. 2849*, 'Statistical Abstract', 78–81.

than five years. About half of those receiving benefit on 27 May had been unemployed for more than one year.[1]

In summary, then, the character of British unemployment in the 1920s showed that William Beveridge's description of the problem in 1909 was after all true and, second, that the planners of the Unemployment Insurance Acts, both in 1911 and 1920, had failed really to understand the nature of the problem with which they were dealing. Unemployment, said Beveridge, was really a matter of 'underemployment'. At any time, no matter what the state of industrial prosperity, there was a segment of working-class society which had less work than it needed. The effect of the declining level of business activity, therefore, was not so much that men hitherto in steady employment found themselves thrown out of work—although this, to be sure, also happened—but that those chronically in need of jobs found them harder to find and, more important, discovered that their spells of joblessness grew longer. Thus at any time rising statistics of unemployment and of applications for unemployment insurance would mean only partly that larger numbers of new men were applying for benefit. The other part, perhaps the more important part, was that fewer men were going off benefit, in effect that those already drawing insurance were remaining on the fund longer. Unemployment insurance had never been designed to deal with this situation. The mistaken assumption of 1911, to use Beveridge's words, was that unemployment was like a chasm with solid ground on either side over which the State might help the otherwise regularly employed working man, with a small subsidy to his savings.

A greater error, however, was the adoption in 1920, hurriedly and thoughtlessly, of the limited principles of the act of 1911. One can excuse Churchill and Sir Hubert Llewellyn-Smith for neglecting the realities of unemployment, which in fact both of them understood, for the 1911 measure remains, nevertheless, a daring experiment in the field of social legislation. But to apply the principles of 1911, which had been formulated for a narrow and carefully calculated industrial context, to the whole working population of Great Britain made no more sense than would the application of the techniques of watchmaking to the mining of coal. By the mid-1920s this fact was becoming clear. While there was only one form of unemployment benefit, there were in fact two types of unemployed. One type for whom the act

[1] PEP, *Report on the British Social Services: A Survey of the Existing Public Social Services in Great Britain with Proposals for Future Development* (London, 1937), 138. A survey made on 14 November 1938, the only occasion when the Unemployment Assistance Board and the Ministry of Labour took an unemployment census on the same day, showed that of 1,678,711 persons receiving assistance on that day, over 16 per cent had been unemployed for more than 12 months. Burns, *Unemployment Programmes*, 179.

presumably had been designed, was the working man in the Midlands or the South-East in new industries, automobile manufacturing, electrical equipment, the chemical industry, or the rapidly growing service industries. His unemployment was usually of short duration and when at work his wages were high enough to permit him to pay a substantial employed contribution. The other was the workman in the textiles, in shipbuilding and in some years, although not in 1924, in coal-mining—the old staple export industries of prewar Britain—in the North or in Wales. Here lived almost exactly half of Britain's working population, but here also was two-thirds of her unemployment and a type insurance could not handle.

The result of the concentration was that a rise in reported figures of unemployment meant less an increase in the number of new claims than an increase in the duration of old claims. An average live register, for instance in 1927, of 1,100,000 unemployed meant about 4,000,000 individual claims for benefit at some time during the year. In effect the average claim was slightly more than three months. But a live register of 3,000,000 meant only about 6,000,000 separate claims for benefit during the year or an average benefit of six months. Almost tripling the number of those receiving benefits at any one time did not mean that three times as many men were unemployed at some time during the 12-month period but rather that about 50 per cent more men were remaining out of work twice as long.[1] The unemployment insurance fund did, to be sure, benefit from the gradually improving employment picture during 1923 and 1924 simply because a larger number of men at work improved the income from contributions. But the basic problem, a problem of principle rather than of finance, continued unsolved. If it were to remain a scheme of insurance it could do little for the chronically unemployed of Wales and the North. Yet if it did not help them what would? Unemployment insurance, fragile as it was, constituted the only tool the Government possessed.

Thus 1922 and 1923 were years when the old unemployment insurance scheme and the new uncovenanted, or 'extended', benefit—really two separate schemes neither of which owed much any longer

---

[1] For a thorough discussion see the address by H. M. Trouncer, 'Unemployment Insurance', *Journal of the Institute of Actuaries*, LXIV (Part II, 1933), 107–20. The 'live register' refers to the number of men actually reporting to the Employment Exchange weekly in search of work. Normally it approximates, but does not precisely equal, the number drawing unemployment benefit. A man for one reason or another not entitled to unemployment insurance benefit, might still report regularly to the exchange and thus remain on the live register. In fact men not entitled to benefit, or those whose benefit had for some reason expired, usually did not come to the exchange. For the next 60 days their names, or in fact their unemployment insurance book, would be transferred to the 'two-month file' and then to the 'dead file'.

G

to insurance—staggered along side by side. Men who had exhausted the standard benefit applied for extended benefit. This, for limited periods of eight or ten weeks, separated by gaps in which no benefit was paid, carried them through to a new insurance year when the standard benefit could begin again. Reams of Cabinet papers and thousands of hours of ministerial time were occupied with the problem of what to do with the unemployed workman who had exhausted his standard benefit, exhausted his uncovenanted benefit and who had, beyond the Poor Law, no alternatives other than starvation or revolution.

The accession to power of Britain's first Labour Government under Ramsay MacDonald on 22 January 1924 might have been expected to bring major changes in the social welfare system. In fact Labour's most successful reforms in this field were in housing. MacDonald was hampered by the fact that the life of his Government depended on the support of 159 Liberals in the House of Commons, disunited admittedly, but nominally under the leadership of H. H. Asquith. Unemployment insurance was above all a Liberal programme and any changes in it were likely to excite even more than the usual suspicion with which the Liberal supporters of the Government treated Labour party projects. At the same time the Cabinet was itself undecided on what to do about unemployment. Sidney Webb strongly advocated a large extension of the Trade Facilities Act while the only other economic expert among his colleagues, Philip Snowden, opposed changes of any kind, including changes in unemployment insurance, that would cost money.[1] Nevertheless, the MacDonald Cabinet and its Minister of Labour, the Lancashire textile worker Tom Shaw, succeeded in putting together and passing the first of several measures that between 1924 and 1927 attempted to reconstruct the tottering unemployment insurance programme. But by changing the basis of unemployment insurance they began also the process that made the programme the focus of the crisis of 1931, destroyed the second Labour Government and came close to destroying the Labour party as well.[2]

Shaw's measure, simple enough by itself, proposed to do two things: to make the uncovenanted benefit indefinite in length and to end ministerial discretion in granting the benefit. This proposal quickly brought to the surface the distrust always latent among the Liberals supporting the Labour Government. On 29 May, after two days of

[1] PRO Cab. 24/164, CP 76, 'Unemployment Insurance, PS', 6 February 1924, Cab. 24/164, CP 83, 'Report of the Unemployment Committee', 7 February 1924, Sidney Webb, Chairman.
[2] On the significance of the Unemployment Insurance (No. 2) Act of 1924 see: Beveridge, *Unemployment*, 276. Labour also increased the amount of the basic benefit from 15s. to 18s. for a single man and from 12s. to 15s. for a single woman, with proportionate increases for dependants.

acrimonious debate, a motion to reduce Shaw's salary was defeated by fewer than 50 votes, well below the normal Labour party majority.[1] Then on 30 June a committee resolution by C. F. G. Masterman was carried terminating Shaw's changes on 30 June 1926. The Cabinet accepted this amendment as the price of continued Liberal support for the measure as a whole. Even so, a motion during the report stage to revive ministerial discretion was defeated only 216 to 201.[2]

The amendment limiting the life of the act of 1924 made inevitable, as was intended, the appointment of a committee to review thoroughly unemployment insurance. Accordingly on 10 November 1925 the second Baldwin administration appointed the 'Unemployment Insurance Committee' under the chairmanship of Robert Younger, Lord Blanesburgh, a Lord of Appeal in Ordinary and brother of George Younger, still President of the National Union of Conservative Associations. The committee's terms of reference were the widest: 'To consider, in the light of experience, what changes, if any,' ought to be made in unemployment insurance.

While the Blanesburgh Committee conceived of insurance in the most generous possible terms and worked for more than a year before presenting its unanimous report, any assessment of the committee's work must conclude that its effect on the insurance programme was almost entirely bad. Instead of recognizing that Britain was faced with two virtually separate problems of joblessness, one of short duration and one nearly permanent, one frictional and one structural, the committee concluded that no useful distinction could be made among various kinds of unemployment. If a man were genuinely without work, the committee concluded, he ought to be relieved at the time his need occurred and for the period of his need. Nor did the need become less because he had been without work for a long period. The contributions that qualified an individual for unemployment insurance, therefore, ought to be regarded not as a means by which the man built up credit in the fund to carry him through periods of unemployment, but simply as a way of certifying that he was ordinarily in an insurable trade.[3]

---

[1] *H of C Deb.*, CLXXIV (29 May 1934), cols. 2451–2560.

[2] *Ibid.*, CLXXV (8 June 1924), cols. 2296–2320.

[3] 'It will be conceded that in the generality of cases persons with so poor a record of employment (as having done less than 15 weeks' work in 52 weeks) could scarcely claim still to be in the insured field; that there is grave doubt as to the genuineness of their search for work; and that the exclusion of such individuals is only fair to the general body of insured contributors.' *Report of the Unemployment Insurance Committee*, 1927, I, 75. For some reason the Blanesburgh Committee Report was published as a separate Stationery Office paper. It was not a Command Paper, nor is it to be found in Accounts and Papers. The report was signed on 31 January 1927.

To these ends, then, the Blanesburgh Committee proposed to alter the entire actuarial basis of unemployment insurance, in fact to discard it. The safeguards and stipulations that had been a part of the programme since 1911, the Committee argued, had destroyed the usefulness of insurance for millions of workers who had never been able to obtain the six months' continuous work necessary for standard benefit. As a consequence, to prevent hundreds of thousands of citizens from either starving or becoming paupers, the Government had been forced to waive rules that had been established to protect the insurance fund. The result was the morass of uncovenanted benefits, the fiction that workers would eventually pay back the loans they had contracted against future credit in the fund, the semi-annual struggles within the Cabinet between the Minister of Labour and the Chancellor of the Exchequer over the search for new money to grant further uncovenanted benefits lest men be forced on to the Poor Law, and finally the struggle with the Poor Law Guardians themselves who, in defence of the rates, lobbied the Government to resume its responsibility toward the unemployed. Instead of forcing the workman to suffer through the vagaries of a scheme established in another era and upon a different set of assumptions, Blanesburgh now proposed to set up a programme that would be adapted to the needs of the individual unemployed workman. It recommended sweeping away the distinctions between uncovenanted and covenanted benefit. Henceforth, the standard benefit would be unlimited in duration. The workman would fully qualify for the standard benefit if he could show that he had paid 30 contributions in the previous two years, or 15 in one year. Therefore, over the protests of Sir Alfred Watson, the chief Government actuary, the committee recommended abolishing the central regulation safeguarding the standard benefit since 1911: that no man could receive more than one week's benefit for each six weeks of contribution.[1]

After having established 30 contributions as an adequate test for an individual applicant's membership in the insured work force, the Blanesburgh Committee admitted that even this stipulation might prove to be too onerous under existing conditions of unemployment. As a consequence, it diluted the whole of its own argument against the uncovenanted and extended benefits by recommending the establishment of yet another special benefit, the 'transitional benefit', which would provide aid for those unable to meet the new work test. It would be given to those who were able to show that they had paid either eight contributions in the previous two years or 30 contributions at any time, under the same terms as the standard benefit. The transitional benefit was to be available only for a limited time—the recom-

[1] *Report of the Unemployment Insurance Committee*, II, 'Minutes of Evidence', 105–108.

mendation was one year—on the assumption that industrial conditions would soon improve. Finally the Blanesburgh Report urged that contributions be divided equally among the three participating parties, the employer, the employee and the Government.

These recommendations had a kind of four-square simplicity that commended them to many insurance experts.[1] But also they excited the hostility of important vested interests, the national health insurance approved societies. The Blanesburgh proposals for equal contributions toward benefits would have meant, in fact, an increase in the Government contribution toward unemployment insurance. Among the first acts of the Baldwin Government after its return to office in the autumn of 1925 was a concerted programme of Government economy which meant particularly a review of Government contributions towards the social services. One result of this had been a reduction in the Treasury contribution to health insurance and a reduction in the contribution to unemployment insurance from 6¾d. to 6d.[2]

The reduction in the contributions to national health insurance had been carried only over the strongest protests from the approved societies whose jealousy of any expenditure on welfare toward services other than their own was so important a determinant of British social policy in the interwar years. Now fear of a reaction from the societies caused a controversy in the Cabinet which held up for nearly a year the introduction of a bill to give effect to the Blanesburgh recommendations. Arthur Steel-Maitland, Baldwin's Minister of Labour, urged the Government to stand firm against the threats of the approved societies. 'It would be a bad precedent,' he wrote, 'if the influence exerted by the approved societies in one field of social insurance were allowed to deflect policy which might otherwise be approved by the Government in quite a different field.' The societies, he reminded the Cabinet, were fought and defeated at the time of the Economy Bill and the Government could, if necessary, defeat them again.[3]

---

[1] Writing in 1930 W. H. Beveridge, in his discussion of the Blanesburgh Report. remarks that 'with this the ten-year chaos since 1918 may be said to have ended', Beveridge, *Unemployment*, 276.

[2] Baldwin's economic ideas were of the simplest. A memorandum by him to the Bonar Law Cabinet less than a month after he became Chancellor of the Exchequer in 1922 illustrates his notions of the place of the government in the national productive system and his innocence of any taint of Keynesianism. Remarking that trade was improving, he lectured the Cabinet on the duty of now balancing the budget. In no case should there be any increase in taxation, nor any borrowing by the State. 'Money taken for Government purposes', he concluded, 'is money taken away from trade and borrowing will thus tend to depress trade and increase unemployment.' PRO Cab. 24/140, CP 4314, 'The Necessity for National Economy, Note by the Chancellor of the Exchequer', 20 November 1922.

[3] PRO Cab. 24/187, CP 166, 'Unemployment Bill', Arthur Steel-Maitland, 25 May 1927.

Maitland was opposed by the Minister of Health, Neville Chamberlain, already emerging as one of the most influential figures in the Baldwin administration, and the Chancellor of the Exchequer, Winston Churchill. Churchill may have been over-sensitive to the power of the friendly societies as a result of his own knowledge of them derived from the passage of the 1911 insurance act. In any case he argued with characteristic vigour that the Government, while attempting to provide a permanent structure for the ramshackle unemployment insurance system, should do nothing to antagonize these powerful organizations and should not suggest therefore that it had any preference for the unemployment programme over health insurance. If the Blanesburgh proposals were accepted without change, he pointed out on 31 May, the Government might have to rescind provisions for health insurance that were saving £3 million annually.

> The Minister of Health will bear me out in saying that this is not a negligible risk to be lightly dismissed by the arguments in the Minister of Labour's memorandum. The political power of the approved societies, with ramifications extending into every village and their agents calling at most of the houses of the working classes, is immense, as more than one Government have found out to their cost.

There was no way to remove the measure from the party arena, he continued. Labour was already coupling the Unemployment Insurance Bill and the Trade Disputes Bill as a package, both being part of the Conservative attack on the working class. It would not be expedient to bring in the approved societies also. Because of lack of parliamentary time the chances were that the measure could not be enacted in 1927 and would have to wait until 1928, dangerously close to a General Election. His personal preference, Churchill concluded, was to do nothing about the Blanesburgh recommendations and simply to pass a measure extending the current scheme.[1]

In the end, fear of the approved societies prevailed. The Unemployment Insurance Act of 1927 provided for contributions of 7d., 8d. and 6d. for the worker, the employer and the State respectively, continuing contributions as they had been before. The benefit for single men was reduced from 18s., at which the Labour Government had set it, to 17s., while dependants' benefits were increased slightly. The act specified that contributions from each party would be reduced by one penny per week when the debt in the Unemployment Insurance Fund was retired.

Most significantly, the requirements for eligibility for all benefit under unemployment insurance, the standard benefit and the new

[1] PRO Cab. 24/187, CP 168, 'Unemployment Insurance, memorandum by the Chancellor of the Exchequer', 31 May 1927.

'transitional benefit' were made identical. The applicant for benefit was required to show that he was 'genuinely seeking work but unable to obtain suitable employment'. The latter part of this phrase had been the basic stipulation for benefit under the act of 1911 and the requirement of 'genuinely seeking work' had been introduced in 1921 as an additional proof for eligibility for the uncovenanted benefit. Now that, theoretically, there was no uncovenanted benefit the entire phrase became applicable to all benefit. The importance of the change for this study derives from the fact that it left with the applicant for benefit the responsibility for proving that he was in fact eligible for benefit. Now that the Blanesburgh recommendations had made benefit unlimited in duration, the requirement of 'genuinely seeking work' provided the only legal check left in the hands of the Government for controlling the cost of unemployment insurance. The removal of this stipulation in 1930 would become an important cause of the crisis in unemployment insurance the next year.[1]

Unfortunately, the Blanesburgh Committee and the measure that embodied its recommendations, had assumed that unemployment would continue to decline and level off at about the rate of 6 per cent.[2] This did not occur and as a result the transitional benefit, which was supposed to end for new claimants in April 1929, was still in January of that year providing support for about 120,000 or 10 per cent of all men receiving unemployment benefit and so had to be extended for another year until April 1930. By February 1930 the number of transitional benefit had increased to 140,000, still about 10 per cent of the total number on the live register. Hence the Labour Government now in power extended the transitional benefit again until October 1931.[3]

The act extending the transitional benefit in 1930 made a most important change in eligibility for unemployment insurance which contributed largely to the crisis of 1931. After the report of a committee under the chairmanship of Sir Harold Morris, an eminent

[1] During the debates on the passage of the measure, Steel-Maitland admitted that he did not like the phrase 'genuinely seeking work', but he could think of nothing else and offered to accept any amendment that would provide a more reasonable and more easily understood requirement. *H of C Deb.*, CCX (9 November 1927), col. 214. It should be noted that the Government took seriously the danger of allowing a controversial unemployment insurance bill to come into effect on the eve of a General Election and so passed the measure in a special session in the autumn of 1927. The bill received the Royal Assent on 22 December 1927 and came into force on 19 April 1928.

[2] In June 1927 just as the act was in its final stages of preparation, insured unemployment in Great Britain reached its interwar low of 8·8 per cent with the live register going below one million for the only time in 20 years. Statistics do not suggest that the General Strike had any permanent effect on general unemployment.

[3] These statistics are taken from *Cmd. 4185*, 'Royal Commission on Unemployment Insurance, Final Report', 1932, 29.

Labour barrister, the act repealed the stipulation that an applicant for benefit give evidence that he was 'genuinely seeking work'. Instead an applicant would be disqualified for benefit only if he failed to accept a vacant situation of which he had been notified and would be disqualified for six weeks if he disregarded written instructions about work given to him by the Employment Exchange.[1] The effect of this change was to make unemployment benefit a right unless the Employment Exchange officer could show that it should not be given. It transferred the burden of proof from the man to the State. From the point of view of Labour and Fabian theorists this was all to the good. Here at last was the right to work or maintenance which Labour had always demanded.[2] On the other hand, the immediate effect of the new rules was to overstrain dangerously the already chaotic finances of unemployment insurance by depriving the insurance administration of any legal control over the cost of the programme.

The act of 1930 caused a larger increase in clients for transitional benefit than occurred at any other time during the period of this benefit. Between March and May 1930 the number of transitional benefits more than doubled, rising from 140,000 to 300,000. Of this 160,000 increase, 60,000 had never been registered at a Labour Exchange before. This was not solely the result of generally worsening economic conditions because the total live register grew only from 1,539,000 to 1,770,000, an increase of 231,000 or about 15 per cent.[3] In effect the growth of unemployment benefit during this period, at a time when general unemployment was certainly increasing steadily, but slowly, was almost completely due to the change in benefit regulations. The act of 1930 made virtually impossible any check on the cost of unemployment insurance. Without questioning the social desirability of this change, in terms of government finance it led directly to crisis.

The act of 1930 also transferred from the Unemployment Insurance Fund to the Treasury the whole burden of the transitional benefit and so for the first time it became possible to delineate precisely the

[1] For a good review of the Morris Committee thinking see: Sir Frank Tillyard, *Unemployment Insurance in Great Britain, 1911-48* (Leigh-on-Sea 1949), 92–8. See also: *Cmd. 3430*, 'Unemployment Insurance Bill, 1929, Explanatory Memorandum on Clauses', 1929. The bill was introduced in November 1929.

[2] William Beveridge, who became increasingly critical of the administration of unemployment insurance throughout 1930, 1931 and 1932, nevertheless approved the recommedations of the Morris Committee. Beveridge, like the Webbs, wanted to expand the role of the Employment Exchange in the administration of industrial welfare. See: Beveridge, *Unemployment*, 279.

[3] The most significant statistic concerning the effect of the act of 1930 may be that between March and June of 1930, while unemployment was growing steadily, the number of heads of families receiving poor relief, which had likewise been increasing regularly, dropped from 92,000 to 43,000. Burns, *Unemployment Programmes*, 53.

cost of the new form of what were, in fact, uncovenanted benefits. Between April 1929 and April 1930 the Treasury paid about half the cost of transitional benefits including administrative expenses. To 31 March of that year the Treasury paid £3,985,000, which suggests that the transitional benefit to the end of that fiscal year was slightly less than £8 million, in a total insurance expenditure of about £46 million. In the next fiscal year to the end of March 1931 after the 1930 changes transitional benefits cost £19,247,000 in a total insurance expenditure of £92,416,000. In effect the cost of the transitional benefit grew from somewhat more than 14 per cent to about 20 per cent of the total insurance expenditure. The £19,247,000 was considerably more than had been spent on the Royal Air Force in any year since the end of the war, and approximately half the customary appropriation for the Army.[1] Without counting the cost of unemployment insurance as a whole, the transitional benefit alone had become a major item of Government expenditure. In effect, the Government had opened the Treasury to certain classes of citizens almost without condition. Relief of the unemployed through the transitional benefit, even more than the cost of the standard benefit, was at the core of the budget deficit that brought England to near-bankruptcy in 1931.

---

[1] The actuary had estimated that the changes would cost about £3,250,000. *Cmd. 3437*, 'Unemployment Insurance Bill, 1929, Report by the Government Actuary on the Financial Provisions of the Bill', 1929.

3   The battle for reform - phase 1: a ministry for health?

Potentially the establishment of the Ministry of Health could have been the greatest achievement of the reform programme of the Lloyd George Government. Before the war, such a ministry, responsible for the national physical welfare in the broadest possible terms, had been regarded by serious reformers as being the culmination of the campaign to improve the 'condition of the people'. This was particularly true for thinkers of the Fabian school who were interested first of all in the prevention of poverty. Because the poor were a wasted social resource whose very existence harmed society, the prevention of poverty through the prevention of its chief cause, sickness, was a large step toward an ideal state. As sickness caused poverty, so poverty caused sickness and for the State to interrupt these reciprocal disasters appeared to be perhaps the most important possible government activity. As early as 1907, at the time of the establishment of school medical inspection, the little group of scientific reformers who hoped to create a comprehensive school medical service—Sir Robert L. Morant, Sir George Newman, Margaret McMillan and Sidney and Beatrice Webb—had already begun to plan for the day when all national public and personal medical activities would be concentrated in a single ministry for health.[1]

The momentum achieved with the early success in the school medical service and feeding of school children was somewhat lessened with the passage of the National Insurance Act of 1911 which founded the British national health insurance scheme. Sidney and Beatrice Webb opposed both health and the accompanying unemployment insurance because the benefits were paid as of right and were not dependent upon improvement of personal habits. Still worse was the transfer of Robert Morant, who generally agreed with the Webbs on the importance of 'conditional relief', from his post as Permanent Secretary of the Board of Education to the Chairmanship of the English Insurance Commission, becoming in effect, civil service head of the insurance scheme. Thus Morant left the school medical service which, with the health activities of the Local Government Board, he had hoped to make the nucleus of a ministry for health and was set to work at building up a competing and independent health service of which

[1] For details of early planning on a ministry for health see Bentley B. Gilbert, *The Evolution of National Insurance in Great Britain* (London, 1966), 131–47.

neither he nor his friends entirely approved. Progress toward a health ministry was considerably slowed.

At the same time occurred another event which was perhaps even more unfortunate for the progress of plans for the consolidation of government health activities. This was the breakdown of friendly relations between Dr George Newman, the Chief Medical Officer at the Board of Education and Dr Arthur Newsholme, the Chief Medical Officer at the Local Government Board. Newsholme had been appointed to the Local Government Board in January 1908. His selection for that important post was a victory for the reformers, principally Sidney and Beatrice Webb, who had supported his candidacy.[1] Newsholme was one of the leading medical officers of health in the country. Until his appointment he had been editor of *Public Health,* the journal of the Society of Medical Officers of Health, and most important was a close friend and in some ways the patron of George Newman, whom he had supported for the school medical service. Newsholme was expected to bring life and the light of reform to the unimaginative routine of the Local Government Board and to collaborate with Newman in public health activity. For a time, the two worked in friendly cooperation. Board of Education Circular 596 of 17 August 1908, as important as a parliamentary statute, which provided the charter for the school medical service, shows clearly the hands of both men. Nevertheless, in the next four years, certainly before 1913, a coolness had appeared between the two. Probably the bad feeling was caused by Newsholme's plans to bring the administration of national health insurance into the Local Government Board. An entry in Newman's diary tells of a long talk with the Webbs about the unification of British medical services and concludes with the remark that the 'present Government is not interested in P.H. development. A P.H. Ministry would be formed soon of Insurance and Poor Laws—not a unity of all medical departments.' Newman blamed this on Newsholme, who had been a 'failure' at the Local Government Board although he had been an excellent man at Brighton where he had been Medical Officer of Health.[2] Newsholme's published memoirs essentially confirm this. He hoped also to concentrate all Government health activities in one ministry but wanted to see it done under an expanded Local Government Board, perhaps under another name. Just before the war he was attempting to bring medical care of children—at that time Newman's responsibility—under himself. There was no useful way, he argued, to distinguish between child ill-health due to disease and due

[1] Beatrice Webb, *Our Partnership* (London, 1948), 394.
[2] Newman Diaries, II, MS entry 18 December 1911.

to environmental cause. It was impossible, he felt, to dissociate successful maternity and child welfare work.[1]

In the controversy between the former friends appears the division of opinion that would hold back the establishment of the Ministry of Health and would ensure, when the ministry was finally set up, that it would be a weak rather than a strong department. While everyone agreed that a ministry for health was desirable, there was sharp controversy about its focus, or core, a controversy that grew from the almost indefinable nature of 'health' itself. Should the ministry be, as Newsholme wanted it, simply an expansion of the Local Government Board? This would mean that the ministry would take on the supervision of the despised Poor Law and would include the general supervision of British municipal authorities. Arguably, thought Newsholme, the Poor Law, which ran a large and important medical service, was an important health activity; almost no activity on behalf of England's poor was unconcerned with health. Nearly every work of British local government, from filling holes in streets to fighting fire, affected the environment and hence the health of the nation's citizens.

Yet from Newman's point of view, and as it turned out from the point of view of most of the enthusiastic advocates of the health ministry in both the medical profession and the Labour party, an attempt to build a new ministry on the old, unimaginative, tradition-bound foundations of the Local Government Board would be both futile and disastrous. The ministry for health was to be concerned with health alone; it should have nothing to do with the Poor Law. It should be scientific, experimental and, above all, free from the parochialism that stifled thought in Local Government Board administration.

Before the war these issues were matters of contest only among a few experts. Outside the narrow circle of the Fabians and their friends in the higher echelons of the civil service, the grand concept of a ministry for health evoked little interest. For the general population, and indeed for the ordinary political world, the excitement and tumult surrounding the establishment of national health insurance seemed to show that the Government was already doing quite enough for the physical well-being of the ordinary citizen. Finally with the coming of the war, national attention was completely diverted. Newman himself was drawn into the Board of Liquor Control. Morant and John Anderson struggled, almost alone, to keep in operation the vast machinery of national health insurance. Christopher Addison, appointed

[1] Sir Arthur Newsholme, *The Last Thirty Years in Public Health* (London, 1935), 197.

parliamentary secretary to the Board of Education after the resignation of Charles Trevelyan, followed Lloyd George in May 1915 into the newly created Ministry of Munitions of War as parliamentary secretary. Here he had, in addition to his other duties, the task of maintaining liaison with his chief's former radical friends and of keeping himself informed of their whereabouts and plans.[1] At last, with the reconstruction of the Government in December 1916 Addison became Minister of Munitions while presiding over most of the Liberal domestic appointments to the Coalition Ministry.

The first attempt

One of several unconventional appointments for which Addison was responsible was that of David Thomas, Baron Rhondda, as President of the Local Government Board on 10 December 1916, which marks the beginning of the drive that by 1919 would give Britain a ministry for health. In Rhondda, the trio of Addison, Morant, and Newman had at their disposal for the first time an LGB chief who was, or at least could be, sympathetic with their plans. He was in addition an influential public figure, a businessman with no political ambitions of his own, and one not hypnotized by the atmosphere of negativism and reaction that seemed always to overcome previous presidents of that board. Within days after Rhondda's appointment, Addison sent Rhondda a memorandum that he, Newman, and Morant had drawn up during the optimistic summer of 1914 arguing the need for the concentration of Government health activity in a single ministry. The document showed particularly that, despite the widespread curative services available to the British population in the Poor Law Medical Service and in national health insurance, preventive medicine in the United Kingdom, especially maternity and child welfare services, still received very little attention, with the result, among other things, that 50,000 children died needlessly each year.[2] Soon afterwards, on 16 January 1917, Morant, Newman, and Rhondda lunched at the Reform Club. Here Rhondda and Newman met for the first time and Rhondda allowed himself to be convinced—with some little hesitation, because he 'did not want to upset people more than necessary'—that a ministry for health was politically feasible. Apparently the reformers had already drawn up a tentative draft bill. Its simplicity suggests the

---

[1] In planning the 1915–16 budget, his last as Chancellor of the Exchequer, Lloyd George agreed, under the urging of Addison, to authorize substantially increased grants for schools, meals, and medical care. Christopher Addison, *Four and a Half Years* (London, 1934), I, 38, diary entry 2–3 December 1914.

[2] This memorandum unfortunately appears to have been lost.

work of Morant whose invariable political technique was to effect large changes quietly.[1]

Rhondda was clearly much impressed by the information laid before him by the two medical men. As a businessman accustomed to using statistics, he found the fact of 50,000 children dying needlessly each year (or as he usually put it, 1,000 each week) both poignant and impressive.[2] In any case, on 24 January 1917, he wrote to Lloyd George asking for an appointment to talk to the Prime Minister about 'the reorganization of this department'. He asked also that Addison be present.[3]

By the middle of February, the reformers were jubilant. In Rhondda they had an agent of considerable political potency—because he was a wealthy Liberal without political commitment—who seemed as enthusiastic as themselves for the unification of health services. The Local Government Board seemed at last to be remodelled. 'Rec'd. letter from RLM [Morant],' wrote Newman in his diary, 'that R. [Rhondda] had sent for him and that R. and Addison were bent on big changes and that RLM and I were to go to LGB and that Monro [the incumbent permanent secretary] and Willis had been informed —that Newsholme's KCB was sent by the P.M. to be a "parting gift".'[4]

This elation was premature. Rhondda was a businessman. He looked on his department as a business which he could manage as he pleased. The subtle exigencies of politics and still more subtle calculations of his fellow Welshman, David Lloyd George, he never understood. Newsholme received his KCB, but he did not leave the Local Government Board. Neither did Newman nor Morant go there for over two years. The ministry of health, which seemed early in 1917 to be upon the verge of establishment, would not come into existence until 1919. Rhondda, its most effective advocate, did not live to see it.

Although on 27 March 1917 Rhondda sent the War Cabinet a memorandum on 'the urgent need' for a ministry of health, he had by now stirred into life opposition to his proposals that for a time seemed likely to make his measure impossible to enact.[5] Among

---

[1] On this meeting see: Newman Diaries, III, MS entry 16 January 1917. At the luncheon Rhondda asked Newman whether he would like to come to the Local Government Board. See also: Christopher Addison, *Politics from Within, 1911–18* (London, 1924), II, 55. Before the meeting Addison had talked to Rhondda privately and had urged the appointment of Newman as well as Morant to the new ministry of health.

[2] Margaret Haig Mackworth, Viscountess Rhondda, *D. A. Thomas, Viscount Rhondda* (London, 1921), 264–5.

[3] Rhondda to Lloyd George, 24 January 1917. Lloyd George Papers, F/43/5/5.

[4] Newman Diaries, III, MS entry 20 February 1917.

[5] Public Record Office, Cab. 23/2, War Cabinet 115, meeting 6 April 1917, appendix.

all the things he had been told about the need for preventive medical care apparently the figure that had affected Rhondda most was the statistic on the death of children. Therefore, even while he considered the establishment of a ministry of health, indeed before he submitted the much overemphasized Cabinet memorandum of 27 March, he requested from his Chief Medical Officer, Dr Newsholme, a special report on child mortality in England and Wales, broken down to the smallest local authorities and he succeeded in inserting into his budget an increased appropriation of £200,000 for maternity and infant welfare.[1] The increased appropriation and Newsholme's report which concluded with the recommendation that the local authorities should he brought to the assistance of the working-class mother and her baby, caused a stir in the House of Commons on 8 March.[2] Particularly apparent was the fear expressed by spokesmen of the industrial insurance companies that the local authorities, by entering the field of maternity and infant care, would intrude upon the highly profitable work already carried on by those companies in the course of their administration of national health insurance. Whatever may be said of Rhondda as a humanitarian—and his claims to distinction in this area are very great—his expertise as a politician and his knowledge of political pressure were negligible. By invading the field of maternity care he aroused resistance among powerful vested interests that would for a time appear to make the enactment of a ministry of health dubious.

Beyond the Poor Law medical service, Britain's only official provision for maternity care in 1917 was the 30s. paid upon confinement to the wives of the 13 million working men of the country covered under national health insurance. (In cases where the wife herself was a worker and also covered under national health insurance, the payment was doubled.) This service, the benefits of which began on 15 January 1913, covered virtually every working man in the United Kingdom. (About five-sixths of the adult male population as well as, by 1917, about five million women, a total of about 15 million, were insured.) This great mass of people carried insurance providing for general practitioner medical care, a sickness benefit of 10s. per week plus a lower disability benefit, and the aforementioned maternity benefit. They were insured not directly with the Government, but with agencies designated by law 'approved societies'. There were nearly 20,000

---

[1] Cd. 8496, 'Supplement in continuance of the Report of the Medical Officer of the Board for 1915–16, containing a Report on Child Mortality of Ages 0–5 in England and Wales', 1916. Introduction to report by Newsholme dated March 1917.

[2] Cd. 8496, 84. Official Report, House of Commons Debates, series 5, XCI (8 March 1917), cols. 645–6.

approved societies. About half of the insured were affiliated with the old fraternal benefit societies, the friendly societies, organized to keep the working man and his family off the Poor Law in case he should fall sick. Most of the remainder were under sections of the modern industrial insurance companies, run for profit, which earned their money by selling small life insurance policies, 'funeral benefits', to the industrial worker on the argument that no working-class household could afford the £10–15 necessary to bury the head of the family in case of a sudden death and that the alternative would be burial by the parish—in effect, the potter's field. This form of insurance was known as industrial insurance and these companies, at the beginning, had not been considered appropriate agents for the administration of national health insurance. But by 1910 industrial insurance had begun to insist that it too had the right to administer benefits under the Government scheme and had by 1911 forced its way into the programme.[1] By 1917, industrial insurance approved societies had as members about half the total number of the insured and by far the great majority of newly insured women. They had been unquestionably the most active in recruiting new members after the establishment of national health insurance. Industrial insurance had been able to do this because of a peculiar characteristic of this form of insurance, the industrial insurance salesman-collector. This man was the insured person's contact with the insurance company and with the industrial insurance approved societies which had been formed after the advent of national health insurance. He visited the home of each of his clients weekly collecting the 1d. or 2d. premium for the burial policies and administering the benefits of the national health insurance scheme at the same time. With over 40 million industrial policies in force by 1917, handled by over 70,000 collector salesmen whose commissions and livelihood depended on their contacts with the industrial working class, simple arithmetic suggests that each of the fewer than 10 million working-class families in the United Kingdom must have owned at least four industrial insurance policies.

The connection between the insurance salesman and his client families was a thing to be jealously guarded. Any interference by a competitive institution, public or private, had to be resisted. Among the most important privileges gained for the industrial insurance salesman by his connection with health insurance was the right to deliver the 30s. maternity benefit which amounted to more than a week's wages for the ordinary working man at the beginning of the war. This was usually the occasion for the sale of a new policy on the life of the infant. (Although the law prohibited the sale of policies on children under the age of six months, this stipulation was widely evaded.)

[1] Gilbert, *Evolution of National Insurance*, 319–83.

This valuable and extremely profitable area of business Lord Rhondda unwittingly threatened early in March 1917 in his eagerness to inject the local authorities into maternity care.

The proposals made public on 8 March and the Rhondda memorandum to the Cabinet at the end of the month merged into a confused debate over precisely what should be the nature of the new ministry of health and more particularly what should be the scope of its administrative activity. The issues were more obscure because Rhondda himself had no particular notion of the form the ministry should take.

On one side, privately, he was propelled by his advisers within the Government, notably Newman and Morant—who had disapproved of national health insurance in the first place and particularly of the approved society form of administration—toward a thoroughgoing reform of all government health activity. They hoped the new ministry of health would take over and reconstruct the administration of national health insurance. Because its functions would be preventative as well as curative and would reach every citizen in the kingdom, local governments would be required to establish a local health authority with broad powers in all fields.

From the other side came the public and private political pressure of the powerful approved societies connected with the industrial insurance industry. These groups reacted immediately to the suggestions that the Local Government Board was moving into the sacred preserve of maternity and child welfare and had requested on the day of the debate that the Prime Minister receive a deputation.[1] Then, as the proposals for a full-scale ministry of health became known, they began to fear not only for the safety of their monopoly of contact with the individual citizen in health matters, but for the security of the approved society system itself. While always saying publicly that they supported in principle the idea of a ministry of health, industrial insurance nevertheless carried on privately a highly effective campaign against any concrete proposals for such a ministry. As their spokesman in the Government they had Sir Edwin Cornwall, Comptroller of the Household who, although not a man of great political capacity, was able to convince the Prime Minister—who knew all too well from his struggles over the passage of the National Insurance Act of the political power of the issue of national insurance—that in order to establish a ministry for health the approved societies would have to be satisfied with their position within it.

Outside the political world industrial insurance reacted quickly to the intimation that the security of its happy position as a purveyor of both Government health benefits and private insurance policies was

[1] Rhondda to Lloyd George, 8 March 1917, LG Papers F/43/5/13.

H

threatened. The *National Insurance Gazette,* the organ of the approved societies, warned its readers in the weeks following that there was danger that the Local Government Board intended to take over the important maternity grant. Furthermore it had come out in debate, said the *Gazette* in a leading article, that there were plans for the unification of all health services in a single department and that F. Handel Booth, 'the insurance man's M.P.', had made a speech attacking the maternity proposals.[1]

On 27 March Rhondda submitted to the Cabinet his memorandum on 'the urgent need for a Ministry of Health'. These proposals, which had caused so much uproar even before they appeared, began by pointing out how much present overlapping in Government health activities existed, using as an illustration a mild proposal for a maternity and child welfare bill that had already excited opposition from the insurance authorities. Basically Rhondda argued for a simple three-clause bill establishing a ministry of health superseding the Local Government Board. He proposed to transfer medical and sanatorial benefits of national health insurance from the local insurance committees to the major local authorities and money would be given to the local authorities to begin their activities. Rhondda's memorandum was referred to a Cabinet committee consisting of Milner and Arthur Henderson but including also, outside the War Cabinet, Rhondda, Cornwall, Addison, H. A. L. Fisher, G. N. Barnes, E. S. Montagu, with G. M. Young as secretary.[2]

Rhondda's memorandum received almost immediate support from Addison who wrote on 2 April that so far as it went it was a fine statement. The new ministry could have a 'health side' and a 'local administration side'. He hoped the Prime Minister would support it and suggested again that George Newman should be chief medical officer. He concluded with: 'I warn you not to let Kingsley Wood & Co. do anything to block it.'[3]

---

[1] *National Insurance Gazette,* 17 March 1917. The *Gazette* had come into existence in the spring of 1912 as a professional and house journal for the scores of thousands of people connected with the national health insurance administration. It was published by the Insurance Publishing Company (now Stone and Cox) which also published the *Insurance Mail,* the professional journal of the industrial insurance salesmen.

[2] PRO Cab. 23/2, War Cabinet 115, 6 April 1917. The local insurance committees were bodies representing chiefly the local authorities and the approved societies which had under their control the administration of the general practitioner service, and the so-called 'sanatorial benefits' which gave each insured the right to go to a sanatorium in case of affliction by tuberculosis.

[3] Addison to Lloyd George, 2 April 1917, LG Papers, F/1/3/11. Kingsley Wood, who had begun public life as a solicitor for the Liverpool Victoria and Royal London Mutual Insurance Companies before 1911 had become by 1917 the most powerful spokesman for the industrial insurance industry.

Rhondda was by this time seriously worried about his project for a ministry of health. Although on 5 April he lunched with Newman and Robert Morant at the Bath Club, telling them that Lloyd George had approved the appointment of both of them to the new ministry and that Newsholme and Willis could work under both of them or leave, the bulk of the conversation was devoted to ways of frustrating Sir Edwin Cornwall.[1]

The first meeting of the committee of the War Cabinet which had been appointed on 6 April occurred just six days later in Lord Milner's rooms in Westminster Palace. It soon degenerated into an unpleasant dialogue between Cornwall and Rhondda. Addison was mystified and distressed by all this. For reasons 'which I could not divine', Cornwall appeared to assume that a ministry of health would be 'inimical' to approved society interest.[2]

The first meeting was inconclusive, as it was bound to be. The only concrete decision was the appointment of Addison, upon Arthur Henderson's suggestion, to head a subcommittee to report on the health aspects of the new proposals.[3] When this committee reported on 15 May, Cornwall returned to the attack. Addison refused to take seriously the opposition provoked by the proposals for a ministry for health. 'Cornwall', he said, 'was obsessed with the views of a small section of industrial societies.'[4] A few days later after another inconclusive meeting of the War Cabinet subcommittee on 23 May, Milner announced that he had heard enough and decided, chiefly upon his own responsibility, to endorse in principle to the War Cabinet the idea of a ministry of health.[5]

Addison's report on the ministry of health had been accepted by all of the Cabinet committee on 15 May except for Cornwall. Milner's decision eight days later at the meeting of the 23rd to take the matter to the Cabinet, notwithstanding the presumed approved society objections, seemed to presage the quick establishment of a ministry.[6] The industrial insurance world now had to act. They were vulnerable, but they were well prepared and organized. They also understood what had already become a maxim of politics: legislation for social welfare cannot be directly opposed. By itself, a ministry of health, like legislation for the welfare of mothers and children, was unexceptionable.

[1] Newman Diaries, III, MS entry 5 April 1917.

[2] Addison, *Politics*, II, 222.

[3] Addison, *Four and a Half Years*, II, 355.

[4] Addison, *Politics*, II, 222.

[5] *Ibid.* Through the seemingly endless series of meetings and hearings of April and May, much of Addison's work was delegated to a young civil servant who eventually emerged after Morant's death as the chief administrator of national health insurance, Michael Heseltine. Addison, *Four and a Half Years*, II, 366.

[6] Margaret I. Cole, ed., *Beatrice Webb's Diaries 1912–24* (London, 1952), diary entry 3 June 1917, 87–8.

Moreover, they had no reason genuinely to oppose a larger department particularly concerned with the operation of national health
insurance. The insurance administration had suffered severely in 1914
and 1915 from the lack of a minister of Cabinet rank to defend it in
the House of Commons. On the other hand, the position of the joint
insurance commission, as an independent board in the American sense,
carried with it certain advantages. Most important, its income was
derived from the contributions of the insured and their employers and
independent of parliamentary vote. This position was worth protecting
and in a strong ministry it might disappear. All approved societies,
both those of industrial insurance and the old friendly societies, were
determined to fight for the maintenance of this independent status.
Hence the Ministry of Health Bill, which Milner had enthusiastically
recommended to the War Cabinet on 23 May 1917, and which by any
normal rule of politics should have been speedily enacted, became
stuck in the mire of political exigency, postponing the creation of a
ministry for nearly two years. By this time the war had ended and the
planning for reconstruction which ought to have been part of the new
department's work had not been accomplished. The failure to establish
a ministry of health during the war was one of the principal causes of
the failure of the Lloyd George Government to provide the land 'fit
for heroes' that the Prime Minister promised the nation, and the
resistance of the insurance world must be examined.

The intervention of the approved societies

The reaction of the approved societies to the bare announcements in
the House of Commons on 8 March during the supply debate for the
Local Government Board that £200,000 were to be appropriated for
a child welfare service showed that they had not been placated by
assurances from Rhondda on 13 March 1917, denying that he had any
intention of taking over the maternity grant. Clearly change was coming.
Their intelligence inside the Government, which appeared always to
be excellent, told them that there were plans for a complete overhaul
of all departments dealing with popular welfare. Inevitably this would
touch national insurance at many points. The truculence and suspicion
manifest in the speeches of industrial insurance approved society
leaders and in the lead articles of the *National Insurance Gazette*
reflect the fear and jealousy with which they regarded any Government
activity in their field. In assessing their attitude and the events of the
next two years, a salient fact was the great industrial insurance victory
of 1911 over the Government and over their colleagues in the friendly
societies. They had forced a virtual remodelling of national health
insurance to permit their entry into the scheme. In 1917 this event

was only five and a half years old. Many leaders in that struggle, most important Howard Kingsley Wood, A. R. Barrand of the Prudential, Thomas Neill of the Pearl, and Percy Rockliff (in 1911 a spokesman for the unregistered dividing societies), were still active. To be sure, many of them now had posts in the national insurance administration but they were insurance men first and government officials only incidentally. Moreover they expected, with ample justification as it turned out, that David Lloyd George who had surrendered to their power in 1911 and had betrayed his friends in the fraternal societies in the process, would not now, in the midst of a great war, care to force the comparatively minor issue of the establishment of a ministry of health over their open opposition. They could expect that he would seek to find a compromise and the establishment of the ministry of health would be held up until they were accommodated. 'Accommodation' would mean the maintenance of the independence of the national health insurance administration at the local level, particularly the maintenance of its separation from any public health activities that might be assumed by the local authorities under the urging of a new health-oriented central ministry.

By the end of March, the organization of the opposition of the industrial insurance societies of national insurance was under way. Its leader was a noisy, and, according to the accounts of several civil servants who had to work with him in the period between the wars, unsavoury little man, Percy Rockliff. In 1911, during the struggle to secure the entry of industrial insurance into the national insurance scheme, Rockliff had been a distinctly second-rate figure, a lesser associate of Kingsley Wood who had been the chief lobbyist for industrial insurance.[1] Now he was far more significant. A frantic organizer, Rockliff specialized in the creation of shadow groups with portentous names. Three of them—the Standing Committee of Approved Societies, the Faculty of Insurance, and the National Insurance Advisory Committee—existed principally on Rockliff's stationery, although in the next two years the Government would apparently take all of them quite seriously. To mobilize opinion he indefatigably wrote letters and issued statements to the press.

Howard Kingsley Wood, who in 1911 had succeeded first in defeating and then in making himself almost indispensable to Lloyd George, was by 1917 detaching himself from the insurance world and beginning a second career as a politician. Increasingly in the next two years, he would serve as a mediator between the men of industrial insurance and the Government. While his only office was that of a member of the London County Council, he received a KB in the New Year's

[1] On Rockliff see: Henry N. Bunbury, ed., *Lloyd George's Ambulance Wagon. Being the Memoirs of William J. Braithwaite, 1911–12* (London, 1957), 97.

honours at the end of 1918, dropping at the same time his first name and becoming simply 'Sir Kingsley Wood'.[1] At the same time he entered Parliament as a Coalition Unionist. Kingsley Wood was the principal speaker at the first of many meetings promoted by the industrial insurance approved societies to coordinate their opposition to a ministry of health. This meeting at Central Hall, Westminster on 31 March 1917 was promoted and sponsored by Percy Rockliff. Kingsley Wood emphasized, as would all industrial insurance spokesmen in the future, that there was no objection to a ministry of health as such. Lloyd George, he said, had always been interested in a ministry of health and now that he was Prime Minister there was a good chance that one would come into being. He assured his audience also that the Prime Minister had always been aware of the dangers of associating health matters with the Poor Law.[2]

During the next few weeks, the *National Insurance Gazette* was filled with reports of letters back and forth between the Local Government Board and various leaders of the industrial insurance world and with letters from insurance men to other members of their profession urging organization and resistance. Sir Edwin Cornwall was consistently applauded. Rockliff termed him 'champion' of national health insurance but warned that he 'had a powerful opponent in Lord Rhondda ...'.[3] Meanwhile, the *Gazette* in lead articles warned the rank and file of industrial insurance to be continually on their guard. While they admitted nothing but praise for the idea of a ministry of health, the men of national health insurance did not want 'to be submerged in a huge department' which also administered the Poor Law. Nor could national health insurance 'trust every county and county Borough Council with National Health work ...'. 'Lord Rhondda hopes that the question of the approved societies will be "taken in hand very soon",' wrote Rockliff in a typically unpleasant letter. 'Both he and the Government will find they are made of far sterner stuff than the Association of Insurance Committees, and that any attempt to merge Health Insurance into the LGB will prove to be the most contentious of proposals.'[4]

The attacks on Rhondda really meant very little. Despite Rockliff's endless snarling letters denouncing the 'Bumbledum' of the Local

---

[1] After 1918, in addition to dropping his first name, Kingsley Wood sought to erase also all of his previous life. *Who's Who* carries no mention of his earlier connection with insurance. Two pamphlets that he wrote against the National Insurance Act are not in the British Museum Catalogue nor indeed are they any longer in the files of their publisher, Stone and Cox.

[2] Association with the Poor Law became a euphemism for association with local authorities generally. *National Insurance Gazette*, 7 April 1917.

[3] *Ibid.*, 14 April 1917.

[4] *Ibid.*, 21 April 1917.

Government Board, the more responsible and intelligent leaders of industrial insurance, particularly Kingsley Wood and A. R. Barrand of Prudential, knew well that the only man for whom to prepare a case was the Prime Minister, David Lloyd George. There was no point in a deputation to the Local Government Board, they continually argued. Accordingly, at a meeting on 21 May they approved a statement welcoming the idea of a ministry of health but insisting that it should be a separate ministry, that a national health insurance department should be an 'integral' part of it, and that a Government committee, upon which presumably national health insurance interests would be represented, should be appointed to plan it. Finally, a deputation to the Prime Minister was named. Although theoretically representing all approved societies, in fact it was made up almost exclusively of men from industrial insurance, Kingsley Wood, Rockliff, Barrand, Neill, Arthur Henri of the Liverpool Victoria, and A. C. Thompson, general manager of the Prudential, together with a few friendly society men. The chairman of the deputation was J. H. Thomas, general secretary of the National Union of Railwaymen and MP for Derby, whom the insurance industry had managed to interest in its cause. An important feature of the 21 May meeting was the announcement by Rockliff that a War Cabinet committee was about to report on the Ministry of Health and that the subject was on the agenda of the War Cabinet. The surprising thing about Rockliff's statement is that it occurred on 21 May although Addison's diary records that Milner did not state until 23 May, two days later, that he intended to endorse a ministry of health to the War Cabinet.[1]

From whatever source, Rockliff's information about the presumably secret agenda of the War Cabinet was as usual excellent. That body received the report of its subcommittee on 6 June 1917. Essentially the proposals were those of Rhondda's previous memorandum of 27 March: the amalgamation of the Local Government Board and the English and Welsh National Health Insurance Commissions in a single ministry with some expansion of local authority public health powers. Cornwall, who in addition to Addison and Rhondda was present, attacked the report again arguing that it would break up national health insurance. Rhondda replied that it would not. Addison, whose responsibilities as the custodian of radical Liberalism within the Coalition were becoming extremely heavy, urged that something be accom-

---

[1] *National Insurance Gazette*, 2 June 1917. Addison, *Politics*, II, 222. Addison's diary notes that Rockliff had written to Milner in 'most truculent' terms demanding to see Lloyd George. The diary contains an implication that it was anger with Rockliff which caused Milner to recommend the ministry of health to the War Cabinet. Addison, *Four and a Half Years*, II, 390. Milner may have answered Rockliff's letter. In any case, Rockliff knew the minister's intentions before his colleagues did.

plished before the war was ended. But the Cabinet decided that before any decisions could be made, the Prime Minister must meet the deputation of approved societies that had been appointed at the meeting of 21 May.[1]

Even before the War Cabinet meeting of 6 June 1917, Lloyd George had begun to bring pressure on Rhondda to leave the Local Government Board and assume the difficult and unpopular office of Food Controller. This was not a ministry for a man with political ambitions and Rhondda, now in his sixty-first year, had none. Nevertheless the President of the Local Government Board was reluctant to leave his present position. 'I have taken the initial step in the establishment of a Ministry of Health', he wrote Lloyd George on 26 May 1917, but then he concluded by suggesting that his decision would be easier to make if the War Cabinet could make a decision upon the health ministry.[2]

Eventually, on 14 June, against his doctor's advice, Rhondda agreed to leave the Local Government Board to become Minister of Food Control. Before doing so, he elicited from the Prime Minister a promise, which he did not forget, that the ministry of health would not suffer from the loss of his personal support: 'Further, it is understood between us,' he wrote, 'that the Cabinet accept in principle the proposal submitted by me in a memorandum of 27 March, for the establishment of a Ministry of Health, and will authorize early steps to give effect to the proposal.' He offered to handle the bill himself in the Lords and suggested that the bill on maternity and child welfare (which had first awakened the approved societies) should be shortly introduced. Finally, he reiterated his pleasure in the work of the Local Government Board—becoming perhaps the only president, save John Burns, to do so.[3]

Rhondda learned a lesson in the ways of politics within the next few days. In answer to a question by a Labour MP, William Collins, about statements by Lord Rhondda that a ministry of health was 'about to be established,' Andrew Bonar Law replied in the House of Commons that the Government had made no decision on the subject.[4]

---

[1] PRO Cab. 23/3, War Cabinet 156, meeting 6 June 1917. Apparently the members of the War Cabinet were by now constant readers of the *National Insurance Gazette*. The issue of 2 June 1917 was mentioned frequently in their discussions.
[2] Rhondda to Lloyd George, 26 May 1917, LG Papers, F/43/5/20. Lloyd George's reluctance to trade a commitment on the Ministry of Health in return for Rhondda's acceptance of the Food Controllership is suggested by the fact that the office was hawked about for nearly a month after Rhondda was first offered this post. Addison reports that he was pressed to take the post early in June. Addison, *Four and a Half Years*, II, 399.
[3] Rhondda to Lloyd George, 14 June 1917, LG Papers, F/43/5/21.
[4] *H of C Deb.*, XCIV (19 June 1917), col. 1614.

Rhondda immediately wrote to Lloyd George demanding an explanation of Bonar Law's statement. Five days later he wrote him again saying that he would not allow the ministry of health to remain where Bonar Law had left it and enclosed a copy of his letter to Lloyd George of 14 June. Two days later, on 27 June, he wrote Lloyd George a third time insisting upon making a statement to the press either along the lines of his memorandum of 27 March, or following the proposals of the subcommittee of the War Cabinet committee report, the 'Addison Report', which he knew Lloyd George liked. He noted that he knew the Prime Minister was pledged to receive on 9 July an insurance deputation headed by Percy Rockliff and agreed to say nothing until that date. He included a draft of newspaper releases.[1]

Disillusion and delay

Bonar Law's statement in the House of Commons on 19 June that the Government had not yet decided about a ministry of health simply announced to the world the fact of the War Cabinet determination of 6 June. The ministry of health which had seemed to its advocates about to be established was put off for 18 months.[2] Basically the decision now turned upon who would control the new department—the Local Government Board with its old and well-entrenched connections among the local authorities or the newer but equally well-entrenched health insurance commissions. The Prime Minister, as Lord Rhondda stated in a bitter speech on the prevention of infant mortality later on in the year, was unwilling to introduce into Parliament any measure that would excite controversy.[3] Therefore, the Local Government Board and the health insurance authorities would have to settle their differences and agree upon a bill. If there was controversy there would be no bill. Essentially the insurance world insisted, as the *National Insurance Gazette* explained on 9 June, that the 'pressure of public officials' would be used within the new ministry to reconstruct

---

[1] Rhondda to Lloyd George, 20 June 1917, LG Papers, F/43/5/23. Rhondda to Lloyd George, 25 June 1917, LG Papers, F/43/5/25. Rhondda to Lloyd George, 27 June 1917, LG Papers, F/43/5/26. The 'Rockliff deputation' does not appear to have been received by the Prime Minister in July.

[2] On 3 June 1917, Beatrice Webb, in one of her frequent outbursts of enthusiasm and self-congratulation, had commented in her diary upon the work of the Reconstruction Committee subcommittee of which she had been a member. The committee had, in three or four meetings, 'completed a report merging the Local Government Board and the Insurance Commission in a new Ministry of Health—a report which seems to have been accepted by the Cabinet. If the Insurance Companies don't defeat it, we shall have a Ministry of Health in a few weeks.' Cole, ed., *Webb's Diaries 1912–24*, 87, diary entry 3 June 1917.

[3] *National Insurance Gazette*, 10 November 1917. Speech at Mansion House 20 October 1917 to the National Association for the Prevention of Infant Mortality.

insurance. All the problems of approved societies would 'disappear if the societies themselves disappear'. If the local authorities began to use their own agents to distribute benefits, say to mothers, or to the elderly, what would prevent them from demanding, quite reasonably, that they should also distribute all approved society benefits?[1]

In effect, the approved societies demanded an independent position for the Insurance Commission within any new department. With long experience in the grim and bitter world of local authority politics, they could see precisely that the establishment of a unified ministry for health would, indeed should, result in the unification of all government functions in this field, including their own. As they could not reasonably oppose a ministry for health, they fought to solidify their position within any new ministry so as to prevent precisely the kind of unification of functions that the health reformers hoped to see effected once the ministry was established. In the end they were successful. Although a ministry of health was established, health insurance remained potent and independent, in every way its own master, administering government benefits and maintaining the profitable and important connection with the working population of Great Britain, until at last, with the powerful weapon of the Beveridge Report, the societies were swept away by the National Insurance Act of 1946.

The approved societies had succeeded in holding up the proposals for a ministry of health. Conceivably without their support there would be no ministry of health. But they had proclaimed from the beginning that in principle they were in favour of such a government department, and so, in the summer of 1917, Kingsley Wood drew up a draft for a parliamentary bill that would become the basis of the industrial insurance bargaining position until a ministry of health was finally established. This measure was of some importance for the future. It provided for the regionalization of hospitals, which finally became a public proposal with the Dawson Report in 1920, and ultimately was incorporated into the national health service in 1948. More important, the draft bill injected into the negotiations between the approved societies and the Government a new element—the break-up of the Poor Law. It would have taken from the Poor Law all of its medical services and transferred them to the proposed ministry. The bill was in effect a precursor of the Local Government Act of 1929, put through Parliament by Neville Chamberlain whose parliamentary secretary was Kingsley Wood.[2]

---

[1] *Ibid.*, 9 June 1917.

[2] The bill appeared in the *National Insurance Gazette* accompanied by two memoranda, one written in the crabbed, pompous style of Percy Rockliff, although signed by all members of the Faculty of Insurance, and a second signed by Kingsley Wood alone. *Ibid.*, 22 September 1917. There appeared also a letter by Rockliff

Although the *National Insurance Gazette* had warned him on 11 August not to mistake approval of *a* ministry of health for approval of *his* ministry of health, Rhondda wrote to the Prime Minister on 3 October, asking whether he had noted the change in attitude of the approved societies.[1] Reading perhaps too much into Kingsley Wood's draft bill, Rhondda noted that the approved societies had now changed their tactics. While admitting that he did not agree with some parts of the approved society plan and that he did not like breaking up the Local Government Board nor the 'preferential treatment' demanded for health insurance, he felt, in spite of all this, that movement was now possible.

> It removes, so far as I can see, the difficulty which made you hesitate to accept my proposals for a Ministry of Health last Spring, and postponed the fulfilment of your promise to me, when I accepted the post of Food Controller.
>
> The Insurance people, I understand, are asking you to receive a deputation before the end of the recess. Their publicly proclaimed desire for a Ministry of Health marks a forward step, and makes it easy for you to give effect to your understanding to me.

After reviewing the course of negotiations, he urged Lloyd George to see the deputation, accompanied however by himself, W. Hayes Fisher and Cornwall. Lloyd George could tell the approved societies that he was ready to compromise. This would be popular, Rhondda thought, in Labour circles.[2]

The rather tawdry politics surrounding the attempts to establish a ministry for health in the late summer of 1917 were obscured in the thought of most British politicians by the events and pressures of the great war. The failure of the Nivelle offensive, which Lloyd George had specifically approved in January 1917, and the subsequent mutinies of the French army in May and June, combined with the clear decay by August of the provisional government in Russia, culminated in October with the ghastly failure of the British Passchendaele offensive and brought the Allied cause close to desperation. Yet on 11 October, just a week after British and Anzac divisions, floundering in the mud and rain of Flanders, took the main ridge east of Ypres, giving Haig his last important success in the much too prolonged battle, the

---

saying that copies of the draft bill had been sent to the Prime Minister, the War Cabinet, and heads of Government departments concerned. However, the only copy of the proposal that this writer has found is in the *National Insurance Gazette* of 22 September.

[1] *Ibid.*, 11 August 1917.
[2] Rhondda to Lloyd George, 3 October 1917, LG Papers, F/43/5/38.

Prime Minister found time to confer with a deputation of the approved societies.

Lloyd George had with him Rhondda, Milner, Hayes Fisher, Addison, Cornwall and Morant among several others. In proportion to
expectations, the results of the meeting were unimportant.[1] The industrial insurance forces were anxious to keep the proposed ministry
of health as small as possible. Poor Law activities would be excluded
and even housing, much to the distress of Addison who now as Minister
of Reconstruction was beginning to worry about this aspect of the
post-war Liberal programme. Perhaps the most important result of the
meeting was an agreement between Addison and Kingsley Wood to
begin, at the latter's suggestion, negotiations for a compromise plan
which the Government could then submit to Parliament.[2]

These negotiations began on 5 November 1917, with the blessing
of the Prime Minister who absolutely refused Government approval
for any bill until all affected parties were satisfied. So far as Addison
was concerned, the meetings were harmonious enough. As a good
radical he sympathized privately with the approved society desire to
separate the ministry of health from the Poor Law. On the other hand,
as a member of the Government, he was well aware of the political
strength of the Poor Law Division of the Local Government Board
and of its ancient ties of sympathy and mutual interest among the
thousands and thousands of borough and urban district councillors
throughout England and Wales who had provided for nearly a century
the grass roots support for English Liberalism. Thus he could not agree
unreservedly to a demand for the establishment of a ministry of health
in such a form that it would automatically entail the break-up of the
Poor Law. Hence the first few meetings of the negotiating committee,
which included Addison, and usually Morant, for the Government
and principally J. H. Thomas and Kingsley Wood for the approved
societies were amicable but unproductive. Addison was forced to re-
iterate the point that to tie a proposal for a ministry of health to Poor
Law reform might indefinitely delay the bill and he insisted that any
Government commitment on reform would have to wait until the
report of the MacLean committee. Countering this, the approved
societies stated in the words of J. H. Thomas at the second meeting
of the conference on 8 November that 'the representatives of Health
Insurance organizations would be unable to secure any public support
for a Bill which gave the administration of Health Insurance to a

[1] For a verbatim report of the meeting see: *National Insurance Gazette*, 20 October
1917.
[2] Addison, *Politics*, II, 223.

Department that was concerned with the administration of the Poor Law'.[1]

The avenue to compromise with industrial insurance opened with the report of the MacLean committee which was signed on 19 December 1917 and published early in January 1918. Basically the committee recommended that the Poor Law guardians be abolished and that the various functions of the Poor Law—care of children, aged and sick— be distributed among appropriate committees of the major local authorities. In effect it was a revival of the minority report of the Royal Commission on the Poor Law of 1909.[2] After spending, as he put it, 'a good deal of time' in January and February eliciting from the Cabinet a pledge that the Government accepted the report and 'regarded it as a matter of urgency,' Addison was quickly able to arrive at an agreement in March with the approved societies on a bill providing for a ministry of health along the lines of Kingsley Wood's draft of the previous August.

But now early in 1918, in place of industrial insurance opposition there appeared from within the Government a resistance to a ministry for health that potentially was as formidable as had been that of the approved societies themselves. The Poor Law guardians, who had paid no attention to the essentially private negotiations between the insurance industry and the official proponents of a ministry for health, were stirred to action by the appearance of a plan for the break-up of their ancient service. The guardians were especially concerned by the Mac-Lean report because it appeared to be, and was hailed as being, a victory for the Fabian reformers and the Labour party. The establishment of a ministry for health and the reform of the Poor Law emerged as two halves of the same programme.[3]

Thus the battle for a ministry of health moved into its second stage. In 1917, the approved societies had feared the competition within a ministry of health that might come from an improved Poor Law medical

[1] The best story of these critical negotiations, which Addison mentions but does not detail in his diary, appears in: PRO Cab. 24/58, GT 5111, 'Ministry of Health Bill and Poor Law reform, note by the Minister of Reconstruction', 15 July 1918. At one point Addison even promised that the Poor Law administration might be in a separate building from the rest of the Ministry of Health. Still the answer was no.

[2] *Cd. 8197*, 'Report on Transfer of Functions of Poor Law Authorities in England and Wales, Local Government Committee, Ministry of Reconstruction', 1918.

[3] In a review of the MacLean Report for the *New Statesman*, Beatrice Webb, herself a member of the committee, boasted that with the report the case for 'an entirely new Ministry of Health and reform of the Poor Law becomes at once easy and irresistible. The same act of Parliament ought to achieve both results.' *New Statesman*, 26 January 1918. A better-informed politician could have told Mrs Webb that by making the two reforms inseparable she was in danger of making them both impossible.

service operated by the local authorities. Their solution had been to demand separation of the Poor Law medical service from the guardians and its incorporation into a ministry of health dominated by themselves. By March 1918, Addison had agreed to this.

But even before final agreement within Addison's negotiation committee, the local authorities and their allies in the Poor Law Division of the Local Government Board, clearly warned of impending disaster by the Government's acceptance of the MacLean report, had begun to fight back. If there were to be a ministry of health, they insisted, it could be nothing more than the old Local Government Board expanded to include the insurance commissioners, perhaps with a new name. Poor Law health activities would have to remain where they were. The real amalgamation of functions at the local level under separate local government committees according to the type of individual relieved—children, the aged, the unemployed—so ardently desired by health reformers could not occur for it would destroy the Poor Law. And if destruction of the Poor Law was the price of a ministry of health, there would be no ministry of health.

Thus for the moment progress toward unification of Government health activity ended. The two powerful vested interests, one private, one official, had arrived at a stalemate. Neither really cared to see any change at all. Both were content to keep the semi-independent position each enjoyed. Neither wished to enter a ministry it did not dominate. Each was, in the last analysis, willing to postpone reform indefinitely. No one wanted reform but a few social theorists and they did not count.

The intervention of the Poor Law

The first reaction of the Poor Law authorities to the impending threat to their security appeared on 11 January 1918, even before the Mac-Lean committee report was published, with an article in the *Poor-Law Officers Journal* quoting the president of the Poor Law Unions' Association, Sir John Spear MP, who announced that the report was now complete and that he had a copy. Beyond making clear that Poor Law authorities were not likely to approve of it, the article said little except to comment that no Poor Law official had been a member of the committee and that Christopher Addison had made clear on a number of occasions that the personnel of the committee itself had been chosen not on 'representative' but on 'personal' grounds. Spear thought Poor Law officials should adopt a more 'determined course of action' on the report and people with 'experience in public assistance' should begin to make plans for expansion of their service. Boards of Guardians should meet MPs so that the Poor Law point of view—

that guardians were subject to public electoral control in a way
statutory sub-committees of the major local authorities could not be—
'could be more exactly explained'. Within a week guardians had begun
to pass resolutions against the 'offensive actions' of Christopher
Addison.[1]

These remarks were supplemented in a long article in *The Charity
Organisation Review*. Together, perhaps, they provide an epitaph for
the nineteenth-century idea of social justice. Like a chronic invalid
seeing the approach of death (*The Charity Organisation Review* did die
within three years) the journal explained the unpopularity of the Poor
Law.

> To honest pride, unwillingness to be under subjection to public
> officials, and the reputation for harshness which all assistance insti-
> tutions inevitably acquire, must be added dislike of cleanliness and
> orderliness, and the absence of alcohol refreshment. All these are
> deterrents which will operate under Public Health just as much as
> under Poor-Law Acts. The inclusion of all forms of assistance made
> available for persons having less than a certain income within the
> activities of what Mr and Mrs Webb call 'the officers of the Town or
> county council' will take away from the recent forms of assistance
> organized outside of the Poor Law such meretricious attractions as
> they enjoy through being outside that administration, and this may
> be fairly set off against the short-lived popularity which Public
> Assistance will acquire from the suppression of the Poor Law.

The article welcomed the transferral of public assistance to a single
authority and the end of overlapping, or competing, services. On the
other hand, it questioned whether changing the name of the 'Poor
Law' would amount to an important change in the system. The
authority of the public assistance relieving officer was bound to be
unpopular. Basically everything turned on the right of the individual.
Did he have a claim on society or did he not? What claim did society
have upon him? On the matter of the able-bodied male, the crux of
the problem, the old deterrent system offered real advantages, admitted *The Charity Organization Review*. 'The work-house test and
the modified work-house test have been used as universal methods
of dealing with able-bodied males. In the unions where they have
been systematically applied they have yielded remarkable results.'[2]

On 10 January the defenders of the Local Government Board and
the Poor Law were stunned by the appearance of the first of two
letters in *The Times* (the second, dated 12 January, appeared on 14
January 1918) signed by a group of ten leading back-bench Conserva-

---

[1] *Poor-Law Officers' Journal*, 11, 18 January 1918.
[2] *Charity Organisation Review*, XLIII (January 1918), 26.

tives headed by Waldorf Astor calling for a ministry of health essentially along the lines of Rhondda and Addison's plan and attacking the
new President of the Local Government Board, W. Hayes Fisher, also
a Conservative, for holding up action upon it.[1]

The public letters evoked a bitter private response from Fisher
who wrote to Astor on 14 January, virtually denouncing him as a
traitor, and saying that

> when the Prime Minister and the War Cabinet desire my considered
> opinion on matters deeply concerning the L.G.B. of which I am
> President at the will of the Prime Minister I have no doubt they
> will seek to elicit those opinions in the official and Parliamentary
> way instead of by the novel procedure which you have thought fit
> to adopt.
>
> I hope that you may one day be the Political Head of a great
> State Department and that you will realize the unfair position in
> which you have put me.[2]

The man who had written in such peremptory terms to Astor
deserves some examination. Although one of the absolutely unknown
figures in Conservative party history of the twentieth century, William
Hayes Fisher was in fact a man of considerable political power. Even
though the Local Government Board was his first ministerial office
when he succeeded Rhondda on 28 June 1917, he had been a Member
of Parliament for Fulham since 1885. More important, he possessed
great influence in the London County Council which the Conservatives
badly needed and had been an organizer of the Moderate party
electoral victory there in 1907.[3] Fisher's importance in the story of
Liberal reconstruction plans during the war is great. Almost single-
handed—with some help from Walter Long whose stature with rural
Conservatives may be compared to Fisher's in the metropolis—he held
up planning for a ministry of health and for housing until the Armistice. By doing so he virtually ensured that health would become a
weak ministry, little more than an expansion of the Local Government
Board by the addition of national health insurance. In housing also he
saw to it that no powers for the requisition of building supplies were

[1] *The Times*, 10 January 1918. Among the signers of the letters were Stanley
Baldwin, W. G. A. Ormsby-Gore, and Edward Wood (better known as Viscount
Halifax).
[2] W. H. Fisher to Waldorf Astor, 14 January 1918, LG Papers, F/15/4/2.
[3] Before the war he was regarded by A. J. Balfour as a more influential figure
than F. E. Smith. Balfour had insisted that Fisher be made a Privy Councillor at
the same time Smith received his surprising PC from the Liberals in 1911. Churchill
in a letter that year to his wife referred to Fisher as a 'wretched Whip's room hack
and county council wire-puller'! Randolph S. Churchill, *Winston S. Churchill*
(London, 1967), II, 342.

available, no land bought, no designs completed. Housing became more than a failure; it was a fiasco. Of all the Lloyd George promises, 'homes for heroes' was the most hollow. The same inertia frustrated plans for reconstruction of the Poor Law until the great postwar depression descended upon the country so that reconstruction was impossible. In all these critical areas planning had to come from within one previously rather despised department, the Local Government Board, whose minister, although neither vicious nor unintelligent —and entirely in sympathy with a large segment of his party—was quite content with things as they were.

Much has been written attempting to explain the failure of social reform after the First World War in comparison with the relative success of reform after the Second. Scholars have tried to show that the extent of reform during postwar reconstruction was in direct proportion to the extent of social participation during the conflict.[1] Equality of sacrifice in war, they argue, demands equality of opportunity in peace. The First World War, the argument runs, was less a people's war than the second, hence less reform.

Against this several points must be made. Even leaving aside the highly questionable assertion about the degree of difference in social participation in the two wars, one is bound to suggest that this interpretation disregards a critical factor—the power of a man in a decision-making office to resist change. He is himself a vested interest. Governments may be established by law, but they are made up of men. At any given moment an office-holder's whim is more powerful than thousands of votes. To ensure that his view will prevail he may delay, he may dissemble; finally, when time is short, he may resist. In politics, where timing is always vital, he may, as did Hayes Fisher, hold up action until the only possible moment for it has passed. Particularly he may do these things if he is comfortable, if he is unimaginative and his knowledge of social problems is slight, and if he is a member of the ruling class and has no quarrel with the society in which he lives. There were many in 1918 who did not wish to see the world change and many of them held office. For them Edwardian England had been good. Indeed, as the popularity of Stanley Baldwin demonstrated through the twenties and thirties, the voters of Great Britain clearly had little desire for a thoroughgoing break with the past. Nostalgia, not religion, may be the opium of the masses. It may not always determine action, but it is always present and an individual who knows how to evoke it has odds in his favour.

Hence, when investigating the reasons for the failure to create the new Britain which the Prime Minister expected he could construct,

[1] For a recent statement of this thesis see: Philip Abrams, 'The Failure of Social Reform, 1918–1920', *Past and Present*, No. 24 (April 1963), 43–64.

I

one must necessarily take into account the character of the men whose ministries would deal with reconstruction and within whose purview lay the duty of planning for the new world. One must ask oneself whether they really looked forward to a new world or to rebuilding the old. Certainly Hayes Fisher preferred the old world.

During the month of February and the first three weeks of March, Addison, labouring to secure the Prime Minister's approval for the MacLean report, the absence of which constituted the only obstacle to successful compromise with the approved societies, found himself engaged in a running battle with the forces of parochial relief. Here he encountered not only spokesmen for the guardians but most seriously Hayes Fisher and Walter Long who warned the Prime Minister of the political danger of opposing the guardians.[1] The Poor Law forces had already begun the more traditional forms of political warfare. In February, the Poor-Law Officers' Association published a pamphlet for the use of speakers. It provided, said the editors of the *Journal*, 'the exact requirements of Boards of Guardians for the defeat of the recommendations made by the Reconstruction Committee: Arguments, examples of Guardians' progressive administration and mistakes made by the committee.' Addison sought to quiet this opposition by assuring the guardians (which was still technically true) that the Government had as yet no policy on Poor Law reconstruction.[2]

The decision that the Poor Law authorities had feared was made on 21 March, the day that the last great German offensive began in France. Addison finally procured the Prime Minister's permission to assure the approved societies that the Government accepted in principle the recommendations of the MacLean report so that the concentration of health powers under the new Ministry of Health would not be entangled with the Poor Law.[3] Four days later on the 25th, admitting that it was 'difficult to work' as a result of the disastrous news from France, he held a concluding and 'most friendly' conference with the approved societies in which agreement upon a bill was reached and later in the afternoon began to dictate a Cabinet minute on the proposed bill.[4]

The measure Addison now recommended to the Cabinet showed the weaknesses of the concessions he had been forced to make. As such it satisfied neither the health reformers who demanded a strong ministry nor the partisans of the Local Government Board and Poor Law who wanted either a weak ministry or none at all. Most important, although Addison emphasized in his memorandum that he had secured

---

[1] *Poor-Law Officers' Journal*, 25 January 1918, 1 February 1918.
[2] *Ibid.*, 22 February 1918.
[3] Addison, *Four and a Half Years*, II, 498, diary entry 21 March 1918.
[4] *Ibid.*, 499, diary entry 25 March.

the concurrence of the President of the Local Government Board, he admitted also that Fisher had three reservations to the Bill as proposed. These were to become critical. First of all, Fisher insisted that the title of the ministry be 'The Ministry of Health and Local Government'. Secondly, he disapproved of the Consultative Council for insurance that national health insurance interests had insisted be established. Addison justified this by saying that it was necessary to conciliate the insurance administration for the loss of the insurance commission. Finally, basic to all else, Fisher disapproved of Schedule One of the draft measure which provided that 'in the event of future provision ... for revision of the Poor Law' all custodial functions of the Poor Law would be transferred to other organs of government.[1] Addison concluded by urging that a bill should be introduced immediately and that upon its introduction he should be authorized to say that the Government 'regarded as a matter of urgency' the recommendations of the MacLean Committee and that 'effect should be given to those recommendations as soon as possible'. Health services for sick and infirm paupers should not be administered as part of the Poor Law but should be made a part of the general health services.[2]

Addison's memorandum brought a retort from Fisher on 13 May, which stated succinctly the Local Government Board's objection to the ministry of health and which the President, in cooperation with a former president of the Board, Walter Long, would supplement by private lobbying against Addison's project. Concerning the Consultative Council, Fisher said that the agreement of the approved societies 'had been purchased too dearly'. The Consultative Council would become an 'active propagandist body claiming a definite share in administration'. It would not be an advisory body at all. In fact, he said, 'it puts the Minister in shackles'.[3]

Addison replied immediately, saying that the Consultative Council would not 'put the Minister in shackles' and whether the councils were the result of British Medical Association or insurance pressure was irrelevant. In any case it was not, Addison argued, what the societies had demanded, 'but what they have been induced to accept. I hope Mr Hayes Fisher will not continue to suspect me of being a party to a conspiracy to undermine ministerial responsibility.'[4] The British Medical Association, it may be noted parenthetically, had also been urging the establishment of a Consultative Council of doctors at the

---

[1] PRO Cab. 24/49, GT 4399, 'Ministry of Health', C. Addison, April 1918.
[2] Addison, *Four and a Half Years*, II, 516, diary entry 24 April 1918.
[3] PRO Cab. 24/51, GT 4533, 'Ministry of Health, Observations by the President of the Local Government Board on the Draft Bill and Memorandum (GT 4399) circulated by the Minister for Reconstruction', 13 May 1918.
[4] PRO Cab. 24/51, GT 4539, 'Memorandum by the Minister of Reconstruction on Mr Hayes Fisher's Memorandum', 16 May 1918.

elbow of the Minister. This became, in 1920, the well-known Dawson Committee. However, the doctors' aim was the opposite of the approved societies'. The doctors wished to influence the Minister; the approved societies hoped to make the Consultative Council a buffer against the Minister. As it turned out, only the insurance Consultative Council remained continuously active after the first few years.[1]

The war in Europe now was in perhaps its most critical stage. On 7 May General F. D. Maurice's letter charging mis-statements by the Government on the British military position appeared in the press and two days later on 9 May occurred the important debate in the House of Commons on Asquith's motion to refer Maurice's charges to a select committee. On 27 May began the third phase of the great German peace offensive. Lloyd George was almost continually out of London and even had he desired to effect a compromise between the contending factions of his Cabinet, he had no time. Consequently, despite endless complaints by Addison to the Prime Minister for lack of decision, no action occurred on the Ministry of Health Bill until the middle of July.[2]

Early in June, after the ministry of health question had been removed from the War Cabinet agenda for the fourth time, Addison decided to threaten resignation on the matter. His double position in the Government as both minister of official planning for reconstruction and custodian of the tradition of radical Liberalism reinforced his responsibility. He must, in effect, save Lloyd George from himself.

> ... the worst of it is that L.G. seems to play up to the obstruction at the expense of his friends. I am probably his best friend in Government and ought to be able to rely on him for support especially as he is continually urging me to get on with various matters and policies he holds up for want not only of a decision but of consideration. He will not be back from France until Tuesday and I must not spoil so important an issue by seemingly unfriendly action, but I must know where I am.[3]

Two days later, on the 5th, Addison wrote a long letter to Lloyd George reminding him of the negotiations with the approved societies, of the fact that the bill had now been postponed four times, of his

[1] On the general importance of the Ministry of Health consultative councils, barring the future importance of the Dawson Report, see: R. V. Vernon and N. Mansurgh, eds., *Advisory Bodies, A Study of their Uses in Relation to Central Government, 1919–1939* (London, 1940), 229–31. See also: *P.E.P. Broadsheet 222*, 30 June 1944, 'Medical Care for Citizens', 22–3.
[2] See Addison diary entries 28, 30 May 1918, complaining of obstruction by Walter Long and Hayes Fisher. Addison, *Four and a Half Years*, II, 534, 535. See also Addison to Lloyd George, 13 May 1918, LG Papers F/1/4/19.
[3] Addison, *Four and a Half Years*, II, 536, diary entry 3 June 1918.

promises to Rhondda, and of the fact that resistance to the bill came from a single Government department. Quite plainly he demanded a decision on his measure and concluded by saying that unless he received some help 'the loyal support which I have always endeavoured to afford you will become of no avail'.[1]

The Prime Minister was not in the least offended by Addison's stern letter. He sent for him the next day and promised support in most cordial terms. Three days later, on 9 July, the Home Affairs Committee under the chairmanship of the Home Secretary, George Cave, had its first meeting.[2] Of the first five meetings of the Home Affairs Committee between 9 and 29 July, three were devoted to the Ministry of Health Bill. Now the opponents of the measure were not only Fisher, but the chairman of the committee, George Cave. The objections were the same as before: the independent position of national health insurance, which Addison defended as being of considerable importance and very difficult to get, and the declaration in the bill that Poor Law functions might be transferred by Order in Council from the new ministry. A ministry of health, the argument went, would break up the Poor Law.

These arguments reflected the dilemma of the Lloyd George administration at the time of the armistice, a problem which would, in the years following, contribute largely to the fall of the Coalition. The promises of peace were promises of domestic social reform. Any dilution of them was bound to be resisted by the left and would weaken further the position of Liberal radicalism, which still hoped to keep its position as the champion of labour. On the other hand, if no concessions were made to the right—if in this case the radicals forced the linking of the ministry of health to the break up of the Poor Law—the measure might never pass the House of Commons. This problem Lloyd George and Addison never solved. Radical Liberal reform was not practical politics.

The Government, by now, was subject to considerable pressure from informed public opinion. With each issue in June and July the *National Insurance Gazette* grew increasingly anxious over the delay in the Ministry of Health Bill. Now that the industry was satisfied with the

---

[1] *Ibid.*, 538, diary entry 5 June 1918.
[2] PRO Cab. 26/1, Home Affairs Committee minutes, No. 1 meeting, 9 July 1918; No. 3 meeting 18 July 1918; No. 5 meeting 29 July 1918. The Home Affairs Committee was to be a domestic counterpart of the War Cabinet, both of which were constitutionally, but not in fact, subsidiary to the general Cabinet. But the Home Affairs Committee did not include the Prime Minister and was always inferior to the War Cabinet. Besides Cave and Addison it included Stanley Baldwin, H. A. L. Fisher, and Hayes Fisher. There is no direct evidence that its creation was the result of Addison's letter although the coincidence of dates is strong and Addison always assumed that the committee was a response to his pressure.

bill, the journal's indignation at local authorities opposing the measure became bitter. 'Writing as calmly as we can, we say it disgusts us.' Also attacking the Government from the opposite point of view was the *New Statesman* which blamed 'certain equivocal types of approved societies' which were making a living from national health insurance. The *New Statesman* condemned by name Hayes Fisher and Walter Long. The Poor Law, it said, was a 'corpse' and a reorganization of the Local Government Board without reconstruction of parochial relief might infuse it with new life.[1]

In order to expedite his measure, Addison agreed at the Home Affairs Committee on 15 July to meet again with the industrial insurance negotiating committee and see whether its members would permit the withdrawal of the reference in the statute to the break-up of the Poor Law and accept instead a simple declaration of Government intention on this policy. The approved societies had been aware for several months of the dangers in their continued obstruction. Certainly there would be an election soon. If there were an election, the Members of Parliament would be under strong pressure from local authorities. Therefore, remarked the *National Insurance Gazette*, 'the longer we delay, the more likely we are to make an unsatisfactory bargain. This is not to suggest that Members of Parliament are without principle but simply that they do with votes what business men do with pounds, shillings, and pence.' 'It is true that the question of delays is not one resting entirely with us, but politicians and governments can be pressed, and the more urgent we are the more likely we are to get what we want. To put it bluntly, we must be importunate.'[2] Not surprisingly, therefore, on 22 July, Kingsley Wood's negotiating committee readily assented to Addison's proposal to drop any statutory declaration about the break-up of the Poor Law.

Basically the industrial insurance companies had little interest in Poor Law reform.[3] Rather their fear was of the competition of an improved Poor Law. For the Government, on the other hand, it was necessary that some bill be put together immediately. The Prime Minister's opening speech of the 1918 electoral campaign was to take place in Manchester on 12 September. His programme was basically social reconstruction. A measure had to be ready. Hence, in a long meeting the day before the Manchester declaration, 11 September, after receiving deputations both from the Royal College of Physicians

---

[1] *National Insurance Gazette*, 15 June 1918. 'Why We Get No Ministry of Health', *New Statesman*, 20 July 1918.

[2] Leading Article, 'Politics', *National Insurance Gazette*, 18 May 1918.

[3] The *National Insurance Gazette* had immediately approved the deletion of the statement in the draft bill that contemplated the break-up of the Poor Law. *National Insurance Gazette*, 3 August 1918.

and from Kingsley Wood, the Home Affairs Committee approved a statement that although nothing would be stipulated in the Ministry of Health Bill about the Poor Law, the minister in charge 'at the appropriate stage' would announce that the Government accepted the 'principle' that health functions of the Poor Law should go to the ministry of health and that the rest should go elsewhere, while maintaining that the Government 'are not in a position to formulate precise proposals at the present time'.[1]

The concession to the Poor Law supporters brought, as Addison had feared it would, indignation from another quarter, the friendly societies and the labour movement.[2] On 24 September, officially recommending the revised bill to the Cabinet with the deletion of the specification that Poor Law duties could be transferred by Order in Council, George Cave warned that the changes would be likely to arouse the opposition of the trade unions and the friendly societies, but to do otherwise, he thought would 'crystallize the opposition of the Poor Law guardians and would seriously prolong discussions on the Bill'. He reported that Addison in his interviews with the insurance organizations and the friendly societies had secured only reluctant acceptance of the Poor Law statement instead of the stipulation for the break-up of the Poor Law in the Bill, and thought that the friendly societies would continue to press for the inclusion of the statement that Poor Law administration was an activity to be transferred away from the ministry of health.[3]

In fact the division Cave warned about had already occurred. Word of the private concession given to the Home Affairs Committee by the industrial insurance negotiating committee quickly spread through the world of national insurance administration. A cleavage between the industrial approved societies, whose concern for the Poor Law centred upon its effect on their own business and the friendly society approved societies, whose membership and hierarchy overlapped extensively with the trade unions and so shared a general interest in social reform, began to appear. On 12 October, in a long editorial entitled 'The Ministry of Health: The Present Position', the *National Insurance Gazette* reviewed the history of the tedious and apparently fruitless negotiations since 1917. In the beginning, said the *Gazette*, the original bill had included only the medical part of the Poor Law upon the

---

[1] PRO Cab. 24/61 GT 5669, 'Statement by Committee on Home Affairs', 11 September 1918. See also PRO Cab. 26/1 Home Affairs Committee minute 11, meeting 11 September 1918; Addison, *Four and a Half Years*, II, 568, diary entry 17 September 1918. Hayes Fisher, Addison noted, was obstructive as usual but he had by this time 'effectively alienated the whole committee'.

[2] On British friendly societies see: Gilbert, *National Insurance*, 165–80, 288–303.

[3] PRO Cab. 24/62, GT 5760, 'Memorandum by George Cave, 24 September 1918'.

insistence of the friendly societies.[1] Later, however, the friendly societies had agreed to compromise by permitting the inclusion of the
whole Poor Law if the bill were so drawn that non-medical Poor Law
activities could be easily removed from the ministry. But now, it
appeared, they were not even to get that. The new bill was to be
called a 'Ministry of Health and Local Government Bill'. The *Gazette*
was now clearly worried. The friendly societies were angry and the
Gazette, and presumably the industrial insurance societies it represented, were inclined to temporize while the friendly societies had
pulled away. In effect, the Poor Law reform and the simultaneous
creation of a ministry of health, which had occupied British reformers
since the beginning of the century, now seemed likely to prevent action
of any kind.[2]

In the next few weeks a rapid realignment of forces occurred. On
one side were the true friendly societies, the Labour movement and
the health reformers, with, surprisingly, Percy Rockliff as their noisy,
if not always effective, spokesman. Rockliff's appearance in the uncharacteristic role of health reformer was almost certainly a result of
the growing estrangement between himself and his former colleague
Kingsley Wood who was about to be adopted as prospective Coalition
Unionist candidate for Woolwich and who would soon receive a KB.
Although he tried, Rockliff was unable to find a constituency.

On the other side were the far better-organized, more efficient, and
more powerful forces of industrial insurance, associated, but not allied,
with the Poor Law. Time was now growing short. Certainly the war
was about to end. Unofficially the electoral campaign had begun on
12 September with the Manchester speech which had featured a call
for national health. But the War Cabinet still had not acted upon the
bill submitted by the Home Affairs Committee. On 24 October Rockliff wrote to the Prime Minister disavowing Kingsley Wood's right to
speak for the friendly societies or even for the industrial insurance
companies in regard to the Poor Law. And in a covering letter to the
secretary of the Cabinet, Maurice Hankey, he asserted that 'the
Friendly Societies are not open to abate their opposition to the Government proposals as a result of a mere discussion of these proposals in
the House'.[3] Addison by this time was nearly frantic with worry.

---

[1] This was not quite true. Rhondda's original bill had assumed that all functions
of the Local Government Board would come into the new ministry although
within the ministry, Poor Law administrative activities and medical activities
would be separated. No doubt Rhondda and certainly Addison, Newman, and
Morant, assumed that sometime, when the Poor Law itself was reformed, all Poor
Law activities except medical relief would be transferred.

[2] *National Insurance Gazette*, 12 October 1918.

[3] Rockliff to Lloyd George, 24 October 1918; Rockliff to Hankey, 25 October
1918; bound in PRO Cab. 24/68 GT 6126.

On 30 October he addressed the War Cabinet in peremptory terms. Noting the Rockliff letter and saying that the objections were based principally on the addition of the words 'and Local Government' to the title of the bill and the deletion of a paragraph about the Poor Law, he insisted that the Cabinet must make up its mind, first whether the changes were to stand, and second, whether the bill was to be introduced at all.

> If this situation is allowed to continue, the misunderstanding and suspicion of the proposals, sedulously fostered by Mr. Rockliff, who does not hesitate to disclose confidential information for his own purposes, will swell to such dimensions that the Bill may become difficult to carry even in the form in which I had secured its acceptance *in April last*. . . .[1]

Already, however, far more powerful forces were moving into line behind the Ministry of Health Bill. With something of the majesty of a column of battleships, the great insurance companies took up positions behind the measure they now determined to have. On the day before Addison sent his memorandum to the Cabinet, 29 October, A. C. Thompson, President of the National Conference of Industrial Insurance Approved Societies, but also general manager of the Prudential Assurance Company, in a rare public speech, announced the industry's unconditional support of the Government's bill. There was no object, he said, in fighting the pauperism taint in the ministry of health. The Government had accepted the MacLean report, but poor food, poor clothing and poor housing were all causes of sickness and would continue to be under the ministry of health. Referring to the fraternal societies, 'with whom we have worked for a long time past on most friendly terms', he asked for understanding of the Prime Minister's position lest there be no ministry of health at all.[2]

Thompson's speech was followed by a resolution put by Thomas Neill, formerly a director of the Pearl, the second largest British industrial insurance company, referring specifically to the Prime Minister's speech in Manchester, approving the MacLean report and reform of the Poor Law. Neill made clear that his resolution had already been forwarded to the Government.[3]

---

[1] PRO Cab. 24/68 GT 6148, 'Memorandum by Minister of Reconstruction', 30 October 1918. In his diary Addison dates this note as 29 October. Addison, *Four and a Half Years*, II, 584–5.

[2] Speech by Alfred C. Thompson, at the annual meeting of the National Conference of Industrial Assurance Approved Societies, 29 October, Staple Inn, *National Insurance Gazette*, 9 November 1918.

[3] *Ibid*. Neill's resolution was seconded by F. T. Jefferson of the Britannic and carried unanimously. A few days later the Assistant Manager of the Prudential, A. R. Barrand, was adopted as a Coalition Liberal candidate for the Pudsey and Otley Division of Yorks.

The next week was crowded with events of importance for the ministry of health. On the first of November, Lloyd George wrote from Paris demanding Fisher's resignation. Fisher, however, was too powerful a man to be so unceremoniously dismissed. He had important friends among leading Conservatives and with an approaching election his political strength in London, as he well knew, could be a danger, more perhaps to the Conservatives than to Lloyd George himself. Hence he delayed his resignation for three days while soliciting protests to Andrew Bonar Law on his own behalf.[1] Although the Conservatives were unhappy about Lloyd George's behaviour, taken without consultation, they were unwilling to challenge his position as Prime Minister. Nevertheless, Fisher was strong enough to make adequate terms for himself. He did not in fact leave the Ministry but became Chancellor of the Duchy of Lancaster and Minister of Information, holding both posts until the 10 January 1919, when the information ministry was abolished. He secured a peerage as Baron Downham of Fulham and, most important of all, he obtained a directorship of the Suez Canal Company, one of the most lucrative and valuable patronage posts within the gift of the Prime Minister.[2]

The important thing was to remove Fisher as an obstacle before Parliament rose.[3] In any case, on the day after Fisher's resignation, 5 November, Addison received permission from Bonar Law, who had just returned from Paris, to introduce the Ministry of Health Bill. So at last, on 7 November, the measure received a first reading under the ten-minute rule.[4] Considering the tumult and alarm that the Ministry of Health Bill had aroused in the past months, the measure was surprisingly simple. It changed little except the name of the Local

[1] Curzon to Bonar Law, 2 November 1918, Bonar Law Papers 84/3/3; memorandum by Walter Long (apparently to A. J. Balfour), 4 November 1918, Bonar Law Papers 84/3/7/.
[2] There is much about Hayes Fisher's resignation that is unclear. Robert Blake's biography of Bonar Law gives the fullest recent account. The trouble is that there were two letters, one of 28 October which was harsh and a second, more temperate, on 1 November and Conservative attempts to save Fisher did not begin until then. Clearly no one but Bonar Law knew of the first letter. See: Lloyd George Papers F/15/4/16 and Robert Blake, *The Unknown Prime Minister* (London, 1965), 381–3.
[3] The much-quoted remark (undated although presumably of 4 November, the day Fisher finally resigned), 'The PM doesn't mind if he (Fisher) is drowned in Malmsey wine, but he must be a dead chicken by tonight', suggests the Prime Minister's anxiety to remove Fisher as an obstacle and his real indifference about the man.
[4] *H of C Deb.*, CX (7 November 1918), cols. 2340–3. The ten-minute rule is an obscure provision, now seldom used, to enable private members who have been unsuccessful on the private members' ballot to obtain leave to introduce a bill. Only two speeches, one from either side of the House, of ten minutes' duration, are permitted. It is technically a first reading debate. There was some criticism of its use for what was supposed to be a Government measure.

Government Board to the Ministry of Health (as a concession to the friendly societies the addition of the words 'and Local Government' had been dropped) and it provided for the transfer of the National Health Insurance administration to the new department. Finally, under subsection three, it permitted, without specifying the activities concerned, the transfer away of any functions not related to health.[1]

The Ministry of Health Bill was of course withdrawn almost immediately, on 18 November. For Addison, the bill represented a personal crusade and he wished to commit the Government to it. This he had done. Its implications for Poor Law reform were still there masked and confused, as were so many measures of the Lloyd George administration, but their intent for those interested was no less clear. The two sides contending were now the Poor Law guardians and against them the true friendly societies supported by the labour movement. Between the lines was industrial insurance represented by Kingsley Wood, now a KB, attempting, more in the name of the Government than in the name of industrial insurance, to placate the friendly societies lest the bill be destroyed.

Everything turned on the election due on 15 December. Both sides attempted to influence candidates. In this, the vast grass-roots organization of the Poor Law had much experience, although the Government did what it could to weaken the Poor Law attack by withholding the coupon from several important spokesmen of the guardians, notably Alderman John Spear, Liberal Unionist at the Tavistock division of Devonshire.[2] The Poor Law authorities watched carefully the work of their opponents in the friendly societies and professed surprise at the fact that the friendly societies would rather have no ministry of health at all than one associated with the Poor Law.[3] The societies themselves were hardly less skilled at influencing Parliament. Although they were uncompromisingly anti-socialist—and would lose most of their Parliamentary influence with the rise of the Labour party—in the issue of reform of the Poor Law they were resolutely supported by Labour and were able to elicit from a 'considerable body of members' of the new House of Commons a 'written pledge against associating the Poor Law with a Ministry of Health and a promise to vote for amendments' in the Ministry of Health Bill.[4] The leader of the friendly society forces was A. H. Warren, past Grand Master of the Manchester

---

[1] Cd. 9211, 'Memorandum on the Ministries of Health Bill, 1918, Ministry of Reconstruction', November 1918.
[2] Poor-Law Officers' Journal, 29 November 1918.
[3] Ibid., 6 November 1918.
[4] National Insurance Gazette, 12 April 1919. This account is taken from a letter by Percy Rockliff to the National Insurance Gazette, undated, but apparently early in April. Rockliff had no reputation as an invariably truthful man, but neither was he able to suppress, to the delight of historians, private information that he knew.

Unity of Odd Fellows, the largest of the true friendly societies. Since 1913, he had been mayor of Poplar. Not surprisingly, at the dissolution of 1918, he received a KB and was adopted as a Coalition Unionist candidate for Edmonton.

The struggle was short and sharp, and the national insurance forces were victorious. The warning from an obscure member of the Holborn guardians, John Bellman (whose area included the Prudential and Pearl offices), given in a letter to the *Poor Law Officers' Journal* before the election that, if the Ministry of Health Bill passed, the new department would be in the hands of the insurance societies and their agents proved to be nearly true.[1] Immediately after the election, negotiations between Warren, Rockliff, and Addison began again and on 3 February 1919 Addison wrote Rockliff saying he was ready to put back into the bill the offending clause which became eventually Section Three (3) of 9 & 10 George V, Cap. 21, the Ministry of Health Bill. This stipulated that 'in the event' of provision being made by Parliament for the revision of the Poor Law 'there shall be transferred' all non-medical powers away from the Ministry of Health. This was not quite as much as the friendly societies had hoped for but on 10 February, after consideration, they agreed 'not to oppose' the bill.[2] As a result, the Ministry of Health Bill included in it a virtual promise for the break-up of the Poor Law.

The failure of Poor Law reform

The Ministry of Health was Addison's triumph, perhaps his only triumph in public life. On 10 January 1919, he succeeded Auckland Geddes as President of the Local Government Board and so at last was able to speak with authority for the ministry he hoped to reconstruct. Why Addison had not been appointed immediately to the Local Government Board upon the resignation of Hayes Fisher on 4 November is not clear. He was asked at this time whether he would like to become Minister of Health and had accepted. No doubt Lloyd George wished to keep him free for political duties during the election. On the other hand, he had not been consulted on the appointment of Auckland Geddes which appeared to have come to him as a rather unpleasant surprise. Even during the busy period of the election he watched carefully Geddes' activity at the Board and wrote to Lloyd George trying to direct the policy of the interim president toward reconstruction. 'Now that agreement had been obtained with the local authorities,' he wrote at the end of November, 'the trade unions and

---

[1] *Poor Law Officers' Journal*, 22 November 1918.
[2] *National Insurance Gazette*, 12 April 1919. These details also were in Rockliff's letter.

insurance uproar ought not to be allowed to start again.' In his own constituency in Shoreditch his speeches were devoted almost entirely to the Ministry of Health and to the reform of the Poor Law, which he promised unconditionally.[1]

One of Addison's first acts as President of the Local Government Board was the discharge of the two chief officers of that department, the Permanent Secretary, Sir Horace Monro, and the Chief Medical Officer, Sir Arthur Newsholme. Monro was inoffensive but unimaginative, simply a prisoner of the routine of one of the least vigorous of all Government departments with which he had been connected since the beginning of his career in the civil service in 1884. Newsholme, on the other hand, the reformers now regarded as a menace even though they had been instrumental in bringing him to the Local Government Board in 1908.[2] The dismissal of Newsholme apparently caused an unpleasant scene and left the former medical officer with a residue of bitterness that he carried with him to the end of his life.[3] In none of Newsholme's later writings does the name of George Newman appear and indeed, in one of the most important of his books, he began to resurrect the figure of Dr James Kerr, the long-forgotten Chief Medical Officer of the old London School Board with whom Newman had fought a bitter contest at the time of the establishment of the school medical service.[4]

With Monro and Newsholme gone, Addison could appoint as his chief assistants the two men who had worked steadily at his side for nearly a decade toward the establishment of the Ministry of Health— Sir Robert Laurie Morant and Sir George Newman. With Sir John Anderson as Second Secretary and Michael Heseltine, whom Addison felt was as capable as Morant, as Assistant Secretary, Addison had at his disposal a team that should have made the Ministry of Health one of the most potent departments of Government.[5] Unfortunately this was not to be.

The parliamentary story of the Ministry of Health Bill, like many measures with which Lloyd George was connected, was a minor political event. The Prime Minister disliked controversy and, although a skilled debater, had perhaps a basic distrust of the House of Commons. His aim was to avoid public political controversy. He was a 'fixer'. This certainly had been the story of the National Insurance Act

[1] Newman Diaries, III, MS entry 8 November 1918. Addison to Lloyd George, 25 November 1918, LG Papers, F/1/4/41. *The Times*, 6 December 1918.
[2] Newman Diaries, III, MS entry 29 October 1918.
[3] See the description of Newman's last interview with Newsholme; Newman Diaries, III, MS entry 16 January 1919.
[4] Arthur Newsholme, *Fifty Years in Public Health, A Personal Narrative with Comments* (London, 1935), 382–4.
[5] Addison, *Politics*, II, 230–1.

which, even though highly controversial, was worked out in its essential details in private. By 1920, acute political thinkers like the Webbs had begun to doubt whether Parliament still fulfilled its basic function.

> ... the real government of Great Britain is nowadays carried on not in the House of Commons at all nor even in the Cabinet, but in private conference between Ministers and their principal officials and representatives of persons specifically affected by any proposed legislation or by any action on the part of the administration.[1]

The Ministry of Health Bill received the Royal Assent on 3 June 1919, and Addison was appointed minister just three weeks later. Addison's short tenure of this office is dominated by two themes: the Poor Law and housing. The story of the Poor Law may be told quickly. It is clear that Addison kept alive, so long as he was Minister of Health, plans for the reform of the Poor Law. Regularly, at approximately six-month intervals, he would release statements of his optimism for the fulfilment of his promises in the near future.

> It is understood that one of the first tasks to be undertaken by the new Ministry of Health is the long overdue reform of the Poor Law. A scheme is now in preparation and Dr Addison may even introduce a Bill this session.[2]

> Since last year the policy of the Government has remained unaltered. Boards of Guardians and the Poor Law Unions are to be abolished and the functions of Poor Law authorities are to be merged in the County Councils and County Borough Councils.[3]

'In reply to a question in the House of Commons on whether legislation for Poor Law reform would be introduced this session Addison replied "I hope so".'[4] Later on in the year, in August 1920, again in answer to a question in the House of Commons on whether the Government intended to bring legislation for Poor Law reform in the sitting Parliament, Addison answered: 'Yes sir.'[5]

Even at the end of 1920, scarcely three months before he left the ministry, Addison was still optimistic. 'It is understood that the bill to transfer the powers of the Boards of Guardians to County and County Borough Councils will be introduced as early as possible in the new Session.'[6] It should be pointed out, however, that both the Cabinet

---

[1] Sidney and Beatrice Webb, *A Constitution for the Socialist Commonwealth of Great Britain* (London, 1920), 69.
[2] *The Times*, 26 June 1919.
[3] *Ibid.*, 27 December 1919.
[4] *Ibid.*, 25 March 1920.
[5] *H of C Deb.*, CXXXIII (11 August 1920), col. 404.
[6] *The Times*, 28 December 1920.

minutes and the Lloyd George papers show that the matter never reached the highest level of ministerial consideration. Neither did Addison bring pressure on the Prime Minister to make good the promises on the Poor Law reform in the way he had forced action on the Ministry of Health.

As his tenure of office was approaching an end, Addison made a single-handed effort to begin the break-up of the Poor Law with the Ministry of Health (Miscellaneous Provisions) Bill introduced into the House of Commons on 16 August 1920. Here he attempted to repeat the legislative coup achieved by Robert Morant with the Education (Administrative Provisions) Act of 1907. In this earlier measure, Morant, who unfortunately died in the spring of 1920, had obtained for the Board of Education the powers to establish the school medical service by burying the necessary legislation in a large and unexciting measure dealing with routine education department housekeeping measures. Addison now attempted to obtain authority to begin dismantling the Poor Law in the same way. Specifically he aimed at Poor Law medical powers. Among many other details concerned chiefly with housing, Clause 11 of the bill would have given local authorities power to take over any Poor Law hospital or infirmary either with the permission of the Minister of Health or by his direction and operate it as a municipal hospital.[1] He had tried earlier in the year to do this by administrative order, allowing local authorities in Bradford to take over a Poor Law infirmary there. His powers to do this were immediately challenged and in the struggle that ensued he eventually had to withdraw his sanction.[2] In addition, the bill permitted local authorities to make regular contributions to voluntary hospitals, which since the war were in serious financial straits.

Surprisingly Addison's proposals were opposed less by the defenders of the Poor Law organization than by Tory spokesmen, both in and out of the House of Commons.[3] For the Tories Addison was, by this time, the chief villain in the Government. The proposal to give local authority money to voluntary hospitals was denounced as an entering wedge for the municipalization of these institutions, while the proposal to attach Poor Law infirmaries to the County Councils was looked upon simply as a way to increase the power of the Ministry of Health. After serious objection, the bill barely passed the House of Commons and on 14 December 1920 was defeated in the House of Lords.

In a leading article on the day following the defeat of the bill in the Lords, *The Times* noted: '... the rejection of the Bill is tending to

---

[1] *Cmd. 898*, 'Memorandum on the Ministry of Health (Miscellaneous Provisions) Bill', 1920.
[2] *Ibid.*, 10 November 1920.
[3] See for instance: *Charity Organisation Review*, XLVIII (September, 1920), 57.

raise the whole question of the future of the Ministry of Health. Dr Addison's position is that he has contrived to bring his department to a point at which it incurs a maximum of unpopularity while it reveals also a minimum of efficiency.' Even though Addison announced that day he intended to stick to his bill and that he had the support of the Prime Minister for doing so, *The Times* predicted that Lloyd George would allow the bill to die.[1] The only important result of the Miscellaneous Provisions Bill's defeat was the appointment, in January 1921, of a committee under Viscount Cave to look into the financial position of voluntary hospitals. Very likely the defeat of the Miscellaneous Provisions Bill marked the end of Christopher Addison's influence as a Coalition Liberal. Notwithstanding Addison's assertions to the contrary, the Prime Minister allowed the bill to drop and may well have decided at this point that his former friend was an encumbrance to the Government at the Ministry of Health.

From the beginning of 1921, the general enthusiasm that had been so apparent in 1918 for the reform of the Poor Law had nearly died. Far from being an anachronism attempting to keep alive narrow Victorian ideals on poverty in the more spacious and enlightened age of twentieth-century welfare, the guardians now, as depression grew daily worse, were defenders of the nation against revolution. *The Times*, which since the beginning of 1920 had consistently attacked both Addison and Newman, summed up the new trends and opinions in a bitter leader on 16 February 1921, referring to a speech of Addison's attacking the guardians for lack of imagination and inefficiency. The paper remarked:

> The country will scarcely, we think, share Dr Addison's dislike for parochial thinking of this kind, but will, on the contrary, recognize the merits of a system which keeps the spenders of public money in such intimate touch with public opinion. Nor is it likely to be spellbound by the vague picture which the Minister presented of an England exempt from the plagues that razed continental nations — if only we will consent to pay a sufficiently large number of experts.[2]

With the resignation of Addison and the appointment of Sir Alfred Mond to the Ministry of Health on 1 April 1921, Government discussion of Poor Law reform abruptly died. Word quickly passed through the tight-knit world of English parochial relief that the danger to the Poor Law was over. At the West Midland Poor Law conference on 20 June 1921 Sir James Curtis, clerk of the Birmingham union, announced with some relief that 'the constant threats to break up the Poor Law system' now seemed to have come to an end.

[1] *The Times*, 16, 17 December 1920.
[2] *Ibid.*, 16 February 1921.

... there was reason to believe that Sir Alfred Mond, the new Minister of Health, was prepared to give an impartial consideration to the Poor Law and other public assistance problems. If so, he hoped Sir Alfred Mond would come to the conclusion that any reconstruction of the Poor Law must, if it was to produce efficiency and economy, proceed side by side with, and as a definite part of, reconstruction of other forms of local government.

He concluded by suggesting that Mond make an announcement postponing for a considerable period, say five years, all action on the transfer of the duties of guardians to the County Councils and that the entire question of local government be referred to a departmental committee of experts among whom would be a majority of men with practical experience in local government.[1]

Mond himself effectively closed the question of Poor Law reform so far as the Coalition was concerned in June 1922 by going out of his way in supply debate to give high praise to the work of the guardians 'in difficult times'. In response to a shout from the benches behind him, 'They saved you from a revolution', Mond retorted that, while that statement was perhaps too strong, the guardians had certainly done much devoted work.[2]

Housing and the City

The second great problem of Addison's administration concerned a question nearly as old as the Poor Law. It had occupied the minds of social thinkers since the 1830s when Edwin Chadwick had discovered that deaths from cholera were highest in slum areas. By the 1870s it had become a serious public political question. But always until the coming of the First World War, Government interest in housing had been restricted to regulation of sanitary arrangements and to abatement of nuisances involving public safety—in effect to questions of eliminating the slums. Building of new houses for the working class, it had always been assumed, was a matter for private philanthropy, and the work of Octavia Hill and Victorian reformers like her seemed to prove that, given properly energetic management and good will, decent private housing could be provided at a profit even for the poorest. Only in the last few years before the war did the Government begin to show some interest in the building, as opposed to the regulation, of housing for the poor. In 1909, John Burns,

[1] *Ibid.*, 21 June 1921. In fact, as the Poor Law reformers, even the Webbs, never seemed to understand, the question of abolition of the guardians and the reconstruction of local government, particularly the financial side of it, were intimately connected. One could not go on without the other.
[2] *H of C Deb.*, CLV (13 June 1922), cols. 299–300.

K

then President of the Local Government Board, carried through Parliament the Housing and Town Planning Act which invited the local authorities to submit plans for urban development and permitted them, technically, to build new houses. Unfortunately both the drafting of the measure and its administration reflected the sterility and immobility of Local Government Board administration before the war. Thus, although the bill at the time was considered an important one and occupied many Parliamentary days in debate, its effect on house building was negligible. English and Welsh local authority expenditures on housing rose from £580,000 in 1910 to £640,000 in 1913. Although this represents a 10 per cent increase, the wholesale price index rose by about 8 per cent in the same period. Much of the increase can probably be traced to this increased cost of local authority borrowing during the great prewar surge of capital export. At the most perhaps 5 per cent of the British population lived in houses let to them by public authorities, and official figures show that only about 11,000 houses were built by all public authorities in England and Wales between 1909 and 1915.[1]

Just before the war, in 1913, David Lloyd George began a far more important, but less well-known, campaign to take the British government into the business of house building. This promotion, usually referred to as the 'Land Campaign', grew out of the then Chancellor of the Exchequer's long-standing interest in doing something toward the revival of the English countryside and English rural life. As a beginning, he hoped to see the national Government lend money to local authorities (specifically he expected to use the reserve funds of national health insurance for this purpose) for the purchase of land and for the building of agricultural labourers' cottages. In the minds of the radical reformers the land programme was the natural corollary of the national health scheme. As health insurance had provided security for the city worker, so the purchase of cottages would give security to the agricultural labourer. Clearly he hoped also to regain for the Liberals, in the general election scheduled for 1915, a number of the rural constituencies that had been lost in the election of 1910.[2]

The Land Campaign, like all other thoughts of public housing and indeed the building of houses, was cut short by the war. But the problems of adequate housing for the British working classes remained and before the conflict was many months old, well before Lloyd George began his programme of focusing national aspirations on a better Britain to come with the peace, the Government had begun tentatively, and on the whole ineffectively, to think about housing after the war. Certainly, housing occupied more time and commanded

[1] Cmd. 1446, 'Second Annual Report of the Ministry of Health, 1920–21', 1921, 57.
[2] On the Land Campaign see: Gilbert, National Insurance, 444–7.

more thought at the beginning than did the questions of employment and unemployment. For the Prime Minister this was especially true and his failure in this area may be accounted as the most serious of the opportunities that the Coalition Government allowed to slip away. The first Committee on Reconstruction, set up by Asquith on 18 March 1916 made a survey of housing needs by circulating the appropriate ministries on their opinions, but made no plans. Perhaps its most significant conclusion was that there was little hope of private enterprise meeting the building needs of the nation and that somehow the local authorities must be induced, possibly by Government grants, to enter the field.[1]

Even before the appointment of the Reconstruction Committee, the Government had already, unwittingly, ensured that no speculative builders would enter the field of working-class houses. The Rent and Mortgage Restriction Act of 1915, passed as a result of the outcry against rising rents in Glasgow, had frozen rents of dwellings with rateable values of £35 in London and less elsewhere at what they had been at the outbreak of war.

The effect of the Rent Restriction Act was to make unsubsidized building of working-class houses virtually impossible. With the inevitable inflation that war would bring, no speculator could afford to build houses to rent at prewar levels. Yet, conversely, so long as a shortage of houses existed, rent control would have to be kept, otherwise there would be no inexpensive houses. The facts of the case after 1915 were, therefore, that subsidized house building either privately or by local authorities was inevitable and that rent control would have to be maintained until a sufficient number of inexpensive dwellings were in the marketplace to permit competition to have its effect. The surprising thing about government planning for house building after the war was not that the principle of a subsidy was rejected but that the necessary concomitants of large government expenditures in the inevitably disorganized consumer market after the war—the control of supplies, the control of non-residential building, perhaps most important of all, the preparation of administrative apparatus to supervise the spending of taxpayer's money—were so little considered.

The story of house planning during the war needs little discussion in detail except as an example, first, of the extraordinary power of a single Cabinet member to delay action should he desire to do so, and second, of the unbelievable pressures and distractions within the Lloyd George administration in the last year of the war which caused the

[1] 'Local Government Board Memorandum on Housing and the War', 29 June 1916. Reconstruction Committee, quoted in: Paul Barton Johnson, 'Post War Planning in Britain, 1916–19, The Committees and Ministry of Reconstruction', unpublished Ph.D. dissertation, University of Chicago, August 1954, 27–40.

almost complete frustration of planning that the Prime Minister himself ardently desired. Even though a Local Government Board memorandum of 24 July 1917 stipulated that 'the Government recognize that it will be necessary to offer substantial financial assistance from public funds to the local authorities who are prepared to carry through without delay ...' the construction of houses, this promise was diluted by a warning that Treasury assistance would depend upon financial circumstances which could not yet be foreseen.[1] Between the summer of 1917 and March 1918 Addison fought—while being distracted by continuous negotiations with the approved societies—for a Cabinet statement saying, in effect, either that it would become the *duty* of the local authority to build houses themselves or that the national Government would appoint housing commissioners to undertake the work in their place.[2] He was able to obtain sanction for neither policy. As he was not President of the Local Government Board he could not give orders to the local authorities himself. However, as he expected from month to month in the spring of 1918 to see the creation of a ministry of health of which he would become head, he was content to wait upon housing plans. The achievement of the larger goal would encompass the smaller. Meanwhile he put the Ministry of Reconstruction to work making plans which would become his own. In the end long delays in the creation of a ministry of health destroyed any possibility of viable preparation for housing; destroyed Addison's reputation as a social reformer and his position as a radical Liberal; destroyed the possibility of keeping perhaps the most important postwar promise of David Lloyd George's administration; and possibly, in the last analysis, destroyed Lloyd George himself.

In the Ministry of Reconstruction, Addison did what he could. His ideas of what preparations for housing should be came principally from two committees—the Salisbury committee and the Carmichael committee. The Salisbury committee included, besides the Marquess of Salisbury, Thomas Jones (later biographer of Lloyd George and at that time a member of the Cabinet Secretariat), B. Seebohm Rowntree and Beatrice Webb, among several others. Generally it was to make an estimate of what conditions could be expected in the building industry after the war, what would be the problems in obtaining building materials, and in what way priorities could be established, and 'to consider and report upon any conditions affecting the building trade which tend to cause unduly high prices, and to make recom-

---

[1] PRO Cab. 23/3, War Cabinet 194, 24 July 1917. Specifically mentioned was aid of at least 5 per cent of the cost of houses above the produce of a penny rate. Addison himself felt the commitment meant nothing. Addison, *Four and a Half Years*, II, 447–9, diary entry 29 November 1917.

[2] See: PRO Cab. 23/5, War Cabinet 364, 12 March 1918.

mendations in regard to any measure of control which it may be desirable to exercise over the purchase, production, transport, or distribution of materials'.[1] The Salisbury committee reported in August 1917. It estimated that 300,000 houses would be needed immediately after the war and suggested that the local authorities plan for them and prepare to buy sites at an agreed valuation. The State would pay the difference between the valuation and the actual cost of the site after the war as part of the war cost. It urged that preparations be made beforehand suggesting the appointment of regional housing commissioners to locate sites and prepare for supplies of building material.[2]

Most important the Salisbury committee urged that housing be made a *duty* of the local authorities and that they be charged, even after the initial deficit was made up, with ensuring a supply of adequate living accommodations within their area. Finally, it was emphasized that the greatest problem for all housing after the war, either public or private, would be the matter of cost of labour and materials.[3]

Salisbury's report made clear that, if a scramble for building materials and labour after the war were to be avoided, steps would have to be taken before the conflict ended. Accordingly, in September 1917, Addison induced Lt. Col. James Carmichael, who had been assistant director of the Material Department in the Ministry of Munitions and an engineer in the Colonial Office, to head a committee to begin making substantive arrangements for ensuring a supply of labour and materials for house building. Technically, much of this work was clearly outside the powers of the Ministry of Reconstruction, which was a planning, not an administrative, department.[4] Without question Addison expected a ministry of health to come into existence well before the end of the war which he would head and which could legalize Carmichael's arrangements. By the summer of 1918, the Carmichael committee had secured promises from building suppliers; had guaranteed, apparently on its own authority, finance for new brickyards; had secured, in conjunction with the demobilization committee

---

[1] Addison, *Four and a Half Years*, II, 495.
[2] Even though the Salisbury committee estimated the need of 300,000 dwellings only as the target for a basic, emergency programme, its estimate of housing needs, the one Addison customarily used thereafter, was ridiculously low. Marian Bowley calculates that the increase in the number of families between 1911 and 1918 was 848,000 and that the number of houses actually built in that period was 238,000. Thus even assuming an adequate number of houses in 1911, which was certainly not the case, there existed an absolute shortage after the war of 610,000 houses. Marian Bowley, *Housing and the State, 1919–1944* (London, 1945), 12.
[3] *Cd. 9087*, 'Housing in England and Wales, memorandum by the Housing Panel', 1919. The date of publication of the Salisbury committee report underlined the power of Fisher who was able to hold up its general circulation until after he was ejected from office. Addison, *Politics*, II, 215.
[4] Addison, *Four and a Half Years*, II, 427, diary entry 6 September 1917.

of the Ministry of Reconstruction, a priority for the release of brick-makers from the army; and generally had planned at least a tentative legal apparatus to ease the shortages which would occur at the end of the war.[1]

As it turned out all the planning came to nothing. The delay over the ministry of health made it impossible for Addison personally to implement his proposals. Of critical importance was the appointment of Sir Auckland Geddes as President of the Local Government Board for the short period between 4 November 1918 and 10 January 1919. At this time, at a meeting on 2 December 1918 with the representatives of the building trades the proposals of the Carmichael committee were scrapped over the sharp protests of Addison and Carmichael. Although the Government proposed to continue to control prices of building materials, without rationing price control meant little. 'The difficulty', Addison bitterly wrote in his diary, 'is that, apart from the trade, the LGB has been solidly against us and as I am not yet Minister, I can do little with them. Their defeat over the Ministry of Health makes them hostile to anything with the name "Addison" attached to it.' Apparently the building industry succeeded in convincing Geddes that there was no need for controls. 'There was ... no adequate reply to the people who said, "We are ready to use the material, the Government is not".'[2]

As a result, when he became President of the Local Government Board, Addison had to report to the Cabinet that for practical pur-poses no planning had been done and that despite 18 months of argument and negotiation the situation was virtually as it had been in the middle of 1917.[3]

Nevertheless, houses had to be built. For many, housing *was* re-construction. Not only were there the endless promises of the general election, but there was also, overshadowing the political danger, the threat of domestic unrest and revolt if something were not done in the field of housing. Although Lloyd George may have ignored do-mestic affairs during the war, by the spring of 1919 he was thoroughly aroused to the importance of social reform and backed Addison strongly in the Cabinet debates while the measure that would become the Housing and Town Planning Act of 1919 was in preparation. In a speech on 3 March 1919, at the end of his only extended stay in England during the Paris Peace Conference, the Prime Minister ex-pounded upon the necessities of a full-scale government housing

---

[1] Addison, *Politics*, II, 219. The arrangements for the release of men with critical skills from the army, which the Government intended in any case, was one of the first of the reconstruction plans to go awry.

[2] Addison, *Four and a Half Years*, II, 597.

[3] Addison, *Politics*, II, 216.

programme before a Cabinet already beginning to show the fears about the expenses that housing could entail. He cited the disorders already apparent in Europe and the dangers of Bolshevism. People no longer believed, he felt, the promises of their leaders. Britain's leaders must show that they meant their promises. The Government, he said, must be prepared to meet the charge that would inevitably be made: when there was a war and the nation needed munitions, it got them, but 'when it came to the question of providing houses the Government was still talking and meanwhile people were without homes'. He estimated the cost would be not more than £71 million.[1]

This speech, made during the last days of preparation of the Housing and Town Planning Bill, as well as much other evidence, suggests that the Prime Minister, in the spring of 1919, was seriously concerned to promote the construction of houses at all costs and that he was quite willing to use peremptory war-time powers to see that the task was accomplished.[2]

Meanwhile, Addison had introduced his bill in the House of Commons.[3] Basically this measure, which became law on 31 July 1919, accomplished only two things. First it laid upon the local authorities the *duty* of providing houses where they were needed. To this end, it required them to make a detailed survey of their areas and to report to the Minister of Health upon housing requirements. Second, it gave sanction to the principle of a State subsidy toward the retirement of the loans that local authorities would contract for the construction of houses. In effect, the difference between the capital cost of the house spread over a period of years and the amount of income the house earned when let at rents that the working class could afford above the proceeds of a penny rate which the local authority would levy itself, would be made up by the Treasury. This provision is important. It meant that the local authorities, although having the cost of their loans guaranteed by the State, had to borrow on their own credit with each raiding the British capital market in competition with all others. On one hand there was no obligation for any individual authority to hold down the cost of houses. Its own liability was small and fixed, and the Treasury stood behind everyone. On the other hand, the Treasury, or the British taxpayer from whom the money would eventually come,

---

[1] PRO Cab. 23/9, War Cabinet 539, 3 March 1919. In fact this speech was during consideration of one of Lloyd George's favourite projects, land settlement, which was always associated in his mind with housing.
[2] On 29 March 1919, the Coalition lost a second by-election at Hull, with a huge turnover of votes. Lord Riddell recalls Lloyd George remarking: 'I really think we should have dealt with housing as we did with factory construction—just have gone ahead. The people are bent on social reform—I am sure of that.' Lord Riddell, *Intimate Diary of the Peace Conference and After, 1918–1923* (London, 1933), 49.
[3] *H of C Deb.*, CXIV (7 April 1919), cols. 1713–40.

lost the advantage of centralized borrowing and would have to pay the inevitable penalty for the disruption of the capital market that would result from the uncoordinated scramble for house building money. In the end the cause of the destruction of the Addison housing programme lay in this provision. It was less the high cost of building, which had indeed fallen drastically by the time the programme came to an end, that destroyed Addison's plans than the high cost of borrowing money.[1] To be sure, if builders' tenders had been lower, local authorities would have had to borrow less. But, as will be seen, by the spring of 1920 financial pressure from the London banking community was seriously interfering with the local authorities' ability to borrow money and not until the spring of 1921, after Addison was dismissed from office, was this pressure relaxed. Briefly from spring 1920 to spring 1921, the British Government was forced to choose between the claims of the City of London as the central financial market of the world and the claims of domestic reconstruction. In this struggle, the City prevailed and one of the important casualties was housing.

There are two ways of looking at the Addison housing programme. As the first British experiment in large-scale public housing, it was by no means an unmitigated failure. From beginning to end, from the summer of 1919 until 30 June 1921—bearing in mind that no commitments for new houses were made under it after the latter date— it brought into existence over 170,000 new dwellings. Of these, 80,000 were completed in 1922. This was the largest number of houses to be completed under government sponsorship in any year in the interwar period except 1928 when slightly more than 90,000 houses were built under the Wheatley Act. If however the 30,000 houses built under the second Addison Act (the Housing (Additional Powers) Act) by private enterprise with government subsidy are added to this, the Addison Act stands, as a sheer creator of living accommodations, the most successful measure of its kind that Britain saw until after the Second World War. Moreover, it should be remembered, that these houses were built in a period during which building was disorganized and supplies and materials uncertain.[2]

[1] In order to calculate the Treasury contribution towards the cost of building, it may be noted for example that the yield of a penny rate in Manchester in 1924–25 was £26,213 while the Treasury contribution to Manchester houses built under the Addison scheme in the same year was £131,124. Bowley, *Housing*, 25–6. Only about one quarter of the money borrowed by local authorities to finance houses under the Addison scheme was borrowed at short term and so able to take advantage of the decline of interest rates that came in the 1930s. The rest cost the local authorities, or the Treasury, an average of more than 6½ per cent. *Ibid.*, 26n. By the mid-thirties, local authorities could borrow at 3½ per cent. *Ibid.*, 278.

[2] One of the most convenient sources for statistics on British housing in the inter-

Politically, on the other hand, the Addison housing programme was a clear failure, which reflected not only upon the political career of Addison himself but upon the credit of the Lloyd George Government. Addison certainly promised too much. He may have been led to expect too much but it is clear also that some of the fault must lie with Addison himself. Testy and uncompromising, he was, at this period at least, a poor negotiator as he had proved at the Ministry of Munitions, and as many of his letters show he was excessively blunt and discourteous to his colleagues and to the local authorities he was supposed to supervise.[1] At bottom lay Addison's chief sin: taking seriously the intentions so long held by himself and his friends of developing the Ministry of Health into a strong department that would bring within its purview all government activities concerned with social welfare.

In addition to Addison's problems resulting from his own personality and promises, he was faced from the beginning with a mass of obstacles not of his own making. Before the war the building industry had been depressed and many workers had left it. During the conflict it had not been among the industries protected from conscription and so had been further depleted. The difficulties of the industry that had caused men to leave it similarly held up the intake of new apprentices. As a result the number of journeymen available even in 1920 was scarcely half the number available at the beginning of the century.[2]

Despite the depletion of their industry, the building trades were unwilling, after the serious struggle during the war on the same subject, to relax apprenticeship regulations and permit the entry of large numbers of new apprentices who in the future might become redundant.[3] This kind of obstruction kept Addison in a continuous rage.

war period are the tables at the end of Marian Bowley's book, *Housing and the State*, 271–83. See also the Ministry of Health return: *Housing, House Production, Slum Clearance etc. England and Wales, 1934*, for more specialized data until 30 September 1934.

[1] He tended to lecture the Cabinet on radical principles. Curzon particularly disliked Addison and thought him a bore. Beaverbrook, *The Decline and Fall of Lloyd George* (London, 1963), 41n.

[2] Conditions in the building industry are well described, from Addison's point of view, in PRO Cab. 27/89, CP 1593, 'Housing Committee, Report by the Chairman of the Committee', 10 September 1920.

	Census Returns		Board of Trade Estimates	
	1901	*1911*	*1914*	*1920*
Masons	73,012	52,188	34,381	19,310
Joiners	265,000	208,995	126,345	108,199

[3] The building trades had been covered by unemployment insurance since 1911 and as a result exact unemployment figures are available for them before October

In a bitter report to the Cabinet of the sort that must have earned him much unpopularity, he cited letters of February 1920, from Holloway Brothers Ltd builders in London, to T. H. Goddey, the district secretary of the Operatives Builders' Society, in which Holloway had asked permission to hire a man 29-years-old who had five years in military service and who agreed to work for apprentice wages in order to learn bricklaying. He was unemployed, had a wife and family, and was willing to join the union, but the union refused to permit it. At the end of March, continued Addison, there were only 3,645 bricklayers at work on local authority schemes, or one bricklayer for each 12 houses presently under contract. At the rate of 400 bricks per day allowed by union rules, one bricklayer could provide four houses per year. The implication was clear: it would take ten years to complete 40,000 houses.[1]

The union's replies, enunciated in innumerable meetings between Addison and the building trades, were always the same. Dilution was both harmful and unnecessary. The Government was asking the union to suffer the disadvantages of slack periods without the compensation of good periods. 'The law of supply and demand is to be suspended to the disadvantage of the building trades. . . .' Nevertheless, the builders insisted they were as interested as anyone in seeing houses constructed. This could be done if the Government guaranteed employment so as to lure back skilled builders from other trades; released building workers from the forces; suspended non-essential building; insisted that all houses under the scheme should be rented at a maximum of 10s. per week and continued the Rent Restriction Act. Finally when every man was employed, the trades would 'consider' permitting overtime.[2]

Addison's troubles with the building industry were only part of his difficulty. He was continually embroiled in struggles with the local authorities, who contrived to be at once tradition-bound and financially carefree. Part of the problem with the local authorities was, as Addison had pointed out many times during the war, that most of them had no experience in house building. Yet suddenly laid upon them was the responsibility for carrying out the most important, expensive and perhaps most complicated of the Coalition reconstruction promises. At the

---

1920. These show for instance that during the spring and summer of 1920, there were fewer than 200 unemployed masons in all of England and Wales. *Ministry of Labour Gazette*, quoted in Bowley, *Housing*, 275.

[1] 'Extracts from Minutes of Meetings of Housing Committee' (subsequent to PRO Cab. 27/89 (Ad hoc committees), CP 1593, 10 September 1920).

[2] 'Housing Operatives Reply to the Speech Delivered by the Prime Minister to the Industrial Council for the Building Industry at Central Hall, Westminister, on 16 December 1919, submitted in Behalf of the National Federation of Building Trades Operatives . . .', signed by W. Bradshaw, no date. *Ibid.*

same time a man had been appointed over them who was the representative of a point of view which almost uniformly they distrusted and disliked, who was a radical Liberal and worst of all a reformer who proposed to do away with one of the most ancient local government institutions which had been the political nursery of endless generations of borough and county councillors—the Board of Guardians. Addison fully understood the hostility of the local authorities well before his appointment to the Local Government Board. But for the first nine months of his administration, at least until the end of 1919, secure in the backing of a Cabinet being deluged with alarmist reports from the Director of Intelligence which seemed to be confirmed by every by-election, he felt safe in his combination of promises, cajolery, and threats to spur them to build houses at all cost. A sampling of remarks from the Directorate of Intelligence may serve to illustrate the atmosphere in which the Cabinet lived in regard to housing:

> The need for houses grows more acute as the weather grows colder. The unrest caused by lack of houses cannot be exaggerated: it is further accentuated by evictions and by the erection in certain districts of Kinematograph Theatres instead of houses. The unrest caused by the housing space difficulties has frequently been alluded to in my reports: it is certainly increasing. In fact, there is probably no more active cause of discontent than this. There is an outcry against the proposal to legalize increased rents, and my correspondent at Leeds states that if rents are raised there will be extensive 'rent strikes'.[1]

Inevitably, with a frightened Cabinet nagging financially uncommitted and hostile local authorities to solicit tenders from building contractors who had no workmen and who could get no materials to build houses upon land they did not own, prices were bound to go up. The more pressure Addison brought to bear, the higher prices went. Everything was done 'under the worst possible conditions', remarked E. D. Simon, who had been Lord Mayor of Manchester in 1921–22 and chairman of the Manchester Housing Committee from 1919 to 1924. Everything was scarce. Prices rose so rapidly that a house that had cost £250 in 1914 was now worth £1,250.[2] Although their economic rent

[1] PRO Cab. 24/89, GT 8228, 'Report on Revolutionary Organizations in the United Kingdom', 25 September 1919. Cab. 24/92, CP 32, 30 October 1919. Arnold Bennett noted in his journal in March 1920, that many estate agents had signs on their doors: 'No unfurnished houses or flats of any description to let under £160 a year'. Arnold Bennett, *The Journal of Arnold Bennett* (London, 1932), II, 302.

[2] *Cmd. 1446*, 'Report of Ministry of Health, 1920-21', 57. The 11,000 houses built by the local authorities between 1905 and 1911 had cost an average of £235 each. In 1920 the purchasing power of the pound was smaller than it would be again until 1945.

was 30s. per week they could not be let for more than 12s. 6d. Addison was in a continual state of near hysteria. 'Use brutal methods', Simon reported he was told by the Minister of Health.[1]

Inevitably, with the rising costs and administrative inexperience among the local authorities, there would be corruption and mistakes. Simon reports a contract for £2,000,000 let without enquiry by the Liverpool Housing Authority to a firm with a paid up capital of £3,000. In spite of an overpayment of £350,000, the firm went bankrupt leaving Liverpool with huge losses to be made up by the ministry. Simon estimated that if the subsidies given under the Addison scheme were applied at the time of writing, 1933, the amount of money paid would build not 176,000 houses but 1,000,000 houses which could be let at about half Addison's average rent. In summary, between 1919 and 31 March 1939, the British Government spent in England and Wales £208,424,183 to subsidize the building by either local authorities or private builders of about 1,542,100 houses. Of these totals, £130,740,246 or about two-thirds, was spent to build 209,300 houses under the two Addison Acts. By 1939 each Addison house had cost the British taxpayer £625, about ten times the outlay for each house built under subsequent acts. The £625 is of course in addition to the rent paid by the householder himself and in addition also to the local government subsidies toward the house collected under the rates.[2]

The forces that would eventually bring an end to the Addison housing programme began to appear in the spring of 1919 even as the housing programme was making its way through Parliament. In August 1918 a committee of representatives of the Treasury and of the Bank of England headed by a former governor of the Bank, Baron Cunliffe, issued an interim report (little changed in its final report several months later) giving its recommendations for government financial policy after the war. These proposals turned generally on the assumption that London ought to resume as quickly as possible its position at the centre of international credit. A free gold exchange standard should be restored without delay, and that as prerequisities for this, government borrowing, and the issuance of Treasury notes should be brought immediately to an end.[3] Although the Cabinet did not officially accept

---

[1] Ernest D. Simon, *The Anti-Slum Campaign* (London, 1933), 11–12. Simon was no enemy of Addison's but a convinced radical Liberal.

[2] These figures are derived from calculations in *Cmd. 3937*, 'Twelfth Annual Report of the Ministry of Health, 1930–31', 1931, 112–7. Put another way, the economic rent for each Addison house based on a £1,000 cost was about £70 per year. Renters by the early thirties paid in fact about £25 per year. Deducting another £5 for administration and repairs, the average annual loss per house was about £50. Appendix Table XVIII, *Cmd. 6089*, 'Twentieth Annual Report of the Ministry of Health, 1938–39', 1939, 253; and from Bowley, *Housing*, 271.

[3] Technically Britain did not go off the gold exchange standard until after the spring

the Cunliffe recommendations until the autumn of 1919, the Bank of England itself began to take steps immediately to put them into operation. Particularly the Bank was concerned by the huge floating debt of over £1,000 million which necessitated repeated Government incursions into the money market upsetting all forms of normal financial business.[1] At the same time the Bank resisted heavy pressure from the Treasury to reduce bank rate which had stood at 5 per cent since April 1917. 'Money is too cheap already', wrote Sir Brian Cokayne, then Governor at the Bank. It would be 'impossible to preserve our international credit unless we have comparatively dear money after the war....'[2] On 6 November 1919 the Bank raised its rate to 6 per cent.

The increase in Bank rate in November brought Addison into angry collision with the Cabinet. In a series of bitter Cabinet meetings in the last weeks of the month, he admitted that through the first week of November only 43,299 houses had been approved out of the 500,000 needed and virtually none completed. The local authorities, he charged, 'whether from inertia, inexperience, or inability to raise the necessary funds' were not proving equal to the task of building houses.[3] But it was becoming clear that the fundamental reason the local authorities were unable even to submit schemes for approval was that they were unable to borrow money. Addison insisted that they must be given credit support or houses would not be built in many places. This demand was immediately resisted by the Chancellor of the Exchequer,

---

of 1919 but the export of gold was in fact nearly impossible for anyone but the Government during the war.

[1] The cost of interest, emphasised by some recent historians, appears to have been of smaller importance in the Bank's objections to the size of debt than was the necessity of continual refinancing. See for instance: A. J. P. Taylor, *English History, 1914–1945* (Oxford, 1965), 124. Taylor states that debt service absorbed 'nearly half the yield from taxation'. In fact the figures were:

	Tax Income	Debt Service
1919–20	£998,960,000	£332,033,708
1920–21	£1,031,725,000	£340,598,616

Cmd. 2849, 'Statistical Abstract for the United Kingdom', 1927, 109, 111. The level of the Bank's concern over excessive government borrowing may be estimated by a serious proposal made by Montagu Norman in a memorandum of 15 April 1919 that the floating debt be taken up by a compulsory loan assessed *pro rata* among income tax payers. Sir Henry Clay, *Lord Norman* (London, 1957), 117–18. One may speculate on the surprise this suggestion would have elicited from the Labour Party had it known that the Bank joined it in urging a capital levy.
[2] On the dealings between the Bank and the Treasury see the almost unbelieveably frank reports in Clay, *Norman*, 111–13.
[3] PRO Cab. 23/18, Cabinet 7 of 1919, meeting 14 November 1919. Up to 31 March 1920, despite endless debates in Parliament, innumerable conferences with builders, and mounting tides of public discontent, only 715 houses had been completed in all of England and Wales. *Cmd. 1446*, 'Second Annual Report of the Ministry of Health, 1920–21', 1921, 57.

Austen Chamberlain, who would become as will be seen one of Addison's most effective enemies in the Cabinet. The Treasury, said Chamberlain, could not without great difficulty render any assistance to the local authorities beyond what had already been committed—£60 million in the next ten months and £160 million for the two following years. In a terse statement, on 20 November, he revealed the desperate position of government finance. 'The best opinion in the City has been consulted, and was found to coincide with the view of the Treasury, namely, that at the present moment the Government could not borrow any more money.' Things might be better the next spring but 'no definite opinion could be obtained as to prospects'. The local authorities would have to borrow on their own credit and the Government, the Cabinet agreed, should hold out no hope to the local authorities of borrowing assistance even if this meant that no borrowing would be done.[1]

Conditions did not improve the next spring; indeed they grew worse. Although the Government succeeded in reducing its floating debt by about one-half in 1919, in April of 1920, with banks rationing credit the Government found itself unable by about £63 million even to refinance its own debt at the existing rate of interest and on April 15 raised the Treasury bill rate to $6\frac{1}{2}$ per cent. The next day, Bank rate went to 7 per cent.[2] The events of the spring of 1920 threw local authority borrowing into unbelievable confusion. In April 80 per cent of a London County Council issue of £7 million was left in the hands of its underwriters. Other counties, Addison reported, were now paralysed.[3]

Throughout the summer and well into the autumn of 1920, Addison struggled with the local authorities and the builders to reduce the costs of house construction and with Austen Chamberlain and the Bank of England to reduce the cost of borrowing money. Chamberlain faithfully reflected the point of view of Montagu Norman, Governor since 31 March 1920 of the Bank of England: that local authority

[1] PRO Cab. 23/18. Cabinet 8 of 1919, meeting 20 November 1919.
[2] London merchant bank discounts were by this time higher than they had been in three-quarters of a century. A number of economists, notably R. G. Hawtry, who was carrying on inside the Treasury a lonely fight for more flexible policy, date the beginning of the great postwar depression from these events in mid-April 1920. For a discussion of Hawtry's position see: A. C. Pigou, *Aspects of British Economic History, 1918–1925* (London, 1948), 188–90. Pigou generally supports Hawtry's analysis but feels that this is too narrow an explanation. On Hawtry's work, see also Douglas Jerrold, *Georgian Adventure* (London, 1937), 239. Jerrold was at this time in the Seventh Division of the Treasury which dealt with health, education and national insurance, labour and pensions.
[3] Addison to Lloyd George, 22 April 1920. LG Papers, F/1/6/8. Addison was no economist and was clearly not aware of the existing gap in Treasury refunding. He attributed the rise in the bill rate to 'some reason of uncanny contrariness' on the part of the Chancellor of the Exchequer. *Ibid.*

demands, which were the chief domestic pressure on the capital market, were wasteful.[1] The answer, Chamberlain continually argued, was not to make borrowing easier but to bring pressure on the builders, and especially upon the building trade unions, to accept dilution of labour, to abolish the awkward and exclusive apprenticeship regulations and to bring large numbers of unskilled workers, particularly ex-soldiers, into the building industry. Further he urged that the Government coerce the building industry by publishing the facts about its stubbornness.[2]

By the winter of 1920–21, with some members of the Cabinet already speaking out freely against building trades employers and workers—bringing upon the Lloyd George Government the denunciations from hitherto staunchly Liberal journals like the *Nation*—Addison was beginning to urge upon the Cabinet a still more costly expedient for building houses, the direct employment of labour by the local authorities themselves.[3] Certain Conservative local authorities, notably the City of London, had been proposing that they try such an experiment for some months, although 98 per cent of local authority building had hitherto been done by private builders. The proposal came up in the Cabinet when the building trade unions, ignoring the threat that the Government would publish in the press an account of two years' negotiations, rejected on 3 February a Government proposal asking that they take on 50,000 unemployed ex-servicemen as apprentices immediately in return for certain concessions such as a guaranteed work week. Addison had doubts about this plan. He knew it would propel him into further disputes particularly with the Labour-dominated local authorities who would probably refuse to hire workers on any other than union terms while none of the authorities had much experience in the direct employment of labour. It was on the other hand particularly supported by the Conservative members of the Cabinet.[4]

As it turned out, by this time the decisions had already been made that would bring the Addison housing programme to an end. In November 1920 Chamberlain, still determined to reduce Government

[1] Clay, *Norman*, 130. 'The financial position is full of difficulties, but not one of the problems that confronts me gives me more cause for anxiety than the drain which housing already makes upon national finances.' Chamberlain to Addison, 4 November 1920. LG Papers, F/1/6/14.

[2] 'Minutes of a Conference of Ministers Held 21 October 1920', in PRO Cab. 23/23, Cabinet 59, 1920, meeting 3 November 1920, appendix VII. As a coal strike was in progress, the Chancellor urged however that 'ministers should be careful in their speeches to avoid a deliberate attack upon Labour at this juncture in order that the policy of the Government in relation to the coal strike might not be interpreted as a general attack upon trade unionism'.

[3] *Nation*, 20 October 1920.

[4] PRO Cab. 23/23, Cabinet 75 of 1920, meeting 22 December 1920, appendix 1. *Ibid.* Cab. 23/24, Cabinet 5 of 1921, meeting 7 February 1921, appendix 1.

short-term borrowing and fully supported by the Bank of England, announced that he hoped in the next budget to apply at least £250 million if not £300 million to reduce the floating debt. He intended to ask for a decrease of 20 per cent in spending in all departments and suggested that some limit be put on the number of houses that the state would be responsible for.[1] Addison immediately responded with a memorandum saying that housing commitments could not be cut and the taxpayer would be fortunate if the Ministry of Health was not forced to ask for an increase. The decision came quickly on 30 January 1921 at a Finance Committee meeting with the Prime Minister in the chair, at which Addison was not present. The committee report to the Cabinet announced with regret that it had decided 'there was no alternative open to the Government but to decide housing questions not on merit, but on financial consideration only'.[2]

The lessons of the previous winter and spring had profoundly affected Chamberlain. Squeezed between the converging pressures of a high interest rate necessary to control inflation at home, the knowledge that for practical purposes the British Government could borrow no more money without driving the rate still higher, and the fact that the service of the existing debt was taking almost 35 per cent of the national budget and 7 per cent of the national income, his conventional mind could conceive of no solution except the production of huge budget surpluses. Income from taxes was still high, higher than at any time during the war (and would indeed remain high until the Bonar Law administration). On the other hand, government expenses would have to come down. Among those to be pared was housing, a most notorious example of government waste which seemed to incur at once a maximum of disruption of the financial market, an inordinate amount of political unpopularity, and yet to produce a negligible number of dwelling units.

There is no way of telling whether the Prime Minister's decision to dismiss his Minister of Health proceeded finally from the difficulties over housing, which were after all of long standing, or the more incisive but less widely understood political failure over the Miscellaneous Provisions Bill. The decision to cut the housing programme and the dropping of the Miscellaneous Provisions Bill occurred at almost precisely the same time. Generally the burden of evidence would seem to indicate that Addison's dismissal from the Ministry of Health came not as a result of public failures in the housing programme but because of his personal loss of power within the increasingly savage world that surrounded the Coalition ministry. The reduction in the Government commitment to housing was the result of factors beyond

[1] Finance Committee meeting, 29 November 1920. PRO Cab. 27/71.
[2] Finance Committee meeting, 30 January 1921. PRO Cab. 27/27.

Addison's control although in fact the amount of money to be saved in the 1921–22 budget on housing would be small, and just before his resignation on 11 March, Addison had reached an agreement with Chamberlain 'on the basis of 250,000 houses' down to June 1922.[1] But the important thing was to end local authority demands on the capital market beside which the building of houses or the employment of ex-servicemen was unimportant.[2] The correspondence surrounding Addison's resignation from the Ministry of Health and the periodical comment suggests that his failure lay in his capabilities as a political operator. Ten months before his departure the *New Statesman*, which had at first strongly supported the health minister, remarked:

> Our advice, then, to the Government is that, if it really wants to give us houses (or even if only it wants to remain in power), it should have a new financial policy, a new labour policy, and a new Minister of Health. Dr Addison may have excellent intentions: he has, we believe, worked hard. But he has most emphatically not proved equal to his task. He has, possibly, not been given a free hand by Mr Lloyd George. There would, perhaps, be political conveniences in having a strong man at the Ministry of Health, who would be as firm for getting houses as other Ministers are for getting swords for airmen or soldiers for Ireland, who would stand up to the Treasury misers or to the profiteers in building materials, and who would even risk his reputation of bold experiments with Labour. If Mr Lloyd George wants weakness at the Ministry of Health, that is Dr Addison's misfortune for which the public is at present paying, and it is time that somebody else paid.[3]

The Times attacked Addison from precisely the opposite point of view just after his resignation.

> The disappearance of Dr Addison from the Ministry of Health affords an opportunity to rescue that institution from its present position and make it of real use to the country and the doctors. Dr Addison's fault was that he gave the impression of playing second fiddle all along to his chief medical officer Sir George Newman. His departure, therefore, ought to mark the end of the 'Newman policy', as laid down in Sir George Newman's numerous writings.
>
> The Newman policy, so far as it is understood, is the policy of special departments centralized in Whitehall. They were to be, and

---

[1] Christopher Addison, *The Betrayal of the Slums* (London, 1922), 27.
[2] By the time borrowing under the Addison Acts ended, the local authorities had succeeded in raising upon their own credit about £152 million for housing, or slightly more than one-fifth of the entire national debt in 1914. *Cmd. 1713*, 'Third Report of the Ministry of Health', 44.
[3] *New Statesman*, 8 May 1920.

L

now are, 'services' with senior and junior medical officers who are pensionable officials. These officers, like the planets, revolve around the central sun, the chief medical officer. In this way, little by little, the whole health work of the country was to be controlled by White-hall, which would possess all the available statistical information.

The paper warned that the same thing would happen to Addison's successor, Sir Alfred Mond, if he continued his 'thoroughly vicious' system.[1] Essentially a weak man politically, at the head of a second-rank department, Addison's administration had attempted too much and had accomplished too little. He antagonized both the supporters and the enemies of reform. He and the men around him had believed, too sincerely, that he could create a ministry for the health of the nation.

But Addison's troubles had not deprived him of all value. The Prime Minister chose to retain him in the Cabinet and to gamble a sub-stantial proportion of the Coalition Liberals' remaining political capital on this decision. Lloyd George asked Addison to resign from the Ministry of Health on 31 March, using as an excuse Bonar Law's resignation as Lord Privy Seal a week earlier. This enforced, wrote the Prime Minister, 'considerable changes in the Ministry' (Lloyd George might have added that it also made his own position weaker). He asked Addison to give up the Ministry of Health and to take instead a Ministry without Portfolio which, he reminded Addison, he had suggested a year earlier in April 1920, so that Addison would be free to help the Liberal leadership with 'general political work'. Addi-son's task now would be 'coordinating the political effort of the Govern-ment and adjusting it to the needs and sympathies of the new elec-torate'.[2] Addison's reply showed clearly the request to resign came to him as a surprise. He said he was 'grievously disappointed' and that he was most unhappy about leaving the Ministry of Health. He loved and understood the work there but was grateful for the offer of a Ministry without Portfolio. As further evidence that the change, at least so far as Addison himself understood it, was not the result of the failure in housing he concluded his letter by reminding the Prime Minister that he had just submitted to the Cabinet committee pro-posals for reforms in values and ratings as a necessary preliminary to the reform of the Poor Law 'to which we are all committed'. He hoped, he said, to deal with the Poor Law in 1922. Was it 'unwarranted' to ask, he concluded, 'whether his change in Cabinet status involves any desire or inclination on your part to depart from our intentions in

[1] *The Times*, 4 April 1921.
[2] Lloyd George to Addison, 31 March 1921. LG Papers, F/1/6/20.

these matters or to entrust the execution of the policy involved to anyone' not informed or unsympathetic.[1]

As these letters indicate, Addison's translation from Minister of Health to Minister without Portfolio was reasonably amicable. Whether or not the Prime Minister wished to keep him in an administrative department, at the end of March at least, he certainly wished to keep Addison at his side. Addison was the sole survivor in the Cabinet of the old prewar days of pioneering radical Liberalism and remained, with T. J. Macnamara, one of the few bits of evidence of the Prime Minister's increasingly dubious affection for social reform. Addison was useful as a piece of window-dressing if nothing else.[2]

Addison's purgatory was not yet at an end. His value to the Prime Minister as an authentic radical and indeed his attempts, however clumsy, to carry out the programme of radical reform while Minister of Health, were precisely the aspects of his personality and position that made him unpalatable to most of the Conservative press and to the Conservative supporters of the Coalition. He was to be sure an easy figure to attack, but the historian cannot help feeling that behind the enthusiasm with which the backbenchers of the House of Commons rushed in to participate in his destruction there lay a feeling that an adequate display of brutality on this occasion might convince the electorate that all the failings of the Government in the past 30 months were the fault of this man alone. By allowing him to remain in the Cabinet the Prime Minister made a surprising political error. In effect the translation to the Ministry without Portfolio weakened rather than strengthened the Government's position. Whatever had been Addison's failures in office, most of the errors had been in the direction of attempting to do too much. Now, however, Lloyd George would have to explain to a hostile Parliament what circumstances continued to justify his enjoyment of a salary at the taxpayer's expense when, at least so far as many Conservative MPs affected to see, he would be doing nothing.[3]

Over the question of Addison's salary as Minister without Portfolio Lloyd George allowed the House of Commons to erode further the waning prestige of his administration. Both the Prime Minister and Austen Chamberlain were hesitant in view of lobby comment and

---

[1] Addison to Lloyd George, 31 March 1921. LG Papers, F/1/6/21. Typically, Addison's biographer confuses for his readers Addison's resignation from the Ministry of Health and his virtual ejection from the Government three months later.
[2] Addison was replaced by Sir Alfred Mond, the founder of the Imperial Chemical Industries and a large contributor to the Liberal party. Lloyd George had promised him the previous year that he could have the first major office that became available. Hector Bolitho, *Alfred Mond, First Lord Melchett* (London, 1933), 215.
[3] For a survey of backbench opinion see: *Evening Standard*, 14 June 1921.

attacks in newspapers to regularize Addison's equivocal position in the Cabinet by asking the Commons for a vote upon his salary.[1] The backbenchers did not like the Ministry without Portfolio office, wrote Chamberlain to Lloyd George on 9 June, even when it had been held, as a year previously, by so unimpeachable a Tory as Laming Worthington-Evans, and they were doubly angry to see it revived to give a job to a man who had failed in a regular department. Chamberlain reported he was being pressed to assign a day for the debate of Addison's salary and was reluctant to do so because he feared the outcome of a Supply Committee vote.[2] His own influence, he thought, would not be enough to carry the question, and he urged Lloyd George to take charge of the matter himself.[3] The Prime Minister answered the same day agreeing it was hard to defend Addison with the lesson of recent by-election losses still fresh. Addison, he thought, regarded himself as a martyr to the cause of public health and that the only question was whether it would be possible to spare him the humiliation of a rebuff by Parliament. 'He has not behaved very well since his dethronement', concluded Lloyd George. 'He had thought it necessary to be sulky and resentful. Winston can afford these little exhibitions, but in Addison they are quite intolerable.'[4] In the next few days Chamberlain, who was keenly aware of the growing and reckless disaffection within the Conservative ranks, subjected Addison to considerable pressure to resign as Minister without Portfolio before his salary came to a vote.[5]

Lloyd George's belief that Addison did not understand the precariousness of his position was strikingly confirmed on 15 June when the former Minister of Health, probably thinking he would strengthen his resistance to an enforced resignation, allowed a long statement by him to be published in the *Evening Standard*. Addison reiterated throughout the interview that he would 'not be driven from office'. He suggested further that most of the Conservatives opposing his appointment were not hostile to him personally but were 'sincerely anxious to destroy the Coalition' and attacked him only because of what he stood

---

[1] 'If the division on his salary were perfectly . . . free and secret he could hardly expect to secure a dozen votes', remarked the *New Statesman* on 18 June 1921.
[2] When the debate finally occurred the Government put out a three-line Whip commanding attendance at the vote. *H of C Deb.*, CXLIII (23 June 1921), col. 1622. Chamberlain's difficulty in maintaining ordinary discipline lay in the fact that the real power of enforcement was with the constituencies, which were by now almost uniformly against the Coalition.
[3] Chamberlain to Lloyd George, 9 June 1921. LG Papers, F/7/4/5.
[4] Lloyd George to Chamberlain, 9 June 1921. LG Papers, F/7/4/6.
[5] Chamberlain to Lloyd George, 10, 13 June, 1921. LG Papers, F/7/4/7–8. Officially the Government still maintained that the Tory revolt was unimportant. The *Evening Standard*, which at this time was generally supporting the Coalition and Addison, insisted that the back-bench unhappiness was of no concern to the Ministry. *Evening Standard*, 14–23 June 1921.

for in the Government. Finally, misapprehending entirely Lloyd George's attitude toward him he boasted that the Prime Minister's decision to move his salary personally was a measure of the support he possessed within the Government.[1]

Addison's interview enraged Chamberlain who wrote to Lloyd George on the day the article appeared. He denounced Addison for twisting facts. Addison had turned, said Chamberlain, 'what was partly a genuine movement for economy and partly a real attack upon his own administration into a revolt of the Unionists against the Coalition Liberals'. He was not sure any longer whether he would be able to promise enough Conservative votes to carry Addison's salary even if Lloyd George did exert all his influence. In any case, Chamberlain reported, he intended to write to Addison and to tell him that he had destroyed his own position with the Unionists.[2]

In the midst of the storm over Addison, a short revolt occurred in the Cabinet led apparently by Birkenhead, who tried to take advantage of the Unionist disaffection to install Churchill as Prime Minister. Churchill, although a close personal and political friend of the Chancellor, declined to be drawn in. Outside the Government Lord Salisbury continued to foment discontent by a letter to the electors of East Hertfordshire, who had on 16 June chosen an Anti-Waste candidate, supported by Horatio Bottomley, over a Coalition Unionist by a majority of more than 2 to 1. Salisbury was not a member of the conspiracy although he may have been aware of it. Nevertheless his letter repeating the formula of the previous year: that 'the Coalition Government no longer possesses the full confidence of the Unionist Party' served to underline the disaffection among Conservatives in the country and so weakened the Government's position.[3]

There can be little doubt that by his intemperate behaviour Addison had seriously harmed himself not only with the Conservatives but with the Coalition Liberals. As a consequence the debate on his salary, which finally occurred on 23 June, resulted in a substantial defeat for the Government. As the *Manchester Guardian* put it, Addison was dismissed 'with the three months notice that a senior clerk would get

[1] *Evening Standard*, 15 June 1921.
[2] Chamberlain to Lloyd George, 15 June 1921. LG Papers, F/7/4/17. Chamberlain's statement was an accurate estimate of the temper of his following and not solely the result of personal anger. During the salary debate a week later, Addison was severely criticised by Conservative spokesmen for resorting to the press instead of the House of Commons to state his case. *H of C Deb.*, CXLIII (23 June 1921), col. 1618.
[3] See: *Manchester Guardian*, 20, 23, June 1921. See also: Beaverbrook, *The Decline and Fall of Lloyd George*, 61–81. Birkenhead later denied vehemently that he had ever intrigued against Lloyd George. Riddell, *Diary of the Peace Conference*, 209, diary entry 2 August 1921.

if he had not done anything actually criminal'.[1] During the debate Lloyd George allowed the Government resolution proposing a salary of £5,000 for Addison to be amended to provide a reduction to £2,500 while announcing himself that the appointment would last only until the end of the existing session of Parliament.[2]

The debate on Christopher Addison focussed the bitterness that had surrounded the Lloyd George reform programme since the 1918 election and concentrated it on a single man. More than any other individual, except perhaps the Prime Minister himself, the former Minister of Health represented the tendencies toward administrative centralization, political control in Whitehall of local authorities, and profligate expenditure, that the Coupon Parliament had come to associate with the term social reform. Among several misapprehensions, Addison's assumption that the Conservatives at bottom objected to 'what he stood for in the Government' was remarkably accurate.

'Mr Addison did not realize that the war had not changed the rules of economy', asserted Lieutenant-Colonel W. E. Guinness, moving the amendment which reduced the salary of the Minister without Portfolio to £2,500.

> Justly or unjustly his Departmental activities at the Ministry of Health have become identified in the public mind with the blight of bureaucracy and interference in the extremest form, and it is viewed with consternation that this bureaucratic blight which is associated with him may be communicated to the general activities of the Government.

In contrast to what Addison was trying to do, Guinness called upon the Commons 'to devote our energy for a great many years to get back to the conditions we enjoyed before the War'.[3]

In the end the resolution to give Addison a salary of £2,500 per year until the end of the session was approved 250–40 with many abstentions. Lloyd George was not present for the division. He had been forced to declare necessary to his Cabinet a man whom by now he wished to see out of it and then to admit his perjury by agreeing to the man's dismissal. Addison's own feelings at this juncture may be imagined.

No homes for heroes

After the brutal treatment dealt Addison as an individual, there was little chance of mercy for his programme. On the day before the salary debate, 22 June, the new Minister of Health, Alfred Mond, outlined

---

[1] *Manchester Guardian*, 24 June 1921.
[2] *H of C Deb.*, CXLIII (23 June 1921), cols. 1593–1654.
[3] *Ibid.*, col. 1606.

in a Cabinet paper the prospective needs of the housing programme for the coming budgetary year. All in all, Mond admitted, the financial commitments were pretty well fixed by policy and could not be reduced unless the policy were changed. And giving what may have been the mortal blow to the Addison housing programme he ended his memorandum: 'I may say it once again that on the above housing policy I cannot see how my total estimates for next year are to show any material decrease, much less such a decrease as the 20 per cent desired by the Cabinet.'[1] Thus the alternatives were clearly laid out. Present housing expenditures were already fixed by contract with the local authorities and for practical purposes could not be reduced. No money, in fact, could be saved on housing. The most that could be accomplished would be the avoidance of future commitments.

The end of the housing programme came with a swiftness that surprised even the Minister of Health himself. Eight days after the submission of the Mond memorandum, on 30 June, the Cabinet Finance Committee, which included Lloyd George, Chamberlain and Robert Horne, the Chancellor of the Exchequer since 23 March, but with neither Addison nor Mond, resolved to end all Government subsidized housing and place a limit of 176,000 dwelling units as the maximum for which the Government would be responsible. (This was approximately the number, so far as could be determined, for which the government had already contracted). Addison did not, even though his biographer suggests the contrary, resign immediately. He remained a member of the Government for nearly two weeks trying vainly to restore the programme. Beginning on 4 July, in a series of increasingly violent memoranda and letters to the Prime Minister, he upbraided the Government and Lloyd George himself for broken personal promises and public bad faith.[2] He agreed, he insisted, on the need for economy and had reached what he believed was an understanding with Austen Chamberlain on the matter who, although by now Lord Privy Seal, apparently remained the principal financial authority and principal advocate of economy in the Cabinet.

The Finance Committee decision of 30 June was confirmed in Cabinet on 11 July, the last meeting that Addison attended. Here Addison produced again his familiar arguments about broken promises and Mond urged that he be allowed simply to announce that the

---

[1] PRO Cab. 24/125, CP 3067, 'Reduction of Public Expenditure, Memorandum by the Minister of Health', 22 June 1921.
[2] Addison to Lloyd George, 4 July 1921. LG Papers, F/1/6/29. PRO Cab. 24/126, CP 3108, 'Housing Policy, Memorandum by Dr Addison', 4 July 1921. Mond himself was surprised by the decision of 30 June, and also protested although in much more moderate terms. PRO Cab. 24/126, CP 3111, 'Housing Policy, Memorandum by the Minister of Health', 7 July 1921.

problem of working-class housing was to be 'reviewed in view of the financial difficulties of the nation', in effect smoothing over and blunting the peremptoriness of the decision. Nevertheless, all protests were rejected and Mond was ordered to make the announcement without equivocation except that the date for the ending of Government responsibilities was moved back from 1 July to 15 July.[1]

Mond's announcement came in the House of Commons on 14 July.[2] It was followed by a bitter statement from Addison who had resigned the same day and who read parts of his resignation letter to the House. Earlier that day, Addison had written to the Prime Minister denouncing the Government and Lloyd George personally for dishonesty: for breaking the promises made to Addison himself that the Ministry of Health policy would not be changed with his resignation and for the Cabinet's unwillingness to deal frankly even with the House of Commons. Mond, he charged, had been refused permission to 'make it plain that the action he will be required to take is based upon a decision that he "should cancel contracts for building houses" and that whilst "in no event shall the number of houses built by the local authorities exceed 176,000" this figure is "to be reduced to the utmost possible extent".'[3]

Addison's letter appears to have thrown the Prime Minister into a rage and forced him into prevarication. Answering Addison's letter of resignation, he stated:

> I cannot accept your description of the Government decision as an abandonment of our housing policy. The financial situation has forced us to cry a halt in the development of your housing plans. Meanwhile time will be given to the new Minister of Health to put these schemes on a more businesslike footing.[4]

The almost incredible bitterness between the two former colleagues, particularly Lloyd George's now undisguised hatred of Addison which would continue through the rest of his life, clearly indicates that the

---

[1] PRO Cab. 23/26, Cabinet 58 of 1921, meeting 11 July 1921. By this time, rumours of the impending Government decision were widespread and innumerable protests were flowing in from local authorities.

[2] *H of C Deb.*, CXLIV (14 July 1921), cols. 1504–5.

[3] Addison to Lloyd George, 14 July 1921. LG Papers, F/1/6/30.

[4] Lloyd George to Addison, 14 July 1921. LG Papers, F/1/6/31. As he frequently did, the Prime Minister vented his rage in a letter that he did not send. Attached to the copy cited above is a second letter, apparently not sent, which concluded with the following paragraph: 'If you had intended resigning, it would have saved a good deal of worry and trouble at a busy time, had you done so before the recent Debate on your salary and as your tenure of office is at any rate coming to an end in a month's time, it hardly seems worthwhile entering into this elaborate explanation.'

Prime Minister understood the importance of the change now being forced upon himself and upon Coalition policy.[1] Within two weeks all pretence of further reform disappeared with the appointment of the Committee on National Expenditure, the so-called Geddes committee, which crudely and ruthlessly pruned all forms of public expenditure in every direction, but particularly in government welfare activity.

Thus ended any possibility that Lloyd George might at some time become leader of a coalition of the non-socialist, but social reforming left. Although the Conservatives did not yet realize it, he was now their prisoner.

Thus ended also the most ambitious attempt to build the better Britain that might have helped make the sacrifices of the First World War worthwhile. The hopeful political climate of 30 months before was now dissipated. There would be useful and imaginative reform measures in the future, but essentially they would deal with specific problems: the aged or the inefficiency of local government. The ideal of national reconstruction, the use of state power to build a fuller and more secure life for all citizens, which above all the Ministry of Health had represented, was dishonoured. Overriding all else now the single problem of massive industrial unemployment, the cost of which had helped to bring down the housing programme, would be for the next decade and a half the incubus of British social politics. This study must return, therefore, to unemployment. It caused directly the second great Parliamentary crisis of the interwar period. As Lloyd George destroyed his political career in an attempt to provide Englishmen a more spacious life than they had ever known, Ramsey MacDonald's second Labour Government nearly drove the State to bankruptcy trying to keep living conditions tolerable.

[1] Lloyd George seldom lost an opportunity in later life to denounce Addison either publicly or privately. He convinced himself that Addison had 'botched' the housing programme and he blamed himself only for protecting Addison so long out of personal consideration. See for instance his letters to Winston Churchill on 1 October 1921, quoted in Beaverbrook, *Men and Power* (London, 1956), 400–4.

4 Unemployment and politics in the thirties

The coming of the depression in Great Britain can be described most simply, and is best remembered, as an explosion of unemployment. In December 1929, three months after the American stock market crash, the live register contained about 1,304,000 names, slightly, but not significantly, above the average of the previous seven years. A year later, by December 1930, it had grown to 2,408,000, higher than any report except June 1921, and amounting to 19·6 per cent of all insured persons. In terms of unemployment insurance finances the debt in the insurance fund had grown from £39,042,000 at the end of the previous March to £57,290,000. By the end of March 1931 the insurance fund debt was £75,472,000 and the fund's expenditures exceeded its income by £36,430,000.[1]

The crisis of 1931 and unemployment insurance

The most surprising thing about the onset of the 1931 crisis is the suddenness with which it appeared and, despite the warnings of a few, by no means all experts, the lack of steps by the Government to meet it. The appointment under duress of the Royal Commission on Unemployment Insurance, the 'Gregory Commission', on 9 December 1930 to consider the future scope of unemployment insurance and the 'means by which it may be made solvent and self-supporting', was not a response to the crisis into which unemployment insurance was slipping.[2] Warnings by some low-ranking Treasury officials to the effect that the fund could not continue indefinitely its borrowing from the Treasury received little notice either inside the Government or out of it.

The Government considered briefly and discarded the possibility of reducing benefits by 2s. for adults and 1s. for dependent children.[3]

---

[1] See: *Minutes of Evidence Taken Before the Royal Commission on Unemployment Insurance*, 1931, 7. Ministry of Labour Memorandum. See also: Eveline M. Burns, *British Unemployment Programmes, 1920–1938*,(Washington, 1941), 69. The ballooning Unemployment Insurance Fund debt required an increase in the borrowing power of the Fund in March to £90 million from the £60 million at which it had been set by the act of 1930, and a second increase in July 1931, to £115 million.

[2] For a discussion of the origins of the Royal Commission see: Robert Skidelsky, *Politicians and the Slump* (London, 1967), 263.

[3] PRO Cab. 24/219, CP 31, 'Unemployment Insurance, Emergency Financial Measures, 5 February 1931, MGB'; This document is not bound with other

But the only changes in unemployment insurance approved before the crisis was the removal of 'anomalies', that is benefits paid to contributors who were working part time which in some cases gave them a higher total income than their colleagues, the restoration to ministerial discretion in transitional benefits, although only for the making of general rules, not in individual cases, and the extension of transitional benefit until April 1932.[1] This was the fourth extension. The third would have run out in October 1931. It was calculated to cost about £20 million. The Cabinet's public position for the first six months of 1931 was to defer all consideration of substantial changes in unemployment insurance until the interim report from the Royal Commission on Unemployment Insurance. But in the meantime, in response to demands by both Conservatives and Liberals and spurred by a projected minimum budget deficit of £37 million, it appointed in March the Committee of National Expenditure under the chairmanship of George May, secretary of the Prudential Assurance Company. Philip Snowden, the Chancellor of the Exchequer, refused to take the matter seriously. 'I have no objection to setting up a committee', he told the House of Commons. 'The Government has already set up 72 and one more will not hurt.[2]

The May Committee scarcely had begun its work when the first of the series of events that brought the crisis of 1931 occurred. On 11 May the Rothschild Bank in Vienna, the Kredit-Anstalt, suspended gold payments. Because it was the central bank not only for Austria but for a substantial part of Southern Germany—which meant that it held deposits of other, smaller banks in the area—its collapse immediately put in jeopardy the solvency of all financial institutions depending upon it. Two weeks later, in order to stop the growing flight of money from the country, the Austrian Government froze all foreign assets. A large proportion of these funds were German and the consequence of this action was simply to transfer the crisis to that country. Therefore, on 15 July 1931, attempting to protect its own threatened banking system, the German Government prohibited the export of gold or foreign currency and so transferred the pressure to its largest creditor, Great Britain.

For Britain 15 July rather than 11 May was the critical date. Until

Cabinet Papers, but is in a separate volume entitled 'Confidential Annexes'. See also: Margaret I. Cole, ed., *Beatrice Webb's Diaries, 1924–32* (London, 1956), diary entry 4 February 1931, 265.

[1] PRO Cab. 24/222, CP 153, 'Report of the Unemployment Insurance Committee', Arthur Henderson, 16 June 1931. Employers in effect were using unemployment insurance to subsidize wages. Skidelsky, *Politicians*, 233.

[2] Robert Skidelsky, 'Crisis, 1931', *The Times*, 2 December 1968. It is important to remember that the second Labour Government, like the first, maintained a majority in the House of Commons only with the help of Liberal votes.

this time not only the Government, but almost unbelievably the City and the Bank of England had taken little notice of the events in Central Europe.[1] The Bank prepared to stem the drain on sterling in the traditional way and on 28 July obtained credits of £25 million each in the New York and Paris money markets. Until this date the crisis was entirely financial. The Government was not informed and appears to have found no reason for taking an interest in the affairs of the City on its own initiative. On 30 July at the last meeting before the August holidays, the Cabinet took note of the problem only to remark that as a result of the fiscal crisis in Germany there was some danger of dumping of German goods in the British market.[2]

Despite the temporary steadying influence effected by the Bank of England's easy discovery of foreign credit, the political phase of the 1931 crisis was about to begin. Unquestionably, the effect of the closure of the German Banks upon confidence in the pound had been heightened by the publication of two days before, on 13 July, of the report of the Macmillan Committee which gave for the first time authoritative estimates of London's short-term foreign indebtedness which amounted to £407 million.[3] Against this amount the City could call immediately only £153 million and this was only technical, for of this amount £90 million was now frozen in Austria and Germany. Like an insolvent contractor, the City's assets, large as they were, were tied up in long-term investments while its credit and capital depended, in effect, on the goodwill of pawnbrokers.

Far more important, however, was the publication, on 1 August, just two days after the Cabinet had calmly parted to enjoy the August Bank holiday, of the May Committee Report, estimating that the budget deficit for the current fiscal year would be £120 million, the insurance deficit £105 million, and recommending drastic economies in all government departments including above all the saving of £66 million in unemployment insurance.[4]

[1] Sir Henry Clay in his unfinished but extremely useful biography of Montagu Norman, the Governor of the Bank of England, quotes a cable of 15 July from George L. Harrison, Governor of the Federal Reserve Bank of New York to Norman asking about the sudden and unexplained drop in the sterling exchange on that day. Could Norman account for it? Norman replied on the same day that he could not and that it was 'sudden and unexpected'. Sir Henry Clay, *Lord Norman* (London, 1957), 383–4.
[2] Cab. 23/67, Cabinet 40 of 1931, meeting 30 July 1931.
[3] *Cmd. 3897*, 'Committee on Finance and Industry Report', 1931, 299–301.
[4] *Cmd. 3920*, 'Committee on National Expenditure Report', 1931, 145–52. The Cabinet considered advance copies of the May Committee report at its meeting on 30 July. With the kind of systematic ineptitude that it seemed determined to display at this period, it took note of the report simply with the casual remark that all departments 'affected by the report should send in their observations not later than 18 August', Cabinet 40 of 1931, meeting 30 July.

The May Report dissolved whatever reassurance the Bank of England's credit of 28 July had given foreign investors. On 6 August Sir Ernest Harvey, Deputy Governor of the Bank, reported to the Chancellor that the Bank has lost £60 million in gold and foreign exchange in the past four weeks and that the rate of liquidation now was increasing. Most significant was the loss of confidence by foreign financial centres in the ability of the City to meet its commitments much longer. He reported a statement to him by the Governor of the Bank of France—confirming the argument in this study that more dexterity in the Government and at the Bank might have averted the crisis—that three weeks earlier it would have been easy for Britain to float a large, long-term loan and so to steady the pound. Now it was impossible. The implication of all this was that the Bank itself was no longer in a position to save national credit and was abdicating this responsibility to the Government without, however, giving up its authority to tell the Government what to do.[1]

The message from the Bank of England on 6 August finally alerted the Government to the disaster impending. Prime Minister Ramsay MacDonald now returned to London and the Treasury was ordered to collect from government departments recommendations on possible economies. On 12 August the Cabinet Committee on National Expenditure—MacDonald, Philip Snowden, Arthur Henderson, J. H. Thomas, the Dominions Secretary and former Secretary of the National Union of Railwaymen, and William Graham, President of the Board of Trade, who with Snowden possessed a substantial training in economics—set to work on an economy programme. The next day, through the Treasury, the Committee asked the Bank of England to enquire from George Harrison of the Federal Reserve in New York whether a large loan could be raised there on the credit not of the Bank of England but of the Government itself. The sums now needed were too large for inter-bank transfers.[2] Harrison replied saying that the British Government ought to be able to raise loans in New York and Paris of about £50 million each but that such a loan would be practicable in America only provided a 'programme of economy was adequate and would receive the approval of Parliament'.[3]

On 19 August the full Cabinet met for the first time since 30 July in a sitting which lasted from 11 in the morning until 10.30 in the evening. It had before it the report of the Cabinet Committee on

---

[1] Clay, *Norman*, 386. It is important to note that Norman, who subsequently became something of a monster from the British Labour point of view, suffered a nervous breakdown at the end of July which kept him completely detached from affairs during the entire period of the crisis until 23 September.

[2] *Ibid.*, 387.

[3] *Ibid.*, 390.

National Expenditure drawn up as a result of the discussions of the previous week.[1] The report bore little resemblance to the May Committee recommendation. First there was Snowden's terrifying revelation, intimated to the Cabinet Committee on 12 August, that the prospective budget deficit was not £120 million as estimated by the May Committee, still less the £37 million expected in the spring, but £170 million. Moreover, whereas the May Committee had recommended economies of £66,500,000 in unemployment insurance, of which about £28,900,000 would have come from a reduction in the rate and duration of benefits, the Cabinet Committee had been able to recommend a saving of only £48,500,000 in unemployment insurance of which in fact only £28,500,000 represented genuine reductions.[2]

The May Committee Report had made the cost of unemployment insurance a public question; the Cabinet of 19 August made it a problem. At this meeting the final agony of the Labour Government began. Suddenly the gap appeared between social justice and fiscal responsibility. What the government could afford according to accepted economic tenets and what the working population needed in order to keep alive could not be reconciled in financial terms.

In the course of the discussion it became clear that while the Cabinet

[1] PRO Cab. 24/222, CP 203, 'Report of the Committee on National Expenditure', n.d. This is not to be confused with the report of the May Committee.

[2]
Deficit	£170,000,000
Total Economies	78,575,000

Reduced Deficit to be made up from taxation	91,425,000

Of the economies, the £28,500,000 from unemployment insurance was divided as follows:

Removal of anomalies (legislation already drawn)	£3,000,000
Reducing duration of benefit to 26 weeks (recommended by May Committee)	8,000,000
Increased contributions to 10d. each from worker, employer and government	15,000,000
Premium (tax on those drawing standard benefit to help pay for transitional benefit)	2,500,000
	£28,500,000

In addition:

Transitional benefit to be transferred to local authorities	£20,000,000
	£48,500,000

Most of the other economies would have come from reductions of pay in Government employees in the Civil Service, the fighting services, and particularly in education. CP. 203

were prepared, though with reluctance, to accept as a temporary measure to meet the emergency, certain of the economies set out in C.P. 203, ... the Cabinet were not prepared to entertain the main recommendations of the May Committee in regard to Unemployment Insurance, including the proposal (rejected by the Cabinet Committee) for a reduction of benefits, and also a suggestion that persons who have fallen out of insurance should be handed over to the Public Assistance Authorities.[1]

The next day, Thursday, MacDonald and Snowden met Neville Chamberlain and Herbert Samuel whom they had already seen on 13 August.[2] The Conservative and Liberal leaders effectively closed one avenue of escape from the crisis by refusing to join the Government in supporting the budget cuts proposed in the Cabinet Committee memorandum. They had 'doubts as to the feasibility of securing' the reductions contemplated in the fighting service budgets. Ominously, Chamberlain emphasized that the economies in unemployment insurance 'would fail to satisfy expectations', and that unless larger cuts were made in the programme 'the whole scheme would be rendered ineffective'. In a private conversation with MacDonald after the general meeting, Chamberlain restated the Conservative refusal to offer any support without 'more drastic action' in cutting unemployment insurance. Neither could there be further taxation. Chamberlain suggested that about £100 million was the fee his party would demand for aid to the Labour Government.[3]

The Labour Government's dilemma now was apparent. Foreign support for sterling, as communications from the Bank emphasized, was dependent upon the confidence of foreign bankers in the intentions of the Government to cut national expenditure. This confidence would not be restored by a simple declaration from the Government itself, but must be the result of action by Parliament encompassing the agreement of all parties. But the consensus of Parliament, specifically of the Conservatives who controlled 263 seats to Labour's 280, was con-

---

[1] PRO Cab. 23/67, Cabinet 41 of 1921, meeting 19 August 1931.

[2] Neither the Conservative nor the Liberal Parliamentary chief was present on 20 August. Lloyd George was ill, recovering from a prostate operation, and Baldwin, taking his customary August holiday at Aix-les-Bains, had returned to France. As a consequence, Herbert Samuel and Neville Chamberlain represented their parties. Herbert Samuel, *Memoirs* (London, 1945), 202. Far more important, the Deputy Governor of the Bank of England, Ernest Harvey, after having requested on 6 August permission to do so, had met the Opposition leaders and given them the facts of the crisis. Clay, *Norman*, 386.

[3] PRO Cab. 23/67, Cabinet 42 of 1931, meeting 20 August. Hastings Lees-Smith, President of the Board of Education reported that he had spoken privately to Samuel who, speaking for Lloyd George, had also demanded further cuts in unemployment insurance.

tingent upon the near-destruction of the unemployment insurance programme which at last had come close to embodying society's responsibility for the maintenance of livelihood that Labour had demanded since the First World War. A Labour Government could not cut the programme and remain a working man's Government.[1]

Soon it became clear that even the modest reductions proposed by the Cabinet Committee were unpalatable to the Labour movement. After the Cabinet of 20 August, Snowden and MacDonald met a committee of the General Council of the Trades Union Congress headed by Ernest Bevin and Walter Citrine. The TUC leadership, Snowden reported the next day, appeared to have no conception of the crisis. They refused to contemplate any cuts whatever in unemployment insurance, teachers' salaries, or fighting services' pay, or even reductions in the modest expenditure for road works. The only economies to which they were not completely opposed were savings in the salaries of Cabinet ministers and judges.[2] The MacDonald administration was caught. Steps that were necessary for it to take as the executive of the nation in order to save the national credit, it was prohibited from taking as the representative of the working class.

The next day, before the Cabinet meeting, MacDonald and Harvey met again. Harvey, MacDonald reported, said that one half the budget deficit must be offset by economies. One third would not be enough to restore confidence. But this was not all.

> It was, in the Deputy Governor's view, essential, particularly from the point of view of foreign interests concerned, that very substantial economies should be effected on Unemployment Insurance. In no other way could foreign confidence be restored. The Deputy Governor had also impressed upon the Prime Minister the great danger of further delay, and had reported the views of a distinguished and very friendly foreign financier on the vital need of securing our budgetary equilibrium by bringing our expenditure within our

---

[1] The only member of the Cabinet who showed any enthusiasm for substantial reductions in the unemployment programme was the Chancellor of the Exchequer, Philip Snowden, who lectured the Cabinet on 20 August, pointing out that unemployment insurance was likely to cost £143 million in the 1931–32 fiscal year and that 'of this great sum, real savings proposed to date, as opposed to increases in contributions and the transfer of the responsibility for the transitional benefit to the local authority, amounted to only about 5 per cent'. Cab. 42 of 1931, meeting 20 August.

[2] PRO Cab. 23/67, Cabinet 43 of 1931, meeting 21 August. See also: Alan Bullock, *The Life and Times of Ernest Bevin* (London, 1960), I, 476–503. The TUC informed the Cabinet simply that it opposed 'any worsening of the position of the unemployed'. Walter Citrine, *Men at Work* (London, 1964), 283.

revenue and by abstaining from borrowing and from using capital as income.[1]

The Cabinet was now under orders to act. The restoration of confidence did not mean simply economies, but specifically economies in unemployment insurance. For practical purposes this meant a reduction in the 17s. and 15s. benefits for men and women. For several hours the Cabinet unhappily debated the alternatives. Everyone agreed that a 5 per cent cut in benefits would be too small to do any good. It must be 10 per cent, amounting to about a £12 million saving, or nothing. There was virtually no discussion of the 20 per cent cut recommended by the May Committee. So appeared the rock upon which the Labour Government would founder. The Cabinet finally parted about equally divided upon whether there should be a 10 per cent cut or no cut at all. After the Cabinet, MacDonald saw the Bank and the leaders of the Opposition again. He had little more to show them than a revised version of CP 203, promising economies of £56,375,000 of which the genuine total savings on unemployment insurance were £22 million. Theoretically the Exchequer deficit was only £93 million, but £20 million of this was achieved on paper by the transfer to the rates of the £20 million cost of the transitional benefit, leaving a real deficit of £113,625,000.[2]

Again, MacDonald left the Cabinet to plead with the Opposition and the Bank. He received answers supplementing each other so well that the historian is driven to the conclusion that there was regular communication between them. Morgan's had already cabled stipulating that a public loan would require prior parliamentary action. Although 'agreement of Party Leaders on a supporting programme might be adequate for a private credit transaction', it 'is going to take a great deal more than simply a joint declaration of three Party Leaders to convince the investment and banking public here that real amendment has been undertaken and that the Government is in a position to command heavy foreign favours'.[3] To this, Ernest Harvey of the Bank of England had added that if the economies of CP 203 were the Government's 'final word' it was 'of no value'. The real saving, said the Bank, was only about £42 million. Other 'so-called economies' were really new taxation which would ease the Exchequer but which would burden the employer and the workman. A saving on unemployment insurance, the symbol of Government sincerity, was imperative: 'It could not be too clearly recognized that foreign leaders regarded the heavy financial burdens on industry of the Unemployment Insurance

---

[1] Cabinet 43 of 1931, meeting 21 August 1931.
[2] Cabinet 43 of 1931, meeting 21 August 1931, Appendix.
[3] Clay, *Norman*, 390.

M

scheme as impairing the security for their loans.' The present proposals, concluded the Bank, would worsen confidence rather than improve it.[1]

Unquestionably Opposition leaders knew of the importance attached
abroad to their public support of the Government and understood the
power this fact gave them. If their public participation was necessary
to save the pound perhaps they could exact a price that would force
the Labour party to disavow its own principles. On the other hand, if
the Labour Government failed to maintain the national credit, the
responsibility would be its own. Hence, both Conservative and Liberal
leaders, Chamberlain, Sir Samuel Hoare, Herbert Samuel and Donald
Maclean, refused any help. Parliament, they insisted, must be summoned.[2] Everything, said the Opposition leaders, was the Government's sole responsibility and the Liberals served notice that they
would no longer support the Cabinet. 'All party leaders', MacDonald
reported to the Cabinet, 'looked for economies which in the aggregate
would be greater than the figure of £56 million. They urged, however,
that the real weakness of the proposals was the failure to secure adequate economies on Unemployment Insurance.'[3]

Meeting the next day, on 23 August, MacDonald informed the
Cabinet that the game was up. Could he inform the Opposition that the
Government would save a further £20 million—£12,250,000 by a
10 per cent reduction in unemployment insurance benefits and
£7,750,000 in other ways? In the first of two critical votes—with only
two members dissenting, Snowden and J. H. Thomas, who asked that
their votes be recorded—the Cabinet refused to commit the Government to the new reductions. However following a long lecture by
Snowden warning that going off the gold standard would mean a
50 per cent cut in the British standard of living, the Cabinet agreed,
apparently unanimously, to permit the Prime Minister to discuss the
benefit cuts with the Opposition, as a principle only, specifically without committing the Government to it in any way.[4] On this unheroic

---

[1] PRO Cab. 23/67, Cabinet 44 of 1931, meeting 22 August.
[2] Cabinet 44 of 1931, meeting 22 August. Baldwin, enjoying the waters of Aix,
did not yet feel called upon to return. Lest Labour capitulate too easily, Chamberlain had told MacDonald the day before that he was certain the cooperation of his
party would not be attained by the cuts in unemployment insurance so far proposed.
Even if the Conservatives agreed to support the Government in Parliament he was
certain that they would demand 'more drastic action' in cutting unemployment
insurance. Cabinet 42 of 1931, meeting 20 August.
[3] Cabinet 44 of 1931, meeting 22 August. Should the Cabinet deceive itself into
thinking that it could fool the financial world by false economies, the Conservative
leaders curtly warned against suspending the Sinking Fund. 'Any attempt of this
kind to camouflage the true position would be at once detected.' The budget
would have to be balanced 'in an honest fashion and not by recourse to borrowing'.
[4] Cabinet 44 of 1931, meeting 22 August 1931.

note the meeting adjourned, agreeing to meet again after the Prime Minister and the Chancellor of the Exchequer had seen the Opposition.

Thus the Labour Government put itself entirely in the hands of the Opposition. It could resolve neither to take action nor to refrain from action. It had offered a plan which it hoped would save the pound without agreeing to, indeed decisively rejecting, the implementation of the plan should it be accepted. The power for effective decision, the Opposition leaders well understood, lay with themselves in their power to impress the New York money market. But in talking to Mac-Donald, the Conservatives refused responsibility for decisions the Government itself was unwilling to take. Specifically, they told Mac-Donald and Snowden that they would not make any commitment about the effect of a further £20 million reduction in Government spending but said that the question should go to the bankers anyway. As MacDonald told the Cabinet when it reassembled at 2.30 in the afternoon, both he and Snowden had 'derived the impression that if the banking interests were ready to regard the proposition as adequate and satisfactory the Party Leaders would accept it...'. Chamberlain had again reiterated that the real Conservative interest was in reductions in spending on unemployment insurance.[1]

The final action of the short Cabinet on Saturday afternoon was a request for authorization by MacDonald to tell Sir Ernest Harvey of the Bank of England of the hypothetical £20 million cut in spending, upon which the Cabinet had not agreed, and to permit the Bank of England to transmit confidentially this proposal to New York. Norman's biographer makes clear that Harvey saw the Conservative leaders after his interview with MacDonald and that they gave him the assurances they had refused MacDonald: that if Morgan's considered a further £20 million cut acceptable the Conservative party would support the Government programme, although they reserved for themselves the right to move amendments increasing the amount of economies.[2]

It was now Sunday and because of the time difference between London and New York a meeting of bankers in North America was hard to organize. As a consequence, at 7.00 p.m. when the Cabinet assembled, the Government had no response to its question of the

[1] PRO Cab. 23/67, Cabinet 45 of 1931, meeting 22 August. This was the second Cabinet of this day.
[2] Clay, *Norman*, 390. This supposition tends to be confirmed by MacDonald's report to the Cabinet on 23 August, Sunday, saying that while he had not seen the Opposition leaders since the previous day they had already 'undertaken' to support Government proposals if they were acceptable to the American bankers. This amounted to an acceptance of the £20 million reduction which he and Snowden together had been unable to obtain the previous day. In effect, the Bank was now mediating between the Government and the Opposition. PRO Cab. 23/67, Cabinet 46 of 1931, meeting 23 August.

previous day. Morgan's answer, sent through the Morgan Grenfell Partners in London, transmitted to Harvey, finally arrived at 10 Downing Street at 9.10 p.m. The message was helpful but unclear. 'Tell your friends,' Harvey was instructed,

in the event that they should desire financial co-operation we shall always do our utmost to meet their wishes. If the suggestion were to take the form of a public loan offering we are confident that until Parliament convenes and acts and until we have had an opportunity to feel out our own investment community we could render no favourable opinion whatsoever. If the suggestion however were to take the form of a short-term Treasury operation that would be less difficult and if the British Government should desire us to canvass among ourselves and our immediate friends such a suggestion we should take the matter up vigorously tomorrow morning and be able to give you an answer by our closing tomorrow afternoon.

Kindly let us know subsequent to the results of the Cabinet meeting which you said will be held this evening whether the Government wishes us to explore promptly this possibility. The furthest we have gone today has been to discuss among ourselves the possibility of a short credit in this market from \$100,000,000 to \$150,000,000 and we have as above indicated assumed that as a condition the French Banking Market would do an equivalent amount. When we speak of short-term we have roughly in mind Ninety Day Treasury Bills subject to renewal for an inclusive period of one year.

While the cable said nothing about a cut of £20 million in expenditure it concluded with the remark: 'Are we right in assuming that the programme under consideration will have the sincere approval and support of the Bank of England and of the City generally ... ?'[1]

This, then, was the answer. It was ambiguous and equivocal, but the implication was reasonably plain. £20 million, of which £12,250,000 would come from unemployment insurance, would secure the confidence of French and American investors provided all parties agreed upon the course of action. But the banking confidence was dependent upon the party agreement and the party agreement was dependent upon the cut in unemployment insurance. The proposal for the insurance cut had come, without any commitment to be sure, from the British Cabinet itself. The Cabinet had now either to accept or reject its own proposal.

MacDonald had already reminded the Cabinet on several occasions that while several of the members might object to a 10 per cent cut in unemployment insurance, failure to make any cut would certainly

[1] Cabinet 46 of 1931, meeting 23 August. Clay, *Norman*, 391-2.

bring the Conservatives to office who would likely reduce benefit by 20 per cent. In general this now was the burden of his argument attempting to secure approval of the Cabinet for their own proposal of two days previously. The Cabinet must approve or reject. If there were any 'important reservations' all must resign. He asked each member of the Cabinet to express a view. When he had finished a majority favoured the cut in unemployment insurance, but a substantial minority, including several of the strongest men in the Cabinet, remained opposed.[1] MacDonald announced immediately that now he would have to advise the King to hold a conference, consisting of Baldwin, Samuel, and himself, because the Cabinet could not agree upon a course of action. After requesting the resignations of his colleagues he visited the King for half an hour that evening.[2]

Although the Labour administration met once again at noon on 24 August, for practical purposes the Government was dead. Essentially, it had been destroyed by its own doctrine. What a cut in unemployment benefits meant in September 1931 in terms of the 2,700,000 insured men and women who were drawing benefits, whether the difference between 17s. and 15s. per week meant much in terms of human privation, or indeed whether the £12,250,000 saved by this reduction in benefits produced a significant economy in the British budget is really irrelevant. Modern economic analysis suggests that spending this sum rather than saving it would have been more beneficial to the British capital structure. The fact was that the foreign bankers, led by Morgan's of the United States, dealt in symbols precisely as did the General Council of the Trades Union Congress. In quite the same way they were prisoners of their beliefs and demanded the insurance cuts with the same insistence that the Labour movement resisted them. They saw unemployment insurance as the epitome of government extravagance and the reduction of its cost as a sign of responsible intentions. Thus £12,250,000 saved in this area meant far more than £12,250,000 saved elsewhere.

But in this connection it is important to emphasize that the New York bankers were concerned with unemployment insurance only and not with British politics. While one may seriously question whether many practising socialists were to be found on the board of J. P. Morgan and Co. in 1931, there is no evidence that the American

[1] The *Daily Herald* reported the next day that the vote was 8–12 for cutting the budget, although with the exception of MacDonald, Snowden and J. H. Thomas, most of the influential Labour leaders, including Henderson, Lansbury, Adamson, were in the minority. More recent scholarship has suggested that the vote may have been nine to eleven with Clynes also opposed. R. Bassett, *Nineteen Thirty One, Political Crisis* (London, 1958), 139. See also: Skidelsky, 'Crisis', *The Times*, 3 December 1968.
[2] Cabinet 46 of 1931, 23 August.

banking community was hostile to the Labour Government as such. Indeed, the evidence is quite the opposite. International banks do not like devaluations of currency and the continual protestations from New York that the banking community there was anxious to help Britain solve her financial problems must have been perfectly genuine. Still more important were the repeated statements that the act which would do most to restore confidence abroad was a Government of all parties, including Labour. One may imagine that this argument, that a Government of cooperation must mean cooperation of the left as well as the right, carried the most weight in inducing a none-too-reluctant Ramsay MacDonald to remain on as Prime Minister.

More equivocal is the part played by the Liberal and Conservative party leaders, particularly the latter. Unquestionably Chamberlain knew the importance of his party's support in securing the foreign confidence necessary to produce a loan. Therefore he raised the price of cooperation above what he expected the Labour Cabinet would be willing to pay. He was by no means opposed to unemployment insurance nor to social reform generally, but he was opposed to extravagance, and he was a committed party man.[1] If unemployment insurance was the exposed nerve of Labour, it was at this point that Chamberlain tormented them. In touch with opinions in British and American banking circles, he understood the importance attached to the symbol of unemployment insurance. The fact that Chamberlain's supporters did not carry out their threat to make further deep cuts in the unemployment benefits when they were in power tends to confirm the supposition that reductions in insurance had been a political weapon rather than a party principle.

In summary then one comes to the conclusion that the Opposition parties deliberately forced the crisis over unemployment insurance, that the Labour administration, by refusing any compromise on this matter, simply connived in its own destruction. By itself, unemployment insurance, and its cost, was hardly significant. The important factor, after all, was the restoration of foreign confidence and this happened once the National Coalition was formed.[2] Even though the Labour Govern-

---

[1] Chamberlain's biographer reports that even before the crisis, in July, MacDonald had proposed a coalition to deal with tariff reform and unemployment insurance. Chamberlain had strongly opposed coalition at this time and had written Baldwin warning him that MacDonald would eventually come to plead for help because of lack of support in his own party. In fact this is what happened. Keith Feiling, *Neville Chamberlain* (London, 1946), 190–1.

[2] At the time of the final run on gold which took Britain off the gold standard on 21 September, Ernest Harvey of the Bank of England explained that besides the dramatic but relatively unimportant event of the Invergordon mutiny, the most important cause of foreign loss of confidence and of the drain on gold was the fear abroad that after the General Election then scheduled for 27 October, the National

ment had been warned that no simple economy statements by the leadership of the three parties would be sufficient to inspire confidence abroad and that an act of Parliament, supported by all parties, would be necessary, in fact the required loan was made immediately after the announcement of the National Government without any reference to insurance or anything else. Whether the same loan would have been granted had the Labour Government been able to agree unilaterally upon a cut in unemployment insurance, without the formation of a Coalition, is uncertain. The messages from Morgan's, filtered through the Bank of England, always assumed that the two would come about together. Conservative betting was that the first, the cuts in unemployment insurance, would not happen without the second, the formation of a Coalition. They were right.

The beginnings of a social policy

Once the National Government was announced on 24 August, the question of unemployment insurance benefits suddenly became unimportant. Not surprisingly, the loans from abroad, £40 million from New York and Paris, which had been the subject for so much anxious consideration three days before, appeared as if by magic on 27 August, not only before the Cabinet announced any economies but before it had decided upon the economies it would make.[1] Eventually, on 2 September, the new administration agreed, with very little discussion on the matter, to save about £35 million on unemployment insurance. This was in fact a smaller amount from unemployment insurance alone than the Labour Government Cabinet had proposed in CP 203. It included the £12,250,000 saving from a 10 per cent reduction in benefits, a £3 million saving from the removal of anomalies as the result of a bill which the Labour Government had already introduced, and £10 million in new income by increasing contributions to 10d. a week for both employer and workman. The other £10 million was intended to come from the introduction of a means test into the transitional benefit,

Government would break up. PRO Cab. 23/68, Cabinet 59 of 1931, meeting 17 September. In a review of the dealings with foreign bankers given the Cabinet on 15 September, dealing, however, only with negotiations since the formation of the National Government, Snowden specified that 'no political or other condition of any was made in connection with the credits'. PRO Cab. 24/223, CP 230, 'Negotiations of the British Treasury Credits in the United States and in France', September 1931.

[1] The new Cabinet Economy Committee, made up of MacDonald, Baldwin, Donald Maclean and Philip Cunliffe-Lister, made its first report on 28 August. PRO Cab. 24/223, CP 208, 'Economy Committee Report'. MacDonald and his colleagues still hoped to keep the support of the Labour party and strongly resisted pressure from Chamberlain and Sir Henry Betterton, the new Minister of Labour, to transfer all persons on transitional benefit to the Public Assistance authorities.

now to be styled the 'transitional payment'. The test would be administered by Public Assistance authorities, although the money for the payment would come from the Treasury. In addition the standard benefit was limited to 26 weeks per year.[1] It must be noted that because under the new plan the Treasury supported the transitional payments and made up all deficiencies in the insurance fund, limiting the standard benefit to 26 weeks did not, by itself, save the National Government any money. It simply transferred the cost of relief to another account. The savings appeared only when the applicant 'failed' his means test. The Labour Government would have put the cost of transitional benefits on the rates. Thus the expense of those who had run out of the standard 26 weeks benefit would have been saved by the Exchequer, not by the taxpaper.

Overall, the National Government economies were not quite £10 million less than those proposed by Labour and over £25 million less than those recommended by the May Committee. At the Cabinet meeting dealing with unemployment insurance it was asked whether there might not be some comment on the contrast between the approximately £70 million actually saved by the National Government and the £96½ million presumably needed. The answer, it was agreed, would be that about £22 million of the May Committee savings were simply transfers from the Exchequer to the rates, and members of the Cabinet were urged to explain this publicly whenever they were challenged on the subject.[2]

Parliament finally reassembled on 8 September and immediately passed the National Economy Act which specified that, for one month following 30 September 1931, the Government could make economies in specified ministries by Orders in Council. Among many other orders issued under this act were the Unemployment Insurance (National Economy) Orders, No. 1 and 2, dated 1 and 7 October 1931. The first of these set, from 5 October, a new 10d. contribution from employee, employer and the State alike and provided for reduced benefits of 15s. 3d. for single men and 13s. 6d. for women with proportionate reductions for dependent wives and children, all to go into effect three days later. The second Order outlined a number of substantive changes in the insurance programme itself. On 12 November 1931, the transitional benefit would be replaced by a new

[1] PRO Cab. 23/68, Cabinet 52 of 1931, meeting 2 September. The comparable figures in CP 203, it will be remembered, had been £28½ million in direct savings on insurance plus a saving of £20 million on the transitional benefit by transferring it to the rates. The chief differences were that the Labour Government had intended to limit the standard benefit to 26 weeks which would have saved £8 million, and had considered increasing contributions to 1s., which would have brought in an extra £5 million.

[2] Cabinet 52 of 1931, meeting 2 September.

'transitional payments' scheme based on a test of need to be administered by the local Public Assistance authorities, although the money
for the benefits themselves would come from the Exchequer. In no
case could the total amount of the transitional payment benefit be
greater than the ordinary standard benefit which would be appropriate
for the same family. Public Assistance authorities were specifically
enjoined to 'deal with the case as if they were estimating the need of
an unemployed, able-bodied person who had applied for public assistance, but as if such assistance could be given only in money'. In
effect, the applicant was to be treated as if he were requesting old-
fashioned Poor Law relief except that the guardians were prohibited
from using the workhouse test. Although the Government did not
wish to emphasize the differences between the transitional payments
scheme and unemployment insurance, the order provided that the
decision of the Public Assistance authority in every case was final and
that there would be no appeal to referees under the insurance scheme.

The changes effected in unemployment insurance under the National
Economy Act of 1931 were proclaimed at the time to be only temporary.
While it is a tradition of politics that temporary institutions often
display a surprising durability, the Government found little satisfaction
in the hurried arrangements made in the autumn of 1931 and soon was
preparing what must be counted as the fifth major reconstruction on
unemployment insurance since its establishment in 1911.[1] The most
serious problem was the administration of the transitional payment
programme by local Public Assistance authorities. Here standards varied
widely, being affected both by the political philosophy of the authority
and by its attitude towards the national administration. The critical
factor was that the funds disbursed by the Public Assistance authority were provided by another level of administration, independent
of local rateable values, and limited only by ordinary book-keeping
accountability. The upshot was a wide variation in the assessment of
means of applicants for relief and in the rate of relief itself. During
1932 over the country as a whole only about 50 per cent of persons
receiving benefit were found to have no resources at all, although
among approximately 200 Public Assistance authorities only about ten
made consistent trouble by over-generous grants of relief. Eventually
two authorities, Rotherham and County Durham, had to be suspended

---

[1] By way of review the others were:
1. The adoption of universal insurance under the act of 1920.
2. The adoption of the principle, if not the practice, of benefit as of right and
   in proportion to need with the uncovenanted and dependants' benefits in
   the three Unemployment Acts of 1921.
3. The Blanesburgh revisions of 1927.
4. The termination of all Government control over the granting of benefit by
   the act of 1930.

and superseded by special commissioners appointed by the Minister of Labour who administered transitional payments until the establishment of the Unemployment Assistance Board in 1935.[1]

From the beginning the Treasury, which traditionally disliked disbursing money through any other than its own agents, had brought pressure to wind up the transitional payments scheme. Its antipathy was increased by the Transitional Payments (Determination of Need) Act of 1932, which increased the cost of the scheme by requiring Public Assistance authorities to disregard portions of pension and investment income belonging to an applicant, and by the continual pressure from both sides of the House of Commons to restore the 1931 cuts in standard benefit. Transitional payments, during both 1933 and 1934, already consumed a larger amount of money and supported more people than did unemployment insurance and any proposal for an increase in the standard benefit, which would raise automatically the transitional payments ceiling, was bound to cause unhappiness among the custodians of the national revenue.[2] Hence, by the autumn of 1932, civil servants in the Treasury and in the Ministry of Labour were at work on a measure to establish a government network of relief officers that would supersede the local authorities.

Out of these considerations the Unemployment Assistance Board evolved. The UAB was not, as frequently has been suggested, a result of the Royal Commission on Unemployment Insurance. Indeed well before the signing of the report on 27 October 1932, Neville Chamberlain, assisted by Horace Wilson, was at work on plans for restoring Treasury control of the huge expenditures for transitional payments.[3] As its own proposals for handling need-related relief outside unemployment insurance, the Royal Commission had recommended a new local committee to be called the 'Unemployment Assistance Committee', adjunct to the local authority but closely supervised by the Ministry of Labour. But fundamentally the Commission had been more concerned with restoring solvency to the unemployment insurance fund and with

---

[1] See: Ronald C. Davison, *British Unemployment Policy* (London, 1938), 22–5.
[2] In these two years, transitional benefit cost, with administration, £101 million. Insurance benefit during the same period cost £91½ million although with the removal of the burden of inconvenanted benefits the insurance fund by 1934 had begun again to pay its way. Registered unemployment did not go below two million until the beginning of 1935.
[3] In a letter to his sister, dated 15 October 1932, Neville Chamberlain, by now Chancellor of the Exchequer, said that he and the Minister of Labour were at work in a scheme to remove the relief of the able-bodied unemployed from the local authorities and to put it outside of party politics. Ian Macleod, *Neville Chamberlain* (London, 1961), 164. On this basis Macleod gives Chamberlain credit for the original idea of the Unemployment Assistance Board.

removing all discretionary payments from labour exchanges than with considering the general problem of workers' relief.[1]

Basically, the Unemployment Bill, introduced on 30 September 1933 by the Minister of Labour, Sir Henry Betterton, was a well-meant attempt to remove the critical problem of unemployment relief from politics. The bill proposed the creation of two new non-political boards, the Unemployment Insurance Statutory Committee and the Unemployment Assistance Board. The first, dealt with in Part I of the bill, was to be a body of seven unpaid members and a secretary which received as its principal duty the task of overseeing the solvency of the unemployment insurance fund and of recommending to the Minister of Labour changes in the rate of benefit and contributions that would guard the fund. It took over, thus, duties which had always lain with the Treasury. But unlike the Treasury, the new board was to be concerned not only with saving money but with seeing that unemployment insurance worked smoothly. It was charged with supervising the efficiency of the programme from a social, as well as a financial, point of view. The act provided also for the funding of the huge debt that unemployment insurance owed the Treasury so that the scheme could have, in a sense, a new beginning unburdened by the financial weight of accumulated past mistakes. The funded debt, amounting to £105,780,000 was to be repaid at the rate of £5 million per year, including principal and interest, over the next 37 years. With the burden of the debt removed, the scheme was expected to be self-supporting.

All in all the Unemployment Insurance Statutory Committee did its work well, although it would be false to say that its independent, semi-judicial, position insulated it altogether from all pressures. By September 1939 it had reduced the fixed obligations of Unemployment Insurance from £105 million to £77 million. At the same time the insurance fund itself possessed a balance of £57,555,000 and was earning about 2 per cent of this figure.[2] Even with these savings the Board was able to extend both the coverage and the amounts of the unemployment insurance standard benefits. In 1935 children's benefits were increased from 2s. to 3s. per child, at a cost of about £1 million per year, and in 1936 the contribution was reduced from 10d. for employee, employer

[1] *Cmd. 4185*, 'Royal Commission on Unemployment Insurance, Final Report,' 1932. The Commission, appointed in December 1930 with a good deal of fanfare, was supposed to be a successor to the Commission on the Poor Laws of 1909. Unfortunately by the time its final report was signed, the May Committee, which used much of its data, the preliminary work on the Unemployment Assistance Board, and generally the convulsions of 1931, had rendered much of it out of date.
[2] 'Report of the Unemployment Insurance Statutory Committee on the Financial Condition of the Unemployment Insurance Fund on 31st December 1939', *Accounts and Papers, 1939/40*, VII, No. 81, Appendix B, 24–5.

and government to 9d. each, resulting in a loss of insurance income of about £6,500,000 per year. In 1936 also the Statutory Committee recommended reducing the waiting time for unemployment benefits from six days to three. Most trade unions required a week's wait, but since labour exchanges paid benefit only on Thursday and Friday an unemployed man could conceivably go for nearly two weeks between his last week's wages and his first benefit. Finally in March 1938, adult dependants' benefit was increased from 9s. to 10s.

Although the Unemployment Insurance Statutory Committee was able to conduct its business, as a general thing, without interference from Westminster politicians, it never was entirely safe from ordinary intra-governmental skirmishing. Thus, as W. H. Beveridge pointed out rather astringently in his last report at the beginning of the war, although it received only 2 per cent on its own funds, it was required to pay 3⅛ per cent upon its funded debt to the Treasury. Again, when the unemployment insurance contribution was reduced by 1d. for employees, employers and the government in July 1936, this change coincided with an increase of 1d. in the contribution for old-age pensioners. There was no saving for either the employer or the employee contributor but the Treasury saved £2 million. Finally, the date of the reduction in the waiting period for unemployment insurance from six days to three days, 1 April 1937, coincided with the appointed day for the Unemployment Assistance Board's assumption of responsibility for those of the able-bodied unemployed who previously had been clients of the Public Assistance authorities. Because of the six-day requirement, the waiting period might well run to nearly two weeks and many unemployed men with an unquestioned right to standard benefit were driven to apply for tax-supported Unemployment Assistance Board relief while waiting for their insurance benefit to begin. A shortened waiting period therefore meant a good deal in terms of Treasury savings. So the Treasury which, in the 1920s, had always supported longer waiting periods or any expedient which might result in savings for the unemployment fund, now threw its considerable influence behind a shorter waiting period, keeping men off unemployment assistance for which it was completely responsible. The fact was that the growing surplus in the unemployment insurance fund was nearly as embarrassing politically as had been the deficit in the previous decade.[1]

Despite the tendency of the Treasury to take advantage of the new prosperity of the Unemployment Insurance Fund, Part I of the Unemployment Act of 1934 must be considered a substantial success. Part II of the act establishing a national Unemployment Assistance

[1] For a discussion see: Davison, *Unemployment Policy*, 52–4.

Board to administer benefits through local offices to those receiving transitional payments and to able-bodied paupers on public assistance encountered many more problems. From the beginning, the bill was fiercely contested by the Labour party in Parliament so that the House of Commons spent 27 days discussing the measure, the longest period spent on any single piece of legislation before the House since the First World War. (The record was soon broken by the Government of India Act.) Labour's argument was the thesis of the Labour movement itself: that the welfare of the working man was, or should be, the chief concern of democratic politics and that to attempt to remove it from parliamentary contention was in effect to remove from popular control the most important of all issues. The measure was inspired, the party argued, by political and financial calculation, not social needs.[1]

The Unemployment Act attempted to insulate the Unemployment Assistance Board from political pressure in every conceivable way. The salaries of its six members, to aggregate not more than £12,000 per year, were to be determined by the Treasury at the time of its appointment and to be drawn directly from the Consolidated Fund. Its members would hold office at the pleasure of the Crown and be eligible for reappointment. The Minister of Labour, while responsible for answering questions in Parliament on the board's activities for general policy and for obtaining money, would have no control over its day-to-day operation. On the other hand its regulations would have the force of statutory rules and orders in that after having been laid before Parliament they would be the law unless they were rejected by that body. More important, unlike other existing semi-official corporate bodies such as the British Broadcasting Corporation or the London Passenger Transport Board, the Unemployment Assistance Board would have no income of its own and, while being virtually independent of Parliament for purposes of question and control, would be spending large sums voted by the House of Commons.

The board was given wide powers, not only to give assistance indefinitely according to need to any individual applying to it who qualified as being regularly in insurable employment, but also to set up training schemes and work schemes all supported from taxes. In effect, it could deal not only with unemployment resulting from economic factors but from personal failings as well.

Through its local staff, the board would become virtually a centralized Poor Law for all working people in the country. It would take over the relief of all workmen not receiving unemployment insurance: those on transitional payments, and the remaining able-bodied poor on

[1] See: Davison, *Unemployment Policy*, 45; John D. Millett, *The British Unemployment Assistance Board, A Case Study in Administrative Autonomy* (New York, 1940), 36–43.

public assistance—agricultural labourers, self-employed, or those under 16, anyone who for one reason or another, although theoretically available for employment, had not hitherto been covered by the unemployment insurance acts. Finally, the act restored the cuts of 1931 and extended the coverage of unemployment insurance by dropping it to 14 years, the school-leaving age.[1]

A lesson learned: the Unemployment Assistance Board

The act received the Royal Assent on 28 June 1934 and the next day the membership of the UAB was announced. The new board was composed of the previous Minister of Labour, Sir Henry Betterton, as Chairman, who became Baron Rushcliffe of Blackfordby, Sir Ernest Strohmenger of the Ministry of Health as Vice-Chairman, together with Violet Markham, H. M. Hallsworth, Thomas Jones, and M. A. Reynard, as members. Considering the widely-advertised non-political position of the board, Jones' appointment is important. Although he would become a biographer of Lloyd George, he was at this time a friend and close confidant of Stanley Baldwin. When Strohmenger, who was not popular on the board and received much of the blame for the difficulties into which it fell, resigned in 1937, Miss Markham took his place as Vice-Chairman. Hallsworth was a Professor of Economics at the University of Durham and Reynard had been Director of Public Assistance in Glasgow.[2]

The act stipulated that the board's activities on behalf of the two groups of unemployed for which it was responsible would begin on two separate 'appointed days' which would be set by the Minister of Labour. On the first appointed day the board would take over the 800,000 people on the old transitional payments scheme and on the second it would assume care of the 200,000 or so more of the able-bodied unemployed presently supported from the rates by the Public

[1] In 1936 after long and anxious consideration an unemployment insurance scheme for agricultural workers was established. Both contributions and benefits were substantially lower than those for the rest of the working population. As it turned out, the plan was scarcely needed. In July 1936 after the act had made the first accurate count of agricultural unemployment possible, it was discovered that only about 17,000 or barely 3 per cent of the total agricultural labouring population of 588,000 were unemployed as opposed to 12·6 per cent for the rest of the insured population at the same time. The acturial calculations of the act had assumed an agricultural unemployment of 7·5 per cent. On this act see: Wilbur J. Cohen, *Unemployment Insurance and Agricultural Labour in Great Britain* (Washington 1940), SSRC pamphlet.

[2] Betterton's salary was £5,000 per year, £1,500 more than the salary of Warren Fisher, the Permanent Secretary of the Treasury and Head of the Civil Service, while Strohmenger's was £3,000. When Strohmenger resigned he was replaced by Violet Markham, however at a salary of £750.

Assistance authorities. The first appointed day was set as 7 January 1935 and the second as 1 March of the same year.

A far more complicated duty devolving upon the board itself rather than the Minister of Labour, was the drafting of regulations under which the new assistance would be offered. The act specified that the board should give draft regulations to the minister within four months and that these would be laid before the House of Commons to be accepted or rejected as a whole. The regulations were submitted to the House of Commons on 11 December and debated on 17 December. Although the act had stipulated that in determining an applicant's needs the board should disregard a number of important items of income such as friendly society and health insurance benefits, military pensions, and certain private savings and investments and despite the insistence of the new Minister of Labour, Oliver Stanley, that the proposed scale of benefits would cost the State about £3 million more than the present aggregate outlay for transitional payments, Labour argued that the scale was below that presently being paid by some Public Assistance authorities and moved an amendment rejecting the scale on this basis.[1] Generally, however, the UAB scales received little attention and even though Labour and the Liberals asserted later that they had warned of disaster from the beginning, there was very little intelligent criticism of the UAB scales before the appointed day.[2]

Meanwhile, the board was establishing a vast service for the administration of relief. It recruited some 6,000 officials from government departments and local authorities. The country was divided into 28 districts which in turn were subdivided into 239 areas. Local office accommodations were found and 140 local appeals tribunals appointed. So far as was reasonably possible everything was ready on 7 January 1935 when the board assumed responsibility for the first 800,000 unemployed who until that time had been receiving transitional payments based upon means tests assessed by the local Public Assistance authorities according to their own scale of relief.

The uproar that began during the second week of January was thus entirely unexpected. At first no one seemed sure what was the cause

[1] H of C Deb., CCXCVI (17–19 December 1934), cols. 829–927, 967–1088, 1163–1284. The most frequent and vigorous speaker on the Labour side was Aneurin Bevan.

[2] In the words of the PEP Broadsheet published four months later, although the new regulations were 'criticised as being a little harsh in some particulars, the general consensus of opinion was that the new scale and means test were reasonable and adequate. The Government which had declared its intention that the unemployed as a whole should be better off as a result of the new arrangements, estimated that an additional £3,000,000 would reach those who come under the Board.' Planning, PEP Broadsheet 47, 'Inquest on the Unemployment Act', 26 March 1935, 4–5.

of the discontent. The *Economist* suggested that perhaps the new machinery was working 'a bit stiffly' and the board itself was inclined to suggest that reports were all exaggerated.[1]

Nevertheless, throughout the country, particularly in Wales and in the North, MPs about to return from the Christmas recess were overwhelmed with complaints from deputations of workmen's organizations. Public demonstrations occurred almost daily. The theme of the protest was always the same: that the payments under the new UAB scales, far from being more generous than had been given by the old Assistance authorities, were in fact smaller and the incomes of many recipients of relief were being drastically cut. When Parliament reassembled on 28 January, its members, Government as well as Opposition, were in a state of near-panic. The Minister of Labour, Oliver Stanley, attempting to defend a vote of £5 million to operate the board until 31 March, suddenly found himself nearly shouted down by denunciations of the expensive new service over which he officially presided, but which he did not control. He was forced to listen to unpleasant comparisons between the new scientific and presumably intelligently run Assistance Board and the old, until now despised, Poor Law authorities. At no time in the recently completed century of its existence had the new Poor Law been so popular.[2]

The parliamentary clamour and the disturbances through the country unnerved Stanley, the board, and also, uncharacteristically, Neville Chamberlain. Because of what were really elementary administrative errors the Government's chief domestic legislative accomplishment of 1934 had been thrown into disrepute. Not only the Opposition, but members of the Conservative back bench, many holding marginal seats won in the landslide of 1931, demanded publicly the resignation of the Unemployment Assistance Board and privately the additional resignations of Stanley, Chamberlain and, indeed, MacDonald.[3]

---

[1] *Economist*, 2 February 1935; Davison, *Unemployment Policy*, 67.

[2] *H of C Deb.*, CCXCVII (28 January 1935), cols. 37–156. By sheer bad luck the Cabinet was at this time distracted by the first of the great crises in foreign affairs which led to the Second World War, Germany's victory of 13 January 1935 in the plebiscite to determine the future of the Saarland. Pleading for support on 30 January about the 'difficult Parliamentary situation which had arisen', Stanley was scarcely able to obtain a hearing from the Cabinet. PRO Cab. 23/81, Cabinet 6 of 1935, meeting 30 January.

[3] *H of C Deb.*, CCXCVII (12 February 1935), cols. 1805–7. Both Betterton and Stanley offered their resignations at the height of the controversy and Stanley did in fact leave the Labour Ministry for Education upon the general reconstruction of the Government in June. *Economist*, 16 February 1935. For a review of press comment see: Ronald C. Davison, 'Unemployment Assistance: The Crisis and the Way Out', *Nineteenth Century*, CXVII (April, 1935), 431–9. On 6 February in the Wavertree Division of Liverpool the Conservatives lost a seat to Labour by 1,840 votes that the party had won in 1931 with a majority of 23,973.

Behind the Government's panic was the figure of David Lloyd George who had chosen 17 January to announce in a well-publicized speech in Bangor his 'New Deal for Britain'. Essentially the new deal was only an expansion of the Gairloch Plan of 1921 and of the Liberal election pamphlet of 1929, *We can Conquer Unemployment,* now polished however with Keynesian terminology and publicity-seeking catchwords. It proposed public investment in industry and a broad programme of public works supervised by an economic general staff paid for—in order to frustrate interference by the Bank of England—by a popularly-subscribed 'prosperity loan'.[1]

The contrast between the optimistic and imaginative new deal and the Government's penny-pinching relief scales was too obvious to be ignored even by the most loyal Tory. As a result, coupled with demands that certain members of the front bench resign, there were strong hints that Lloyd George, and perhaps Winston Churchill, should be brought into the Cabinet.[2]

On 5 February, without previously consulting the Cabinet, Stanley announced in the House of Commons that the UAB scales would be suspended in cases where the applicant for relief would receive more money from the old public assistance scales.[3] This was regularized a few days later on 13 February. Bearing as well as it could the jeers of the Labour party coupled with denunciations of allowances paid to members of the Royal Family, the Government put through the Unemployment Assistance (Temporary Provisions) Act, the so-called

[1] *The Times,* 18 January 1935. See also speech at Glasgow, 13 April 1935, *The Times,* 15 April 1935.

[2] *Economist,* 16 February 1935. The repercussions of New Deal announcement continued long after the Government had surrendered on the UAB scales. Prodded by members of their own party looking for an unemployment programme for a general election and by an increasing awareness of the example of gigantic public sector investment in Germany and the United States, the Cabinet went through the motions in ten meetings between February and June of consulting Lloyd George about his programme. The intermediary was Thomas Jones of the UAB whom Lloyd George had first brought into Government service in 1912. Lloyd George used his fellow-countryman to sound Cabinet opinion and Jones promptly passed along all of the former Prime Minister's thoughts to his new patron, Stanley Baldwin. Thomas Jones, *A Diary with Letters, 1931–1950* (London, 1954), 143–52. However the person most opposed to Lloyd George and to Public works, who finally brought the charade to an end, was Neville Chamberlain. Feiling, *Chamberlain,* 242–4, 260.

[3] *H of C Deb.,* CCXVII (5 February 1935), cols. 971–2. Although there were many suggestions that the low scales were the result of Treasury pressure, both Stanley and Chamberlain had disliked the first UAB draft and had required substantial increases before submitting it to Parliament. *Ibid.,* 971; Feiling, *Chamberlain,* 240. The Cabinet, distracted by Germany, agreed to support this concession virtually without discussion. PRO Cab. 23/81, Cabinet 8 of 1935, meeting 6 February.

'standstill act'. Specifically, the standstill act authorized relieving officers to use either the new UAB scales or the old public assistance
scales, whichever was most favourable to the applicant. The critical
factor in this decision appears to have been that in more than half the
public assistance areas the old assessments for transitional payments
were higher than the new scales. Although Stanley refused to admit
he had been mistaken, it had become clear that instead of spending
£3 million more on the transitional payment class, as had been contemplated, the UAB was likely to show a substantial saving in the
current year.[1]

The question remained: what had happened? The Government had
failed, both in attempting to remove the problem of unemployment
from politics and in providing a stable programme that would care for
those unemployed who could not qualify for insurance. The lessons of
the 1920s had been forgotten. The relief of unemployment *was* a
political question. It touched the most intimate of human needs, food,
shelter and clothing. To suppose that free and politically conscious
British citizens would not react through the ordinary political channels
available to them if they became dissatisfied with the method or the
amount of relief was simply unrealistic.

Secondly, by imposing a means test the Government had, in fact,
committed itself to giving relief adequate to need. The Poor Law,
without ever saying so, had long understood this. A relieving officer
simply could not say to the applicant: 'Our investigation shows that
you need 25s. per week to live, therefore we will give you 15s.' This
was, however, what the new Unemployment Assistance Board had done.
The act of 1934, typical of the neat, logical intelligence of Neville
Chamberlain, had been expected to provide a simpler and less arbitrary
apparatus for relieving the poor. Instead it had caused endless com-
plication and hardship. The act had been framed by men who were
experts in government rather than experts in human needs. In order
to avoid official arbitrariness they had caused personal misery by
regulation. And their effort to remove unemployment from the party
arena had caused a political explosion.

Clearly the difficulty lay with lack of imagination rather than lack
of sympathy. Local officials recruited from Public Assistance com-

---

[1] *H of C Deb.*, CCXCVII (12, 13 February 1935), cols. 1781–1883, 1953–2044
Burns, *Unemployment Programmes*, 217. Davison, *Unemployment Policy*, 67. In
the end about half of the recipients of transitional payments chose the new scales.
A report for England, Wales and Scotland, 17–26 June 1936, showed 227,245
under the new scale and 274,918 under the Public Assistance scale. *Cmd. 5240*,
'Unemployment Assistance Act, 1934, Return of number of payments made at
local offices of the Ministry of Labour in the week ending Friday 26th June 1936
. . . under the Unemployment Assistance Regulations, 1934, and the Unemployment Assistance (Temporary Provisions) Act, 1935', 1936.

mittees were intimidated by the voluminous code of instructions which was supposed to answer every question but which did not. The UAB scales, for instance, gave a man with a small household a rent subsidy if he needed it but a man with a larger household, and hence a higher basic allowance, got none. Again, the UAB regulations assumed that in a household in which several members earned wages an equal proportion of each individual's income would be available for rent. This was in fact unrealistic. Subsidiary members of the household could not, or in fact did not, contribute the same proportion of their incomes to the cost of the dwelling as did the head of the house.

Conversely, the other large group of officials at the local bureaux, Unemployment Insurance Offices, were unused to discretionary relief and appear to have been unable to bring themselves to exercise the administrative latitude which in fact they were allowed. They were unaware of the impact of even a small contraction of income upon a poor family. When discretion would have been advisable, they failed to use even the homely 'kitchen pots and pans' intelligence with which Poor Law officials were well acquainted. 'Thus,' reported PEP:

> a destitute unemployed man whose bedding had been destroyed by the local Sanitary Authority after his child had contracted scarlet fever, was unable to obtain the means to purchase new bedding from the Board's local officer, although this plainly was the Board's responsibility. And in another case of a different kind an unemployed man was refused the supplementary allowance which his Public Assistance Committee had formerly made to him under the transitional payment scheme in order that he might visit his wife who was lying in a hospital several miles away.[1]

For practical purposes the independent existence of the UAB came to an end with the uprising of January and February 1935. The Government learned the lesson of the dangers inherent in allowing so critical a matter as unemployment to escape from its control and the board for its part never again attempted to reassert its practical initiative.[2] The situation was clear almost immediately after the standstill act was passed. The board had been prepared to submit amended regulations by May 1935, but the Cabinet, with a General Election in the offing, was in no hurry to alter existing arrangements. It determined, for in-

---

[1] PEP made a careful survey of the UAB difficulties immediately after the Standstill Order. See also: PEP, *Report on the British Social Services* (London, 1937), 151. For a comprehensive, but partisan statement on the operation of the needs test, giving sample scales see: Wal Hannington, *Ten Lean Years* (London, 1940), 120–42.

[2] For a discussion see: Joan Simeon Clarke, *The Assistance Board* (London, 1941), Fabian Research Series No. 57, 13. Probably only the Bank of England was more disliked by the Labour movement.

stance, that whatever cuts were to be made in the scale of benefits they would be spread over a period of at least 18 months whereas any increases would come immediately. To protect itself from its own ignorance, the board set up, under power given it in the act which had hitherto been neglected, about 120 local advisory committees which had the duty both of educating the board and of educating public opinion. The statement at the end of the UAB's first annual report was in effect a declaration of surrender. While insisting that the existing standstill regulations were, and always had been intended to be, temporary, the board admitted that the permanent scale, when it came, must be acceptable to everyone. 'Any action must be gradual and must be carried out in full association with local opinion, so as to give effect to the considerable differences in the locality.' Henceforth the board would always be guided by experience and the Government would be the final arbiter of the political desirability of the board's recommendations.[1]

The revised code of regulations, which finally became available on 9 July 1936, was so comprehensive that it has been described as 'the negation of a code', or a 'code of exceptional circumstances'.[2] The new regulations were expected to involve an extra annual outlay of some £750,000. The average weekly payment that had been 21s. 10d. before 7 January 1935 would now be 23s. The basic standard of existence for a husband and wife remained 24s., except that if a family had no resources at all they would receive the regular unemployment insurance rate which was at that time 26s. The new appointed days were set at 16 November 1936 for those on transitional payments, and 1 April 1937 for able-bodied men drawing public assistance relief.

By and large the new regulations were well received and the new appointed days passed with little difficulty. Part of this could be ascribed to the now substantially declining unemployment. The live register, which had stood at about two million through the winter of 1934–35, was about 1,600,000 by the autumn of 1936. Even more noticeable, however, was the chastening effect of the political uproar the board had caused. The new attitude towards the unemployed was

---

[1] Quoted in Millett, *Unemployment Assistance Board*, 126. The discussion of the revised regulations in the House of Commons handled by the New Minister of Labour, Ernest Brown, showed that the Minister was himself much involved in the revision of the regulations and that it was not being done by the board as an independent group. Millett's comprehensive study of the board concludes that after the spring of 1935, despite Government protestations to the contrary, its status was little different than that of any other Government department. *Ibid.*, 125–8.
[2] Davison, *Unemployment Policy*, 75. The board discovered for instance that it was practically impossible to describe a single person living alone. Eventually it envisioned 28 different sets of circumstances for giving benefit to boarders. *Ibid.*, 77.

one of accommodation and friendliness. Officials were now willing to make enquiries about adequate bedding and cooking facilities and to make substantial lump-sum payments above regular maintenance for exceptional needs. Relieving officer discretion, the absence of which had been so much a part of the previous trouble, was now used to the fullest. The practice of substantial exceptional payments for unusual family situations—and nearly every family situation was exceptional —which had become common for obvious reasons during the political turmoil of the standstill, continued even though theoretically these were at an end with the introduction of the new regulations. In many cases they continued until the war. The apparently prosperous condition of one household receiving exceptional payments could always be justified by the fact that the family was making good use of the money to improve itself. Conversely, the poor condition of another household receiving exceptional payments might be excused by the argument that if the payment were removed conditions would become still worse.[1]

The generous rate of the UAB relief and the improvement in overall unemployment statistics had the effect of increasing problems growing from the contrast between the chronic depression of Wales and the North and the near-prosperity of the Midlands and the South. Frequently there was now little difference between what a family could receive in State benefits and the local wage rate in a depressed area. The payment of substantial dependants' allowances meant that a man with a large family might well be eligible for more money out of work than in employment. The Assistance Board after all paid for children and employers did not. Here was an anomaly that no amount of reasoning could solve, or rather one which could only be solved by a return to the principle of 1832, of less eligibility. If Unemployment Assistance Board scales were accurate, if its methods of assessing family needs were fair, then wages in many places were below the subsistence level. But the laws of practical politics were no more able to raise wages than they were to reduce the level of benefit.[2]

[1] With the coming of the war the UAB became simply the 'Assistance Board' and received large duties for the care of evacuees and air raid victims. At the same time the hated 'household means test' was superseded by a personal means investigation. This change came not at the initiative of the board, however, but through Labour pressure. For a full discussion see: Richard M. Titmuss, *Problems of Social Policy* (London, 1950), Civil History Series, 89.

[2] In one of the most powerful books to come from this period, *The Road to Wigan Pier*, George Orwell noted a 'recent' census among Lancashire cotton mills which showed that 40,000 *full-time* employees were receiving less than 30s. per week. In Preston the number over 30s. was 640, the number under 30s. 3,113. George Orwell, *The Road to Wigan Pier* (London, 1962), 1937, 67n. Any UAB client with a wife and two children would be receiving more than 30s. by 1937, even without exceptional payments. A 'wage stop' instituted at the end of 1937 stipulated that no family could receive more in UAB assistance than it would earn if all

This situation was well understood by authorities both within the Unemployment Assistance Board and within the House of Commons but among neither group was there any enthusiasm for taking action. Wages in the depressed areas could not be raised and the unemployment assistance scales could not be lowered.[1] The easiest solution, as is frequent in politics, was to do nothing and to attempt to head off criticism before it appeared. John Boyd Orr, for instance, was summoned to see Kingsley Wood, Minister of Health after June 1935, for publicizing the fact that insurance benefits and pensions were inadequate to purchase enough food to maintain human health. The former insurance solicitor informed the nutritionist that 'there was no poverty in the country' and inquired what all the fuss was about. Boyd Orr reports that he received much official pressure not to publish a pamphlet on his findings, which appeared in March 1936 as *Food, Health and Income,* and that the civil servants associated with the investigation asked to have their names withdrawn.[2] Criticism of unemployment assistance was taboo in Parliament.

A second problem, in some ways more intractable than the first, although less politically explosive, lay with the slightly fewer than 200,000 theoretically able-bodied workers which the UAB finally took over from the Public Assistance authorities on 1 April 1937. Here resided a problem of definition. Very many of these men had done nothing at all for years. What was, indeed, their 'normal occupation'? Could one reasonably say that they were 'capable of and available for work'? Many had no homes and in fact did not wish to leave the Poor Law institutions for they had nowhere to go. Immediately arose a series of contests between the UAB and the local authorities. The Public Assistance authorities were anxious to prove that each man at some time had been in employment within the scope of contributory old-age pensions which made them legally working men for purposes of unemployment insurance. The UAB argued that the men were in fact no longer capable of work and should remain therefore legitimate clients of parochial relief. The Public Assistance authorities had the right to appeal to board umpires in case the local UAB authorities rejected any particular individual. In the end many cases were appealed,

members of that family were at work in their normal occupations. Such a stipulation was of course difficult to apply and by December 1937 only about 6,500 allowances were affected.

[1] One effect of the anomaly caused by dependants' allowances in both unemployment assistance and unemployment insurance was to increase pressure, long carried on by Eleanor Rathbone, for some system of universal children's allowances. *Economist,* 30 March 1935.

[2] John, Baron Boyd-Orr, *As I Remember* (London, 1966), 115–16. He received much encouragement from Harold Macmillan.

although the board eventually succeeded in avoiding responsibility for about 45,000 of 130,000 of the former able-bodied paupers.[1]

Although it was less sensitive politically than some other problems, the inability of the Government to settle upon an agreed and permanent policy for the treatment of hard-core indigency, symbolized perhaps the greatest failure of British social policy in the interwar period. Ordinary unemployment, although fraught with political dangers and unbelievably expensive, could be ended, as in fact it was after 1945, by the provision of work. But how was society to treat the portion of its members who because of individual weaknesses—drink, laziness, physical disability or age—could not conceivably take care of themselves and who were producers no longer of national wealth, although they were consumers, and indeed rather large consumers, of custodial services? A man did not become a member of the work force because a Public Assistance authority clerk classified him as 'able-bodied' any more than a sick person became healthy because he chose to apply, as many did, for the more generous unemployment benefits rather than sickness benefit.

The conclusion that must be drawn from the experience of the UAB in the three years of its mature life before the Second World War, is that it closed most of the alternative doors to the creation of a real needs service. As a step away from the Poor Law and the principles of 1834, it was probably more important than the Local Government Act of 1929 usually hailed as the vindication of Sidney and Beatrice Webb. The act of 1929 transferred the duties of the Boards of Guardians to the major local authorities and so adopted an administrative technique recommended by the minority report of the Royal Commission of 1909. But far more important was the UAB's termination of the principle of less eligibility, which after all had been the philosophical undergirding of the act of 1834. With the act of 1934 the British working man substantially achieved what the Labour party had been demanding on his behalf in the previous 15 years: 'work or maintenance' (indeed maintenance that was frequently more profitable than the work). It did not follow, to be sure, that life in the distressed areas was good, nor that the majority of the unemployed, as the countless protest marches and demonstrations showed, preferred life on the dole to employment in their customary occupations. Nevertheless, the UAB, without ever admitting that it was doing so, did provide for the unemployed man, so long as he was technically available for work, a stipend theoretically adjusted according to his need which lasted as long as his unemployment continued.

The difficulty of course was that the UAB solved only a political problem not a social problem. The passing of the Unemployment

[1] Davison, *Unemployment Policy*, 80–1.

Act, in a pamphlet bearing the almost unmistakable style of William Beveridge,

> was due to other considerations than the needs of the people chiefly concerned—the off-insurance class who are in poverty. Politics and Treasury finance smothered the truth of social issues. No specifically *unemployment* service can ever become a *needs* service in the round so long as it is detached from our basic poverty service whether institutional or domiciliary—whether concerned with the able-bodied or the sick, with infancy or old age. Many reforms and many advances are required in these services—not least in the way of their financing—but we do not believe that the poverty of British citizens, either in depressed or in prosperous areas can ever be adequately relieved, still less prevented, by dealing with it in specialized categories, which do not correspond to human needs.[1]

In effect the right to relief for the UAB was a function of status not of individual requirement. The hardship of an unemployed man is no greater than that of a cripple who has never worked or of an aged woman alone in the world and unable to care for herself. But the healthy adult male's political leverage is greater, particularly if his problem is new and if he can combine the ordinary weapons of electoral pressure with the threat of revolution. The Government between 1934 and 1936 did not nearly solve the problem of poverty, rather it bought off the most dangerous group among the poor. Other categories, more numerous and more pathetic, remained. What was done, or in many cases not done, for them constitutes a substantial portion of the remainder of this study. But at no time was the basic problem touched. Qualification for Unemployment Assistance Board relief depended upon stipulations not of need, means or helplessness, but of economic status, of accidents of training and previous employment. The board did not represent social justice but rather was a sign that the nation was not yet ready for social justice.

[1] *Planning*, PEP Broadsheet No. 75, 'Unemployment Assistance Reviewed', 19 May 1936, 8.

Appendix

The question of why the Government in the 1930s gave no attention to public works and the direct promotion of capital investment deserves a brief note. One reason certainly was Baldwin's, and no doubt Chamberlain's, rather simple economic philosophy that State spending was money wasted to the economy. Second, certainly influential, was the fact that public investment to stimulate the economy had been originated in the postwar period by Lloyd George in the national development loans and had reappeared in various Liberal manifestos culminating in the so-called 'New Deal' in 1935. By supporting the idea himself, Lloyd George ensured for practical purposes that Chamberlain and Baldwin would oppose it.

Finally, the existing system of unemployment relief, particularly transitional payments, militated against any publicly supported projects. Workers on transitional payments, although under a means test, chose to regard themselves as being part of a form of subsidiary insurance programme. Work offered them by public authority, which they would not have been able to refuse and retain their eligibility, would have been unpleasantly similar to the ancient labour test required by the Poor Law. The political implications of such development were frightening.

As a consequence, the amount spent on public works was insignificant, even under the Labour Government. The peak year was 1931 when the Unemployment Grants Committee spent £30 million on direct relief work. The largest number of men employed at any one time was 59,000. After this, direct government employment dwindled. By 1937 the Grants Committee had two schemes in operation employing a total of 303 men.

In the last years before the war, as the contrast between Wales, Scotland and the North and the rest of the country grew more marked, the Government undertook development programmes for certain depressed areas. Under the Special Areas (Development and Improvement) Act of 1934 particular efforts were made to attract industry to the areas with the highest and most intractable unemployment. Special commissioners, with considerable power and money were appointed. (By the end of 1937 £5 million had been spent principally in aid of rates.) Except for a few show pieces the results were negligible. Businessmen insisted on making the bulk of their new investment in areas that were already prosperous and although unemployment fell by more than one third in the Special Areas between December 1934 and September 1937, much of this must have reflected emigration from these areas and the national decline in unemployment.

	1934	1935	1936	1937
New Factories (England and Wales):	478	488	551	541
In special areas	7	2	8	17
Expanded Factories (England and Wales):	144	182	201	237
In special areas	2	6	3	5

Davison, *Unemployment Policy*, 93–105; Burns, *Unemployment Programmes*, 287n.; *Cmd. 5896*, 'Report of the Commissioners for the Special Areas of England and Wales for the Year ended 30th September 1938', 1938, Appendix I.

5 The battle for reform - phase II: socialism or social reform

After the resignation of the Lloyd George Government in October 1922, the central figure in British social politics was Neville Chamberlain. From the beginning of his first tenure as Minister of Health on 7 March 1923, presiding over the destruction of Ramsay MacDonald's administration in 1931, supporting the courage of his party at the time of the Unemployment Assistance Board crisis—at least until the reconstruction of the National Coalition on 7 June 1935, when Chamberlain's attention and the world's began increasingly to be devoted to foreign affairs, there were few matters concerned with domestic social policy in which Chamberlain was not involved. Whether as Minister of Health or Chancellor of the Exchequer, he always kept part of his terse, businesslike and not ungenerous mind directed toward what seemed to many the prosaic realities of day-to-day social administration. The traditions of his father's house, his own experience as a businessman and his opinions about the parochialism and incompetence of politicians on both sides of the House, propelled him toward this area of public activity. He enjoyed this work and was good at it. Were he not the heir of the Chamberlain tradition at Westminster, his training, temperament and incredible industry might well have taken him into the Civil Service where he could have become an outstanding Permanent Secretary, even in the age of Morant, Fisher and Anderson. Indeed the personal qualities that sustained him as an administrator—his expertise, clarity of thought and precision in grasping alternatives —proved his undoing as Prime Minister. The Nazi leaders could not be treated as if they were a powerful but fractious Board of Guardians.

That the most successful social reformer in the 17 years between 1922 and 1939 should be a Conservative rather than a Labour party man, one who was essentially a civil servant in politics and whose talents were for handling administrative problems rather than men, helps to explain why the Baldwin Age, although by no means socially reactionary, was not a period of innovation in welfare legislation. Chamberlain's achievements were undeniably important: after 1922 no one else is really of any significance. But even his greatest legislative works—the Widows', Orphans' and Old-Age Contributory Pensions Act of 1925, his comprehensive reconstruction of finance and administration of local authorities culminating in the Local Government Act of 1929, the Unemployment Act of 1934, not to mention his contributions in housing and in the rationalization of national health insurance—all represented simplification, consolidation and adaptation of state machinery. He was concerned less with what was to be done than how it was to be done. If social legislation is conceived as the transfer of wealth to needy individuals in the population, his care was for the method of payment rather than the alleviation of hardship. The quick sympathy of Lloyd George, who knew what it was to be poor and sought always to deal immediately with need while being only slightly concerned about the way in which the need was met, Chamberlain could never understand and indeed despised. Lloyd George's proposals for a solution to Britain's problems by the stimulation of industry through some form of a State guarantee for capital investment, Chamberlain regarded as nothing more than a vote-getting waste of Treasury money on public works. Like many other Conservative public figures he allowed his distaste for Lloyd George's devious and frequently dishonourable methods of political practice to obscure any consideration of the possible utility of his goals.

No-one can fairly blame Chamberlain for not being a different person than he was. Chamberlain was active, courageous, intelligent and, within his limits, compassionate. Given the political climate of Baldwinism and the discouraging precedents from the Lloyd George administration, perhaps no man could have done more than he did to solve the social and economic problems oppressing Britain in the late twenties and thirties. Nevertheless, as a consolidator rather than an innovator, he must bear the burden of the blame, so far as it can be assigned to anyone, for allowing the nation to remain the gloomy place it was for many millions of citizens. The reaction manifest in the election of 1945 against Chamberlain's party was to a large extent founded upon the belief that the Conservatives could not be trusted any longer with the stewardship of social reform. This is not to say that Chamberlain's reforms were not worthwhile; nor that in the thoughtless optimism of the late twenties or the distractions of the early thirties it would have been possible for the party of Stanley Baldwin to do more; nor, above all, that any feasible combination of Labour party leaders would have done more. But the houses, schools, hospitals, and factories which were not built in the middle 1930s, when money, labour, and raw materials were cheap and when an important proportion of Britain's resources were standing idle and when no-one but Chamberlain could have put them to work, were no less a loss to the nation than if they had been destroyed by German bombs. Memories of failures in domestic policy no less than in foreign policy formed a part of the political inheritance of the interwar period and remained for the British electorate a continuing reproach to the party of Neville Chamberlain.

Homes for heroes after all

Chamberlain entered Andrew Bonar Law's Cabinet at the Ministry of Health at the end of the first week of March 1923, little more than two months before the Prime Minister retired, shortly to die of cancer. His appointment illustrated the distinctly ramshackle character of the Conservative Government which had succeeded the Lloyd George Coalition and emphasized the serious shortage of experienced talent possessed by the Conservative leadership, whose strongest men maintained still some loyalty to Lloyd George. He succeeded Arthur Griffith Boscawen, who had been unable to win re-election upon appointment to office, and had been offered the seat in the Cabinet only after its rejection by Robert Horne. Chamberlain himself had been in Parliament only since the Coupon Election. Little was known of him except that he was the brother of Austen Chamberlain and that he had failed badly as Director of National Service in 1916 and 1917.

With the burden of the responsibility for housing and with the absolute certainty that the Conservatives could not leave the housing problem as it stood, the portfolio of health was a dubious honour. Griffith Boscawen's defeat had turned upon housing and the electorate's disappointment not on the Government's policy but upon its apparent lack of policy. The voters, remarked *The Times,* 'see in the first place a Ministry which has not made up its mind on an all-important subject. While the Minister of Health was seeking a seat, the Government appeared to be seeking a policy for him.'[1]

These circumstances gave Chamberlain unusual bargaining power for so junior a man. Before he accepted the office he insisted that he be given a free hand over rent control and that the Government accept the responsibility refused his predecessor for subsidizing the construction of dwellings for the working class. He set to work immediately upon a measure modelled on Griffith Boscawen's proposals.[2]

Like the man himself, Chamberlain's housing act was economical, businesslike, and straightforward. It was also highly successful and

[1] *The Times,* 4 March 1923. This was unfair to Arthur Griffith Boscawen. In fact since January he had been urging upon the Cabinet, unsuccessfully, a subsidy programme much like the one Chamberlain finally induced it to accept.

[2] Keith Feiling, *Neville Chamberlain* (London, 1946), 102–3. Rent control, begun in 1915, had been renewed periodically since. In 1920 the act had been amended to permit increases up to 40 per cent above the 1914 rent but otherwise was little changed. For a short survey of rent control legislation in the 1920s see: Cmd. *4372,* 'Fourteenth Annual Report of the Ministry of Health, 1932–33', 1933, 91. On Griffith Boscawen's work see: PRO 24/158, CP 9. 'Interim Report of the Housing Committee', 8 January 1923; CP 34, 'Final Report of the Housing Committee', 23 January 1923.

laid down the lines along which state-subsidized housing would be conducted henceforth. Although Chamberlain himself had conceived it strictly as an emergency programme to last only for two years, its life was extended by the first Labour Government and in the end the act remained in force until 1929. Chamberlain hoped that his measure would enable private builders to construct houses that could be sold cheaply to more prosperous workers thus releasing capital for more building and allowing the less prosperous working class to move into houses vacated by those above them. This process Chamberlain styled as 'filtering up'.[1]

The bill precisely reversed the premises of Addison's legislation, which had limited the liability of builders either private or local authority, by laying the ultimate financial responsibility upon the Treasury. Chamberlain offered in contrast a strictly limited subsidy of £6 per year for 20 years for all houses begun, in the first instance, before October 1925. Although the bill was oriented toward private builders, it stipulated that local authorities might also qualify for the subsidy if they could convince the minister of their ability to construct houses.

The Housing Act of 1923, passed virtually without change during Chamberlain's brief five months tenure at the Ministry of Health, brought into being in its six year life altogether 438,047 dwelling units. Moreover, these houses cost the Treasury only £6 a year (and £4 on those completed after 1 October 1927, when Chamberlain himself reduced the subsidy) which contrasted with an average of £50 each year for the houses build under the Addison acts. The average cost of the new houses was between £400 and £450 depending on size, compared with an average for Addison of about £1,000.[2]

Chamberlain reluctantly left the Ministry of Health on 27 August 1923 to become Baldwin's Chancellor of the Exchequer. Almost immediately he became involved in the Prime Minister's surprising and unsuccessful attempt to return Great Britain to a policy of tariff protection. The result, on 6 December 1923, was a general election in which the Conservatives lost their majority although they remained the largest party in the House of Commons. As a consequence, after securing Liberal parliamentary support although not Cabinet participation, a

---

[1] *Official Report, House of Commons Debates*, CLXIII (24 April 1923), cols. 303–22. Feiling, *Chamberlain*, 114. The movement of families from older houses to new ones would have begun also the general de-control of rents.

[2] Of the 438,000 total about 363,000 were built by private enterprise usually for sale. Dwellings built for purchase received a lump sum grant of between £75 and £100. This data is taken from *Cmd. 2218*, 'Fifth Annual Report of the Ministry of Health, 1923–24', 1924, p. x; *Cmd. 3937*, 'Twelfth Annual Report of the Ministry of Health, 1930–31', 1931, 114; Ministry of Health, *Housing* (London, 1934), HMSO Publication.

Labour Government headed by James Ramsay MacDonald took power on 22 January 1924.

The new Minister of Health was John Wheatley, a Labour radical and Clydesider who proved, nevertheless, to be one of the strongest and most popular figures on the Labour front bench and whose untimely death in 1930 deprived the party of a leader it badly needed. Wheatley had severely criticized Chamberlain's measure at the time of its passage both for its short period of effectiveness, which gave no support toward building industry expansion, and for the small subsidy that seemed only to give State approval to squalid living conditions. While the Conservative measure had aimed at causing the least amount of interference with building enterprise and had been intended to serve only as a temporary stimulant for private house construction, which would hopefully then be able to proceed on its own, Wheatley looked forward to establishing the government, and particularly the local authorities, permanently in the business of residential construction. Armed with the report of a committee made up of representatives of both building trades unions and employers, appointed within weeks after he took office, Wheatley put together an act promising long-term Government support for local authority housing construction.[1]

Wheatley's act, the Housing (Financial Provisions) Act of 1924, was to run for 15 years. It gave an Exchequer contribution of £9 for 40 years (as opposed to £6 for 20 years under the Chamberlain measure) toward houses to be built either by local authorities or private enterprise, constructed for rent only and to be let at the prevailing prewar rents increased only by whatever sum was necessary to limit the annual cost to the rates to £4 10s. per house. In effect the total Wheatley subsidy for the house from both national and local authorities would be £13 10s. per year and the rent would be the difference between that figure and the sum per year necessary to retire within forty years the loan made on the house.

Chamberlain was not a man with much intellectual generosity nor one to applaud skill in a field in which he considered himself an expert. He disliked the Wheatley Act even though it was founded upon the limited subsidy principles of his own measure. He felt the state subsidy was too large. Nine pounds for 40 years, in capital terms

---

[1] *Cmd. 2104*, 'Report on the Present Position in the Building Industry, with regard to the carrying out of a full Housing Programme, having particular reference to the means of providing an adequate supply of labour and materials', 1924. The report noted that the supply of the labour in building trades had been declining not only since 1914 or since the war, but since the autumn of 1921 when the Addison programme ended. In 1921 the industry had contained 392,500 journeymen; in April 1924 there were 367,030.

amounting to £156, as opposed to £75 in a £6 subsidy for 20 years, meant that a far larger proportion of the total Treasury contribution went toward interest. The larger subsidy, he argued, would not result in lower rents but simply in larger houses while the heavy charge on the rates would subsidize a privileged class of householders at the expense of all others. In this he appears to have been justified by the results. As part of his programme of reducing Government expenses after the Conservatives returned to power he cut the Wheatley subsidy to £7 10s., and his own from £6 to £4. During the debates in the House of Commons on his Draft Order announcing the cut he said that there was no substantial difference between the 1923 and 1924 house rents but that the cost of the smallest houses under his own Act was £386 while the Wheatley houses, somewhat more spacious, were averaging £451.[1]

Nevertheless, of the nine major housing acts passed between 1919 and 1938 (of which the last five were concerned principally with specialized problems—rural housing and slum clearance) Wheatley's measure was by far the most successful. Although as one of his first acts as Chancellor of the Exchequer Chamberlain took his revenge for Labour's destruction of his measure by bringing to an end the Wheatley subsidy on all houses for which plans had not been submitted to the Minister of Health before 7 December 1932, the act of 1924 brought into existence during the eight years of its life a total of 520,298 dwellings, nearly 100,000 more than were built under the act of 1923 and about one-third of all houses built by public authorities between the wars. This was the largest number built as a result of any single piece of legislation during the interwar period. Chamberlain's defence for the withdrawal of the Wheatley subsidy was that building and interest costs by 1932 had fallen to a point where it was possible for private builders to construct houses at rents that the poor could afford and should they fail to do so in any given area the local authorities could now borrow cheaply enough to build themselves without an Exchequer subsidy.[2]

---

[1] *H of C Deb.*, CC (2 December 1926), cols. 1403–4. It should be noted that Wheatley was equally protective of his own measure and attacked violently Chamberlain's modifications of it. *Ibid.*, cols. 1407–20. One of the first acts of the 1929 Labour Government was to restore Chamberlain's cuts while allowing the Chamberlain act to die. For the public politics of the passage of the Wheatley Act see: Richard W. Lyman, *The First Labour Government, 1924* (London, 1957), 110–29.

[2] *H of C Deb.*, CLXXIII (15 December 1932), cols. 543–63. Perhaps the most important result of the abandonment of the gold standard in October 1931, apparently totally unexpected, was the decline of the bank rate to two per cent where it remained solidly until the war. Thus, as if by magic, the chief obstacle to house building disappeared.

The Housing (Financial Provisions) Act of 1924 did not by any means solve all of Britain's housing problems but it may be considered to have brought to an end the political struggle over homes for heroes that had so tormented politics since 1918. The nation had now two workable Government-supported housing programmes, one oriented toward private enterprise and the other toward local authority building, running side by side. The local authorities were now in the business of house building for good, and the 'council estates' which decorate the British landscape were henceforth a fixture of domestic life.

Unfortunately, the disappearance of housing as a first-rank political question did not mean that the problem of living accommodation for the working class had been solved. Between November 1918 and September 1939 almost exactly four million houses were built in England and Wales. Of these about 83 per cent had a rateable value of less than £25 (or £35 in London) putting them within the Ministry of Health definition of working-class houses. But of this large figure, which represented 50 per cent of the number of houses existing at the Armistice and which reduced the average number of persons per house from 5·4 at the beginning of the century to 3·5 by 1939, almost precisely two-thirds were built by private enterprise without any State assistance. Particularly after 1930 the net addition to the national stock of houses by public authorities was negligible. In the nine years before the Second World War local governments built about 273,000 houses under various acts, but demolished at the same time 242,000, mostly in slum clearance.

Although the crude statistics for housing provisions are most impressive, although 300,000 houses were built each year between 1934 and 1939, and although without question the surge in residential construction itself played a substantial part in Britain's emergence from the Depression, the fact remained that the poor section of the population was probably little better housed at the end of the interwar period than it had been at the beginning.[1]

Most simply, Chamberlain's assumption that the reduction of building costs had made profitable the erection of houses by private enterprise for all levels of the working class was mistaken. For the lowest paid section of the working population 10s. per week appears to have been the maximum allowable for rent.[2] Under the best conditions in

---

[1] In 1935, Birmingham had over 50,000 houses without a separate bathroom and 13,700 without a private water supply. In Hull, as late as 1944, 34,000 houses or 39·3 per cent of all houses, had no bathroom. PEP, *Planning*, Broadsheet 218, 'Old Houses' (3 March 1944), 3.

[2] This figure was used by PEP in its housing survey at the end of 1934. It would tend to be confirmed by the UAB experience whose rent allowance for a family of four was found to be inadequate. PEP, *Housing, England* (London, 1934), PEP Report No. 3, 6.

O

1934 a four-roomed house could not be built for less than £350. Given the lowest possible capital costs, average rates, repair and management this meant a rent of not less than 12s. 6d. and more likely 14s. a week.[1] The only area in which the above sum could be reduced was in the cost of building and here costs were rising. For instance the cement industry, which had paid substantial dividends through the entire Depression, concluded in the autumn of 1934 a price-fixing agreement to increase prices by about 20 per cent.[2]

If 10s. per week is accepted as the maximum rent that the lowest paid urban worker could afford, there existed a gap of two to four shillings between the minimum profitable rent for a house built without subsidy and the largest amount that the poor section of the working population could pay. Even though a very large number of houses had been built they had come into the hands of a relatively small part of the population. English builders had produced since 1919 enough dwellings to rehouse 50 per cent of the population, but by 1939 only 30 per cent of the population was living in houses built since 1919.[3]

Overcrowding, as much as poor sanitary conditions, appears to have been a problem which private building in the thirties failed to solve. At the beginning of the decade, just before Chamberlain ended the Wheatley subsidy, the census of 1931 reported that there were 460,000 more families than occupied dwellings in London County and an excess of 1,110,000 families in all of England and Wales. The difficulty encountered by the Unemployment Assistance Board in setting a benefit to give a large family a sufficient rent subsidy without exceeding the prevailing wage in a depressed area reflected the problem encountered by the ordinary wage-earner who found that the size of the house he could afford bore little relation to the size of his family. It provided also an almost unanswerable argument for children's allowances.

A comprehensive survey of overcrowding conducted by the Ministry of Health in 1936 concluded that while, to be sure, the problem was more severe in poor areas than in well-to-do ones, the variation in overcrowding was more nearly proportionate to family size than to

---

[1] In December 1934, when building costs were at probably at the interwar low, PEP estimated that the expenses in the rent of a £350 house broke down as follows:

Loan for 30 years at 6 per cent (4 per cent interest and 2 per cent sinking fund)	8s. 1d. p.w.
Rates	2s. 6d.–3s. 0d. p.w.
Repair, Management	2s. 0d.–2s. 6d. p.w.
	12s. 7d.–13s. 7d. p.w.

[2] PEP, *Housing*, 12–14.
[3] *Cmd. 6609*, 'Housing: Government's Policy and Organization for Carrying it into Effect', 1945, 2.

family income. Only 3·4 per cent of families with four members were overcrowded (although 30 per cent of all English families were living below the subsistence level) but 41·7 per cent of all families of eight were overcrowded and 59.8 per cent of all families of ten. In effect while nearly one-third of the population were in either 'deep' or 'moderate' poverty, overcrowding was not necessarily a characteristic of the condition of a poor family. On the other hand, many of the 70 per cent of the population at or above the subsistence level, living in economic circumstances that did not warrant their description as poor, were unable to find houses adequate for their families.[1]

Nevertheless, at the end of 1937 Political and Economic Planning could write hopefully that finally, after a generation of error, the housing problem seemed to be on the verge of solution. Those who most needed houses were at last beginning to get them.[2] Unfortunately there remained only a little more than a year of normal economic conditions. Whether private enterprise and the eventual satisfaction of the middle-class housing market, particularly of houses for sale, would somehow have brought down costs for working-class rental housing, is impossible to say. 1938 and the early months of 1939 did see the beginning of a gradual drop in private construction. In view of the rising prices of other commodities that had begun in 1936, this condition suggests a gradual decline in demand.

In any case the war intervened. With the coming of peace and the General Election of 1945, the most important and immediately pressing issue in the minds of the electorate, according to all opinion polls, was housing. Of all the missed opportunities of the interwar period, perhaps the failures in housing were the most unpardonable and, for the Conservative party, the most serious for the future.

The Poor Law after the Royal Commission

In any summary of British politics between the wars, unemployment and, for nearly a decade at least, housing appear as continuing foci of political storm. Each in its own way was a part of the new politics of the democracy that emerged after the First World War. Each provided a slogan for working-class militancy and for ruling-class apprehension. Of course they were not new questions for philanthropists or

---

[1] Data for these comparisons is taken from: Ministry of Health, 'Report on the Overcrowding Survey in England and Sales, 1936' (London, 1936), HMSO. Report of a survey carried out by the local authorities, a compilation of 1,472 returns from 1,536 local authorities, x–xiii. See also the investigation by the Pilgrim Trust in November 1936 of 932 families. Quoted Eveline M. Burns, *British Unemployment Programmes, 1920–1938* (Washington, 1938), 253–4.
[2] PEP, *Planning*, Broadsheet No. 107, 'Building and Housing Progress', 5 October 1937.

even for political reformers in Great Britain. But they were new as first-rank political issues. Probably housing conditions were not worse in 1920 than they had been in 1870, nor unemployment graver in 1927 than in 1886, but the attitude of the nation's leaders had changed. What the Boer War did for concern about the physical condition of the British population, the so-called 'condition of the people question', the First World War did for unemployment and housing in making them intractable, recurrent and serious matters of general parliamentary interest.

All this contrasts sharply with the contemporary significance accorded Britain's oldest question of social politics, the reform of the Poor Law. By the early 1920s this matter was ancient and thoroughly discussed. It trespassed upon and confused so many other areas of reform that with the coming of the Depression in the winter of 1920–21 and the consequent sudden importance of every form of public relief no matter how decrepit, most politicians were relieved to see the question die. For the next four years while the nation struggled with an unprecedented burden of unemployment, practical politicians on both sides of the House were inclined to regard Poor Law reformers either as impractical dreamers or old-fashioned cranks, somewhere between advocates of proportional representation and Scottish Nationalism. This is not to suggest that many politicians publicly approved of the Boards of Guardians' administration whether it was carried on with Victorian severity or with the undiscriminating generosity associated with the term 'poplarism'. But the problem was easier to deplore than to discuss intelligently, let alone to try and solve. The Poor Law existed, ugly and dangerous. Those who attempted to disturb it, as Addison had discovered, were inevitably wounded.

Both national and local Poor Law administration of the early 1920s had changed profoundly since the appointment of the Royal Commission a decade and a half before. Although they demonstrated their power beyond question in the struggle over the Ministry of Health, the guardians heeded the warnings of the Commission's reports and in the years just before the war had worked seriously at improving both the realities of their administration and their reputation. They sought to become more businesslike and scientific, to adopt respectable modern methods of social administration, while dispelling the atmosphere of narrow mustiness which had always seemed to hover around them.[1]

For a time before the war it had seemed possible that the Poor Law, at least in its old structure, would disappear either through gradual supersession by the welfare institutions of the New Liberalism or by

[1] Sidney and Beatrice Webb, *English Poor Law History: Part II: The Last Hundred Years* (London, 1929), II, 809–11.

root and branch destruction. Asquith's Government discussed, without any sense of urgency, various modifications of the Poor Law—classification of applicants according to type of relief needed, abolition of Poor Law educational services entirely, and abolition, where it existed, of the general mixed workhouse. As it turned out, nothing happened. The competing social philosophies of insurance-based welfare institutions and 'conditional relief'—benefits dependent upon improvements in personal habits and behaviour—cancelled each other out. In spite of many promises the Liberal reformers before 1914 lacked opportunity, or perhaps the courage, either to abolish or to reconstruct the Poor Law. Neither, however, could they incorporate any of the Poor Law administrative apparatus, for instance its extensive and surprisingly modern medical facilities, into their service. There were very few fixed rules in the planning of national insurance presided over by Lloyd George, but one, always adhered to, was that at no point should insurance administration touch the despised Poor Law.

With the war came radical changes in popular and official attitudes toward social welfare which made earlier proposals for reform of the Poor Law almost completely out of date. By and large the reports of the Royal Commission of 1905-09, both majority and minority, had been concerned first with reform of Poor Law administration, overcoming in one way or another the limitations of the Boards of Guardians. Secondly, each proposed to develop from the Poor Law some sort of apparatus that would prevent, rather than simply treat, the effects of unemployment. Both had thought of unemployment as a disease; something that could be corrected by improvements in the health, training or personal habits of the individual. To be sure, the signers of the minority report, with Beatrice Webb as their spokesman and Sidney Webb as their unofficial researcher and writer, hoped eventually to treat unemployment through the social control of industry. But for the immediate future they, no less than the writers of the majority report, assumed that the productive forces of society tended towards the provision, at some wage, of work for all. If economic equilibrium in those pre-Keynesian days meant full employment, individuals without work were in that condition as the result of personal failings which ought to be treated by social action. It was no longer a matter of assigning blame for the man's condition, or of attaching to him the stigma of 'pauper', or of assuming that his idleness was the result of sloth or drink, although to be sure this might be the case. Making a man employable was assumed to be akin to a process of education and both the majority and the minority reports devoted scores of pages to plans for personal rehabilitation and industrial retraining. As poor health was found to be a cause of unemployment, both reports considered at length means for looking after the physical welfare of the working classes, although in secret the Liberal Cabinet had begun to consider the establishment of the national health insurance scheme nearly six months before the Royal Commission reports were published.[1] Common to both reports, however, was the assumption, hesitantly but explicitly stated, that fundamentally permanent unemployment was the result of the failure of the individual to prepare himself adequately for work. Therefore, if a man refused vocational instruction or neglected the necessary habits of personal cleanliness in order to make himself fit or continued to drink and maintain an irregular mode of life, he was in effect committing a crime against the economic system and as a last resort might be disciplined in some form of detention colony.[2] No one thought that such people constituted a very large group and the detention colonies provided for them had no important place in the general scheme. Justification for mentioning them here lies in the fact that the logic behind the most progressive thinking for the treatment of unemployment in England before the First World War was based on the premise that society had the right to expect a man to prepare himself for work and chastise him if he did not, on the assumption that for the properly trained man work eventually would be available.

Economists had long been aware, to be sure, of cyclical industrial depression which periodically caused many hundreds of thousands of otherwise well-trained and industrious workers to be without employment. Keeping such people off the Poor Law had been the original motive for unemployment insurance in 1911. But nevertheless it was taken for granted that a free economy, allowed to function as it should, would tend to make use of all its resources and that in the long run the prices of those resources would adjust themselves to make this possible. In dealing with the able-bodied worker, then, the reconstructed Poor Law should facilitate preparation for industry and require men to place themselves, beneficially, at the disposal of the economic system. But to repeat, the critical assumption was that economic equilibrium meant full employment. The possibility that economic activity might stabilize at less than full employment—the great riddle that Maynard Keynes set out to solve in the 1920s—was not yet considered. When it became clear that unemployment could be a 'normal' economic condition, the premises for a large part of both the majority and the minority reports no longer obtained and these conclusions themselves became obsolete.

Another characteristic of Poor Law relief that would be important

[1] For a good discussion particularly of this aspect of both Commission reports see: William H. Beveridge, *Unemployment, A Problem of Industry* (London, 1931), 253–62; see also: S. & B. Webb, *Poor Law History*, 539–44, 717–23.
[2] Beveridge, *Unemployment*, 260.

in proposals for reform after the war, and which would be a major weapon of defence in the arsenal of the guardians, was that the Poor Law had become the customary resort for very many thousands of English citizens whose destitution was not the result of unemployment, but of age or sickness or frequently both. This situation did not begin with the war. Indeed the certainty that about one-third of Britain's elderly would spend some portion of their retired lives as clients of parish relief was one of the most potent arguments for the Old Age Pensions Act of 1908. Again, rapidly improving Poor Law medical facilities, particularly after the turn of the twentieth century, were in a way both a cause and a result of the increasing use of the Poor Law medical service by large numbers of the working class who were not economically destitute and whose patronage of Poor Law medicine as a form of embryonic State medical service had been recognized in the Medical Relief (Disqualification Removal) Act of 1885.[1]

By going into detail on ways of strengthening the Poor Law medical service, even though they aimed to remove it from the ordinary destitution authority, the writers of both the majority and the minority reports probably ensured that nothing would be done to implement their recommendations. Particularly Sidney and Beatrice Webb, who hoped to put Poor Law medicine and all other local health activities under a committee of the county and county borough councils, failed to understand the antagonism that their well-meant proposals aroused or to heed the conviction in the working-class mind that any Government activity connected with a Poor Law function became tainted by the association. This fact—one might almost term it a custom—of British politics was clearly manifest in the last two years of the war when the Webbs and other advanced health reformers sought to use the creation of a Ministry of Health as a means of breaking up the Poor Law.

During the war popular interest in the reform of the Poor Law and in most other ordinary concerns of domestic politics came to an end. For the first two years of the conflict, with income from the rates climbing steadily and with unemployment among able-bodied men negligible, the harassed Boards of Guardians enjoyed a spell of un-accustomed neglect. This restful period ended in January 1918, with the publication of the report of the so-called 'MacLean Committee', technically the Local Government Committee of the Ministry of Reconstruction. The MacLean Committee of fifteen members had been

[1] On the conditions of working-class medical care before National Health Insurance see Bentley B. Gilbert, *Evolution of National Insurance in Great Britain* (London, 1966), 311–13. See also: Sidney and Beatrice Webb, *The State and the Doctor* (London, 1910). This is largely a restatement of the parts of the minority report of the Royal Commission relating to medicine.

appointed in July 1917, at the time of the establishment of Addison's ministry to prepare a plan for carrying out one of the most important of the Coalition reconstruction promises, the rebuilding of parish relief. Unquestionably the committee had been deliberately packed with members in favour of radical reform. Beside MacLean himself, its most powerful members, Mrs Webb, Sir Robert Morant, and J. H. Thomas, were all enemies of the Poor Law. So was Lord George Hamilton who had been Chairman of the Royal Commission in 1905–09 and who, although having signed the majority report of his own commission, had been converted by Mrs Webb to the cause of reform.[1]

Inevitably, the committee delivered a report, signed on 19 December 1917, that was virtually a restatement of the minority report of the Royal Commission of 1905–09. It proposed to abolish the Boards of Guardians entirely and to break up the entire parochial administration of relief. The existing functions of the Poor Law, relief itself, support of the unemployed, care of children, medical care, the support and re-training of the unemployed, would be given to appropriate sub-committees of the major local authorities. The whole apparatus would be buttressed by a system of detention for able-bodied men who refused to make the necessary personal adjustments which would make them useful members of society.[2]

The report was not the result of an investigation. The committee had heard no witnesses—saying that ample evidence was available from the Royal Commission reports—and had refused to allow the Poor Law authorities to submit evidence.[3] Most of the six-month life of the committee had been occupied with the writing of the report itself and with skirmishes among committee members.[4]

Not surprisingly, the Government was in something of a dilemma over the MacLean Report. Inevitably it would arouse hostility among the Poor Law forces. But its suppression, equally, would cause suspicion and anger among reformers. Reconstruction of the Poor Law was, to be sure, an important matter but it was not the only reform which the Government had promised and negotiations for the ministry of health were at a critical stage. As a consequence its publication was delayed for over a month.[5]

The explosion of anger among Poor Law authorities over the Mac-Lean Report and the political effects of the guardians' resistance to a

---

[1] On the internal life of the Committee see: Margaret I. Cole, ed., *Beatrice Webb's Diaries, 1912–24* (London, 1952).
[2] *Cd. 8197*, 'Report on Transfer of Functions of Poor Law Authorities in England and Wales, Local Government Committee, Ministry of Reconstruction', 1918, 26.
[3] *Cd. 8197*, 4–5, 20.
[4] Cole, ed., *Webb Diaries, 1912–24*, 99.
[5] Dr Addison's note introducing the report on its publication on 17 January 1918 reflects the Government unhappiness over the whole matter. *Cd. 8197*, 2.

ministry of health, and consequently to planning for housing, are properly part of the story of the Ministry of Health itself. The grass-roots political power of well over 600 Boards of Guardians, each with taxing authority, each composed of a dozen or more substantial local citizens who were usually figures of importance in constituency political associations, represented an electoral force that the Government simply could not dismiss.[1] Had they possessed a more skilful spokesman in the ministry than W. Hayes Fisher, the guardians might have been able to obtain a promise from the Cabinet that the creation of a ministry of health would entail no change in their own status. As it was they were able to forestall any immediate changes in the position of the Poor Law and to force the Government to put off the reformers simply with promises of future reconstruction of paro-chial relief. Meanwhile, under the leadership of the Poor Law Unions Association, the guardians moved ahead rather reluctantly with a scheme of reform of their own which amounted to little more than changes of nomenclature. Poor Law relief would become 'Public Assistance', a pauper an 'assisted person', the workhouse would be 'the institution'.[2]

Although Poor Law forces were active during the 1918 election, re-form of parochial relief was hardly a matter of contention between the parties. Labour explicitly demanded that the whole structure of the Poor Law be abolished and the Coalition, committed to a ministry of health and tied up by the highly equivocal promises concerning the extent of the new ministry's duties, hardly wished to bring the matter up. But with the leadership of both parties displaying at least implied agreement that their ancient service should be destroyed, Poor Law officials and members of the Boards of Guardians were bound to defend themselves. Without much publicity, but with considerable quiet organization born of long experience in such matters, they worked in each constituency reminding candidates that elected Boards of Guardians were traditional in English democracy and extracting from them promises to protect the Poor Law.[3]

The failure to reform the Poor Law during the enthusiastic and optimistic early days of Christopher Addison's tenure as Minister of Health must be counted as a symptom of Addison's political decline. Almost certainly the Boards of Guardians' survival was more the result of accidents of politics and economics than of their own powers of resistance. Addison never gave up his plans to attack the Poor Law,

---

[1] On the political activities of the Poor Law forces in the months following the MacLean Report see: *Charity Organisation Review*, XLIII, XLIV (March-November 1918); *Poor-Law Officers' Journal*, 29 November 1918.

[2] *Charity Organisation Review*, XLIV (November 1918), III.

[3] *Poor-Law Officer's Journal* (29 November 1918).

and until the very end of his tenure as Minister of Health was casting about for ways to begin its reconstruction. But he never was able to make even a serious beginning on the task.

The Poor Law survived because of the enormity of the job of reforming it and because the unexpected death of the Permanent Secretary of the Ministry of Health, Sir Robert Morant, one of the most formidable workers in the Civil Service, deprived Addison of the only person at his disposal capable of the task of reconstruction. Moreover Morant's sudden collapse on 13 March 1920 probably lowered all Ministry of Health efficiency in a way that would be apparent until the end of the interwar period. It ended the preoccupation with health that had been intended for the new ministry. It broke up also the easy working relationship that the Chief Medical Officer, Sir George Newman, had enjoyed with his Permanent Secretary. The new civil service head of the Ministry of Health, Sir William Arthur Robinson, had a Poor Law background and his relations with Newman quickly deteriorated to petty jealousy and mutual dislike. Under Robinson, Newman felt, the position of Chief Medical Officer declined. Previously both he and Morant had envisaged the CMO as having equal status to the Permanent Secretary, with separate access to the Minister. With Robinson the project for concentrating the rapidly growing Poor Law health activities within the Ministry of Health lost its impetus.[1]

Newman alone could do little. He was a serious and dedicated health reformer, who in the next 15 years would build a great reputation in a series of sparkling annual reports, but he was politically untutored. By attempting from the time of its establishment to concentrate under the Ministry of Health medical activities of the local authorities and by sponsoring grandiose plans for reforming Britain's medical services he injected himself and his office into the acrimonious public controversy that attended all Coalition reform plans. Addison was distracted by the struggles over house building and, without Morant's prestige, political astuteness and knowledge of the Poor Law, he was unable to drive reform forward.

It is incorrect to say, nevertheless, that the Government forgot the MacLean Report and the promises it had inserted at such great political cost in the Ministry of Health Act. Addison and Newman personally never altered their intentions in this direction and even in

[1] Symbolic of his lowered status, which Newman found particularly galling even 15 years later, was the fact that when Morant had been Permanent Secretary each had enjoyed the same salary of £2,000, Robinson at the time of his appointment had been given £3,000 while Newman remained at the old figure until his retirement in 1935. Newman Diaries V, MS entry n.d. (page opposite these entries February 1935). See also: Newman's comments on the importance of equal status for the Chief Medical Officer and the Permanent Secretary in Sir George Newman, *The Building of a Nation's Health* (London, 1939).

the winter of 1920–21, when statistics on pauperism began to show the increase that signalled the onset of Depression, the ministry still publicly insisted that the break-up of the Poor Law would occur in the coming session of Parliament.[1] Indeed, at the time of his resignation from the Ministry of Health in March 1921, Addison received from Lloyd George a statement that the Government's commitments on this matter would be honoured. But finally, with Addison's departure from the Government in July coinciding with the enormous growth of pauperism from 664,000 or 1·76 per cent of the population at the end of 1920 to 1,498,000 or 3·94 per cent of the population at the end of 1921, and with the unfortunate precedent of the Miscellaneous Provisons Bill which had tried to introduce Poor Law reform by the back door, plans for reconstruction of parochial relief were allowed quietly to disappear.

The reconstruction of the Poor Law, essentially the integration of Poor Law administration into the rest of local authority activities, was scarcely considered during the Labour administration of 1924 although the party for decades had demanded precisely this reform. So it fell to Neville Chamberlain, with courage that even his enemies recognized, to civilize this untamed area of local administration. His triumph, the Local Government Act of 1929, was perhaps the most characteristic, if not the most useful, of Chamberlain's social reforms. Arguably it was fitting that a man for whom most political problems were problems of administration should undertake the reconstruction of the huge and ramshackle apparatus of the Poor Law. Possibly after the death of Morant, no one in the British national administration except Chamberlain had both the knowledge and the enthusiasm to accomplish the task.

Chamberlain's motives for attacking the Poor Law were far removed from those of the earlier reformers. Whereas Addison, Newman, Morant and the Webbs, as well as the majority of the writers of the MacLean Report, objected to the existing Poor Law because it was an inadequate instrument of social control and sought to increase its effectiveness by making it a part of a general administration for dealing with all forms of economic and social need — the 'Framework of Prevention' as the Webbs called it — Chamberlain simply regarded the Boards of Guardians as an administrative excrescence and thought of reform as the improvement of functional efficiency. The early reformers had been concerned with what the Poor Laws did and with the fact that this one form of public assistance, parochial relief, bore no relation to the multitude of other social welfare institutions that the

---

[1] 'It is understood that the bill to transfer the powers of Boards of Guardians to county and borough councils will be introduced as early as possible in the new Session.' *The Times*, 28 December 1920.

twentieth century had brought to England. Chamberlain cared less about the effect of the Poor Law on economic society than that it functioned badly, that it was a broken piece of administrative apparatus. The writers of the MacLean Report saw relief from the bottom, from the 'consumer's' point of view. Chamberlain looked at it from the top down.

All of this thinking was apparent in Chamberlain's plans for the Poor Law which began to take shape within days after he took office for the second time as Baldwin's Minister of Health, on 6 November 1924. Before the end of the month he had sent the Cabinet a four-year programme of legislation for the Ministry of Health which had as its first major proposal, scheduled at that time for 1926, the reconstruction of Poor Law administration. But most important, Chamberlain understood, and explained in a memorandum accompanying his programme, a fact which appeared to have escaped the notice of all previous reformers, that the Boards of Guardians were also major local taxing authorities and that sweeping them away involved large scale rebuilding of local finance. The key, therefore, to reform of the Poor Law was the reform of rating and valuation. The reconstruction of this single authority of local government would eventually involve the general reconstruction of all local government.[1]

The guardians, above all else in the Poor Law apparatus, were most offensive to Chamberlain's passion for regularity and order. Theoretically Poor Law relief at the end of the First World War was granted on the terms that had governed its administration for nearly half a century. These conditions had been restated most explicitly in Local Government Board orders before the war when the guardians were under heavy pressure as a result of the Royal Commission. The Out Relief Orders of 1910 and 1911 specified that relief should be 'adequate' to support the needs of life and, according to the 1911 order which also served as a consolidating and codifying regulation, relief to able-bodied men could be given only in the workhouse. But, and most important, this stringent requirement was diluted by Article 12 of the 1911 order which provided that 'exceptional' cases—defined in court judgment to exist when a man was on the verge of starvation—could be granted outdoor relief. If such relief was given, a special report had to be submitted to the Poor Law Division of the Local Government Board. In any case, between 1910 and 1914 relief of able-bodied working men was scarcely a problem. Unemployment was below 3 per cent and working men applying to guardians of the poor for aid were ordinarily tramps and casuals, in fact unemployable, although technically able-bodied.

As with nearly every other institution in Great Britain, the First

[1] Feiling, *Chamberlain*, 459–62.

World War cut across the history of the English Poor Law, destroying old usages and abruptly making recent reforms obsolete. The guardians, who in the decade between 1909 and 1919 had tried with reasonable success to lift their rickety service out of its well-worn grooves and to adjust to the fact that many of their clients resorted to them because of sickness or the weakness of old age, by 1920 suddenly found themselves again overwhelmed with a demand for support for the able-bodied unemployed whose need for the Poor Law everyone had assumed was a thing of the past.

The inability of the new Ministry of Health and of the guardians to find a means by which adequate relief could be given to hundreds of thousands of English citizens and their families without debauching every principle of prudent finance in the long run made inevitable the reform of Poor Law administration. Whatever were the political difficulties of the nation's leaders at Westminster in the face of popular pressure, the guardians' problems were immeasurably worse. Since the Representation of the People Act of 1918 their electoral constituencies had more than doubled. In working-class areas they were responsible not only to large numbers of the precariously employed who might become paupers, but also now to the paupers themselves.[1] Thus the guardians found the familiar vice closing up them. 'Adequate' relief for a large family might well be more in monetary terms than the lowest wages in the community. Certainly it contradicted the principle of 'less eligibility'. But the insistence that an able-bodied worker could be relieved only in the workhouse or at the price of daily attendance at a labour yard, cost more in political and social disharmony than did the relief given in social good. The honest labourer restrained by test work was unable to look for a job. And if he was confined in the workhouse his family was broken up as well. Yet if no deterrent were applied, adequate relief surely meant the creation of a large pool of loafers and wastrels who could conclude reasonably enough that there was no object in looking for regular employment if one could receive from the Poor Law larger sums than regular wages.

Behind this reasoning lay the singular and sophisticated motivations of English local politics. By no means all the Boards of Guardians which dropped the workhouse test in the years after the Armistice and began to pay relief competing seriously with the local labour market were Labour-dominated. The fact was that even the most reactionary individual guardian of the poor could tell himself that, however high was his board's scale of relief, any lessening of it might cause a popular reaction by the working class which would result in still a

[1] The act of 1918 swept away the last franchise disabilities upon paupers except that a pauper could not be a member of a Board of Guardians or of a borough council or district council.

higher scale. He could feel also that there were clear party advantages in having the largest spending agency of the local authorities in the hands of Conservatives. Finally it was useful to the publicans, shop-keepers, and indeed to the representatives of the major employers to maintain at least a minimum purchasing power among the unemployed.

The waning of deterrent Poor Law relief then, and the growth of indiscriminatingly generous, even lavish, scales of relief was not con-fined only to the 50-odd Boards of Guardians in which the Labour party had a majority, although this group included the worst offender of all, Poplar, whose responsibility as an example for the rest is des-cribed below. But over twice this number gave, under the dubious legality of Article 12 of the Relief Order of 1911, more or less un-discriminating relief to able-bodied men. The huge West Derby Union, for instance, covering all of the cities of Liverpool and Bootle with a population of nearly a million and regularly paying relief to a maximum of 41s. per week, half again as much as a worker could receive from unemployment insurance, included no Labour members whatever among 106 guardians until 1928.

Whatever one may say about the causes of the breakdown of control over Poor Law relief that came after the First World War, it was not as a result of the rise of the Labour party. Rather, as with the flounder-ing welfare experiments at the national level, the malaise was a reflec-tion of society's fear of the new political democracy demanding but not comprehending social justice, and of the anxiety of an old ruling class which was ready to grant demands made upon it, but was unsure of what it had to give. In any union where between one-quarter and one-half of the adult working population was unemployed, Poor Law relief was almost certain to be open-handed relief, whether the guard-ians themselves were Labour or Conservative. If this conflicted with the rules of the Poor Law Division of the Ministry of Health then any attempt to enforce the deterrents would conflict also with the principle of local control. A Government that could not bring itself to end the chaos in its own programme of unemployment insurance was unlikely to enforce its will upon numerous and articulate Boards of Guardians whose political capacity and contacts with the voting population were as good as its own. So long as the guardians existed they would be independent.

Out-of-doors relief and unemployment

The story of the disintegration of national authority over the adminis-tration of poor relief, which Neville Chamberlain found so deplorable and which led to the Local Government Act of 1929, began with the 'Revolt of Poplar' in the autumn of 1921. 'Poplarism', specifically the granting of outdoor relief to able-bodied men, was not new. Since the turn of the century, the Poplar guardians, under the influence of George Lansbury, had been giving undiscriminating outdoor relief to all who asked for it. For this they had frequently come into conflict with the Poor Law Division of the Local Government Board, but in the last decade before the war with the Poor Law itself under attack and with the general decline in unemployment after 1908, the board preferred to ignore Poplar's infractions of its regulations. However, the explosion of unemployment in the spring of 1921 made the continuance of this easy toleration impossible. When it occurred, the crisis in Poplar came not as a result of the scale of relief, but over a question of finance.

In London Poor Law Unions were not entirely self-supporting. Since the Equalisation of Rates Act of 1893 the Poplar guardians had received from a common fund supported by general rates about £50,000 per year towards the maintenance of paupers in the workhouse and infirmary, although they received nothing at all toward outdoor relief. Poplar's problem, in common with that of most other East End boroughs, was an extremely low property valuation carefully maintained by large employers, particularly the dock companies in the area, which forced borough rates up to 22s. in the pound.[1] Within a few months after the beginning of unemployment, the taxing and borrowing resources of Poplar were approaching exhaustion.[2] As a consequence, arguing that it received no aid at all from the rest of London toward the outdoor relief that was now its biggest expense, the Poplar Borough Council, which included a number of the Poor Law guardians, on 9 April and 10 May 1921 formally declined to levy rates for the support it was required to give to the Metropolitan Asylums Board, the Metropolitan Police and the London County Council. Its argument was simply that as Poplar's expenses towards maintenance of the poor were greater than those of the West End and that as the West End made no contribution toward outdoor relief, the money should be withheld to be set against the extra expenses that Poplar incurred.

Now began the high comedy of the borough council appearance

[1] Raymond Postgate, *The Life of George Lansbury* (London, 1951), 216–20. See also: George Lansbury, *My Life* (London, 1928), 155–62. Lansbury notes that the dock companies customarily kept a man on the guardians until assessing power was transferred to the borough council at which time the representative moved also to the new body. *Ibid.*, 139.

[2] By the end of 1921 Poplar had on its relief roll on *account of unemployment* five times as many men as the average in England and Wales and nearly four times as many as the average in London. The figures were, per 10,000 of population, England and Wales, 197; London, 266; Poplar, 970. These figures deal only with able-bodied paupers receiving outdoor relief on account of unemployment and not with total numbers receiving Poor Law relief. 'Persons in receipt of Poor Law relief' (On the night of 1 January 1922), *Accounts and Papers*, 1922.

before the High Court. The members attended in a body led by the Mayor, Sam March, wearing his chain of office and preceded by the mace. They solemnly declined a court order to make the required appropriations and were imprisoned for contempt, the 24 men going to Brixton Prison and the six women to Holloway. In jail the councillors demanded union guards, organized the other prisoners to demand their legal rights, insisted up being allowed to hold borough council meetings, and enjoyed serenades played by the band of the Poplar Borough Workhouse School.

In any struggle of this sort the Government was bound to emerge appearing both obstructive and ridiculous. Its own plans for relief of distress were not much more tightly controlled than those of the Poplar Guardians. With thousands upon thousands of unemployed ex-soldiers soon exhausting their insurance benefits, the Cabinet could not insist upon restrictions on Poor Law relief which remained for the working class the only barrier to starvation. Government embarrassment, reflected for instance in the fact that no mention of the Poplar affair ever appeared in the annual reports of the Ministry of Health, therefore prevented it from offering much in the way of support to the London County Council. As a result, after allowing the members of the governing body of one of its most populous constituent boroughs to suffer incarceration for unpurged contempt, the LCC, seriously threatened by similar actions by the councils of Bethnal Green, Stepney and Battersea, agreed to permit the release of the Poplar councillors following nothing more than a formal apology. At the same time the Minister of Health, Sir Alfred Mond, hurried through Parliament the Local Authorities (Financial Provisions) Act which passed through the House of Commons at the end of October and received the Royal Assent on 10 November 1921.

So in the end Poplar won. The Financial Provisions Act raised the payment from the Metropolitan Common Poor Fund for indoor paupers from 5d. per day which had been the rule since 1893 to 15d. per day and took over the whole cost of outdoor relief within limits to be specified by the Minister of Health.[1] In all, payments to Poplar were

---

[1] On the politics of the Poplar affair see Postgate, *Lansbury*, 216–20. Hector Bolitho's dismal biography of Alfred Mond never mentions the Poplar affair directly, and remarks only that during 1921 Mond requested from the Cabinet authority to suspend Boards of Guardians but did not get it. Hector Bolitho, *Alfred Mond, First Lord Melchett* (London, 1933), 226–7. The Poplar guardians in fact never did purge themselves of contempt and never tried to do so. Once the Mond scale came into effect they raised their own level of relief and in spite of their quasi-criminal position, borrowed about £500,000 from the Ministry of Health during the next three years. Most of this was written off by John Wheatley the Labour Minister of Health in 1924. Meanwhile in 1927 Lansbury himself was elected to Parliament for Bow and Bromley.

increased from about £50,000 to £300,000 and borough rates were relieved by nearly 7s. in the pound.[1]

As important for the future as the example of Poplar's easy victory itself, was the publication at the beginning of 1922 of what could be regarded as the first officially sanctioned scale of Poor Law relief, the so-called 'Mond Scale'. Theoretically the scale, drawn up under the terms of the Financial Provisions Act, applied only to London and to payments made from the Metropolitan Common Poor Fund. However, the 'Mond Scale' provided an implied approval for relief grants at the same level everywhere and so contributed to the vast expansion in the cost of pauperism which followed. The scale provided a maximum payment of 54s. per week for a family of eight with an additional allowance for fuel in winter which averaged through the year to another 2s. per week. The same family under unemployment insurance would have drawn 23s. 4d., which may help to account for the rapid rise in applications for Poor Law benefit in other London boroughs during the next few months.[2]

Poplar's victory, then, practically destroyed the possibility of central control over the Boards of Guardians. As other East End boroughs followed Poplar's lead in the next few years, London became a haven for paupers. This doubtful popularity continued into the middle twenties when in the south and east of England unemployment had at last declined to five or six per cent, not much more than usual.[3] The situation can be illustrated statistically. After the grim years of 1921–22 during which perhaps 20 per cent of the labour force was idle, British unemployment levelled off at a national average of about 1,250,000 or approximately 10 per cent of insured persons where, with fluctuations, it remained until 1930. However within this crude figure were wide regional variations. After the settlement in the Ruhr, Wales rarely had three-quarters of its available work force occupied. London, on the other hand, fell from about the national average in 1923 to between five and six per cent after 1925, enjoying with the southwest generally the lowest rate of unemployment in the kingdom. But while the general rate of unemployment fell by nearly 75 per cent in London between the beginning and the end of the decade the number of able-bodied

---

[1] The best, and by far the most factual story, of the Poplar rebellion is in Webb, *Poor Law*, 899–900, from which much of the information for this account is taken.
[2] Mond attempted to adjust his scale of relief to local labour conditions by stipulating that, notwithstanding the maximum permissible amount, no relief could be given that was more than 10s. less than the lowest prevailing wage in the district.
[3] The act authorizing the Mond scale expired on 3 September 1922. It was, however, replaced by the Local Authority (Emergency Provisions) Act 1923 which limited the amount that any single borough could charge to the Metropolitan Common Poor Fund as outdoor relief to 9d. per head per night. This restriction did not cut the Poplar Scale of relief.

P

paupers relieved in East End boroughs on account of unemployment remained virtually stationary. Indeed, as the example of Poplar spread, applications in neighbouring districts increased. Poplar for instance, with a total population of 162,578 in 1921, gave outdoor relief to 25,154 able-bodied men on 1 January 1922 and to 25,254 on 1 July 1928. Bermondsey similarly relieved 8,877 in a population of 119,452 in 1922 and 15,303 in 1928. Mile End, not strictly comparable, had 3,527 paupers theoretically available for work in 1922 in a population of 103,121 and six years later incorporated into the Stepney Union and, with Clement Attlee as an alderman, supported 17,418 in a population of 249,657.[1]

So far as it can be ascertained, the numbers drawing unemployment insurance in these boroughs did not vary greatly from the general London rate. The figures, broken down into Poor Law Unions for the first time in September 1929, show live registers of 8, 8·6 and 7·4 per cent for Poplar, Bermondsey and Stepney respectively. In fact, according to a special return order by Chamberlain in June 1928, the percentage of men drawing unemployment insurance benefit as opposed to Poor Law relief was lower in the more notorious London boroughs than it was for the East End as a whole.[2]

Perhaps one may find here not only the explanation for Chamberlain's attack on the Boards of Guardians that resulted in the Local Government Act of 1929, but also the causes of revolt against the Unemployment Assistance Board in 1935. Bermondsey in 1927 gave nearly £1 a week in outdoor relief to a single man. Stepney offered £3 a week to a large family, twice what that same family would have received from unemployment insurance and a third more than the lowest basic wage in the borough. Most of this income was in cash — there was no labour test — and the Poor Law Unions at the same time were hiring men at wages to do the ordinary work of gardening and window cleaning.[3] Until at least 1927, when, even before the abolition of the guardians, Chamberlain began to revive serious supervision through the Poor Law inspectorate, the Ministry of Health made little attempt to interfere, even though on Sidney Webb's estimate some £60,000 was spent on technically 'exceptional' relief, based upon the slender legal basis of Article 12 of the relief order of 1911.[4]

In one form or another 'exceptional payments' continued until the Second World War. Even though the Public Assistance Committees of the major local authorities, which superseded the guardians in 1929,

[1] London County Council, *London Statistics, 1921–23—1928–30*, London, 1924–31.
[2] *Cmd. 3218*, 'Unemployed Persons in receipt of Domiciliary Poor Law relief in England and Wales during the week ending 16 June 1928', 1928.
[3] Webb, *Poor Law History*, 906–7.
[4] *Ibid.*, 909.

were forbidden to make larger grants under transitional payments than those to which the family would have been entitled under unemployment insurance, the assessments of need were made by the subsidiary Guardians Committees who frequently inherited both the traditions and the personnel of the old guardians. Thus, the exceptional payments still existed to help fire the revolt of 1935. The standstill order specifically continued them and they were, as has been seen, written into the revised Unemployment Assistance Board scales which was in fact a scale of exceptions.

Chamberlain, Churchill and the guardians

Writing in 1928, Sidney Webb suggested that the attack upon the Poor Law, both upon undiscriminating outdoor relief and upon the rickety structure of the guardians, was a part of a general offensive against Labour undertaken by the Baldwin Cabinet. It derived, he thought, from reaction to Government weakness in previous years, to the fears of the spread of the Russian Revolution, to disorder at home, and to

> the incessant reports of the Secret Service Departments [which] filled the Ministers' minds week by week (at first accompanied by disquieting bulletins of the Civil War dragging on in Ireland, reporting the horrors of guerrilla warfare on both sides), with all sorts of tales of subversive agitation in South Wales, and on the Clyde, and among both the Irish and the aliens in the Metropolitan Area, agitation which is always so easy to discover, and which it is almost impossible for a secret agent not to magnify both the extent and the importance.

Webb connected all of this with the suppression of the General Strike, Government support of the mine-owners, and even with British diplomatic intervention in the United States to prevent the payment of relief money for striking miners.[1]

There is, to be sure, something to be said for this point of view. By the middle of the decade, the calm of Baldwinism had replaced the agitation of the immediate postwar period. The Labour party's extreme conventionality in office had not been followed by a revival of workers' militancy and the clear failure of union solidarity during the General Strike suggested that the danger of revolution was over.

On the other hand, endless Cabinet documents as well as Chamberlain's own letters and diaries indicate that he saw reform of the Poor Law, together with the rationalization of local assessment and rating, as his most important single legislative goal. To a man with his passion

[1] *Ibid.*, 910, 912.

for order and logic in public affairs, the sprawling Poor Law appeared deplorable. Appropriately for a future Chancellor of the Exchequer, his point of view was basically financial. So far as possible spending authority and financial responsibility should reside in the same body. The habit, so apparent among the London boroughs, of raiding the Metropolitan Common Poor Fund and of bringing upon the Ministry of Health outside political pressure for loans in order to subsidize profligate scales of relief would have to come to an end. As a guide for reform he proposed the use of the report of the MacLean Committee which was, as he told the Cabinet in the spring of 1925, the 'basic statement' on reform of the Poor Law. But emphatically he was not interested in abolishing the Poor Law. Essentially he hoped to disentangle its health activities from its other functions and to concentrate them in a single service. Secondly, but more important, he wanted to put the powers of the guardians in more responsible hands.[1] On 13 May 1925 the Cabinet approved Chamberlain's tentative proposals for abolishing the Boards of Guardians and transferring their functions to major local authorities. The Cabinet was satisfied that it was approving only the transfer, not the reform, of functions. Poor Law activities would be modified only in such ways as the transfer made necessary. It noted, however, looking a decade into the future, that it would be desirable, if possible, to find some way of unifying unemployment insurance benefits with parish relief given working men on account of unemployment. It agreed finally that the distribution of activities of the Boards of Guardians, the apparatus for administering the Poor Law, would be worked out by the major local authorities themselves under the supervision of the Ministry of Health.[2] Chamberlain was authorized to begin negotiations with local authorities immediately.

The key to Poor Law reform, indeed to all reform of local government, lay in the modernization of local authority finance. In his memorandum of 19 November 1924 Chamberlain emphasized that, because valuation and rating were at the time attached chiefly to Poor Law areas and to Poor Law authorities, 'any schemes of Poor Law reform which proceed on the lines of transferring the functions of Poor Law values to other bodies would necessarily involve the reconstruction of the machinery of valuation and rating'.[3] Rating reform, he continued, should come before the larger reconstructions of local government for no changes were possible without it. Hence he proposed to push ahead immediately in this field, particularly as a draft measure

---

[1] See Chamberlain's memorandum of 19 November 1924 in Feiling, *Chamberlain*, 459–60, and PRO Cab. 24/173, CP 219, 'Scheme of Poor Law Reform, Ministry of Health, March 1925'.
[2] PRO Cab. 23/50, Cabinet 25 of 1925, meeting 13 May.
[3] Feiling, *Chamberlain*, 460.

prepared during his previous tenure at the Ministry of Health in 1923 was already in existence.

But even reform of rating and valuation, a narrow and highly technical piece of legislation, could not be passed without contention. Chamberlain's proposal to supersede 12,882 parish overseers, who dated back to 1601 and who actually made assessments, and the more than 600 Poor Law Unions which were the rating areas, and to concentrate the powers of rating and valuation in the 'real living bodies', the county councils, was bound to upset many traditional authorities.[1] Gentlemen of property, who saw the determination of the taxes on their homes and estates being turned over to Labour-dominated county councils, descended upon the Ministry of Health. Conversely the bill aroused Labour by making permanent the 75 per cent rate exemption for agricultural land and machinery which had been established for two years in 1923. The new figure represented an increase in exemption from the 50 per cent established by Lord Salisbury's Government in 1896. By and large, however, opposition to Chamberlain's measure, which was an excellent example of the old Liberal Unionism, came from within the Conservatives.[2]

Even though occupied with rating reform and with his contributory pensions scheme, Chamberlain pushed forward with preparations for a draft bill for Poor Law reform and with less dramatic, but in the short run more effective, administrative changes that would tighten up central control over the troublesome guardians until the boards themselves could be abolished.[3] The attack on the guardians occurred on two fronts. One was a series of measures becoming law between 1926 and 1928 strengthening Cabinet control over the guardians themselves. The first of these, receiving the Royal Assent on 15 July 1926, was the Board of Guardians (Default) Act permitting the minister to supersede any board which acted in such a way that it was 'unable to discharge all its functions'. In practice this meant the appointment of Ministry of Health commissioners to take over the work of a board which bankrupted itself through extravagant scales of relief. Since he took office Chamberlain had complained of the tendency of certain boards to undercut the unemployment scheme by giving relief to men

[1] For a lucid and brief survey of the history of English rating and valuation see Chamberlain's opening speech on the second reading of the bill. *H of C Deb.*, CLXXXIII (13 May 1925), cols. 1873–92.

[2] Feiling, *Chamberlain*, 132–3.

[3] The first draft of the Poor Law reform sections of the Local Government Bill was submitted to the Cabinet at the end of September 1925. PRO Cab. 24/175, CP 410, 'Poor Law Reform', 25 September 1925. This memorandum was little changed from CP 219 of the previous spring. Chamberlain emphasised in the accompanying memorandum that the changes were administrative only; they were not changes in function.

who were out of work because of ill behaviour or to men who had been denied unemployment benefit because of a failure to seek work.[1] Early in the autumn of 1925 he ordered a survey of the incidence of outdoor relief granted on account of unemployment. His conclusion was that in a time of stable or slightly declining unemployment, outdoor relief had increased most rapidly in Unions where the amounts of relief were the most liberal and that this was worst in the Unions in mining areas. He noted that since April 1925 relief given on account of unemployment had increased 77 per cent in Unions where mining was the predominant industry. Other areas were showing no change or a decline in the cost of relief. Unions dominated by metal and engineering had in fact a 17 per cent decrease. Durham was the worst where four of the 15 Unions in the County showed an increase of 254 per cent.[2] The act was a violent and much resented corruption of the English tradition that the care of the poor was the responsibility of the locality. The applications of the Default Act—to West Ham in London and later to Chester-le-Street in Durham and Bedwellty in Wales— were successful financially and administratively. However, the action caused unhappiness not only in the localities but among members of Chamberlain's own party for whom local control, as in rating and valuation, seemed to provide a bastion against socialism.

The other two measures, the Audit (Local Authorities) Act of 1927 and the Local Authorities (Emergency Provisions) Act of 1928, provided the Minister of Health with more flexible instruments for dealing with recalcitrant guardians. In a way both measures were steps toward the centralization of the Poor Law administration that was finally achieved under the Unemployment Act of 1934. Each of them provided instruments by which the Ministry of Health could determine the day-to-day scale of relief provided by the guardians without waiting for a board to run itself into bankruptcy.

The Audit Act of 1927 gave the Minister of Health power for the coercion of individual guardians in a way that struck directly at the cherished independence which for centuries had been the heart of British local politics. It strengthened the minister's legal control over the guardians by permitting him to recover, as a civil debt, surcharges against the guardians assessed by the district auditor. Henceforth, any board might find itself involved in expensive litigation with the central government unless it heeded ministerial orders about the granting of relief. But perhaps more severe—an innovation which Sidney Webb[3] found open to 'grave objection' but which, fortunately, was almost

[1] CP 410, 25 September 1925.
[2] PRO Cab. 24/175, CP 468, 'Administration of Poor Law Relief', 11 November 1925.
[3] Webb, *Poor Law History*, 915n.

immediately superseded by the abolition of the guardians themselves and so was never tested—was the provision stipulating that members of any board upon whom a single surcharge of more than £500 was upheld would be prohibited not only from serving as guardians for a period of five years but forbidden to serve on any other local authority as well. In effect, the individual guardians would find themselves put under the legal disabilities of pauperism if their disregard of ministerial orders was detected by the district auditor.

The second act, the Emergency Provisions Act of 1928, was aimed particularly at London. For practical purposes it reversed the Emergency Provisions Act of 1923, which had been a re-enactment and amendment of the Local Authority (Financial Provisions) Act of 1921, the measure that had signalized the victory of Poplar in its fight with the Ministry of Health. The 1921 act, it will be remembered, had permitted all metropolitan Poor Law Unions to charge to the Metropolitan Common Poor Fund all outdoor relief up to the amount sanctioned by the extremely generous Mond Scale. This act did not prevent any union from offering larger amounts of relief than the Mond Scale but simply stipulated that only amounts up to the Mond Scale could be charged to the fund. The large subsidies which the act provided permitted Poplar, early in 1922, to increase its scale of relief and encouraged other East End boroughs to follow this example. Although the act of 1921 came to an end on 30 September 1922, the Emergency Provisions Act of 1923, repassed in 1926, continued the subsidy while attempting to end the abuse of the previous measure by abolishing the Mond Scale and providing instead only a subsidy of 9d. per head per night for outdoor relief from the Common Poor Fund. In spite of this restriction the East End boroughs were able to increase their expenditures enormously. By 1927 and 1928 all of them were spending between six and ten times the amount they had given in 1921 and even those which had previously been strict in relief, for instance Bethnal Green, were competing with Poplar in generosity.

The Emergency Provisions Act of 1928 extended the act of 1923 for another three years but reversed its effect. Instead of setting a fixed amount from the Common Poor Fund upon which each borough could count, it placed control of the Common Poor Fund under the Metropolitan Asylums Board and gave the Board power to give or withhold reimbursement for any charges that it might decide. The Asylums Board consisted of 55 representatives of London Poor Law Unions of which about half, being those in the West End, had objected for several years to the subsidies that the West End taxpayer had given toward what seemed to be profligate expenditure in the East End. The voting power of these representatives, with the support of 18 Ministry of Health nominees on the board, gave Chamberlain, for practical purposes, control of amounts that the Poor Fund would provide to East End Unions. The act of 1928 was normally regarded as the measure that finally brought 'Poplarism' under control.[1]

While setting the House of Commons ringing by the violence of his fights with Labour, and building a fund of hatred for himself in the party, Chamberlain moved less spectacularly, but perhaps more effectively, through the Poor Law Inspectorate toward controlling the activities of the guardians. Here again he entered fields of administration that surprisingly had been altogether unsupervised. For instance, except for one report made in 1908 at the request of the Royal Commission on the Poor Laws, there had never been any review of the entire administration of outdoor relief at the parish level even though by the 1920s domiciliary paupers were both the most numerous and the most expensive part of the guardians' responsibility. Hence in the last three years before they were abolished, the parish guardians of the poor began to learn, for the first time, what modern, systematic, scientific social administration could mean. Inspectors attended meetings of the boards and of the relief committees and intervened not only in general discussion but, contrary to tradition, in the disposition of individual applications for relief. They visited the homes of paupers and of citizens whose applications for relief had been refused. They inspected case papers and urged the use of the workhouse test or the labour test upon men who appeared to be reluctant to seek work. They urged continually the substitution of relief in kind for relief in cash and harassed Boards of Guardians with terse reports about slackness of record-keeping and inadequate accounting of expenditures of the ratepayers' money. The Chairman of the Bermondsey Board of Guardians gave a wry account of his board's less-than-happy experience with the new technique of inspection.

> They were jogging along in their tin-pot way, feeling happy in what they were doing and sure that it was the right thing and that the majority of the recipients of relief were grateful. They were going along all right, until one day—just after April Fool's Day [1927]—there came into their midst a representative from Whitehall. He was not going to say a word against the Inspector personally. The Inspector complained that the scale of relief was too high, and that too much money and too little in kind was allotted. It used to be 95 per cent in money and 5 per cent in kind, and it was gradually

---

[1] See Chamberlain's explanation of the bill. PRO Cab. 24/192, CP 33, 'Extension of the Local Authorities (Emergency Provisions) Act of 1926', 7 February 1928. After the passage of the Emergency Provisions Act of 1928 the total cost of poor relief in London fell from about £3,000,000 to £2,400,000 and payments from the Common Poor Fund dropped from £2,100,000 to £1,700,000. Sir Gwilym Gibbon and Reginald Bell, *History of London County Council* (London, 1939), 405.

altered to 75 per cent and 25 per cent but that did not satisfy the Ministry. Single men, according to the Ministry, should have two weeks' 'Final' and then look for work anywhere and any how.

The chairman concluded by suggesting that Chamberlain go to the docks himself and see the daily fight among unemployed men for work.[1]

Chamberlain had originally planned to deal with reform of the Poor Law in 1926. In his original programme of legislation put before the Cabinet in November 1924 he had given Poor Law reform a priority over contributory pensions. Political considerations had made necessary the earlier consideration of pensions and the growth of resistance to the first proposals for Poor Law reform submitted to the Cabinet as CP 410 in September 1925, and finally published in December, showed that the achievement of anything approaching a consensus on the measure would be a long process. The Boards of Guardians were of course furious at the prospect of extinction, but the major local authorities, the counties and county borough councils, were by no means enthusiastic about receiving new responsibilities. On the other hand the supersession of the West Ham Guardians, who by July 1926 had succeeded in accumulating a debt of £2,275,000, of which £1,975,000 was owed to the Ministry of Health, and who had been the immediate cause of the Guardians' Default Act, showed more clearly than any theoretical discussion could have the need of transferring the relief of the poor to more viable economic areas. It was 'common knowledge', reported *The Times'* political correspondent two years later, when Chamberlain was deep in negotiations with representatives of contending local authorities, that the Minister of Health had undertaken the suppression of elected authorities only 'with unfeigned regret' and that the desire to make unnecessary such drastic interruptions of normal local administration had reinforced his ambition to reform the Poor Law.[2]

But more serious than the resistance caused by the guardians' struggle for life was the growth inside the Baldwin Cabinet of Winston Churchill's proposals for reform of local government finance which, although not necessarily competing with Chamberlain's plans, threatened to make them politically unfeasible by cutting across the neat concentration of local responsibility and authority. Whereas Chamberlain in 1925 had succeeded in centralizing most taxing power under the major local authorities, Churchill a year later proposed the wholesale de-rating of industry as a means of lowering costs of British

[1] *South London Press*, 4 November 1927, quoted in Webb, *Poor Law History*, 925n. Bermondsey's expenditures for outdoor relief were, in fact, among the largest in the country. *Ibid.*, 939.
[2] *The Times*, 18 September 1928.

manufactured goods, aiming to make them more competitive in world markets, and also, without question, to head off further demands for import duties against lower priced foreign products. The return to the gold standard in 1925 had made British goods more expensive. By how much was, and is, a matter of dispute. But British wage rates were substantially above those prevailing among many of her competitors and the heavy burden of local taxes which in steel, for instance, amounted to about 7s. per ton was a serious matter for a nation in which two out of five workers traditionally were employed by industries in which part of the produce went abroad.

There was substantial logic in Churchill's plan. Not only would it help British price competitiveness abroad, but it would tend to spread the burden of unemployment at home. By 1926 the burden of British joblessness centred in the old export industries, coal, shipbuilding, steel and textiles. These by their nature were restricted geographically. The result was an automatic compounding of the financial burden. Areas in which there was large-scale unemployment had a disproportionate burden of poor relief. Large sums paid out in poor relief meant high rates. High rates resulted in higher costs for the remaining industries in the locality which were either forced out of business or moved away to more prosperous areas where their tax expenditure would be less. Accordingly unemployment in the less prosperous areas increased. All of this was itself compounded by the Government practice of per-centage grants for local authority services which sums were based on the amount of money the local authority had chosen already to spend. Hence, a prosperous area such as Oxford, with booming employment in the automobile industry and low rates, received from the Exchequer more than twice as much money per head of population as depressed Merthyr Tydfil.

Chamberlain knew this problem as well as Churchill, and probably understood it better. But whereas Churchill hoped to solve it by wholesale exemptions of industry and railways, perhaps to the extent of £30 million to be made up by grants from the national Exchequer, Chamberlain intended simply to provide aid on a much smaller scale via block grants to selected local authorities, based not upon what the authority was already doing—itself proportionate to the rate base available—but according to need. Chamberlain's plan, characteristic-ally, was to make local government more effective. Churchill, also characteristically, sought to use taxing power to solve a social and economic problem.

The fight over the two proposals began in the Cabinet at the end of November 1926 when Chamberlain again brought up Poor Law reform. At first he reported to his sister optimistically:

I did not ask for any decision but was allowed to talk for about forty minutes.... There were some murmurings about the effect on the rates but ... they did not go very far. Winston of course was eloquent upon his grand scheme, but it seemed to me that it met a rather chilly atmosphere. On the whole I thought it was not a bad beginning.[1]

So the battle for Poor Law reform began on two fronts. One one side the Minister of Health was beset by the guardians and by many of their allies in the local authorities who wanted no reform at all. On the other, more privately, he fought the Chancellor of the Exchequer, who hoped to make himself the steward of a vast measure of industrial rehabilitation which Chamberlain disliked in principle as an administrator and feared in practice as a politician.

In Churchill, the Minister of Health faced a skilful opponent, far less single-minded than himself, whose proposals appealed always to a wide range of electoral interests even when they lacked the technical refinement upon which Chamberlain prided himself. Churchill's plans, gestating almost from the moment he became Chancellor, were to balance the return to gold and the reduction of income tax carried in 1925 with wholesale rate relief for all productive industry. Basically, he told the Cabinet in a summary of his scheme at the beginning of 1928, this was the only way in which tax reductions in aid of trade could be effected without bringing on the Government the charge of class legislation and without 'dividing the country along lines much less advantageous to the Conservative Party than the present cleavage between Socialism and anti-Socialism'. A tariff on manufactures, for instance, might help unemployment, but would produce also a demand for agricultural protection that would split the party. A reduction in the tax upon beer would be popular but would arouse the newly-enfranchised women, as would a tax on food. However, a reduction of rates on basic producers, which he calculated cost now about 8 per cent of average profits in industry nationally, would interrupt the cycle of unemployment, high rates, bankruptcies and more unemployment, and for agriculture would remove the objection to Poor Law reforms among farmers who feared being thrown upon the mercy of Labour-dominated county and borough rating authorities. Finally, remarked Churchill in a surprising conclusion, rate reduction would continue the great and successful tradition of nineteenth-century Liberalism by 'striking off the out-worn fetters' of an antiquated tax. The whole plan, he esti-

---

[1] Quoted in Iain Macleod, *Neville Chamberlain* (London, 1961), 125, diary 27 November 1926. See Cabinet minutes: PRO Cab. 23/53 Cabinets 60, 66, 67 of 1926, meeting 24 November, 16, 17 December, and PRO Cab. 24/184, CP 30 (27), 'Poor Law Reform', 31 January 1927.

mated, would cost £41 million. He proposed to find part of the money through a tax on motor fuel. If his proposals were to have any political benefit it would be necessary to begin immediately. An election could not be far off.[1]

Churchill admitted that he had Chamberlain's support for 'a great part' of his scheme but privately he knew that there were some important differences of principle. He had from the beginning insisted that his cargo be loaded upon Chamberlain's vessel. '... the opportunity is too good, and safeguards are too necessary', he wrote to Chamberlain in October 1927, 'for a purely departmental solution on my part. I see no reason why your plans and mine should not be interwoven ... you really must not expect me to produce 3 or 4 millions a year for a partial scheme of modest dimensions.'[2]

Inevitably in a Cabinet dominated by Stanley Baldwin, the answer to disharmony would be delay. Therefore through 1927 and early 1928 Poor Law reform was put off while Chamberlain periodically considered whether he should resign. By the spring of 1928 Chamberlain knew that acceptance of his scheme would have to be bought by substantial assent to Churchill's plan. At the end of April 1928, he surrendered to the extent of agreeing that industry and railways should pay generally one-quarter of the normal rates, although he noted in his diary that the plan he had just accepted was

> so utterly illogical, so complicated, and so completely contradictory to the opinion universally expressed a little while ago that State subsidies were economically unsound, that I could not imagine that it would not be torn to pieces at once.... Not a word of criticism has been heard to this most vulnerable proposal. It makes one long to be in opposition.[3]

The essence of the compromise was embodied in the Rating and Valuation (Apportionment) Act of 1928 which began a survey of industries actually to be de-rated and so prevented this potentially dangerous controversy from becoming entangled with Poor Law reform. The bill itself, Chamberlain carefully explained, did nothing. It did not de-rate any piece of property and only prepared the way for further legislation.[4]

To a distressing extent, the necessities of the de-rating scheme determined also the structure of the projected reform of the Poor Law. In 1927 Chamberlain had hoped for a moment to placate the guardians

[1] PRO Cab. 24/192, CP 8 (28), 'Rating Relief', 20 January 1928 (stamped 'Special Care to Ensure Secrecy').
[2] Churchill to Chamberlain 18 October 1927, quoted in Feiling, *Chamberlain*, 145.
[3] *Ibid.*, 145–6, diary entry 29 April 1928.
[4] PRO Cab. 24/195, CP 166 (28), 'Rating and Valuation (Apportionment) Bill', 22 May 1928.

by leaving the boards in existence, slightly reconstituted, with full financial responsibility for the institutional care as well as the outdoor relief of the able-bodied and vagrants. This compromise, however, could not be made to fit a system of block grants. The guardians were too small a unit of administration.[1]

Chamberlain at last introduced his bill on 28 November 1928 in a speech of two and a half hours.[2] It was a vast measure of over one hundred clauses of which only one part dealt with the Poor Law and which could reasonably have been designated like so many others a miscellaneous provisions bill. The Poor Law clauses were in fact relatively simple. The measure provided that the powers, duties and assets of the, at that time, 625 Poor Law Unions were to be transferred to the county and county borough councils, each of which was required to form a Public Assistance committee. The actual administration of domiciliary Poor Law relief would be handled by aptly named 'Guardians' Committees' of not fewer than 12, nor more than 36 members, who would supervise the poor in the various districts into which each county or borough would be divided. Institutional care given as relief would be the duty of the Public Assistance committee and would be administered on a county-wide basis. The councils were authorized, but not required, to transfer from the Public Assistance committee to other appropriate committees, auxiliary functions of the Guardians' Committees — the education of children and the care of the chronically ill. The measure stipulated that schemes for administration would have to be submitted to the Minister and approved within a specified time after the formal transfer, which would occur on 1 April 1930. In effect, the measure transferred the administration of the Poor Law to the major local authorities but left any reform of the Poor Law, beyond certain useful but minor administrative changes such as county-wide supervision of institutions, to the initiative of the local authority itself. Poor Law relief remained Poor Law relief and pauperism remained pauperism except for a few small modifications, notably the removal of certain remaining disabilities which had previously attended Poor Law medical care.[3]

---

[1] For a history of the evolution of the Local Government Bill see: PRO Cab. 24/195, CP 186 (28), 'Proposals for Reform of Local Government', n.d. (printer's mark shows 18 June 1928). Feiling's biography of Chamberlain although valuable for source references gives a confusing explanation of the de-rating controversy and misses the significance of the Rating and Valuation Bill altogether. The best readily available discussion of the act is in Webb, *Poor Law History*, 701–4. Webb estimated that the three-quarters de-rating of industry and the resultant £24 million subsidy to the local authorities underwrote about 2 per cent of the cost of industrial production.

[2] *H of C Deb.*, CCXXII (26 November 1928), cols. 65–107.

[3] The most useful summary of this huge and inchoate measure is not to be found

The bill virtually exempted the County of London from any of the changes required of the other county authorities. The London County Council simply was authorized to take over the duties of the various London Boards of Guardians and to distribute their functions among its existing committees as it chose within the supervision of the Minister. It was not bound, in other words, by the requirement imposed on other authorities of transferring to other committees only those functions covered by existing legislation. In this way, London was given power genuinely to break up the Poor Law if it chose to do so.

The other controversial matter in the bill, grants and de-rating, had been partially settled by the Rating and Valuation Act, which became law shortly before the Local Government Bill was introduced. This act had ordered the preparation of lists of industrial property, which under the Local Government Bill would be exempted from three-quarters of the rate, after 1 October 1929. All agricultural land became totally exempt. Special grants were to be discontinued, and beginning in the 1930–31 fiscal year, annual consolidated grants would make up losses incurred. The Government agreed in addition to provide the local authorities with an extra £5 million subsidy above the estimated £24 million to smooth over the dislocations caused by de-rating and by the changes in local government tax boundaries.

The act did much else. It transferred all highway and town-planning powers from the minor local authorities to the counties and county boroughs, while strengthening powers in these areas. It reorganized the registration of vital statistics. It brought to an end at long last the Unemployed Workmen Act of 1905, which had been Britain's first national legislation to attempt to deal with the problem of unemployment. It extended the pauper disqualification, still the chief legal disability of pauper status, from the membership on the Boards of Guardians to the county and county borough councils.[1]

The guardians were slow to react to this last threat to their existence and they were not entirely united in rejecting it. Moreover the whole question of resistance to the bill was confused by Labour's motion of rejection, which argued that relief of the poor should be a national matter and that the bill did not go far enough.[2] Nor were the counties and county boroughs themselves uniformly enthusiastic about their new powers; an official statement by the Council of the Association of Municipal Corporations generally supported the abolition of the

in the Second Reading Debates which are endless, nor in Sidney Webb's *History of the Poor Law*, which was written before the measure was passed, but in *Cmd. 3273*, 'Local Government Bill, 1928, Explanatory Memorandum on the provisions of the Bill as Passed by the House of Commons', 1929.

[1] Most important, Poor Law authorities remained virtually immune from suits by paupers arising out of the authorities' negligence.

[2] *H of C Deb.*, CCXXIII (26 November 1928), col. 107.

Boards of Guardians and the transfer of functions but viewed the de-rating and grant proposals 'with grave apprehension'.[1] Generally the enthusiasm for the new system varied directly with the amount of unemployment and hence the need for assistance within the area. Authorities in prosperous areas with high rateable values and consequently substantial budgets even with relatively low rate scales already received generous grants from the government. Particularly if there were a large amount of agricultural land within the county, they disliked the block grant system and wanted to see grants made proportionate to the amount of money lost through de-rating. Conversely, authorities in poor areas with low valuations and rates which because of large expenditures for Poor Law relief were sometimes higher than the valuation itself, who thus were unable to give much to health, maternity welfare and education, welcomed the block grants which would be given on a basis of need.

The guardians showed the same ambivalence. At the Northern Poor Law Conference meeting at Keswick the chairman of the Tynemouth Guardians attacked the argument that block grants made the break-up of the guardians necessary. Guardians, he thought, would be glad to surrender the block grants if they could be relieved of the burden of relief to the unemployed and 'he looked upon the whole scheme as typically Churchillian'. There had been in fact no discussion of the unemployed.

> The hospital and health parts of [the guardians'] work would be transferred to council health committees and the children to the council education committees, but he found no single reference to what was to become of the unemployed. At present the family was dealt with on one case paper, but under the new scheme there might be half a dozen committees dealing with different members of the family, and each committee would have its own inspectors and case papers.

Worse, the country would be deprived of the services of a large number of men who had devoted themselves untiringly to the poor and who had done magnificent work.[2]

These very traditional views were widely held but certainly did not represent a consensus. The Poor Law administrators were embarrassed by the fact that, although the Labour party opposed the bill in Parliament, the poorest areas of the nation, those most likely to vote Labour, nevertheless would gain most from the new rating and relief systems. Conversely, the wealthier, and particularly the rural, guardians who

[1] *The Times*, 24 October 1928.
[2] *Ibid.*, 24 October 1928.

disliked block grants found themselves opposing a major piece of legislation put forward by the party to which most of them belonged.

In fact, however, the guardians were fighting almost alone. No one
seriously defended them in the House of Commons and by the middle
of February national leaders of Poor Law associations were urging
parochial officials to prepare to work under the new authorities while
reminding them, as turned out to be the case, that the new Guardians'
Committees under the council Public Assistance committees might not
be very much different from the old boards.

'Under the Bill, each council had to submit a scheme for the Ministry', remarked the president of the Central Conference of Poor Law
Guardians, Lord Richard Cavendish, on 19 February 1929:

> Presumably the Councils would endeavour to draw up efficient and
> business-like schemes, and he imagined they would be willing to give
> a sympathetic hearing to Representatives of those Authorities they
> were about to replace. Those who were in a position to make reason-
> able suggestions ought not to hesitate to do so, and again, when the
> new Committees were formed, they should be ready to serve upon
> them if asked to do so. Although the old principles of democracy,
> and the ideas of Government for the people and by the people, had
> received a shattering blow, it would still be possible for a limited
> number, few indeed, as compared with the past, to identify them-
> selves with local administration.[1]

Although he declined to support a resolution, which eventually
failed, urging the House of Lords to hold up the bill, Cavendish's
closing speech at the conference voiced the regret of a number of his
colleagues that the destruction of the Boards of Guardians should be
the work of a Conservative Government.[2]

The Local Government Bill received the Royal Assent on 27 March
1929. Almost immediately Chamberlain began to issue circulars to the
local authorities urging the most imaginative use of their new powers
particularly in planning for the assumption of Poor Law health activities.[3] This area of administration, Chamberlain expected, would become markedly improved by the measure. In fact, beyond the disappearance of the guardians themselves, the expansion of hospital facilities of some, by no means all, local authorities, turned out to be almost
the only notable change in the durable apparatus of local welfare functions. In London, about one-half of the 800 people recruited by the

---

[1] *Ibid.*, 20 February 1929.
[2] *Ibid.*, 20, 21 February 1929.
[3] *Ibid.*, 11 April 1929.

LCC to handle its new welfare work had been employees of the guardians and one may assume the same occurred elsewhere.[1]

Although the term 'pauper' officially disappeared in 1931, the conditions of relief of the distressed person—unless his application was because of unemployment which, after 1935, brought him under the Unemployment Assistance Board—appear to have changed very little until the war. The last Ministry of Health report before the war commented sadly upon the continuing 'need for an overall service' and noted that, far from disappearing, the latest returns showed an actual increase in expenditure by local authorities for non-hospital Poor Law institutions.[2]

The creation of an embryonic system of municipal hospitals was by far the most important effect of the Local Government Act. Except in London, immediate changes in facilities for institutional medical care were slow to come, but the measure made improvements possible when the local authorities chose to act. The old attitude that a Poor Law infirmary, no matter how well-equipped, remained a Poor Law infirmary and its patients technically paupers could at last be modified. The difficulties with the operation of the Local Government Act lay with the reluctance of county and borough councils in the face of a world financial crisis and mounting unemployment to assume new obligations. As a consequence only in the last three years before the war did English local authorities provide more extensive hospital accommodation under their public health powers than under their Poor Law powers.[3] By far the most active authority was London County which, between 1 April 1930 and 1 April 1931, assumed responsibility for 76 institutions with over 43,000 beds from the London Guardians and from the Metropolitan Asylums Board.[4] Even though the closure of unsuitable beds in the next few years reduced this total to about 37,000, London in 1939 provided nearly three-fifths of total English municipal general hospital space. Particularly county authorities, as opposed to county boroughs, were slow to exercise their new powers. Up to the war, excepting Middlesex, only twelve had taken any action whatever.

The fact was that the optimistic predictions for a coordinated

[1] Gibbon and Bell, *London County Council*, 405.
[2] *Cmd. 6089*, 'Twentieth Annual Report of the Ministry of Health', 1939, 67–8, 70.
[3] In 1936 the Ministry of Health reported that local authorities possessed 106 general hospitals with 55,550 beds and 423 Poor Law 'institutions' with 68,737 beds. By 31 March 1939 the local authorities operated 137 hospitals with 66,805 beds versus 388 'institutions' with 59,910 beds. *Cmd. 6089*, 'Twentieth Annual Report of the Ministry of Health', 1939, 65, 247.
[4] On London's hospital plans see: Lewis Silkin, *The New Public Health Organization of the London County Council* (London, 1930 paperback pamphlet published by London Labour Publications). See also: Gibbon and Bell, *London County Council*, 324.

Q

national hospital service with local authorities taking the initiative in preparing systematic cooperation among all hospitals in their areas, which had been so much a part of Chamberlain's planning for the Local Government Act, never came to pass.[1] County and borough boundaries were not necessarily good hospital areas. Council hospital committees did not become automatically enlightened administrators of the new institutions under their care. The status of medical practice in what once had been a Poor Law infirmary did not immediately acquire the dignity of an honorary appointment in a voluntary hospital after the institution was taken over by the county authorities.[2]

Arguably, this less than complete success of the experiment in municipal operation of hospitals tended to harden—certainly it did nothing to allay—medical suspicion of proposals for the nationalization of hospitals during the war. Writing at the time of the publication of the White Paper on the National Health Service, Political and Economic Planning summarized what were probably the ordinary memories of the professional atmosphere in municipal general hospitals. There was always the

> inflexible and pettifogging control of doctors, out of date methods of appointing and promoting medical staffs. Narrow-mindedness and lack of imagination are still far too prevalent among local health authorities. The doctors practising in municipal hospitals are usually denied the full measure of freedom in their professional work which is the rule in voluntary hospitals, chiefly because local authorities lack one man—in this case the medical superintendent—to be clearly responsible for all that happens in each of their institutions, whether hospitals, workhouses, or schools. Local authorities still commonly expect their doctor to seek their councils' permission before publishing papers even of a purely medical character, and they do not often invite experts' technical advice from practising doctors or other health workers.
>
> Similarly the Ministry of Health has too often allowed the non-health functions which it inherited from the Local Government Board to overshadow its public health duties; it has too frequently combined a meticulous attention to details with a disheartening disregard for fundamentals; in many respects until recently it has tended too easily to forget even the outside expert advice which it invited and to shelve proposals for reform. The smugness of many of its pre-war reports on such matters as malnutrition and the health of children still rankles. Too many Ministers have been more

---

[1] See for instance: *The Times*, 11 April 1929.
[2] For a full and critical discussion see: PEP, *Report on the British Health Services* (London, 1937), 250–63.

interested in party politics than in the nation's health or in the welfare of doctors, nurses, and other health workers. Both the Ministry and local authorities, not to mention the Treasury, have given too little thought to Newsholme's principle—that 'health is worth whatever expenditures are incurred in its maintenance or to secure its return'.[1]

The Local Government Act of 1929, then, was not the landmark in Poor Law history that the Webbs and other social reformers expected it would be. It did not 'break up' the Poor Law. At least, so far as it concerned the able-bodied unemployed, against whom after all the principles of 1834 had been directed, the new Poor Law disappeared with the Unemployment Act of 1934. On a narrower scale, the 1929 act did not nearly accomplish the unification of institutional health facilities that had been the ideal of all Ministry of Health advocates from Robert Morant to Kingsley Wood. Indeed, in passing, it may be noted that the latter, whose service at the Ministry of Health as Parliamentary Secretary and minister was as long as Chamberlain's, contributed little while he was minister from 1935 to 1938. On the eve of the Second World War the local authorities still supported one million paupers of whom nearly half were receiving medical relief. That, in a time of stable prices after three decades of experimentation with social legislation, $2\frac{1}{2}$ per cent of the population of England and Wales should still be dependent upon the oldest and most despised of all welfare institutions for at least part of their needs provides perhaps the strongest indictment of social planning and political leadership in the interwar period.

The problem of the aged

Neville Chamberlain's third great piece of social welfare legislation, more long-lasting than the Housing Act and of far wider popular effect than the Local Government Act, was the Widows', Orphans' and Old Age Contributory Pensions Act of 1925. This measure, put together in something of an emergency atmosphere, and passed within a year of his taking office, was in at least one way the most influential of all Chamberlain's works. With insurance-based pensions, Chamberlain made contributory insurance the customary vehicle for future social welfare. The political motivation behind this, commending such a measure to the Conservatives, was the possibility—more than a likelihood indeed a threat—that the alternative to a contributory pension financed by the working class would be a non-contributory pension financed, it was intimated, by capital levy. Beneficiary participation,

[1] PEP Broadsheet 222, 'Medical Care for Citizens', 30 June 1944, 12.

Chamberlain intended, would help to remove the problems of old age from the political arena while the extension of pensions themselves would go a long way toward alleviating the most common form of pauperism and so make easier the reform of the Poor Law. Finally, for Chamberlain himself, contributory pensions were the realization of a commitment first made by his father in 1891.

At the beginning of the First World War Britain had as a pension system the plan established by the Old Age Pensions Act of 1908 which provided a pension of 5s. per week for any citizen of the United Kingdom over 70 whose income from other sources did not exceed £21 per year, with reduced pensions for those earning more than £21 but less than £31 10s.[1] In 1914 nearly one million people received non-contributory pensions under the 1908 legislation.

The war at first had little effect on the numbers claiming old age pensions. However, in the autumn of 1916 rising prices forced the Government to institute an allowance of 2s. 6d. for those in special hardship. In August 1917 the 'special hardship' provisions were removed and the means test liberalized by excluding income received by the applicant from military allowances and certain voluntary savings while raising the basic permissible earnings for a full pension to 30s. per week. Nevertheless, by this time inflation had so far increased all earnings, even the pittances of old people, that the number of pensioners at the end of March 1919 was nearly 30,000 smaller than it had been two years earlier.

The fear that pensions, civilian or military, would become an issue for which returning soldiers and the increasingly restless working class would auction their votes seriously worried the political leaders in the months immediately after the war.[2] Accordingly, soon after the Government was reconstructed in January 1919, the Cabinet began to examine the possibility of the reconstruction of the existing pension system. On 3 April 1919, the new Minister of Pensions, Laming Worthington-Evans, appointed a strong departmental committee under the chairmanship of W. Ryland Adkins, a senior Coalition Liberal, to consider 'alterations' in the existing statute. The Adkins Committee conducted a very full investigation. Through the summer months it interviewed more than 50 deputations and witnesses whose evidence ranged far beyond consideration of pensions, and who, because of the simplicity of the non-contributory pensions, were able to deal fully with the basic philosophical and social implications of welfare without becoming enmeshed in matters of detail.

---

[1] For the story of pensions before the First World War see: Gilbert, *Evolution of National Insurance*, 159–232. In fact relatively few people, scarcely one tenth of the total number, chose to claim reduced pensions.

[2] See for instance: A. Montague Barlow to Bonar Law, 13 November 1918. PRO Cab. 24/69, CT 6284.

The committee's report, signed on 7 November 1919, was not precisely what the Cabinet had expected from an investigating body
which, except for a few friendly society people, was made up entirely
of parliamentary supporters and civil servants. Its logic demonstrated
a conviction of the rightness of the general principles of social democracy that had been so much a part of the evidence. 'The final object
which we have in view', said the majority report,

> is a system under which complete and adequate public assistance
> would be available in all cases in which it is required, whether the
> need arises from old age in particular, or from invalidity, unemploy-
> ment, or other forms of disability, and whether or not the need
> extends to destitution. Such a system would cover the field occupied
> by old age pensions and National Insurance on the one side, and the
> Poor Law, regenerated as welfare, on the other.

Any kind of a partial system, the report argued, immediately presented difficulties for establishing eligibility. No department of government, so far as pensions were concerned, was really in a position to
assess income. As evidence the committee called attention to the small
number of partial pensions presently paid which suggested either that
many assets were being concealed or that many people who presumably
deserved at least partial pensions were unwilling to reveal what income they had. The use of the income tax limit as a way of establishing
eligibility for a non-contributory scheme would embarrass the Inland
Revenue. On the other hand the obstacles to a universal contributory
pension — principally that it competed with other forms of thrift — were
the same now as they had been when investigated by Asquith during
the preparation of the 1908 act. 'We have, therefore,' concluded the
majority report, 'been irresistibly forced to advocate that the means
limit be abolished altogether, and that old age pensions be given to all
citizens, at the age of 70. We are of the opinion that no other course
will remove the very serious objections to the present system.' In addition the committee concluded, unanimously, that the present payment
should immediately be increased to 10s. per week per person. The
cost for the universal pension would be, if calculated at 10s. per week,
£41 million per year as opposed to the £18 million being spent in 1919.
On the other hand to restrict the grant to those below the income tax
level would save only £3 million. To double the present means limit
would make pensions cost £32 million, in effect about £14 million
more than was presently being spent.[1]

The Cabinet discussed the Adkins Committee Report with an in-
credulity that even the extraordinarily formal language of the secre-

[1] *Cmd. 410*, 'Report of the Departmental Committee on Old Age Pensions', 1919,
7, 9.

tariat was unable to disguise. With the clamour for money from all sides, pensions could only be raised by added taxation which public opinion would not tolerate. The old contradiction between social welfare and responsible public finance appeared again. The international position of the pound depended on financial conservatism at home. Domestic fiscal prudence defined by the City demanded an end to government borrowing, particularly to short-term borrowing, and most specifically to short-term borrowing to meet current expenses. All of this meant that a sizable increase in pensions, however desirable, was out of the question.

> The present state of foreign exchanges was very bad, and this could not be improved until it was possible to fund the floating debt. This, however, could not be achieved until we had ceased to borrow on the revenue account. Even the borrowing for housing policy would be very difficult. All this made additional taxation undesirable in the last degree.[1]

But on the other hand old age pensions were an unexploded bomb. The TUC witnesses before the Departmental Committee, G. H. Stuart Bunting and C. W. Bowerman, had presented a resolution demanding universal £1 per week pension at age 60 and had argued that the war had shown the amount of money the country could raise.[2] If pensions were left to the House of Commons, concluded the Cabinet, 'pressure from the constituencies, as with the out-of-work donation, would make a very large increase difficult to resist. Moreover, where the merits of the argument *against* the dole were very strong, with pensions they were very weak.' But certainly pensions would have to be enlarged. The cost of living was up; profits on manufacturing and wages were high. Even though pensions had never been thought of as the sole support of the recipient, and despite the fact that much of the money would go to Ireland, something would have to be done.[3]

The upshot was the Old Age Pensions Act of 1919, one of the most unusual spending bills ever passed by the House of Commons. Put together in something approaching a panic, it passed three readings in about one and a half hours of a single day under suspension of the rules without any MP, backbencher or Government, having seen a copy of the measure before it was introduced.[4] Beyond raising the basic pensions to 10s., involving by 1921 an additional outlay of

---

[1] PRO Cab. 23/18, Cabinet 11 of 1919, meeting 8 December.
[2] *Cmd. 411*, 'Appendix to the Report of the Departmental Committee on Old Age Pensions including Minutes of Evidence', 1919, 117–22.
[3] Cabinet Minutes, 8 December 1919.
[4] *H of C Deb.*, CXXXIII (19 December 1919), cols. 865–92. This is the entire debate.

about £10 million, and slightly loosening the means limits, the act amounted to little. By 1920 10s. was worth nearly a third less in purchasing power than 5s. in 1914. One of the few benefits conferred upon the Government by the coming of the Depression was the fall in retail prices, which, while not extinguishing Labour party agitation for a subsistence pension, destroyed much of the potency of the issue.

One important change in 1919 was the total removal of the pauper disqualification. The original bill had prohibited payment of a pension to any one who had received Poor Law relief within the previous two years. While this stipulation had been amended to end in 1910, it was still impossible for an individual to receive poor relief and a pension at the same time. The 1919 measure now permitted, in effect, the parish authorities to subsidize the national pension. Unquestionably a certain amount of this did occur in the years after 1920 although the dramatic rise in the figures of pauperism for persons over 70 that occurred between the wars was more likely due to the increasing use by aged people of the Poor Law Medical Service, which did not in any case disqualify a person for a pension even under the 1908 act.[1]

Even though the Cabinet had disregarded all considerations except financial expediency in setting the amount of old age pensions in 1919, after the coming of the Depression the 20s. per week that an elderly man and wife might receive together was not ungenerous when measured against the amounts provided by other welfare legislation. The sickness benefit under national health insurance, no matter how large the family, was only 15s. Through the early twenties the standard benefit under unemployment insurance, except for a few weeks in the spring of 1921, was likewise 15s. Even after the coming of dependants' benefits in November 1921, the unemployment insurance benefit for a married couple was only 20s. plus 1s. for each child. In addition, a pensioner who had been a contributor to national health insurance received general practitioner medical care free of charge.

After 1919, under the threat of financial collapse and with the growing pressure of unemployment, the Coalition Government declined to discuss any further increases in pensions. Indeed one of the most substantial items in the Geddes programme for national economy in the autumn of 1921 was a reduction in the pensions for state school

---

[1] The number of people over 70 receiving Poor Law relief (and after 1931 Public Assistance) increased about 750 per cent between 1919 and 1939, from 43,200 to 337,000. But included in this figure is the far more dramatic rise in Poor Law outdoor medical relief which rose from about 8,000 in 1920 to 267,000 by 1939. Indoor medical relief increased far less dramatically by only about 50 per cent from 18,500 in 1920 passing a peak of 32,000 in 1931 at the time the Local Government Act of 1929 went into effect, and levelling off at about 26,600 in 1939. 'Persons in receipt of Poor Law Relief', *Account and Papers*, 1919–39.

teachers. However, a revival of interest occurred in 1923 under the administration of Andrew Bonar Law with a suggestion by Sidney Webb that despite the relatively large amounts of money being spent on social services there were many, particularly ex-servicemen, who were not cared for, who fell through 'gaps' in the structure of the welfare. This typical Webbian interest in neatness of administration appealed to the Prime Minister. The result, in February, was the appointment of an interdepartmental committee charged, essentially, with looking into the integration of social welfare apparatus. The committee's reports were signed in December, after the Conservatives' defeat in the General Election of 1923 but before Baldwin, who had succeeded Bonar Law, had resigned. Briefly, the report declared that there *were* gaps in welfare administration but that they are to be closed only by a comprehensive rebuilding of the entire benefits structure.[1]

The publication of the committee report coincided approximately with the appearance, in January 1924, of William Beveridge's pamphlet, *Insurance for All and Every Thing*. Beveridge's scheme was published 'under the auspices' of the Council of Liberal Summer Schools by the *Daily News*, at that time owned by David Lloyd George. The pamphlet was hardly the preview of social insurance and allied services that Beveridge later came to regard it; it was more a survey of existing provisions with some suggestions at the end. However, it did call attention to the 'definite gaps' in the national welfare provisions for a large group in the population, particularly for widows and orphans, and it had a considerable circulation.[2] As a remedy Beveridge proposed an 'all in' insurance programme, covering health, unemployment, dependants, disability and widows' pensions. It suggested that pensions for the working man should begin at age 65 not 70 and that a widow's pension of 12s. should be established with perhaps 6s. for dependants.[3] Beveridge supplemented these proposals with a more detailed plan published in the *Nation and Atheneum* on 12 July 1924.

The rising public interest in extensions of the social services and the advent on 22 January of the first Labour Government—whose plans for social reform were unclear but were presumed to be large and expensive—inevitably stimulated planning activity among the Con-

---

[1] *Cmd. 2011*, 'Inter-Departmental Committee on the Co-ordination of Administrative and Executive Arrangements for the Grant of Assistance from Public Funds on Account of Sickness, Destitution and Unemployment', 1924. The chairman of the committee was Sir Henry Betterton.

[2] It became a 'best seller' according to Janet Beveridge, *Beveridge and His Plan* (London, 1954), 76.

[3] W. H. Beveridge, *Insurance For All and Everything* (January, 1924), 26, 27, 33.

servatives.[1] A small group of backbenchers under the leadership of J. A. R. Marriot, the historian, using the advice of a former Coalition Liberal, Mr Thomas Tucker Broad, had been at work for some months on a scheme of comprehensive national insurance which Marriot put down as a Private Member's Bill as soon as Parliament met.[2] Meanwhile the Conservative leadership, not wishing to be outflanked by its own backbenchers, had begun to consider possible extension of welfare services. In March Chamberlain, who was at work privately on a plan of his own, sent Baldwin a memorandum proposing that the Party officially begin to consider comprehensive insurance. The scheme, Chamberlain said, must be contributory and compulsory. It must cover the four main needs of the breadwinner: unemployment, sickness, old age and death. The pensions should be large enough to permit old men to retire and so help reduce unemployment.[3] Baldwin, who a year earlier had publicly doubted whether comprehensive insurance had 'much to recommend it', now gave his blessing and Chamberlain set to work with a Liverpool actuary, Duncan C. Fraser, to draw a plan for an insurance programme that the Conservative party might adopt.[4] Although Chamberlain's project was almost entirely a private venture, by the end of March Baldwin, in his woolly and unspecific way and with very little notion of what was involved, had begun to allude to a large programme of social legislation that his party was preparing.[5]

With MacDonald's sudden dissolution of Parliament on 9 October 1924 the extravagant but unclear statements about a general overhaul of all welfare programmes became rather more specific and at the same time considerably narrower. Both Baldwin and Chamberlain in their addresses to electors announced that they hoped, rather than promised, that the Conservatives would be able to enlarge the existing pension system.[6] Both men publicly deplored Labour's tendency to use the welfare of old ladies and destitute children as a weapon in the class struggle by coupling pensions with a capital levy. Both emphasized that only through a contributory system could a genuine, universal, non-means-tested pension be financed.

[1] In the King's Speech Baldwin's Government, secure in the knowledge that it would be turned out of office within days, promised 'to deal with the discouragement of thrift' involved in the existing pensions means test. *H of C Deb.*, CLXIX (15 January 1924), col. 80. Privately the Cabinet had discussed only the possibility of extending slightly the list of exempted forms of income. PRO Cab. 24/164, CP 19, 'Old Age Pensions', 10 January 1924.
[2] On the Broad scheme see: *Spectator*, 1, 22 March 1924.
[3] Feiling, *Chamberlain*, 114.
[4] *H of C Deb.*, CLX (19 February 1923), col. 604.
[5] See Baldwin's speeches in Edinburgh, 24 March, and to the Junior Imperial League, 3 May 1924.
[6] *The Times*, 15, 16 October 1924.

One could scarcely say that the issue of old age pensions, or indeed any issue of social welfare other than unemployment, figured largely in the General Election of 29 October 1924, which returned the Conservatives to office with a majority of 223 over all other parties. But even with the immediate threat from Labour gone, care for the aged was no less a political than a social necessity. The non-contributory scheme of 1908, however straightforward and simple its operation, could not be expanded except at ruinous cost to the tax-payer. Above all it could not be enlarged by a Conservative Government already beset by clamourings from members of its own party that British prices were too high in competition with foreign goods. On the other hand the increasing proportion of old people in the population was a social fact. Pension coverage ought to be broadened and would be broadened. But the task could not be left to Labour which was now clearly to be considered the normal alternative party. If pensions were to be handled responsibly and soberly, the Conservatives must deal with the question and within their existing tenure of office.

In fact the Government privately had already begun to plan a modest extension of the insurance principle in the form of contributory pensions. After the 1923 election but before Baldwin's resignation, apparently on the initiative of Horace Wilson who was at that time Permanent Secretary of the Ministry of Labour, a small, only semi-official, committee of seven civil servants under Sir John Anderson began to look into ways of coordinating various welfare services. Wilson's particular interest, which he finally saw translated into legislation eleven years later in the Unemployment Act of 1934, was in ending the competition between unemployment insurance and Poor Law relief of the unemployed.

The Anderson Committee was in many ways an unusual body and its two reports had a strange history. Its irregular status was emphasized by the lack of a Treasury representative among its members and by the fact that there is reason to believe, despite his biographer's statement, that the out-going Prime Minister, Stanley Baldwin, had not approved and perhaps did not know of its creation.[1] After a quick interim report in January before the Conservatives left office, the committee presented a fuller report to Philip Snowden, the Labour

[1] G. M. Young, *Stanley Baldwin* (London, 1952), 97. Unfortunately Anderson's biographer only mentions the committee by remarking that its report became the basis of the 1925 Pensions Act. John W. Wheeler-Bennett, John Anderson, *Viscount Waverly* (London, 1962), 114. The members of the committee were, besides Anderson and Wilson, H. P. Hamilton, John Lamb, W. Arthur Robinson, Permanent Secretary at the Ministry of Health, and the Government Actuary, Alfred Watson, with H. D. Hancock, private secretary to Wilson as secretary of the committee.

Chancellor of the Exchequer early in July 1924. Whether Snowden planned to use the report as a basis for a pension plan is not clear—the debates on Chamberlain's bill revealed a wide split on the contributory principle between Snowden and the rest of the party—but certainly the Labour Cabinet never considered, and probably never saw, the Anderson report. So it was not until the Conservatives returned to office, on 6 November 1924, that the report finally was scrutinized by the political leader for whom it had been written.

Chamberlain brought up pensions in the Cabinet a few days after submitting his programme of proposed legislation for the Ministry of Health, in which widows' and old age pensions had been scheduled for 1926. At this time he was requested to communicate with the Chancellor of the Exchequer about his plans bringing together the material collected by his own party committee and by the Anderson Committee. In his interview with Churchill he learned something of the new Chancellor's plans for his first budget in which he hoped to make a large reduction in the income tax. Exactly as in 1906 Henry Campbell-Bannerman and Herbert Asquith had first taken up the original pension act as a means of balancing the Liberal concentration on education, Churchill in November 1924 asked Chamberlain to move forward his own pension proposals so that benefits for the working classes could balance a cut in the income tax. On 3 December the Cabinet determined to make pensions a part of the coming year's legislative programme and Chamberlain was instructed to compose an appropriate sentence for the King's Speech.[1] The greatest importance of the Anderson Committte may be that it made possible within a very few months the preparation of a long, complicated and very expensive parliamentary measure with which Chamberlain had not expected to be concerned for nearly a year.

The Anderson Committee specifically advised against converting the existing 1908 pensions to a contributory plan, principally because such a change would cut out many needy people, particularly women, who had never been wage earners and so would not qualify under any contributory scheme. An alternative, also rejected, was to set up the contributory scheme alongside the present free pensions, but this again would result in an inequity. It proposed therefore the institution of a limited contributory pension scheme beginning at 65 and ending at 70 and noted that the results would be great savings both on national health insurance and on unemployment insurance. The pensionable group, it pointed out, was made up of people with great liability to

---

[1] Feiling, *Chamberlain*, 131. PRO Cab. 23/49, Cabinets 64 and 65 of 1924, meeting 26 November and 3 December.

sickness and unemployment. It might even be possible to reduce the State grants to those funds.[1]

So far as possible the pension programme that came out of the relatively brief discussions in the spring of 1925 was to be integrated into existing services, which would both simplify administration and prevent future tampering. Coverage would be limited to the contributors to national health insurance except that a few groups exempt from health insurance would nevertheless contribute to pensions. The basic pension proposed was 10s. per week for the contributor or his widow at 65. At 70 any individual receiving a contributory pension passed automatically to the non-contributory 1908 pension without further means, residence or nationality tests. Thus the proposal substantially accomplished what Labour had so long demanded. It did not make the 1908 pension universal but it extended coverage to five-sixths of the population. At the same time the incorporation of the 1908 programme into the contributory scheme tended to stabilize the former at the level of the latter, reducing the political volatility of tax supported payments. Other provisions included 5s. for the eldest dependant child up to age 16, reduced in the bill to 14 for economy, with 3s. for all others, and 7s. for orphans. Contributions were to be 4½d. each from the working man and his employer with 2d. from the working woman and 2½d. from her employer. Pensions for widows and children would begin 1 January 1926 and for regular contributors on 1 January 1928.

By early April 1925, a little more than four months after Chamberlain's first visit to Churchill, the Cabinet committee on pensions headed by Churchill and including Chamberlain and the Lord Privy Seal, Lord Salisbury, had proposed a draft bill. Generally the Cabinet committee assumed that the ideal measure would be one in which the beneficiaries would pay nearly the entire cost of their own pensions. This would be 'a good example of Conservative social reform', remarked Churchill.[2] In fact the measure did not achieve this. New entrants at age 16 would pay, to be sure, the entire cost of their insurance based pension covering their lives between 65 and 70 as well as 21 per cent of the cost of the older 1908 pension. Furthermore the proportion of the total pension costs supported by new entrants would increase as rates of contribution were raised at regular decennial intervals so that by

[1] 'Committee on Insurance and Other Social Services', 8 July 1924, bound with PRO Cab. 24/173, CP 204, 'Improved Old Age Pensions and Pensions for Widowed Mothers', 18 April 1925.
[2] PRO Cab. 27/276, 'Widows' and Old Age Pensions, Minutes of Cabinet Committee Meeting 9 April 1925'.

1956 workers coming into the scheme would pay not only the cost of the new pension but of the 1908 pension as well.

On the other hand, in the coverage of widows and orphans, the scheme incurred a considerable actuarial deficit. In the beginning Treasury payments would run nearly half the total income from contributions.[1] This early deficit was compounded by the fact that contributory pensions for the first group over 65 commenced after only two years of payment by contributors while no contributions at all would have been paid for most widows and orphans immediately eligible for pensions. This problem—how to care for those eligible for pensions on account of age but without a credit in the pension fund—had seemed impossible to solve in the prewar discussion of beneficiary financed pensions and had been one of the large arguments in favour of a tax supported pension. Chamberlain's bold solution was to make the cost of the elderly simply a charge upon society.

The financial calculations of the measure were relatively simple. The Treasury payment to the contributory pension fund was set at an annual £4 million for at least the first decade, athough the net outlay by the Government would be about £400,000 less than this because of the suspension of national health insurance sickness benefits to pensioners. At the end of ten years workers' and employers' contributions were to increase, while Exchequer support, it was hoed, could be reduced. In succeeding decades as contributions from workers and employers were increased, the plan, xcept for widows' and orphans' payments, would become self-supporting for new entrants. But in the meantime the broadened eligibility for 1908 pensions, four-fifths carried by the Treasury, would cost an extra £2,700,000 in the first year, making the total new outlay caused by Chamberlain's bill to be about £6,300,000.[2]

The Cabinet approved the plan outlined in CP 204 on 22 April after a speech from Baldwin on the origin of the pension proposals and on the need for 'exceptional secrecy' concerning them.[3] Chamberlain introduced his measure a week later, on 29 April, the day after Churchill's first budget speech in which the Chancellor had displayed an enthusiasm for pensions that had caused some members of the Ministry to comment that he was attempting to take credit for the

[1] CP 204, 18 April 1925.
[2] PRO Cab. 24/173, CP 214, 'Report by the Government Actuaries on the Financial Provisions of the Bill', 25 April 1925. The Anderson Committee had not dealt with the 1908 pension.
[3] PRO Cab. 24/50, Cabinet 21 of 1925 meeting 22 April 1925. Not surprisingly hints on the Government's pension proposals almost immediately began to appear in the press and Baldwin had to give his colleagues another lecture on the subject five days later. PRO Cab. 23/50, Cabinet 22 of 1925 meeting 27 April.

scheme.[1] However the bill was not published until 5 May and the second reading was delayed until the eighteenth.

The resistance to the Contributory Pension Bill originated in two quarters. The least formidable was that of the Labour Party in the House of Commons. Labour attacked Chamberlain's measure over the extension of the contributory principle and for the inadequacy of the pensions themselves. On the other hand the Labour party was hampered by the ingenious financial construction of the scheme itself. Whatever one might say to the effect that in the long run the pensions for new entrants were virtually self-financing and so with the flat-rate contributions represented a regressive form of taxation, for the immediate future the bill's provisions were extremely generous and could scarcely be opposed. Thus the Opposition was reduced to criticism of the scale of the benefits themselves, claiming that they offered inadequate maintenance and were an insult to widowhood while re-iterating their old demands for a living pension paid for from taxes. Above all Labour's difficulty proceeded from the party's failure to arrive at any consensus of its own on pensions. The widely held belief that Philip Snowden favoured a contributory scheme seriously embarrassed Labour speakers.[2]

Far more serious was the opposition of the national health insurance approved societies. The societies customarily saw a threat to themselves in any proposed welfare agency beyond their control. But besides the usual jealousy, widows' and orphans' pensions appeared a particular threat especially to the industrial insurance organizations. Widows' pensions, it may be remembered, had been part of Lloyd George's original health insurance scheme as it took final form in the summer of 1910. His famous Criccieth memorandum of 17 August 1910 proposing a Coalition of the Liberal and Unionist parties had been aimed principally at outflanking the enormous army of industrial insurance collecting agents who threatened to make national health insurance impossible to enact if the measure included widows' pensions.

In 1911 industrial insurance companies themselves did not offer old age protection, selling only the 1d. insurance policies. Neverthe-

---

[1] Feiling, *Chamberlain*, 131, diary entry 1 May 1925. Privately Chamberlain admitted that the scheme, and particularly the introduction of it in 1925, owed a good deal to Churchill. P. J. Grigg, then a civil servant at the Treasury, states flatly that Churchill 'impelled' the Baldwin Government into pensions. P. J. Grigg, *Prejudice and Judgement* (London, 1948), 194–5.

[2] John Wheatley's motion rejecting the second reading never made clear what form a Labour bill would have taken. It simply attacked the contributory principle as an additional burden on industry and argued that the amounts offered were too small. *H of C Deb.*, CLXXIV (18 May 1925), col. 93.

less, the industrial insurance industry—including both the great limited companies and the so-called 'collecting' friendly societies—saw potential competition in any payment to a recently bereaved widow whether it was in the form of a single lump-sum benefit or as a weekly pension. Using the power of a collecting organization, the industrial insurance companies had first forced Lloyd George to drop widows' pensions from the bill and then, in order to secure ground already conquered, had demanded and received the right to form approved societies in order to become administrators of national health insurance. Formation of industrial assurance approved societies was bitterly resisted by the older friendly society movement and the necessary overhauling of national health insurance, entailed by these changes, forced the Chancellor to preside over a number of bitter and extended conferences in which he and his colleagues came to appreciate the power of industrial insurance. His fear of their strength was manifest in the consultations over the Ministry of Health and in the compromises made to the fraternal approved societies—here industrial insurance was less concerned—in unemployment insurance.

Now in 1925, from the insurance point of view, the political situation was less favourable. Lloyd George was out of office and his position within the Liberal Party, of which Asquith was the nominal leader, was equivocal. Adding to the societies' unease was the growing antagonism between themselves and Labour, signalled by the MacDonald Government's appointment in 1924 of a Royal Commission on national health insurance which had not yet reported, but which the societies were well aware was generally unfriendly to the approved society system.

During 1924 the insurance world had shown increasing apprehension at the reviving political concern for social welfare. Especially depressing was the fact that the Conservatives, whom the friendly societies particularly depended upon for allies, were allowing themselves to become committed to widows' pensions. Speeches by Chamberlain, Hoare, and especially Baldwin, received wide notice. With both parties committed to some extension of the pension system ordinary methods of political pressure and resistance were of little use, commented the *Insurance Mail* early in April, after a speech by Baldwin at Edinburgh on 24 March. 'What we should accustom our minds to is the provision by the state of payments to widows—in other words, a death benefit, payable not in a lump sum on the death of the breadwinner, but at so much per week for a period covering at least the infancy of the children left without a father.' Deplorable as all of this was, probably in the long run it would not hurt the insurance business much. Baldwin's statements about security would provide an excellent canvassing argument, thought the journal, and insurance would be needed to supplement any State pension.[1]

The Conservative victory at the end of October calmed approved society nerves a good deal. Although periodicals reflecting insurance opinion, particularly the *National Insurance Gazette* and the *Insurance Mail,* assumed still that some sort of a pension bill would come within six months, they assured their readers that a measure from the Conservatives would be preferable to one from Labour. Even more comforting was the fact that the Conservatives would be in power should the sitting Royal Commission recommend some general overhaul of national health insurance that made both funeral benefits and endowment insurance unnecessary. Finally, most reassuring, was the appointment of Kingsley Wood, on 11 November, as Parliamentary Secretary to the Ministry of Health. He needed no introduction to the approved society world, having played an important part both in the National Insurance Act and in staving off unpleasantness in the Industrial Assurance Act of 1923, noted the *National Insurance Gazette*. He could be depended upon 'to put the views of the Approved Societies' forcibly before the proper authorities.[2]

While the approved societies consoled themselves with the recollection that at least their friends were in office and that if a pension bill had to come this was probably the time for it, Chamberlain was preparing an unpleasant surprise. One of the factors commending the consideration of large extensions of social insurance during 1924 had been a steadily decreasing rate of unemployment which in the summer moved below 10 per cent of the English and Welsh work force for the first time since 1921. The principal reason for this had nothing to do with the British economy. The French occupation of the Ruhr and the resultant strikes in the German coal mines raised world coal prices and reduced unemployment among the one million men in the British coal industry to little more than 3 per cent. Unfortunately in the summer of 1924 the Germans ended their passive resistance to the French occupation, German coal mining revived, world coal prices tumbled and unemployment in British mines leaped up again passing the national average in the spring of 1925.

All this affected planning for old age pensions. At the end of March the Government Actuary, Sir Alfred Watson, submitted a memorandum to the Ministry of Health expressing deep concern. The Ministry of Labour, he said, was beginning to fear contributory pensions because of the heavier than expected unemployment. It would not be possible now, Watson thought, to bring down unemployment insurance contributions to compensate for the extra levy necessitated by pensions. But,

[1] *Insurance Mail,* 12 April 1924.
[2] *National Insurance Gazette,* 22 November 1924.

he contended, the rates of contribution could be reduced for national health insurance as many of the societies possessed large surpluses. Chamberlain supported this view a few weeks later reminding the Cabinet that agricultural workers, while under health insurance, were not covered by unemployment insurance. Consequently this entire class of labour would be excluded from the benefit accruing from a reduction in contributions to unemployment insurance. On the other hand a reduction in the contribution for health insurance would benefit equally all classes of labour.[1]

The upshot was that when the bill was introduced there were no changes in the unemployment insurance contributions but the measure provided for a 1d. reduction in the employed contribution to national health insurance for men and a ½d. reduction in the women's contribution. In effect, while the premium for old age pensions from both the workman and his employer was 9d. for men and 4½d. for women, the actual amount of new outlay demanded of a worker's pay for both health and pension was 8d. or 3½d. The result, as the approved societies looked at it, was a subsidy to the pension programme from their income in the amount of nearly £2,400,000, or about 10 per cent of their revenue.

Until publication of the pension bill on 5 May, a week after its first reading in the House of Commons, the approved societies had been reasonably complacent. A few spokesmen assumed that the societies would be allowed to administer widows' pensions as Lloyd George had originally proposed before the war.[2] Accordingly they reacted violently when they discovered not only that they were excluded from administration but that the coming of pensions would cost them a substantial portion of their income. 'Mr Lloyd George intended pensions from the very start,' asserted the *National Insurance Gazette* on 16 May, 'and only postponed them. There is little doubt that if they had been included, approved societies would have administered them. It will not do to let the Government think we will stand anything.' Generally the societies tended to accuse the Conservative administration of pandering to Labour.

It has long been known that the Trade Unions, for instance, have

---

[1] PRO Pin. 3/19, Bill File 'Widows', Orphans' and Contributory Old Age Pension Bill, 1925', Part I, Memorandum, A. W. Watson, 25 March 1925; 'Memorandum on Administration by Approved Societies', unsigned, undated; CP 204, 18 April 1925. In the summer the Government while restoring ministerial discretion on extended benefit did, in fact, reduce the worker's and employer's contribution to unemployment insurance by 2d. each at a cost to the fund of £6,800,000. But at the same time it extended the waiting period for benefit from three days to six saving £6,500,000. For an explanation see: *H of C Deb.*, CLXXVI (7 July 1925), cols. 251–65.

[2] See the statement by Percy Rockliff, *The Times*, 30 April 1925.

R

been strenuously opposed to the Industrial Assurance Group having any lot or part in the administration of the new Pension benefits, and we believe that in refusing to let Approved Societies administer the new benefits to the pensioners the Government will have the support of the Labour Party.

Such is the gratitude of politicians. We saved the National Health Insurance Scheme from disaster. . . .[1]

After the initial burst of outrage approved society opinion moderated somewhat. The *Gazette* reminded the industry that it might not be desirable to antagonize the Cabinet while the Royal Commission on National Health Insurance was still sitting. Sir Joseph Burn, the General Manager of the Prudential and F. T. Jefferson, formerly of the Britannic, both urged moderation in statesman-like but unspecific terms. Early in June at its meeting at Bournemouth the Manchester Unity of Odd Fellows, the largest of the friendly societies, heard speeches attacking the reduction in contributions as a breach of faith with the approved societies but also approving the reduction of pension age as an unquestioned benefit to society funds.[2] The societies of course were intimidated by the fact that the Labour opposition to the bill had nothing in common with their own position and was based instead on the inadequacy of the proposed pension while attacking the insurance principle. In fact the only consistent friend of the approved societies in the House of Commons was David Lloyd George.

As the bill made its way through the Commons the relation between pensions and national health insurance and the effect of the programme upon the approved societies came increasingly to dominate the debates. Lloyd George introduced the societies during the second reading by recounting his familiar story about the help he had received in establishing national health insurance from the 70,000 insurance agents. In fact this meant aid only from industrial assurance; the friendly societies at that time employed no collectors.[3]

But the administrators of health insurance were in danger from the right as well as the left. One of the features of the debate on the bill was the fierce attacks upon it by several Conservative industrialists and particularly by the former Chancellor of the Exchequer, Sir Robert Horne. In an uncomfortable alliance with Labour, Horne denounced the contributory principle as laying a further burden upon British industry. In July, just before the third reading debate, to the terror of the approved societies it was suggested that the large surpluses ac-

---

[1] *National Insurance Gazette*, 9, 16 May 1925.
[2] *Ibid.*, 23 May, 13 June 1925; *The Times*, 3 June 1925.
[3] *H of C Deb.*, CLXIV (18 May 1925), col. 115. Labour's attitude towards industrial insurance was exemplified by Ellen Wilkinson's shout of 'Spies' at the mention of the collection agents.

cumulated under national health insurance be used either to pay for pensions or to reduce contributions.[1] By the third reading, the debate on contributory pensions had degenerated principally into an attack by the Labour party supported by a few members of the Conservative back bench upon the administration of national health insurance with a reluctant defence of the societies by the Government. William Graham, for Labour, happily associated his party with what he insisted was Horne's contention that pensions should be non-contributory and that the surplus in the national health insurance funds should be used immediately for reductions in contributions. Horne, denying that he had urged non-contributory pensions, admitted that the 1890 Manchester Unity of Odd Fellows tables used in national health insurance assumed a far larger incidence of sickness than now was the case and that interest rates were higher than they had been before the war. Chamberlain, ominously, refused to make any promises about future treatment of the societies.[2]

Even though the Royal Commission had not yet reported, the debates over the contributory pension bill were a clear warning to the approved societies of unpleasantness in the future. The Contributory Pensions Act of 1925, therefore, must be considered a part of the changes in the health programme that came with the Economy Act of 1926 to be discussed in connection with national health insurance. More important, the accumulation of bitterness left by society behaviour in the twenties finally caused the societies to be dropped from State insurance despite William Beveridge's great efforts to create a place in his programme for at least a friendly society portion of the approved society apparatus. Whether the old fraternal orders, which for a third of a century had tried with little success to initiate pension plans among their own members, might have been able to adapt their organizations to fit into a Government pension plan is hard to say. They never had the opportunity again.

Contributory pensions after 1925

The operation of the national provisions for the aged between 1926 and the coming of the Second World War provides two obvious but conflicting conclusions. First the act of 1925 proved to be actuarily sound and nearly, not absolutely, invulnerable to politics. Yet second, in terms of the professed aims of its sponsors, the alleviation of economic hardship among the aged, it was far less than a success.

Concerning the first point, in 1929 the Labour Government added potentially nearly 500,000 people, or obout 50 per cent, to the pension

[1] See: *National Insurance Gazette*, 1 August 1925.
[2] *H of C Deb.*, CLXXXVI (22 July 1925), cols. 2342–7, 2350–4, 2369–76.

rolls by giving pensions at age 55 to the widows of insurable men who had died before 4 January 1926, the date at which the widows' pensions became payable. Benefits under this act began on 1 July 1930 for women already over 60 and on 1 January 1931 for those over 55 bringing immediately about 320,000 new pensioners into the scheme.[1] The act of 1929 greatly extended the immediate State financial responsibility, even if it did not increase permanently the number of individuals pensionable. Benefit payments under the unfunded portion of the widows' pension account leaped up from £3,500,000 in 1929–30 to £7,800,000 in 1930–31 and to £10,500,000 in 1931–32.[2] Of the £764 million capital liability that stood against the pension scheme in its last valuation before the war, £100 million was the result of the extensions in the act of 1929 which, much to Chamberlain's disgust, the Conservatives had chosen not to oppose.

A final extension of Government pensions came with the Widows', Orphans' and Old Age Contributory Pensions (Voluntary Contributors) Act of 1937 which extended pension rights to independent workers whose income exceeded the £250 per year maximum for compulsory pensions but was less than £400 per year (or £250 for women) of which not more than half was unearned. These pensions came into force on 3 January 1938. For the first year only, until 2 January 1939, the plan permitted any individual in the appropriate earnings bracket and under age 55 to subscribe for a 10s. pension at age 65 plus the regular non-contributory pension at 70 in return for a contribution of 1s. 3d. for men or 6d. for women. After the beginning of 1939, however, the maximum age for joining the scheme would go down to 40 and the scale of contributions would increase according to age with a maximum of 2s. 11d. for men or 11d. for women.

Although very generous, the so-called 'black-coated workers' pensions were less than a popular success. The Ministry of Health had suggested that perhaps 700,000 of the slightly fewer than 2,000,000 persons eligible would apply for them.[3] As it turned out, by the end of October 1938 only 272,000 applications had been received of which nearly one-third had to be rejected. In the last months of 1938 the

[1] The best summary of the operation of the pension plan as modified may be found in: 'Widows', Orphans' and Old Age Contributory Pensions Acts 1925–1932, report by the Government Actuary', 1935, in *Accounts and Papers*. (Not a paper by command.) See also: 'Financial operation of the Widows' Orphans' and Old Age Contributory Pension Scheme in Great Britain.' *International Labour Review*, XXXIII (April 1936), 543–51. This study is largely founded on the actuaries' report with some comment.

[2] Government contributions were to increase by an additional £1 million each year to level off at £21 million in 1942.

[3] On the planning on the Voluntary Contributors Act see: *Cmd. 5801*, 'Nineteenth Annual Report of the Ministry of Health, 1937–38', 1938, 185–8.

Government mounted an intensive publicity campaign which succeeded in bringing in about 380,000 more. In all slightly fewer than 438,000 eligible men and women applied to join the voluntary pension scheme before 2 January 1939.

The second, perhaps more important, conclusion to be drawn from any survey of the rather substantial efforts in the interwar period to care for Britain's old people is that the government programme was relatively unsuccessful in providing the nation's elderly with economic independence. Statistics on the numbers receiving Poor Law relief— a term that persisted in official reports despite all legislative attempts to abolish it—showed a regular increase of approximately 5 per cent per year between 1931 and 1939 among persons over 65 even though after 1935 the total numbers at all ages receiving public assistance declined. Specifically on 1 January 1931 about 215,000 persons over 65 received relief. Most astonishing is that these figures grew regularly, almost inexorably, and seemed to be unaffected by the rise and fall of other statistics of distress. There were, in comparison, slightly more than 1,000,000 people of all ages receiving Poor Law relief on 1 January 1931. This number grew to nearly 1,500,000 in 1935 but fell back again to slightly over 1,000,000 on 1 January 1931. Despite all attempts to improve their condition, the elderly were forming a continually larger proportion of those forced to apply for public charity. This problem was recognized after the outbreak of war by the Old Age and Widows' Pension Act of 1940 which lowered the pensionable age to 60 for insured women or the wives of insured men over 65. Most important, however, the second part of the act introduced a supplementary pension based on need and administered by the Unemployment Assistance Board, renamed the Assistance Board, in the same year. Well before the end of the war the cost of supplementary pensions was nearly one-third of the cost of all pensions.[1]

Through the twenties and thirties, it should be noted in summary, attitudes about the care of the elderly evolved along approximately the same lines as attitudes toward the care of the unemployed. In both cases the conception at the beginning had been that State aid was to be given only as a supplement toward private savings and that if there were no private savings or other resources the individual recipient would be kept alive only if he permitted himself to be made a pauper. Support proportionate to need was available only from the Poor Law. By sanctioning Poor Law relief at a higher scale than the sums offered by insurance and pension benefit the nation admitted that pension,

[1] On the problems of the elderly attempting to live on pensions see: *Old People, Report of a Survey Committee on the Problems of Ageing and the Care of Old People Under the Chairmanship of B. Seebohm Rowntree*, a Nuffield Foundation Report (London, 1947), 7–8, 14–15.

unemployment and health benefits were too small. Yet it stipulated at the same time that a man attempting to realize these benefits should commit a form of civil crime. Such a system could not long survive the changes that overcame the British political world in the 1920s. Arguably, in giving aid according to need, what the Unemployment Assistance Board did for the unemployed was finally accomplished for the elderly with supplemental pensions in 1940 under the threat of wartime inflation. Yet although the concept of maintenance according to need had gained at least grudging acceptance by the beginning of the Second World War, the programmes themselves, insurance-based pensions and unemployment benefits, were products of another age when it had been assumed that a low flat-rate contribution was all that the ordinary workman could afford.

No doubt within the context of the economic conditions of the interwar period these assumptions were quite correct. Small increases of 1d. or 2d. in weekly contributions were bitterly resisted. But the consequence was huge subventions by the taxpayer to the pensions and unemployment insurance programmes. If the programmes were to keep any respectability as actuarial propositions, contributions would have to approach expenses. This was particularly true in old age pensions where the cost of supporting a growing proportion of pensioners in the population would fall on a smaller and smaller productive wage-earning and contribution-paying popuation. The question for the future then, one not answered even in the Beveridge report, was how to prevent ever-larger insurance contributions from being regarded simply as a vast and regressive subsidiary income tax system. And if this were the case, would not the wage-earning population retaliate against punitive insurance contributions at the bottom of the scale by imposing equally punitive progressive income tax rates upon the wealthier sections of the community.

6 Towards a national health service

For most people before the war, social reform meant Part I of the National Insurance Act of 1911. In health insurance, David Lloyd George provided 14 million British men and women with general practitioner medical care and payments for the support of members of the family while the wage earner was sick. If not as imaginative and experimental as unemployment insurance, health insurance was by all odds the most expensive and most controversial of the Liberal measures. Through the wage earner, it touched five-sixths of the families of the United Kingdom, bringing them into contact with the national government in an unprecedented way. It began the transformation of relations between British citizens and the State.

In return for a 4d. contribution from working men, or a 3d. contribution from women, with 3d. from the employer, Lloyd George's measure provided unlimited general practitioner medical care for the working man himself and 10s. per week for his family while the breadwinner was incapacitated. The 10s. sickness benefit was available for 26 weeks after which it dropped to 5s. and became, technically, a disability benefit which would continue indefinitely. In addition the plan offered a 30s. lump-sum payment at child-birth for the wife of an insured working man, although she did not receive medical care under the programme. It provided finally institutional care in sanitoria in case of tuberculosis. The cash benefits were administered by the approved societies, either the old friendly societies or the national insurance sections of the industrial insurance companies and collecting friendly societies.

Because the approved societies became so important a factor in subsequent welfare planning about not only health insurance but nearly all other areas of social policy, the reasons for establishing this awkward and somewhat self-defeating system of administration are worth brief examination. Lloyd George's consideration of health insurance had grown out of his experience with non-contributory old age pensions which he had piloted through Parliament in 1908 soon after he became Chancellor of the Exchequer. Privately, he considered the tax-supported pension scheme an inadequate and unduly expensive way of dealing with the problem of distress. Although like many other reformers he looked for some way to supersede the Poor Law through a far-reaching programme of unconditional State payments, such a large plan could not be supported by the Exchequer alone. To a considerable extent it would have to be supported by payments from the beneficiaries. With this in mind, in August 1908, the Chancellor travelled to Germany to look into the widows', orphans' and invalidity pensions established there as part of that nation's general programme of contributory insurance. He returned filled with enthusiasm for the German scheme and in the last month of 1908, very much as a personal project within the Treasury, he began the planning of a scheme of social insurance that would provide pensions for workers' sickness and disability, and for widows and orphans.

Here the government plan would have come into competition with the friendly society movement, which already offered these benefits. Therefore, Lloyd George proposed from the beginning to bring the societies into his programme by offering some sort of a government subsidy which would extend fraternal insurance to that part of the working population which hitherto had been unable to insure for itself. No enlargement of government social insurance would be possible, or indeed desirable, the Chancellor felt, without their cooperation.

An impelling motive for agreement with the friendly societies before invading their field of activity was their reputation for parliamentary influence. The fear of society opposition had destroyed Joseph Chamberlain's attempts to establish a contributory old age pension in the 1890s. Later at the turn of the century, when organized promotion for a non-contributory pension along the lines first suggested by Charles Booth had begun, friendly society attitudes were meticulously canvassed. The need for soothing the friendly societies determined more than any other factor the shape of the Old Age Pensions Act of 1908. The societies would accept only, and that reluctantly, a tax supported pension and even if pensions were paid for entirely from the Treasury, they had to be small, with a severe means test. They could provide, therefore, no base for further expansion of social welfare services.

As a consequence Lloyd George did not have as an alternative the expansion of the non-contributory system even had he been able to overcome the opposition within the Cabinet of the proponents of naval rearmament. Essentially his choices for widows' and invalidity pensions were to try and build within England a Germanized system of social insurance supported by beneficiary contributions in competition with the friendly societies or to bring the friendly societies into his plan and to make them the beneficiaries of a system of compulsory State insurance.

Accordingly, between the autumn of 1908 and the autumn of 1910, interrupted by the tremendous battle over the 'People's Budget,' he negotiated with the National Conference of Friendly Societies a mea-

sure of social insurance which would require friendly society membership for all working men that the societies cared to accept and would
set up some sort of comprehensive State plan for working men who
could find no society. Then in the middle of these negotiations, probably early in August 1910, the Chancellor learned that his plans for
social insurance concerned not only the friendly society movement
but the British industrial insurance industry as well. Because a
widows' and orphans' pension would reduce a wife's financial desperation at the time of her husband's death it would interfere with the sale
of funeral insurance. Funeral benefits themselves, the £10–15 policy
to ensure a 'respectable' funeral for the family breadwinner and avoid
the indignity of Potters' Field, had not been considered from the
beginning as a part of the national insurance scheme partly because
the friendly societies also sold such benefits and partly to avoid precisely the objection that now appeared from the industrial insurance
industry.

Industrial insurance and the collecting friendly societies forced a
major overhaul of Lloyd George's plan. What had been envisioned
originally as an extension of the friendly society movement became
instead simply a government insurance scheme in which part of the
administration was handled by private organizations all of which, in
different ways, hoped to derive some financial advantage from participation. In this way the enormous vested interest of the approved
societies had been built into national health insurance. Neither the
friendly societies nor industrial insurance cared particularly for
national health insurance except as it affected their own business. The
welfare of the programme itself or indeed of the insured population
always remained secondary to the welfare of the administrative society.
Even the democratically run and altogether admirable friendly societies
began to lose their old fraternal character, becoming merely business
operations, with consequential loss of member interest both in the
operation of branches and in the protection of funds.

But probably most serious, an acute and chronic problem after the
war, was each society's concentration on its own welfare and its disregard both for the general success of national health insurance and
for competing approved societies. By the time the plan had been in
operation a decade, some societies, either because of good luck or
better management, had acquired large surpluses in their insurance
accounts while a few were near bankruptcy. Nevertheless each society
regarded its surplus as its own and was absolutely unwilling to share
its funds with others. Worst of all, the prevailing system perpetuated
and accentuated the existing differences among the societies. By the
1920s, more wealthy ones were able to add extra benefits or higher
sickness payments. Thus they attracted new applications, could select

their members more carefully, had a better claims experience, and increased still further their reserves. On the other hand, poorer socie- ties offering only the statutory minimum benefits were forced to take the more marginal risks and sank further into financial difficulty. In relation to the general question of social politics, the problem of the approved societies in the 1920s and early '30s stemmed less from the existence of great society surpluses—although these seemed more and more incongruous in the light of the growing deficit in the unemploy- ment insurance fund—than from the fact that the surpluses belonged to some, but not all, societies. The wealthy societies were unwilling to give up funds they felt they had earned for the benefit of the poorer and, as they saw it, less carefully run societies.

The problem of surpluses was complicated by the fact that the funds were themselves augmented by the government contribution which was not a fixed amount. Although during the passage of the National Insurance Bill Lloyd George had chosen to refer to it as a 2d. contri- bution it was in fact two-ninths of the benefits actually paid. Thus the more extra benefits a wealthy society gave, the greater the amount of money it attracted from the government on behalf of its members, and the larger its surplus became. These surpluses, amounting to £37 million in the last valuation before the war, survived virtually intact and became eventually an embarrassment to the societies. While the true situation was never fully explained to the public, the clear affluence of the societies and the difference between the relatively low rate of sickness benefit from the wealthy health insurance service and the high rate of unemployment benefit under the continually bankrupt unemployment insurance scheme was well known and commented upon.[1]

A second area of contention, particularly as a focus of political criticism, in the health scheme involved the unhealthy connection that appeared to exist between the highly profitable sale of burial insurance policies and the administration of the health insurance. Objection here concerned less the fraternal approved societies than the health in- surance sections of the industrial insurance companies (including al- ways in this definition the collecting friendly societies of which only

[1] See for instance the comprehensive PEP survey of the social services in 1937 which received wide publicity and was in many ways more detached and less polemical than the Beveridge Report five years later: PEP, *Report on the British Social Services; A Survey of Existing Public Social Services in Great Britain with Proposals for Future Development*, London, June 1937. A family for instance of a man, wife and two children, if the breadwinner were unemployed, would receive 32s. per week. However, if he fell sick and ceased to be available for work, the family's income fell to 15s. per week. On the friendly societies and the origins of national health insurance see: B. Gilbert, *The Evolution of National Insurance in Great Britain* (London, 1966), 289–399.

three, the Liverpool Victoria, the Royal Liver and the Scottish Legal, were important). The administration of health insurance benefits by the 70,000 collector-salesmen of industrial insurance, who combined in their visits to virtually every working-class home in the nation the payment of State benefits and the collection of premiums on an exceedingly profitable form of commercial insurance, seemed to many a dangerous way of handling what was supposed to be a public social service. Yet the elements of the system that were most objectionable, the power of the salesman to guide the political thinking of the families with which he was in weekly contact, gave also a political leverage to his employers that made the system almost impossible to change. If, as was charged, the salesman could use his official presence at the delivery of the maternity benefit—which amounted to about a week's income in most working-class households—to sell an additional industrial insurance policy, the same presence made it possible for him to explain to the householders the usefulness of his function and the inadvisability of allowing selfish and ignorant politicians to interfere with him. The network of collector-salesmen had given industrial insurance industry the power to force its way into the health scheme in the first place. In the interwar period it made health insurance almost immune to effective reform.

The influence of industrial insurance, perhaps more than any other factor, caused the continuing demand, particularly within the Labour party, for the abolition of the entire approved society system including the friendly societies. By the time William Beveridge formulated his plan for the reconstruction and unification of national insurance, seeking to keep a place for the friendly societies while dissolving the industrial insurance approved societies, the fraternal orders' long association with industrial insurance had blurred their identity in the public mind as a distinct form of insurance organization. Thus despite strenuous efforts during the General Election of 1945 to secure promises from candidates for Parliament that the Government would find a place for them in the Welfare State and to revive among the public an awareness of their special virtues, the friendly societies were cut adrift when the approved society system was ended.

The third criticism of national health insurance dealt not with the administration but the conception of the scheme itself. It came from Socialists who hoped to see the role of the State in all welfare activity expanded and also from experts in health matters who in other things were politically conservative. Generally, it centred on the narrowness of coverage and the inadequacy of care offered under national health insurance. Health insurance, it was argued, really did little for public health. There was no incentive for the national health insurance panel physician, who by the end of the war received 11s. per year for each contributor he had on his list, to do anything toward prevention of disease among his insurance patients nor indeed to do more than the minimum necessary to keep the patient from transferring to another doctor.

Still more to the point, it was only the contributor himself who received medical care. His wife, unless she was also a contributor, and his dependants were not covered. Finally, the subject of the most general criticism, was the fact that most of the rapidly increasing range of modern curative services coming from medical research were not available under national health insurance. Medical care under the insurance scheme included virtually only the clinical services available in the doctor's black bag. Specialist service and hospital treatment were not covered. Indeed health insurance in some ways caused the contributor's position at a voluntary hospital to become more difficult than ever. As the recipient of a regular, if small, sickness benefit, he could no longer qualify as a charity patient in the ordinary sense. Yet the sickness benefit by itself was hardly enough upon which to maintain a family, let alone to pay in addition for hospital treatment. As a result, one of the most common of the extra benefits offered by the affluent approved societies was the provision of hospital and specialist treatment, usually secured by regular payment made by the society to hospitals in areas where it had large numbers of members. The lack of hospital and specialist benefits resulted also, particularly during the 1930s, in the rapid growth of private hospitalization insurance plans to supplement the inadequate State scheme.

The shortcomings of Part I in the National Insurance Act of 1911 were well understood by the planners of the measure. Before the insurance scheme had been in operation many months C. F. G. Masterman and Addison, with the full approval of Lloyd George, were at work on a plan, unfortunately cut short by the war, to extend coverage to hospital and specialist services for at least the contributor.[1] On the other hand although Lloyd George had said many times that he would be happy to extend his service in any direction that people were willing to pay for, critics of the insurance plan tended to forget that in the beginning the Chancellor of the Exchequer had conceived his measure not as a way of preventing sickness but as a way of preventing pauperism. The medical benefit indeed had only been added to the programme when planning was well under way. The aim after all was not to put the insured man in the hospital but to keep him out of the workhouse and to do this the State had to provide him not with a doctor but with cash. Many friendly societies did not themselves offer medical service but simply provided their members with a sum

[1] Lucy Masterman, *C. F. G. Masterman* (London, 1939), 264; Christopher Addison, *Politics from Within, 1911–1918* (London, 1924), I, 29.

of money from which they could pay any doctor they chose. Indeed the health insurance scheme for Ireland offered no medical benefits but simply an extra sum of money under the sickness benefit. Those who criticized the scheme as an inadequate instrument for building the health of the British nation, and this included the Fabian and intellectual wing of the Labour party as well as men within the Civil Service such as Sir Robert Morant and George Newman in addition to many members of the medical profession, were charging Lloyd George with failing to accomplish something he had never set out to do.

Unfortunately, by the end of the war, when the Prime Minister began to think of improvement of the health of that nation as one of the central reforms in the building of a better Britain, the approved societies were already a well-entrenched vested interest in the administration of national health insurance. They refused to permit the integration of the service they operated into a larger preventative and clinical apparatus handled by the new Ministry of Health. They insisted that the insurance be kept independent of all competing services operated by the State. The amalgamation of preventative and curative services had to wait therefore until the advent of the National Health Service and even at this time the achievement was something less than complete. But in maintaining their independence for a quarter of a century against such experienced political operators as Robert Morant and Neville Chamberlain, the approved societies showed a lobby skill that ought to rank them among the most formidable of modern British parliamentary interests.

War and the prosperity of health insurance

The approved societies profited during the First World War from lack of a permanent departmental home for national health insurance and the absence of a strong minister. Before August 1914 Lloyd George and Charles Masterman had jointly handled explanations in the House of Commons. Unhappily Masterman's position was growing steadily weaker in the last months before Britain's declaration of war on Germany. Lloyd George's patronage had brought him into the Cabinet as Chancellor of the Duchy of Lancaster on 11 February 1914. But he had been unable to win the by-election then required of new appointees to the Ministry and after two attempts, both of which resulted in humiliating defeats, he lingered in the anomalous position of a Minister of the Crown without a seat in Parliament. As such health insurance was virtually without a real parliamentary spokesman, although day-to-day administration remained firmly in the hand of Sir Robert Morant assisted until 1917 by John Anderson. In February 1915 Masterman was replaced at the Duchy of Lancaster and as

Chairman of the Joint Insurance Committee (a committee of politicians and civil servants including the heads of the insurance commissions of the three kingdoms and Wales with a political chairman) by Edwin Montagu who held these posts until the reconstruction of the Government at the end of May. At this time Lloyd George, who was determined to keep health insurance out of the soporific atmosphere of the Local Government Board, contrived to have the joint committee chairmanship transferred to the Comptroller of the Household.

Between May 1915 and December 1916 this ancient sinecure and the chairmanship of the Joint Committee was held by the Liberal Member of Parliament for the city of Lincoln since 1906, Charles Roberts. Roberts' tenure of office, which lasted only until the break-up of the Liberal Party in December 1916, was unhappy. He had neither the knowledge of health insurance possessed by Masterman nor Edwin Montagu's singular influence in the Cabinet. He inherited a mass of friendly society complaints about the increasing uninsurability of women coupled with the demand that, as the government's actuarial calculations for health insurance were inaccurate, the Treasury should indemnify the societies for the extra claims for women, particularly because the large war-time entrance of women into industry had increased the number of women contributors. He allowed himself to be driven to agree to government compensation for above-average claims from women without earning the friendship of the societies.

In November 1916 Roberts was replaced by Sir Edwin Cornwall, Liberal Member of Parliament for Bethnal Green since 1906.[1] In Cornwall the societies had an unimpeachable political spokesman. He was a member of several friendly societies and knew the lines of power in local authority politics at the level at which the societies themselves operated. Through the trucks of his coal business he had a name familiar to the citizens of Fulham and Hammersmith.[2] In cooperation with his fellow-resident of Fulham, W. Hayes Fisher, Cornwall vigorously defended the societies against a threat presented by the plans for a Ministry of Health, and in company with many others was mollified by a place on the 1918 Honours List when the National Health Insurance Joint Committee succeeded the Joint Insurance Committee in the new Ministry of Health.

Unlike its predecessor the new committee was entirely political in membership. It was made up of the Minister of Health, the Secretary

[1] The friendly societies were not sorry to see Roberts leave. The *National Insurance Gazette* remarked that he 'had not had an easy time' as Chairman of the Joint Committee (*National Insurance Gazette*, 23 November 1916). Roberts' withdrawal from heath insurance administration occurred before the break-up of Asquith's Cabinet although he remained loyal to his former chief.

[2] For the societies' reaction to Cornwall's appointment see: *National Insurance Gazette*, 23 December 1916.

of State for Scotland, the Chief Secretary for Ireland (later the Minister of Labour for North Ireland), and someone, usually a member of Parliament, nominated for Wales. Below the level of the formal control of the Joint Committee, effective day-to-day decisions in health insurance administration lay with deputies appointed from the civil service. The most important of these, in effect the permanent head of National Health Insurance after 1919 when Robert Morant became permanent secretary of the Local Government Board, was Walter Kinnear who normally acted for the Minister of Health. The approved societies were represented at the governing level in the insurance administration by the Consultative Council on National Health Insurance which they had fought hard to establish during the planning of the Ministry of Health. On the council, at one time or another, appeared every important figure in the approved society and insurance world. While the Consultative Council had no executive functions, it provided an official platform for the expression of approved society opinion and gave the societies, theoretically the servants of the ministry, what amounted to a permanent lobby deputation with automatic access to the minister. When examining the reasons for the effectiveness of approved society resistance to all efforts to interfere with their activities, their proximity to the seat of executive authority as well as their strength in parliamentary constituencies needs to be remembered.[1]

In common with most other institutions concerned with the economic climate of Great Britain, the approved societies had assumed that the outbreak of war in 1914 would bring on a period of depression and industrial hardship. This, it was thought, would cause the drop in contribution income and the rise in claims which for generations friendly societies had learned to expect in times of bad trade.[2] As it turned out, the war helped to solve a number of problems left over from peace and allowed the strong societies to begin the accumulation of the great surpluses while reducing the number of societies by one

[1] On the formal structure and personnel of National Health Insurance administration after reconstruction at the end of the war see: Cmd. 913, 'First Annual Report of the Ministry of Health, 1919–1920, Part IV—Administration of National Health Insurance 1917 to 31 March 1920', 4. It may be remembered that the Consultative Council was only one of several advisory committees instituted by the Ministry of Health Act. All the others, with the exception briefly of the Medical Advisory Committee, were of little account.

[2] See the leading article, 'The War and National Insurance', *National Insurance Gazette*, 15 August 1914. The *Gazette* noted with approval that the Member of Parliament for West Worcestershire, Mr S. Baldwin, had offered to pay friendly society contributions for all men in his constituency, and also in cities of Worcester and Stourport, serving in the armed forces. This would probably affect over 1,000 men. *Ibid.*, 29 August 1914.

half.[1] Far from suffering from unemployment among contributors, by 1915 approved societies as well as all other forms of enterprise were finding their activities curtailed because of the shortage of staff, while the disappearance of doctors into the forces caused problems for the local insurance committees which administered the medical benefit. The general shortage of doctors tended to improve the bad relations between the medical profession and the approved societies which had been so marked in the negotiations immediately before the war. Lloyd George had in fact used the medical profession's fear of the societies as a way of breaking the doctors' threatened boycott of national health insurance. But as the war lessened competition among doctors, societies were no longer in a position to dictate to the profession and the strained relations between the two groups grew noticeably better.

Perhaps the most important and easily measurable effect of the war came with the relief of the threatened actuarial crisis that had appeared in 1913 over the unexpectedly high sickness liability of women. Although the war did bring, of course, many more women into industry and so increased the problem of female sickness, it also virtually ended unemployment, thus keeping income from contributions high, while generous wages lessened absenteeism due to malingering and probably, by improving nutrition, reduced actual ill-health. After 1915 sickness claims fell dramatically and never again during the war reached the level of 1913–14, even at the time of the 1918 influenza epidemic.[2] At the same time massive government borrowing raised interest rates and so increased the value of the societies' reserve, which had been calculated on a 3 per cent interest rate.

Finally, there are the lugubrious but indisputable statistics showing that war casualties helped the reserves of the approved societies. Statistically societies under normal conditions would have expected 212,000 deaths among men under the age of 40. During the period of the war they experienced, in fact, nearly twice this number of deaths and all indications are that the recorded mortality was far less than the actual losses among society members. Alfred Watson, the Government actuary, calculated that at least 500,000 approved society members died between 1914 and 1918 during the period of their lives when their sickness liability was at a minimum and when contributions on their behalf were paid regularly by the military forces, while at the same time any actual sickness among the group was the responsibility of the State. Consequently the societies' reserves received the benefit of con-

---

[1] Of 2,208 societies granted approval in 1912, 10 years later 1,192 had ceased to administer insurance. Ian G. Gibbon, 'The Public Social Services', *Journal of the Royal Statistical Society*, C (Part IV, 1937), 520.

[2] *Cmd. 1662*, 'Report by the Government Actuary on the Valuations of the Assets and liabilities of Approved Societies as of 31 December 1918', 1922, 27.

tributions of half a million or more young men, for whom no sickness claims in the older, more unhealthy, time of life would ever be made. Due to inadequate reporting, the effect of these deaths was not clear at the time of the first evaluation, begun in 1918. But the unclaimed reserves created by war casualties and by the influenza epidemic of 1918, and the value of the interest earned upon them, probably never can be satisfactorily calculated except as a variation from an actuarial norm. Nevertheless it must be assumed that they greatly affected approved societies' claims experience during the next two decades.[1]

Probably not much less important than battlefield deaths were what might be termed actuarial deaths: the disappearance from the records of approved societies of young men who, having been under insurance for a year or two before the war, disappeared so far as the society was concerned. During the next four years the society received regular contributions on behalf of the soldier who, at the end of the war, returned to uninsured employment or who joined another society probably forgetting over the chasm of war that half a decade earlier he had briefly been a member of some other society or not realizing that five years' reserves had been accumulated for him. In the absence of centralized record keeping, without the existence of a card or the memory of the name of the society, there was no way of tracing the sum he had built up. Similarly, large numbers of women, who entered war work and paid practically uninterrupted contributions for three or four years, left insured employment for domestic duties after the Armistice. Unless the approved society could prove the death of a contributor, either male or female, it was forced to return to the government part of its credited reserve for the individual and the matter was carried simply as lapsed coverage. Nevertheless societies were able to retain as a result of secession from insurance during and after the war a total of £3,541,000.[2]

The cause of most of the postwar problems of national health insurance could be traced to inflation. At the time of the Armistice an immediate need was the revision in the upper limit of coverage of £160 to prevent many non-manual workers from losing their eligibility as a result of the growth of wages during the war. (Manual workers were covered at any wage.) Often employers had continued to pay their 3d. contribution as a gift in order to prevent workers from losing

---

[1] For the best, virtually the only, authoritative statement of the effect of the war on national health insurance see: Alfred W. Watson, 'National Health Insurance and Friendly Societies during the War', in James T. Shotwell (ed.), *War and Insurance* (London, 1927).

[2] *Cmd. 1662*, 38–9. In all, the actuaries discovered that, up to 31 December 1918, societies with surpluses had earned £4,964,000 over expectations on men's sickness and £1,622,000 on women's. Societies with losses showed a deficit of £228,000 on men's sickness and only £57,000 on women's. *Ibid.*, 17.

s

eligibility under the health scheme. But technically this was illegal. With recollections of the struggle with the British Medical Association at the time of the passage of the National Insurance Act for even a lower income limit, the Government in 1919 hurriedly passed a bill raising the maximum income for health insurance purposes to £250, where it remained until the beginning of the Second World War, when it was increased to £420.

The problems of adjusting benefits to the new value of money were far more serious. Involved here was the fact that the health scheme was after all a plan of reserve insurance. In effect the money available to pay benefits for any single group of contributors throughout the term of coverage was only the amount paid in by the same individual or group, plus interest, during the same period. This was one of the disadvantages of approved society administration and resulted partly from the fact that W. J. Braithwaite, who almost singlehandedly had written Part I of the National Insurance Act, was himself a friendly society man. During the planning of the national health insurance scheme Braithwaite had eventually convinced David Lloyd George that, given the necessity of administration through self-governing societies, the only way to enforce prudent handling of contributors' funds was to provide each society with a separate reserve for which it would be the guardian and from which it would receive the benefits of any surplus. Most simply, each insured invested his money with the society, received the increased value of the government contribution and the interest, and throughout his insured life was paid benefits from the global sum. Theoretically the reserve build up through the healthy early period of an individual contributor's life—or in actuarial terms, the reserve derived from all men and women of a given class of insured entering into the scheme at the same time—was extinguished as the class passed the age of 70 and disappeared from the scheme. Consequently, if a society through prudent investment, administration, or better-than-expected claims experience (such as the death in war of a large number of contributors) had money left over in its reserve it would begin to accumulate a surplus which could be used for the payment of extra benefits. If on the other hand the reserves accumulated for each individual or class of individuals were not sufficient to support those individuals throughout their insured lives, it would show upon each evaluation a reserve deficiency. Most important, the government would have no trouble assigning responsibilty to the administrators of the society itself.

The alternative plan, never considered seriously by Braithwaite, was the form of non-funded insurance used with the unemployment scheme. Here there was no necessity for the accumulation of a reserve. In any given insurance year the amount of money coming in to the scheme had only to balance the amount being spent. The contributions of the men at work at any moment paid the benefits of those out of work. With some modifications this was the plan of insurance used in the Widows', Orphans' and Old Age Contributory Pensions Act of 1925. It could not, however, have been used successfully in national health insurance with administration in the hands of approved societies. A non-funded benefit scheme depends for its existence upon a sure and predictable supply of new entrants. The competition among societies, upon which Lloyd George depended for careful administration, assumed above all competition for members.

The argument here is not that a funded system is unworkable, or indeed undesirable, but rather it was part of the price paid for the political decision to administer national health insurance through many small and competing units. It destroyed the flexibility that competition of small units should have provided. The great weakness of the system lay in the fact that under it the amount of money available for the payment of benefits at any given time depended upon past contributions rather than on present prices and wages. It put the contributors at the mercy of inflation. The reserves they accumulated in hard money paid benefits in cheap money. More important, because benefits were proportionate to the size of the reserve and not, except over a period of years, to the amount of the contribution, a simple increase in contributions without some other adjustment of resources did little for benefits.

Accordingly, when the Lloyd George Government began to consider the problem of how to make national health insurance benefits slightly more appropriate to the price and wage scale that prevailed after the First World War, it was faced with the question of how to provide the capital value upon which the larger benefits could be based. All benefits needed to be increased. Sick pay was still at the 10s., at which it had been set in 1911. The maternity benefit was 30s., almost a week and a half's pay for a shipyard or engineering labourer before the war. In 1920 he would earn nearly that much in two days. Although the health insurance sub-committee of the Cabinet decided quickly that anything less than an increase to 15s. in the sickness benefit would be derisory, while anything more would be financially impossible, the problem of what to do about the doctors seemed almost unsolvable. In the last months of 1912, after breaking with consummate skill a threatened strike of the medical profession, Lloyd George had set the capitation fee for national health insurance general practitioners at between 8s. 6d. and 9s. per head, depending upon whether the doctor provided his own prescribed medicines. This rate had substantially increased medical incomes and nearly doubled the price of medical practices offered for sale, but it had done no more than most thoughtful critics felt the profession deserved.[1]

However, in the months immediately after the war standards of medical practice under national health insurance declined sharply. During 1919 Dr Addison repeatedly warned the Cabinet of complaints received from Insurance Committees about the low standards of attendance and casual treatment by doctors in their employ. If doctors were genuinely dissatisfied with their conditions and the government failed to give them a substantial increase in income, he insisted, the likely result would be a strike which would do nothing for national health insurance medical service, nor for the reputation of the Coalition Government.[2]

It was easier to admit that the doctors deserved a raise in pay than to find the money for it. Part of the agreement with the profession in 1912 had been the addition by the State of about £1,700,000 annually to the fund set aside for the panel practitioner. This sum, above the amount ordinarily contributed by the Treasury to national health insurance funds, had been paid regularly for eight years. The doctors were already getting more than the approved societies had in their reserves for the purpose; any increase would be the government's responsibility. During the last months of 1919 and the early months of 1920, while Lloyd George was struggling to force an increasingly reluctant Parliament to honour his promises for social reform, the subject of national health insurance received one of the few Cabinet-level reviews it would enjoy in the interwar period. Here the reconstruction of British medicine and Addison's goal, the establishment of a separate medical service, were put off for a quarter century.[3]

The economizers in the Cabinet were Austen Chamberlain and Robert Horne, who, as in unemployment insurance and housing, attempted to reduce the State's support for the funds of the approved societies and to raise instead the workman's and employer's contributions above the amounts Addison proposed. However the main problem

[1] It should be noted that the official investigation commissioned by the government on the ordinary income of non-specialist physicians showed that they received on an average 4s. per patient per year. *Cd. 6305*, 'Existing conditions in respect of medical attendance and remuneration in certain towns', 1912.

[2] PRO Cab. 24/94, CP 285, 'National Health Insurance', 5 December 1919, memorandum by Christopher Addison; Cab. 27/54 (Ad hoc Cabinet Committees), Health Insurance Committee 17 December 1919; Cab. 21/181, Health Insurance Committee File (unsorted), Minutes of a conference on 8 January 1920.

[3] At the end of May 1919 the *National Insurance Gazette* warned its readers that a full-time State-salaried medical service was a definite possibility and that there was a strong current of opinion in the medical profession for precisely such a measure, while hinting that Addison, supported by health reforming radicals, was thinking of such a bill. (*National Insurance Gazette*, 31 May 1919.) A Labour party committee headed by Beatrice Webb had advocated such a plan in 1918.

was not the increase for which there could be little argument, but the payment to doctors, the 'medical benefit'. Addison produced evidence to show that 75 per cent of medical practitioners working for national health insurance received less than £500 per year from the scheme.[1] Physicians were not growing rich from the government subsidy. On the contrary, they felt that they were being badly treated by the government, hence the poor service. A strike of health insurance doctors was always a threat.

But the most telling argument against increasing workers' contributions enough to make possible a reduction in the State subsidy was the political difficulty. Younger members of approved societies did not use the medical benefit a great deal and disliked it. The societies themselves would resist having to pay an extra amount without having control of the doctors, which the doctors themselves would resist. There was really no possibility of separating the cost of medical benefit from other insurance costs. Health insurance, after all, covered a form of risk in which the exposure varied directly with age. Proportionately the older portion of population would receive the bulk of the increased benefits. Yet the young would provide most of the money. In a statement that answers many questions about the basic assumptions of social insurance, the committee agreed on 18 December 1919 that the object of the State subsidy was to secure a flat-rate contribution. If the subsidy were reduced, the premiums would have to be varied according to age, or the flat rate increased overall. To vary by age would be hard. Employers would be unable or unwilling to discriminate, and with a scheme of the vast proportions of the insurance act, a machine-like uniformity was essential to its smooth working. Generally, thought the Health Insurance Committee in a conclusion that would remain forgotten until the Second World War, the 'Medical Benefit was not an appropriate benefit in an insurance scheme, and was difficult to measure in cash'.[2]

In the end, over the protests of the Chancellor of the Exchequer and Robert Munro, Secretary of State for Scotland, the Cabinet agreed to raise the doctor's capitation fee from 8s. 6d. to 11s., retroactive to January 1920 as Addison had requested, and to relieve the approved societies of the contribution to the tuberculosis sanitoria, which amounted to an annual sum of about £550,000.[3] The sanitoria now became a responsibility of the local authorities and a charge on the

---

[1] Minutes of Conference of Health Insurance Committee, 9 January 1920, Cab. 21/181.
[2] PRO Cab. 27/54, Meeting of the Health Insurance Committee, 18 December 1919.
[3] PRO Cab. 23/20, Cabinet 8 of 1920, meeting 4 February. These changes were incorporated in the National Health Insurance (Amendment) Act of 1920.

rate payer. At the same time, although increasing the normal work-man's contribution from 4d. to 5d. and increasing the employer's contribution from 3d. to 5d., the level at which it would remain until the coming of contributory pensions, the government continued its two-ninths cost of benefits contribution to national health insurance.

In effect, the Lloyd George Government neglected the opportunity to overhaul national health insurance. Although documentary evidence is lacking, the reason, beside the obvious pressure of other business and the Prime Minister's probable unwillingness to embark upon what would have been a large and highly controversial project in the re-construction programme that he had himself established, must be Addison's assumption that the health scheme would be rebuilt as a part of the general reconstruction of government health services which would come when the Poor Law was broken up. It is significant that the same Cabinet that accepted the minor changes incorporated in the National Health Insurance Act of 1920 also decided to delete from the King's Speech a phrase announcing that bills would be presented for dealing with the services administered by the Poor Law authorities.

Finally, by 1920, the surge for reform had nearly run its course. The rebuilding of state medical and health activities might have been possible at the end of the war with thousands of doctors without established practices returning from the armed services, but such changes would have been incredibly expensive. With relentless City pressure upon the Cabinet for the reduction of the cost of housing and unemployment programmes, there was little chance of the expansion of any government activity which seemed to be working at least reason-ably well. This is particularly true of a programme that was largely supported by the working-class beneficiaries themselves. The transfer of the burden of the medical benefit from national health insurance contributions to the income surtax payer would have caused a political explosion among the Government's backbenchers in the Coupon Parlia-ment, who detested the Minister of Health and all his works and who were fighting with every weapon to have government expenditures and taxes reduced. The reasons for the failure to reform health insurance, therefore, parallel the reasons for the maintenance of the unreconstructed Poor Law. Even if the suggested changes had been unopposed, which was far from the case, they would have been expen-sive for the national exchequer and would involve the Government in conflicts with the British financial world, whose well-being, all agreed, was paramount.

The approved societies and their enemies

The advent of widespread industrial unemployment in the fall and winter of 1920 and the growing pressure for governmental economy by the spring of 1921 affected national health insurance as it did nearly every aspect of British social policy. Most immediately hit was the medical profession. The settlement in the spring of the previous year of 11s. as the capitation fee had satisfied no one. The doctors had asked for 13s. 6d. while the approved societies had believed that 7s. 3d. was ample. Like a man with two masters, the Government was able to serve neither well and found that only by contributing from its own funds was it able to force an agreement.[1]

The new higher medical benefit had scarcely taken effect before it came under attack from the Treasury. The financial crisis in unemployment insurance of the spring of 1921, that also destroyed the housing programme, forced the Ministry of Health to notify the Insurance Acts Committee of the British Medical Association that after 1 January 1922 the doctors would be paid 9s. 6d. per patient. It should be noted that the health ministry's action was the result of a Treasury circular of May 1921 and was not caused by the more dramatic Committee on National Expenditure, the so-called 'Geddes Committee' which although appointed in August had not yet reached that department.

The doctors accepted the reduction in their fees grudgingly, but without overt protest as a recognition of the need for national sacrifice. The Ministry had promised them that the new scale would be guaranteed for two years and that before the end of that time there would be a general inquiry into the subject of professional remuneration. Approved societies, on the other hand, had always felt that the doctors were overpaid. This prejudice on the part of the societies gained unusual force in the spring of 1922 when, as the result of Geddes Committee recommendations, the Government announced that it intended to end the grant of £1,700,000 toward the cost of the medical benefit that David Lloyd George had procured in 1913 as a means of breaking the doctors' strike at the inception of the health insurance programme. This decision was the result of long and anxious consideration within the Ministry of Health and came only after protracted and angry consultations with the approved societies. £1,700,000 represented approximately the difference in cost between the 9s. 6d. per head that the doctors actually received and 7s. 3d. which was the amount that the increase in insurance contributions would in fact permit toward the payment of the capitation fee. If the money did not come from the government the societies would have to take it from their own reserves which, unfortunately for their own argument, now showed substantial surpluses. The Minister of Health, Alfred Mond, had hoped briefly to increase workers' contributions again. But a second increase within two years was resisted even by the societies

[1] *British Medical Journal*, 5 June 1921, Supplement, 341–4.

themselves. In March 1922, however, the societies agreed to carry the extra cost of the medical benefit for two years but warned the Government that at the end of 1923 they intended to reduce further the cost of the medical benefit if they were to carry it themselves. Their own surpluses, Watson had assured both the societies and the Cabinet, would permit no more, while the general poverty of the working class and the fierce competition for contributions from unemployment insurance precluded raising any other money from the beneficiaries themselves. Insurance reserves calculated in prewar pounds were simply inadequate to pay the cost of inflated postwar benefits.[1]

Mond's bill reducing the capitation fee, the National Health Insurance (Amendment) Bill of 1922, received a second reading on 24 May. Although the minister paid high tribute to the 'wise and statesman-like' contributions of the National Health Insurance Consultative Council which he termed 'an important and representative body', the Consultative Council immediately came under attack within the House of Commons as an evil influence within the Ministry of Health and the debate degenerated into the customary skirmish over the role of the approved societies within the Government welfare programme.[2]

Most unhappy of all with the bill were the doctors themselves. During consideration of the measure in the Cabinet Mond had warned his colleagues, who could by that time think of little but economy, that

> to remove all State assistance above the statutory two-ninths [that proportion of the cost of benefits that the government bore under the terms of the National Insurance Act of 1911] would be to surrender the weapon which the State can use in dealing with the doctors and to hand them over to the approved societies. To do this would raise a storm of opposition in the medical profession and gravely endanger the structure of the medical benefit now embodied in the National Health Insurance Act.[3]

The doctors were indeed apprehensive. Although they possessed no official knowledge of the negotiations between the approved societies and the government, they could guess easily enough that at the end of the two-year contract societies, without any help from the government, would seek to reduce the capitation fee still further. The societies, if left to themselves, would have paid the doctor 7s. 3d. per patient. Distrusting both the profession which they considered rapacious and the government which they thought pusillanimous, they prepared to defend their own funds by soliciting actively from parlia-

[1] PRO Cab. 24/31, CP 3838, 'National Health Insurance Bill, memorandum by the Minister of Health', 14 March 1922.
[2] House of Commons Debates, CLIV (24 May 1922), cols. 1277–1376.
[3] PRO Cab. 23/29, Cabinet 20 of 1922, meeting 22 March.

mentary candidates in the election of 6 December 1923 pledges not to touch society funds for payment of doctors beyond 7s. 3d. They went about this with efficiency of long practice and appeared to have succeeded in obtaining promises from about 400 MPs of all parties.[1]

The doctors on the other hand were perfectly correct in assuming that the approved societies would urge the Ministry of Health to reduce the capitation fee as far as possible. The government offer, made in a letter to the Insurance Acts Committee on 4 October 1923, offered a capitation fee of 8s. 6d. for three years or 8s. guaranteed for five. The letter pointed out that the cost of living had dropped considerably since the reduction in the fee made on 1 January 1922 and that even with this reduction a net of 552 doctors had entered the national health insurance service since that time and that the average salary of a full-time doctor in the health scheme was about £1,200.[2]

The panel practitioners lost little time in rejecting this offer and at a meeting on 18 October prepared to strike. This was a bold step in view of the disastrous failure of the attempted medical strike in 1913 just ten years before. But according to Dr Alfred Cox, the Medical Secretary of the British Medical Association, 97 per cent of all panel practitioners put their resignations at the disposal of the Insurance Acts Committee within the next few weeks.[3] At the same time the doctors demanded an independent court of inquiry to examine the entire question of medical remuneration.

This was a shrewd move. An arbitration panel in 1920 had suggested the capitation fee of 11s., the highest the doctors received at any time during the interwar period. But for the same reasons the government was loathe to submit its case to an independent tribunal, this distaste being reinforced by the reluctance of both the Treasury and the approved societies to permit judgement on the dispersal of their funds to be handed to agents which they did not control. Nevertheless, by the end of the month with the clear threat, and probable success, of a medical strike, to the disgust of the approved societies the Ministry of Health capitulated. A letter from the permanent secretary of the ministry, W. A. Robinson, agreed, after making a final offer of a capitation fee of 8s. 6d. for five years, to appoint an impartial court of inquiry whose findings would be binding both on the government and the profession.[4] The letter promised at the same time the appointment of a Royal Commission to look into all aspects of the national health service. The Court of Inquiry finally was appointed towards the end

[1] *H of C Deb.*, CLXXI (31 March 1924), col. 1867.
[2] *The Times*, 5 October 1923.
[3] *Ibid.*, 19 October 1923. Alfred Cox, *Among the Doctors*, London, n.d. (1950), 124–5.
[4] *Ibid.*, 1 November 1923.

of the month a few days after the dissolution of Parliament. It was headed by T. R. Hughes, Chairman of the General Council of the Bar, and included also F. C. Goodenough, Chairman of Barclay's Bank, and Sir Josiah Stamp, the eminent statistician and civil servant. Because he had been a member of the 1920 arbitration panel, Stamp was strenuously opposed by the approved societies who were now reminding the Government at every opportunity that they possessed pledges for the protection of their funds from a 'considerable majority' of the new House of Commons.[1] Stamp resigned early in January 1924 and was replaced by Sir Gilbert Garnsey, a well-known accountant.

The Court of Inquiry announced its award on 24 January 1924. It gave the doctors a capitation fee of 9s. This was 6d. less than they had asked for, but 6d. more than the last government offer. It recommended moreover that the new fee remain in effect until the end of 1927. The court urged also the appointment of a Royal Commission to consider possible changes in national health insurance. The doctors were overjoyed by the award while the approved societies contented themselves by remarking only that there remained in their reserves nevertheless only 7s. 3d. per contributor per year for the payment of a capitation fee. The award as it stood, they argued, threatened all other benefits and further raids upon their funds would be dangerous. Therefore, remarked Percy Rockliff their usual spokesman in political matters, 'it is not unreasonable to predict that the Treasury will be invited now to find the whole difference between 7s. 3d. and 9s. . .'.[2]

Baldwin's defeat in the House of Commons by a combination of Liberal and Labour votes occurred just three days before the Court of Inquiry's decision. It fell therefore to Joynson-Hicks' successor at the Ministry of Health, John Wheatley, to solve the problem of finding the 9s. per contributor that the government had bound itself to give without taking money either from the approved societies or the Treasury. The total amount needed was about £1,762,000 per year, in effect an addition of nearly 25 per cent to the approximately £7 million that the government normally paid to national health insurance as its part of the contribution towards benefits. The discovery of money to pay the Court of Inquiry's award was one of the major triumphs of the statistical magic of Sir Alfred W. Watson, the Chief Government Actuary, who to the relief of Members of Parliament was able to uncover the necessary funds in three insurance accounts that the rest of the insurance world had not only been unaware contained such sums, but had scarcely known existed. Of the approximately 2s. 4d. per head that were altogether required for the capitation fee and administration, 2d. came from the approved societies who were in

[1] *Ibid.*, 15 December 1923.
[2] *Ibid.*, 25 January 1924.

turn relieved of the necessity of paying the salaries of the Regional Medical Officers, the referees who examined patients suspected of malingering. Sixpence per head was found in an unknown fund accumulated as a hedge against a drop in the interest rate which would reduce the value of the societies' reserves. This fund had been completely unused and seemed unlikely to be called upon in the future inasmuch as the actuarial calculations for national health service were based on an assumed 3 per cent while the prevailing interest rate in the mid-twenties was nearly twice that. The rest came from the so-called Central Contingencies Fund which had been established under the act of 1911 to pay standard benefits to contributors in societies that went bankrupt.

John Wheatley produced his solution to the medical problem on 31 March 1924 with obvious relish before a mystified but relieved House of Commons. He insisted from the beginning that the measure providing the new capitation fee, the National Health Insurance (Cost of Medical Benefit) Bill had been put together in agreement with the Consultative Council. He announced further that he intended to appoint a Royal Commission on health insurance. The Commons, with many expressions of approval for the wizardry of Alfred Watson and unquestionably anxious to be rid of an embarrassing and potentially dangerous political issue about which a majority of them had given pledges, gave the measure a quick passage.[1] Except for a short period after the May Committee report in 1931, the capitation fee remained at 9s. until 1946.

The Royal Commission which had been the subject of so much discussion was finally appointed on 11 July 1924. Its terms of reference and membership were of the contradictory sort usually found in an investigating body when the appointive authority hopes that nothing will be done while wishing to avoid the charge of obstruction. On one hand the commission had the right to recommend almost anything it cared to. The terms of reference specified only that it report 'what, if any, alterations, extensions, or developments should be made in the scope of [the national health scheme] and the administrative, financial and medical arrangements set up under it'. On the other hand the personnel of the commission were hardly of the sort to find radical changes necessary. The most expert members were civil servants, Sir John Anderson and Sir Alfred Watson. There were a number of important figures from the insurance world headed by Charles Napier Lawrence, Baron Lawrence of Kingsgate, but no one from any of the major companies or orders connected with the approved societies. The only commissioners among the thirteen who might be said to combine both an expert knowledge of national health insurance and some

[1] *H of C Deb.*, CLXXI (31 March 1924), cols. 1861–1919.

interest in changing the scheme were Professor Alexander Gray of the University of Aberdeen who had been involved as a civil servant in its establishment and Fred Bramley, Secretary of the Trades Union Congress since 1923, who, however, resigned from the commission on 11 March 1925 because of ill health.[1]

There are really only two things to be said about the Royal Commission on National Health Insurance. As a source for the historian, the report, and more importantly the minutes of evidence, are of great value. For virtually the only time between the establishment of national health insurance in 1912 and its supersession 36 years later, the vast, diffuse, and expensive machine was examined publicly and critically in all its parts. The commission could do what Parliament never seemed to be able to accomplish: to lift its examination above narrow questions of finance and approved society politics. These struggles, no less fierce on that account, were nevertheless of special interest only. Indeed health insurance provides probably the best example of the rule of modern welfare politics—that welfare machinery, because of its sheer size and complexity, dealing as it does with every citizen at the most personal level of private economics, becomes almost invulnerable to general criticism in ordinary public parliamentary bodies. It may be compared in this sense to modern tax legislation, which similarly is of most intimate personal concern while being at the same time virtually incomprehensible to anyone but the expert.

The Royal Commission was able to say what no one with any authority could legitimately have stated before—that national health insurance *did* work and given the established inconsistencies and inequities of the system, that it worked reasonably well. Building upon this premise the majority of the commission argued that the system was worth continuing and, in fact, expanding. Both majority and minority reports urged that coverage of the scheme be widened to give certain benefits to dependants of contributors, notably medical care at the time of childbirth, and that the benefits themselves be extended to include dental and ophthalmic as well as other specialist treatments, although not in-patient care in hospitals. It proposed also that dependant allowances be added to the sickness benefits. These suggestions obviously were hardly of a revolutionary nature and represented nothing that many approved societies were not already doing. Generally they proceeded from a conviction that national health insurance was an adequate instrument of social policy as it existed. They reflected the evidence that the commission had received from groups that it was bound to consider among its most expert witnesses, particularly the British Medical Association, that medical care and conditions of prac-

[1] *Cmd. 2596*, 'Report of the Royal Commission on National Health Insurance', 1926.

tice under national health insurance were at least as good as similar conditions outside it. 'A comparison of the conditions of practice among the classes to which insured persons belong', the Insurance Acts Committee had told the commission,

> before and since 1913, leaves no doubt in the minds of the profession (a) that large numbers, indeed whole classes of persons, are now receiving medical attention which they formerly did not receive at all; (b) that the number of practitioners in proportion to the population in densely populated areas has increased; (c) that the amount and character of the medical attention given is superior to that formerly given in even the best of the old clubs, and immensely superior to that given in the great majority of clubs which were far from the best; (d) that illness is now coming under skilled observation and treatment at an earlier stage than was formerly the case; (e) that speaking generally the work of practitioners has been given a bias toward prevention that was formerly not so marked; (f) that clinical records have been or are being provided which may be of great service in relation to medical research in public health; (g) that cooperation among practitioners is being encouraged to an increasing degree; and (h) that there is now a more marked recognition than formerly of the collective responsibility of the profession to the community in respect of all public health matters.[1]

This was extremely satisfactory, particularly coming as it did from a body whose approval of the health scheme and its administration had been highly conditional many times in the past. It indicated that as at least an instrument of welfare policy health insurance was successful. On the other hand the commission was less satisfied, and indeed its hearings were far more preoccupied, with the apparatus of health insurance administration. As was perhaps inevitable, the commission found itself providing a forum for attacks upon the approved societies.

This leads then to the second thing to be said about the report of the Royal Commission on National Health Insurance: that while it generally believed the concept of health insurance to be satisfactory and recommended a number of modest but important extensions, the Government discovered, as with many other reform proposals, that the approved society system made growth almost impossible. Hence the report was of no effect.

Basically the situation was this. The extensions in coverage and increase in benefits recommended by the commission's report of course would have to be uniform for all societies. Some societies could well afford an increase in benefits having already shown a substantial

[1] *Royal Commission on National Health Insurance, Minutes of Evidence*, II, 'Statement of the British Medical Association', 445.

surplus of contributions over expenses. But a number of them could not. Therefore, to effect the recommended extensions, the Royal Commission also proposed a pooling of one-half of all approved society surpluses. The more prosperous societies would help to pay for the new benefits to be given by the poorer societies. Partial pooling of surpluses, then, was by far the most important recommendation of the majority report of the Royal Commission on National Health Insurance. Without it there could be no wholesale extension of benefits. And if it occurred, it could well mark the beginning of the break down of the competitive approved society system.

The Royal Commission majority report, therefore, may have been less 'barren' than the New Statesman styled it at the time of its publication.[1] Given the assumption that the existing system was far better than anything that had come before it and confronted with the fact that an ideal system would involve abolition of approved society administration, which would not only be difficult but absolutely impossible to effect under present circumstances, the best compromise was to break down the fiscal independence of the approved societies using as an argument the eminently reasonable proposal of the extension of benefits. The money was available. The approved society surpluses were more than 'embarrassing' as the Economist termed them.[2] The paradox of the situation lay in the fact that if there had been no surpluses, if the administration of health insurance had not proved to be, as at least it appeared in 1925, so eminently profitable, the proposals for merging these profits might not have been so distasteful. But because the surpluses belonged to a few societies and not to all, pooling had to be resisted. The same fact that made the health scheme's extension in the direction of a true national health service economically feasible made it politically impossible.

A feature of the Royal Commission investigation was the opportunity it provided for a public attack on the approved society system. The struggle was on altogether a different plane from the perennial Labour party's denunciations in the House of Commons of the industrial insurance monopoly. Labour fought the insurance industry because it represented a concentration of private wealth and power and because the existence of approved societies, whether industrial insurance or fraternal, prevented the extension of socialism. Before the Royal Commission, however, the discussion was at another level. Here the question turned upon whether the industrial insurance approved societies had not perverted the original plan of national health insurance. In effect, even if one left aside the larger question of the industry's place in an ideal socialist society, did it not represent also an administrative

[1] New Statesman, 21 March 1926.
[2] Economist, 21 March 1926.

sham, connived at by the State, within the context of national health insurance?

If there existed an ideological or doctrinal weakness in national health insurance as the chief edifice of prewar Radical Liberalism it lay in the decay of the approved societies. David Lloyd George's original conception of national health insurance in 1908 had been that of the expansion of the friendly society system through the entire nation. His romantic mind had conceived an English nation free of economic deprivation and fear, united by the ancient principle of mutual providence, protected by the 'magic of averages'. Every working man would be required either to join a friendly society or to participate in a slightly less advantageous State programme. The two plans—one State-subsidized, the other entirely State-operated—would be democratically controlled as were the friendly societies and much of the administration would be handled by the members themselves. Hopefully the societies would inculcate also in their members the moral and educational values that had been so much a part of the old fraternal provident movement.

All of this changed with the entry into the health scheme of the industrial insurance industry. The great commercial insurance corporations had no intention of converting themselves into approved societies and indeed it would have been impossible for the limited companies to do so, for the act of 1911 stipulated that an approved society could not be run for profit.

Industrial insurance had insisted on the right to set up dummy friendly societies that could apply for approval. These societies employed on their own behalf the sales force of the company with which they were connected. Each salesman administered State benefits and also sold profitable funeral insurance. The dual role of the collector-salesman as a species of civil servant administering State-controlled funds and also as a semi-independent entrepreneur in a highly profitable and more than dubious business, had of course been the subject of innumerable political attacks. In every case the collecting insurance industry had been able to forestall both the attempts to alter the basic structure of national health insurance and to dilute proposals for competing welfare programmes that would make the salesman-administrator role less profitable.

Lloyd George, to his credit, had attempted immediately after the war to bring some regulation into the almost uncontrolled business of collecting insurance. In 1919 he had appointed a strong and radical departmental committee under Lord Parmoor which issued a scathing report on the incredible profitability of the sale of funeral benefits.[1]

[1] *Cmd. 614*, 'Report of the Departmental Committee on the Business of Industrial

In the summer of 1921 Lord Onslow had introduced into the House of Lords on behalf of the Government a measure setting a limit of 40 per cent of premium income as the maximum permitted for its management expenses in industrial insurance and providing, among other things, that at least one-half of any surplus should be divided among policy holders. The logic of these two together was that if management expenses were held down it simply would build up the surplus for stockholders. The insurance companies, apparently through Kingsley Wood, quickly informed the Cabinet that they found even these mild restrictions unacceptable and in the summer of 1922 Edward Shortt, the Home Secretary, was forced to report to the Cabinet that to pass a bill including these provisions would be politically impossible.[1]

Thus industrial insurance and the industrial insurance approved societies were even more than usually controversial during the Royal Commission investigation which began two years later. Although the commission included a number of representatives of the insurance world it had also as members Sir Alfred Watson and Alexander Gray, both of whom had been involved in national health insurance at the time of its establishment and Watson by 1924 was Chief Government Actuary. Both men were seriously concerned by the perversion of the approved society system that had resulted from the interests of industrial insurance. The approved sections of the profit-making companies were nothing more than fictions, they argued. Their annual meetings, which were supposed to be their plenary organization, were imaginary and their rules were so drawn that control of these several vast organizations, which among them controlled many millions of pounds of the government and the contributors' money, rested in the hands of a few officials. The National Amalgamated Approved Society for instance, with a membership of two and one-quarter million, had a quorum of 50 for its annual meeting and the annual meeting was usually attended by not more than 250 people, all of them members of the staff of the approved society's head office.[2] In order to criticize the management, forbidden at an annual meeting, Gray pointed out that National

Assurance Companies and Collecting Societies', 1920. The Parmoor report is an easily accessible source for a full and critical examination of the entire industry.

[1] PRO Cab. 24/137, CP 4038, 'Industrial Assurance Bill, Memorandum by the Home Secretary', 16 June 1922. 'These proposals . . . are strongly opposed by the Societies and Companies and by their Agents' organizations and having regard to the strength of this opposition I have come to the conclusions that it is necessary to omit them from the new bill.' The companies, Shortt reported, had succeeded in stirring up business interests generally against them. On Kingsley Wood's work see: *Insurance Mail*, 19 May 1923.

[2] *Royal Commission on National Health Insurance, Minutes of Evidence*, I, Oral Evidence, 225–6. This admission was drawn from Sir Thomas Neill by Gray after a number of acrimonious exchanges. Neill was also a former director of the Pearl Assurance Company.

Amalgamated rules required a district meeting attended by one-third of those in the district. The National Amalgamated's district in Manchester, for instance, included 60,000 people. There was no hall in the country that could hold the required 20,000 necessary to impeach the society's administration.[1]

The attacks on the industrial insurance approved societies may be reduced essentially to one point. No one suggested that approved society administration was corrupt in any ordinary sense, or even incompetent. At bottom the difficulty was that approved society administration turned national health insurance in a direction never envisioned by its founders. The idea had been that the service would grow, that the interests of the population themselves would generate demand for wider benefits, for increasing preventative medical care, and generally for a larger conception of what was necessary for the health of a nation. Instead the approved societies had fought, usually successfully, every extension of public medicine. They were not instrumentalities of the government, still less of their members. To be sure they worked the machinery for paying benefits with ordinary business efficiency and they were extremely sensitive to competition from each other in the development of member-catching plans for the enlargement of personal health payments. But their orientation of policy was always toward the welfare of their private business and their interest in public health insurance was always subsidiary to the profits of stockholders.

These charges were the burden of the minority report of the Royal Commission. Badly written and neglected by the press, it was a scathing indictment of the approved society system.[2] The minority report went far beyond the Labour party's ideological objections to insurance companies' financial power and to the pernicious influence of the collector-salesman. It said simply that while health insurance was adequately administered as it stood, no further development of it was possible under the present system. If Britain were ever to have a comprehensive national health policy the fundamental administrative apparatus of health insurance would have to be reconstructed. These considerations underlay William Beveridge's plan for the rebuilding of the British social service system 16 years later. The tumult of applause that accompanied publication of the Beveridge report in December 1942 drowned an important voice of dissent from the approved societies whose work was to be taken over by a new ministry of social security. Beveridge devoted a section of his report and a major appendix to a denunciation of collecting insurance.[3]

[1] *Ibid.*, 230.
[2] *Cmd. 2596*, 299–329.
[3] *Cmd. 6404*, 'Report on Social Insurance and Allied Services', 1942, Appendix D, 'The Problem of Industrial Assurance'.

It is frequently forgotten that Beveridge's concern was solely with the industrial section of the approved societies. While he intended to administer his scheme through a central government ministry and the local authorities, he hoped to keep a place in it for the payment of supplementary benefits through the genuine friendly societies whose worth he thoroughly appreciated. In a way, therefore, the original Beveridge plan was a step backward toward David Lloyd George's original conception of state insurance—a compulsory State plan upon which voluntary thrift could build. In the end, nevertheless, the long identification of both fraternal and industrial insurance proved to be too much. In 1945, despite strenuous efforts from the fraternal organizations and from Beveridge himself, the Labour Government dropped all forms of private social security administration.

The reports of the Royal Commission were signed on 22 February 1926 but Baldwin's Cabinet was in no hurry to act upon them. The principal reason was that the Government had begun an assault on the approved societies with the Economy (Miscellaneous Provisions) Bill which it introduced in March of that year, just after the commission reported. The bill itself was the work of Chamberlain and Churchill, with Chamberlain its principal sponsor in the House of Commons.[1] The debates over it were even more acrimonious than was the custom when Chamberlain and the Labour party fought each other. On several occasions Labour members had to be suspended and Chamberlain suffered personally from the continual denunciations he was forced to undergo.[2]

The measure included a wide range of cuts in domestic expenditure but, so far as national health insurance was concerned, the most important change in the Economy Bill was a reduction in the regular government contributions to the health scheme from one-ninth of the cost of benefits to one-seventh and to one-fifth for women. This would save, it was expected, £2,750,000. Chamberlain's argument was that because of the swollen surpluses which the societies still enjoyed, because old age pensions would relieve the societies of responsibility for elderly members between age 65 and 70, and because of the high interest rates which the societies had enjoyed since the war, they could well afford this loss of income.

As with old age pensions the societies were almost helpless against unfavourable legislation by a Conservative Government. The party in power contained most of their friends. They could expect no help or support from Labour. Baldwin refused to meet their deputation and Chamberlain, who did meet a deputation on 14 April 1926, would

[1] For an explanation of the bill on the second reading debate, see: *H of C Deb.*, CXCIII (16 March 1926), cols. 273–99.
[2] Keith Feiling, *Neville Chamberlain* (London, 1946), 134.

promise nothing.[1] A cut in the government contributions, as it was pointed out several times, usually by Liberals, in the House of Commons, had nothing to do with the Royal Commission report nor with any improved efficiency in national health insurance. It had been planned since the previous year and was simply a matter of saving money.[2] The approved societies estimated that the reduction would amount to about 36 per cent of the State contribution as it had been before. The *National Insurance Gazette* referred to the Economy Bill simply as a 'raid' on the approved society funds. But there was, the *Gazette* continued, one advantage. 'The present feeling is, however, that the Government will want a little rest from Approved Society troubles and that legislation upon the Royal Commission Report is most probably a matter of the distant future.'[3]

The *National Insurance Gazette* estimate of the political effect of the Economy Bill on the Royal Commission report was perfectly accurate. The Cabinet waited until 1928 before dealing with the Royal Commission investigation and then it approached the subject with reluctance. Even Chamberlain's unquestionable political courage deserted him on the occasion. Introducing his draft to his colleagues he admitted that it did not transfer any functions to the ancient enemies of the approved societies, the local authorities, nor did it contain any proposals for extension of services or coverage, nor for the partial pooling of surpluses. All of these were absolutely opposed by the insurance interests. 'The political power and influence of the Approved Societies', he concluded, 'make it desirable in present circumstances to meet their views if possible, especially as they are still very sore over the economy Act of 1926.'[4]

So the two years' labour of the Royal Commission on National Health Insurance came to nothing. The National Health Insurance Bill of 1928 embodied a number of very minor housekeeping changes recommended by both the majority and minority reports, but the essential recommendation, the enlargement of health insurance and the break-down of approved society financial autonomy, was missing. The most important item in the bill, the relaxation of the requirement for contributors' payment of arrears, was the result of the growing problem of long-term unemployment and had not even appeared in the commission's reports.[5]

---

[1] *National Insurance Gazette*, 1 May 1926.
[2] *H of C Deb.*, CXCIII, 16 March 1926, col. 311.
[3] *National Insurance Gazette*, 24 April 1926.
[4] PRO Cab. 24/192, CP 9, 'Provisional Programme of Legislation, Ministry of Health', 23 January 1928.
[5] *Cmd. 3051*, 'National Health Insurance Bill, Memorandum Explanatory of the Bill', 1928.

The approved society victory over the Royal Commission did not end their disappointment about the cut in the government contribution toward benefits. Their bitterness was enhanced because the competition among societies prevented any of them from making large cuts in extra benefits to balance the loss in government revenue. They took an active part, of course, in the General Election of 1929, attempting to solicit promises from candidates to oppose pooling of surpluses and to fight to restore the Treasury contribution toward benefits. Apparently the Parliamentary Agent for the Manchester Unity of Odd Fellows was able to secure a pledge from David Lloyd George, again leader of the technically united Liberals and still a consistent friend of the approved societies, that a Liberal Government would reinstate the two-ninths.[1] Commenting upon this with its usual political sense, the *Gazette* noted that, while the Liberals' pledge was an easy one to make as they would not be likely to come to office, there was nevertheless a good chance that they would hold the balance of power in the next Government and so be able to protect the societies whichever party won. The Labour party, the journal noted, had endorsed the Royal Commission recommendations and among the Conservatives Chamberlain had particularly liked them. So the danger of pooling was not past. Chamberlain might even have insisted upon the recommendations, the *Gazette* concluded, quoting almost verbatim from the Minister of Health's Cabinet paper of 23 January 1928, 'if he had not already given sufficient offence to the approved Societies by halving the Economy Act moneys (sic)'.[2]

Unemployment and malingering

In the Economy Act of 1926 the approved societies suffered their only important political defeat of the interwar period and even this loss was mitigated by the immunity from further interference that it appeared to give them. But by the late twenties it was becoming clear that the societies' funds were threatened by danger from another source that was not to be turned aside by political manoeuvering. This was the cost of long-term industrial unemployment.

The national health scheme was probably saved from the bankruptcy which overtook unemployment insurance by the fact that after the spring of 1921 the sickness benefit was lower than the unemployment benefit and that the approved societies acted to insulate the Government from direct political pressure to increase it. Perhaps here lay the most important, although unnoticed, service of the approved societies system.

[1] *Odd Fellows' Magazine*, June 1929, quoted in *National Insurance Gazette*, 25 May 1929.
[2] *Ibid.*, 25 May, 8 June 1929.

In all other social services, unemployment insurance, pensions, and later even in children's allowances, the ordinary politician was defenceless against demands for the expansion of social welfare. Only the threat of national bankruptcy, as in 1931, could force a wholesale downward revision of the unemployment payment. Again, as the standstill surrender showed in 1935, the most elaborate political defences were useless in matters of social welfare. In national health insurance, on the other hand, there was within the ministry itself, in the Consultative Council, a well-organized pressure group committed to economy in the protection of what it considered its own funds, and possessing, unlike the Treasury, its own contacts with the electorate.

The approved societies were well aware of the advantages of keeping the national health insurance sickness benefits lower than the unemployment insurance benefit. They knew the advantage that accrued to their funds from the tendency of an unemployed man who had fallen ill to try and maintain so long as he could the fiction of being available for work so as to draw the more generous unemployment benefit.[1] This situation the societies publicly deplored while working privately to maintain. Although the Government was subjected to endless criticism for lack of coordination among the various welfare programmes, until the Second World War the national health insurance benefit remained serenely at 15s. for men and 12s. for unmarried women, while in fact being reduced to 10s. for married women in 1932.

Nevertheless the control of benefit exercised by the approved societies did not insulate entirely national health insurance from the deteriorating economic climate in which the scheme had to operate. Malingering clearly grew as unemployment grew worse. Statistical evidence about the increase is inadequate for several reasons. The societies always were reluctant to publicize any unfavourable data about themselves and pre-1911 friendly-society experience, although recognizing malingering as a threat, had never shown any important correlations between it and unemployment.[2] In addition, the lack of centralized record-keeping among approved societies made it difficult, except at the triennial valuations, to determine whether abnormal claims experience in any given society was the result of malingering or simply of poor administration in the society. Finally, there was the unmeasurable but indisputable fact that unemployment itself caused ill health and that the line between sickness and well-being for a man suffering economic deprivation was likely to be unclear even to the individual, without health insurance sections of all of the large industrial insurance

[1] See testimony of Percy Rockliff, 15 February 1925, Ministry of Health, *Royal Commission on National Health Insurance, Minutes of Evidence*, I, 1925, 381.

[2] *National Insurance Gazette*, 15 August 1914. On the other hand the societies had little experience with women members.

taking into account any conscious efforts on the part of the claimant to dissemble.[1]

Until the mid-twenties it appeared that so far as men were concerned, widespread unemployment might not be beyond the approved societies' ability to handle. This was not, however, the case among women. As has been discussed, sickness claims from females had been a problem for national health insurance from the beginning of the payment of sickness benefits in January 1913. Part of this certainly was the result of mistaken actuarial calculation in the framing of the act. The Manchester Unity of Odd Fellows, whose experience tables for the 1890s were used as a basis for national health insurance, did not offer membership to women, nor did most friendly societies. The few women's societies were too small to be of much help. Therefore, the planners of the health scheme could do little beyond assuming that women's sickness experience would be 10 per cent greater than men's, which itself, on a national basis, was expected to be 10 per cent greater than the experience tables of the Manchester Unity.

These rather primitive calculations were quickly proven to be incorrect. Well before the end of 1913 it had become clear that even in the largest and best-run societies, allowing for each society's natural reluctance to admit that it was in difficulty, the cost of women's sickness was as much as 25 per cent above the reserves allotted to it.[2]

Generally the experience in the 18 months that national health insurance had to run before the outbreak of the First World War seemed to show that working-class housewives, especially employed mothers, were never really well and were not perhaps an insurable risk. Whether pregnancy constituted a sickness or whether the various minor ailments associated with pregnancy qualified for the sickness benefit was a question that the administrators of national health insurance never really succeeded in answering. The remarkable demand for women's sickness benefit continued for about a year after the war began and necessitated a special government grant to maintain the solvency of a number of societies. Then, surprisingly, in 1915 women's sickness claims began to decline. Even during the influenza epidemic of 1918 claims were not as high as they had been in 1913-14.

The reappearance of excessive sickness and disablement claims among women coincided exactly with the onset of postwar unemployment, although the general alarm that resulted from this phenomenon did not become public until about the middle of the decade. The reason for this, as with most unanswered questions about the adminis-

[1] See testimony of Thomas Neill of the National Amalgamated Approved Society, 26 February 1925, RC on NHI, Minutes of Evidence, I, 499.
[2] See: Cd. 7687, 'Report of the Departmental Committee on Sickness Benefit Claims Under the National Insurance Act', 1914.

tration of national health insurance, lay in the disconnected system of insurance administration through approved societies which, when combined with the jealousy among the societies themselves, made any unfavourable statistical information almost impossible to obtain. Consequently, the marked revival of women's sickness claims that began in 1921, although apparently no secret to some of the better-run societies, became a public matter only in 1925. It evoked no official recognition until 1926 and, because of the huge surpluses possessed by the societies, caused no remedial action until the early 1930s.

The problem of 'over-certification' for women illustrated what was perhaps the most important weakness in the entire administrative structure of national health insurance, a fault that William Beveridge determined to eliminate when he insisted in his report that the administration of cash support payments for sickness be divorced from the apparatus for medical treatment. Under national health insurance the panel doctor was a dispenser not only of medicine but of money. Upon his word that a patient was unfit for work the contributor was entitled to claim a sickness benefit from his approved society of 15s. for men and 12s. for women, which would be paid for 26 weeks, or a disablement benefit of one-half each amount which would last indefinitely. This responsibility put the health insurance practitioner in a difficult position. Symptoms of illness were not always clear. But to acquire a reputation for refusing sickness certificates meant the loss of patients. Friendly societies had recognized this problem before the advent of national health insurance and had combated it by insisting always that patients eligible for sickness benefit attend a specified doctor employed by the society. However, during the passage of the National Insurance Bill, the British Medical Association had demanded and received the concession that contributors under the national scheme be able to choose any physician from the list, or 'panel', of medical men in the area who had agreed to accept patients under the scheme. By insisting upon competition among doctors the health insurance practitioners had put themselves in a position either of closing their eyes to what might be perjury on the part of some of their patients or of risking the loss of patients.

By 1921, then, sickness and disablement among all classes of contributors had begun to grow. To be sure not all societies were seriously affected at first and for several years claims from men and unmarried women still remained below actuarial expectations but, significantly, societies whose membership was largely drawn either from the unskilled working class or from areas in which unemployment was most serious showed the largest increases in claims. For instance the National Amalgamated Approved Society, a huge organization incorporating the health insurance sections of all of the large industrial organizations

except the Prudential, was almost immediately hurt by unemployment.[1] Records of the National Amalgamated showed that, while
sickness experience for men between 1920 and 1923 had remained
relatively stable, sickness experience for women had gone from 87
per cent of expectation in 1920 to 101 per cent in 1921, and in Wales
alone from 93 per cent in 1920 to 113 per cent in 1921, and 123 per
cent in 1923. Men's disablement experience increased from 54 per
cent, barely half of expectation in 1920, to 85 per cent in 1923.
Women's went from 120 per cent to 201 per cent in 1923, while
Welsh women's claims increased from 164 per cent in 1920 to 214
per cent in 1921 and 256 per cent by 1923.[2] More important, the
society discovered that nearly all its excessive sickness experience
among women resulted from claims from married women. Even in
1923, widows' and spinsters' sickness claims were only 91 per cent
of expectation while married women's claims were 125 per cent of
expectation.

Commenting upon these figures, the chairman of the National Amalgamated, Sir Edward Neill, stated under questioning that, while he felt
his society's claims experience was the result of real incapacity, it was
hard to apply the test of sickness to married women. Women could
appear to be genuinely ill when a doctor called and perhaps were
unwell in fact, but they carried on with household duties nevertheless.
Neill suggested that abnormal unemployment might cause an increase
in sickness experience among men brought on not by malingering but
by the ill health that attended unemployment.[3]

Neill's evidence was supported by the report of an actuarial committee of the Royal Commission which Chamberlain appointed as one
of his first official acts after taking office as Minister of Health in
November 1924. The committee, headed by Watson, surveyed the sickness experience between 1921 and 1923 of a sample of about 900,000
insured and produced a report 11 months later in October 1925. The
report noted principally a serious increase in the rate of claims of
married women over those of unmarried women. Still worse, the varia-

[1] As a rule the industrial insurance societies drew membership from the poorer
part of the working class and from women, in effect the groups which had not
been members of friendly societies before the coming of national health insurance.
Dr Harry Roberts, who claimed to have the largest panel practice in the United
Kingdom, told the Royal Commission on National Health Insurance that in the
East End of London, where he maintained his office, nearly all insurance patients
were members of industrial insurance approved societies. He testified that he saw
only 'an occasional' Forester or Odd Fellow. Ministry of Health, *Royal Commission
on National Health Insurance, Minutes of Evidence*, I, 1925, 771–2, 776–7, Oral
Evidence, Dr Harry Roberts.
[2] *RC on NHI, Minutes of Evidence*, II, 289, Written Statements, National Amalgamated Approved Society.
[3] *RC on NHI., Minutes of Evidence*, I, 490–9, Oral Evidence, Sir Edward Neill.

tion was continually growing larger and was increasing most rapidly not among elderly women, from whom sickness could be expected, but among younger women. Between the ages of 20 and 25 the rate of sickness claims among married women was three times that among unmarried.[1]

Surprisingly the commissioners' report made no comment upon the growth in sickness experience. This was after all an approved society problem, not therefore one likely to command much sympathy in a group investigating ways of improving the efficiency of national health insurance. But more to the point, the actuarial committee reports, presented in October 1925, may have come too late to be incorporated in the commission's report which was signed on 22 February 1926.

The Royal Commission had scarcely reported when the slow decay of unemployment which had already undermined nearly every other social service suddenly became serious for national health insurance. The immediate cause was the stoppage in the coal industry which had precipitated the General Strike at the beginning of May and which by summer had increased unemployment figures to nearly 50 per cent over the spring. At the end of July the Insurance Committee addressed a memorandum to panel doctors calling attention to the sudden alarming rise in sickness claims during the past two months. There had been no outbreaks of epidemic disease to account for the increase. On the contrary the distribution of claims throughout the nation corresponded closely with the incidence of unemployment. Doctors must understand their responsibility in the matter of certification. The document warned 'No practitioner is justified in allowing the economic position of the applicant [for sickness benefit] to influence him' in professional judgment.[2]

On 21 October 1926, addressing the annual conference of panel physicians, Sir Walter Kinnear, Controller of the Insurance Department of the Ministry of Health and deputy chairman of the National Health Insurance Joint Committee, reiterated the official belief that doctors were allowing the unemployed to turn the national health insurance sickness benefit into a form of dole. Medical men, he suggested, ought not to allow themselves to be intimidated by demands for sickness certificates. He proposed that he might be able to help protect them by making it more difficult for the insured to change doctors. Approved societies, he continued, ought not to be afraid to

---

[1] *Cmd. 2596*, 'Royal Commission on National Health Insurance', 1926, 336–67, Appendix A. There was no reason to assume that the disparity was the result of maternity confinement, for childbirth was not sickness under the terms of national health insurance and in any case the difference between married women and spinsters continued, if slightly reduced, well into middle age.

[2] Memorandum 3041C, July 1926, reprinted in *National Insurance Gazette*, 7 August 1926.

send all certification cases to medical referees. Some, he noted, were already doing this and the work of referees was three times what it had been three months ago. In this connection, referees during the past three months had discovered that only 66 per cent of the cases they examined were still unfit for work, whereas in the first quarter of 1926 this figure had been 91 per cent. Kinnear cited a recent case that had come to his attention of two men certified as ill attending a local sports meeting. One had won a race, the other a boxing match.[1]

The problem of sickness claims, first noted in 1925 and 1926, did not disappear with the brief drop in unemployment the nation enjoyed in the next two years, and by 1929, even before the onset of the great world depression, Kinnear had found it necessary to begin planning corrective action. The problem of malingering on account of unemployment itself had been compounded by the reduction of the pension age to 65 which, although relieving approved society funds of liability for the payment of sickness benefit to a substantial portion of the elderly population, also affected funds adversely. There had always been a tendency for contributors, as they passed from insurance, to attempt to recover their payments by declaring on the funds. As the number of English males reaching 65 was about 25 per cent larger than the number reaching 70, the five-year reduction in eligibility for sickness benefit meant a substantial increase in the number of men who would attempt to get back their contributions for sickness benefit before they became ineligible for it.

Early in 1928, Kinnear asked Sir Alfred Watson to make a special survey of approved society sickness experience covering the years 1921 to 1927. Watson's report, completed in January 1930, was profoundly disturbing not only to the approved societies but to the Government as well.[2] Put very simply, it appeared that a large number of working-class households, indeed nearly half of them—far more than the number unemployed—were using national health insurance sickness or disablement benefit as a supplementary for ordinary family income. Claims in all categories had risen steeply since 1921. Men's sickness benefit claims

[1] *National Insurance Gazette*, 6 November 1926. Medical referees, officially Regional Medical Officers, were employees of the government, not of the approved societies. The establishment of such a staff had been recommended by the Departmental Committee in 1914 although the first appointments were not made until 1920. Their duty was to protect approved society funds from malingerers by examining paitents whose claims record appeared to warrant it. In this way also they shielded doctors from pressure by patients. The doctors themselves supported the system privately although they were frequently harassed by irate patients after an RMO had examined an individual and declared him fit for work. For a discussion see: AGP, *This Panel Business* (London, 1933), 46, 47, 363.

[2] *Cmd. 3548*, 'Report by the Government Actuary on an Examination of the Sickness and Disablement Experience of a Group of Approved Societies in the Period, 1921–27', 1930.

were 41 per cent larger in 1927 than in 1921, having passed actuarial expectation in 1926, while disablement benefit claims were 85 per cent larger. Worse, married women's sickness claims had increased 106 per cent between 1921 and 1927 and claims for disablement benefit by 159 per cent. Perhaps the most distressing conclusion to appear in Watson's report was the discovery from a special analysis of 7,155 cases of sickness benefit in 1927, that nearly three-fifths of this number, 3,997, had 'declared off' sickness benefit at the end of 26 weeks when it was reduced to the disablement benefit. This quick recovery at the end of the stipulated sickness benefit period, when the amount of money received was cut in half, was common to all classes but was much heavier among younger workers and was 'specially marked' among married women under 50. The impact of the Regional Medical Officer was manifest by the fact that between 55 per cent of men and 65 per cent of women went off the funds immediately when this official was called in. In all, 380 married women of every thousand claimed sickness benefit in 1927 (as opposed to 21 per cent of unmarried women and 23 per cent of men) and 92 of every thousand claimed disability benefit. If, in order not to count them twice, the 42 married women per thousand who drew both sickness and disability benefit in 1927 were deducted from the total of 472, the statistician was still left with the disconcerting result that of every thousand women, nearly half, or 430, drew either sickness benefit or disablement benefit or both in 1927.[1]

All in all, the results of the Watson Report were distressing, and were the more frightening because they covered the period only up to 1927. By the time they were published in the spring of 1930, and widely attacked in the Labour press, unemployment was approaching twice the rate that had prevailed in the last year of the sudy.[2]

Through the rest of 1930 and on into the grim year of 1931, the problem of control of claims increasingly occupied columns of insurance and medical journals and the time of officials in the Ministry of Health. Generally, approved society spokesmen tended to blame dishonest contributors who connived with lazy or incompetent doctors to

---

[1] *Cmd. 3548*, 5, 7. For a discussion of the findings see: Kinnear's speech to the Annual Conference of the Faculty of Insurance, 5 April 1930, in the *National Insurance Gazette*, 12 April 1930. See also: Joan Gibbon, 'The Public Social Services', *Journal of the Royal Statistical Society*, C (Part IV, 1937), 523–7.

[2] The report was clearly most embarrassing to the new Labour Minister of Health, Arthur Greenwood. When it was discussed during the supply debate of April 1930, he was caught in the dilemma of either disavowing the statistical work of respected civil servants in his own department or of accusing English working men of abusing a valuable social service. During hours of persistent questioning he refused to admit that he knew of any malingering and suggested instead that unemployment itself caused sickness. *H of C Deb.*, CCXXXVIII (29 April 1930), cols. 71–167.

obtain fraudulent sickness certificates. Moreover, felt the societies, other organs of government welfare administration, particularly unemployment insurance and Poor Law officers, sought to protect their own funds by passing clients along to the wealthy approved societies. Men who had run out of unemployment insurance were urged to apply for sickness benefits and even the Poor Law authorities were reported to have used their own well established medical service to help paupers to qualify for health insurance. The *National Insurance Gazette* in the spring of 1931 reported a story of the secretary of a local approved society asking a man who brought in a certificate marked 'bronchitis' to describe his symptoms. The man described a pain in his stomach. It developed that the man had exhausted his unemployment insurance benefits and had gone to the guardians who had ordered their doctor to examine him. The Poor Law physician had told the man that he had bronchitis and that he should go to his panel doctor to get a certificate which would entitle him to sick pay. Apparently the panel doctor had given the certificate without an examination.[1] The problem, concluded the societies, was that even if the patient reported unobservable symptoms, most doctors simply would not refuse to give certificates to their regular patients and there were not enough medical referees available to handle the great surge of sickness claims. Most society records seemed to show that scarcely one-third of the contributors claiming sickness benefit were in fact ill. Among industrial insurance approved societies in 1930, of 423,000 cases referred to Regional Medical Officers nearly 154,000 immediately went off the funds and of those who did submit to a physical examination about 118,000 were certified as capable. For the two years 1929 and 1930 only 36 per cent of the cases examined by the medical referees were confirmed as genuinely ill.[2]

For its part, the British medical profession declined to accept entirely the blame for the growing crisis in national health insurance. The fault lay with the system. Societies ought to protect the profession by the appointment of more medical referees, the doctors argued. There was on the other hand little unanimity on the question of malingering. Dr Alfred Cox, Medical Secretary of the British Medical Association, insisted in the summer of 1930 that his correspondents all agreed that there was little or no malingering, 'pretending to suffer from diseases which one does not have'. Rather there was widespread feeling that the existence of sick pay magnified the importance of symptoms and made possible absenteeism on account of minor ailments that might otherwise be ignored. Clinically, Dr Cox argued, all of this might be entirely

[1] *National Insurance Gazette*, 7 March 1931.
[2] *Ibid.*, 27 June 1931.

desirable. The insured were, he thought, getting three times the medical attendance that was the rule among the general population.[1]

Other doctors took issue with Cox. The anonymous author of a widely read pamphlet, *This Panel Business,* reported a number of examples taken from discussions at the annual panel conferences of the hard, mercenary attitude manifest among national insurance contributors toward the health scheme. He cited the case of a doctor whose cook had demanded a bottle of medicine simply on the basis that she wanted 'something for my 8d.' and of another case where two men had sold a sickness certificate for 5s. in order to obtain money to attend a football match. 'Is there any single panel doctor who cannot point to similar incidents in his own experience?' he concluded.[2]

As regards medical referees, the anonymous author emphasized that while they were helpful their numbers were totally inadequate—there were only 82 for al England and Wales in 1930—and that their usefulness was limited because the doctors feared that patients would believe that it was they who had ordered the examination. In fact the doctors rarely did this. Of 530,000 referee examinations in 1930, only 1,800 had been requested by panel practitioners.[3]

The crisis over the abuse of national health insurance climaxed in 1931 with the issuance of Insurance Commission Memorandum 329 which was itself the result of an intensive investigation of certification practices conducted by the Regional Medical Officers. In bluntest terms the health insurance administration accused the panel practitioners—always insisting however that it did not intend to condemn every single individual—of using their power to issue sickness certificates as a means of building or retaining practice. The rise in claims for sickness and disablement benefits was now 'so continuous in its operation and of such magnitude as to occasion grave concern among all engaged in the administration of these benefits'.

The fact that cessation of benefit after reference is most frequent in

---

[1] '17 Years of National Health Insurance Medical Service', paper read before the Royal Sanitary Institute, June 1930, printed in *National Insurance Gazette,* 24 January 1931.
[2] AGP, *Panel Business,* 42.
[3] *Ibid.,* 46, 47, 363. On references to Regional Medical Officers see also: R. W. Harris, *National Health Insurance, 1911–1946* (London, 1946), 109–16, 156–8. In this connection, telling more of cultural than administrative differences, it may be noted that, with even more unemployment, there was less evidence of malingering in Scotland than in England and Wales. Whereas in 1930 only 34 per cent of those referred to Regional Medical Officers were certified as incapable of work in the south, in the north 45 per cent were so certified. Of the 377 references made by doctors themselves to Regional Medical Officers in 1937, no less than 361 were referred by doctors in Scotland which had an insured population scarcely one-eighth as large as England and Wales. *Ibid.,* 158–60.

294 TOWARDS A NATIONAL HEALTH SERVICE

the classes in which claims had increased the most between 1921–27, and least in the class which showed the least increase in claims, tends to reinforce the belief that the increase in claims has been mainly an increase in claims by persons who were not incapable of work.

The memorandum went on to quote reports from the medical referees summarizing explanations they had received from the insurance practitioners. Panel doctors had said:

... they found themselves unable to certify strictly in accordance with their medical judgment for fear of losing patients.

... when their patients complained of their illness and inability to work they did not feel justified, even in the absence of any signs of disease, in refusing certificates.

... although they might believe a patient to have recovered and become able to resume work, they preferred to leave the duty of saying so to the examining officer of the Department.

... although a patient might legitimately be considered not incapable of work, the doctor knew how difficult it would be for the patient to find work under the prevailing conditions of employment, and he allowed himself to be influenced by compassionate considerations.[1]

It was easier to define the problem of sickness claims than to decide how to solve it. Generally officials in the health insurance administration, led by Walter Kinnear, tended to be reluctant to look for a solution in a change of policy among the medical profession.[2] Even though the profession needed continual warning and supervision, at bottom there was little that the lonely insurance practitioner, himself affected by the depression and desperate for patients, could do. The easier response, one clearly supported within the Ministry of Health, and tacitly supported by the approved societies, was to drop or to limit health insurance coverage for the unemployed.

The position of an unemployed contributor to health insurance was precarious. An act in 1918 had provided one year of free health insurance at full benefit for any working person in an insured trade should he lose his job. At the time this had been considered adequate for ordinary periods of unemployment. By the end of 1921, however, with large numbers of working people in danger of losing all health insurance coverage because they had paid no contributions for a year, Parliament hurriedly passed a prolongation of insurance act continuing full medical benefit and reduced cash benefits, which in any case could

[1] 329/IC, 1931, quoted in Harris, *National Health Insurance*, 113, 114, 157.
[2] See for instance Kinnear's speech to the Annual Conference of the Faculty of Insurance, 5 April 1930, quoted in the *National Insurance Gazette*, 12, 26 April 1930.

not fall lower than one-half cash benefit, 7s. 6d. for men, for those unemployed longer than one year. The Act of 1921 remained in effect through annual renewals until 1928. In 1926 the Royal Commission on National Health Insurance had commented in strongest terms upon the inequity of a system in which an unemployed head of a family might receive well over a pound a week in unemployment insurance benefits, but after a year should the deprivation of unemployment cause him to fall sick, this unavoidable accident reduced his income to slightly more than 1s. per day. Although the commission made no formal recommendation on arrears, in the National Health Insurance Act of 1928, the act of 1921 was amended to extend the period of full benefit for, on the average, a further nine months, the period of the extension depending on the amount of arrears of contribution with another 12 months at half benefit. As with many other changes in the welfare programme during the second Baldwin administration, notably the Unemployment Insurance Act of 1927, Chamberlain justified his relaxation of rules by the argument that unemployment appeared to be diminishing.[1] The extra concession would be paid for by government contribution from the surplus stamp fund: income accrued from the purchase of insurance stamps against which for one reason or another no claims had been made. Friendly society reserves would continue to support the unemployed during their first year.

Like so many other social plans the Great Depression soon made obsolete this easy, self-financing way of supporting the long-term unemployed under national health insurance. By the end of 1930 a substantial number of men had been without work for more than the 22 months provided under the act of 1928 and were again in danger of losing benefits. In most cases the friendly societies were carrying them from their own reserves, but these surpluses, suffering from reduced contributions and the lower Treasury payments following the National Economy Act of 1926, were no longer so large as they had been in the 1920s. Through the Consultative Council the societies began to bring pressure on the Government either to support the unemployed from the Treasury or to allow the societies to drop men most seriously in arrears from benefit. Thus the MacDonald Government was caught again in its familiar dilemma of being forced to choose between the demand of socialist ideology and prudent finance. The Cabinet was badly divided on the issue and after apparently determining early in December to drop all cash benefits for men unemployed more than two and a half years, the Government reversed itself, allowing Arthur Greenwood to announce on 11 December that a measure would be introduced providing for an exchequer grant of about £100,000 to

[1] *H of C Deb.*, CCXV (3 April 1928), cols. 1815–20.

allow half benefits for the 100,000 or so contributors who had been unemployed more than two and a half years.[1]

When compared to unemployment insurance, national health insurance received little direct harm from the financial crisis of 1931. The Committee on National Expenditure treated the programme tenderly, perhaps, one may speculate, because its chairman, George May, was himself a former secretary of the Prudential Assurance Company. In any case, beyond recommending the cessation of the government contribution of £142,000 to the Central Contingencies Fund, the ending of the grant for prolongation of insurance, and the reduction of the doctors' capitation fee from 9s. to 8s., there was little that economy-minded body could find to cut. Moreover the committee took note of the fact that Exchequer payments to the health insurance scheme had fallen from £10 million in 1921 to only £6 million in 1930 while total expenditures of the scheme in the same ten-year period had increased from £28 million to £36 million. The insurance world was aware that it had been treated generously in comparison with the wreckage left among other welfare programmes and the *National Insurance Gazette* urged its readers to move quietly.[2]

More serious, however, was the introduction of the means test to be administered by the local authorities for applicants for transitional benefits. This appeared to be a real danger to national health insurance. It should be remembered that the fundamental, if seldom noticed, safeguard to the reserves of the approved societies was the fact that even with the abuse of sickness certification the amount of the national health insurance cash benefit was scarcely more than two-thirds the benefit available under unemployment insurance. It represented usually a less desirable alternative to any unemployed working man. But there were some loopholes. For instance a man working a theoretical five-and-a-half-day week for 44s. would receive only 32s. and no unemployment insurance if he were able to obtain work for only four days. If on the other hand he malingered on the fourth day and worked only three days he would get 24s. in wages and 15s. in sickness benefit for a total of 39s.[3]

Even though the National Government reduced the basic unemployment benefits from 17s. to 15s., the generous provisions for dependants'

[1] *H of C Deb.*, CCXLVI (11 December 1930, 11, 17 December 1930), cols. 507–8, 1363–97. For a discussion of the pressures brought by the Consultative Council and the politics involved see: *National Insurance Gazette*, 29 November, 20 December 1930. The Conservatives opposed the bill as a dilution of the contributory principle arguing that it constituted perhaps a first step toward the creation of a tax-supported medical service.

[2] *National Insurance Gazette*, 15, 22 August 1931.

[3] For a description of various malingering techniques see: J. Redman Ormerod, *National Insurance: Its Inherent Defects* (London, 1930), 29–35.

allowances kept the ordinary grant of unemployment insurance well above the national health insurance sickness benefit. But now, in September 1931, this fixed amount was no longer available to the nearly 1,000,000 heads of families who would have to apply to the public assistance authorities and whose relief would be dependent upon a means test. A large number of them, the *National Insurance Gazette* felt, might well prefer the 15s. theoretically available under national health insurance which could be obtained without the humiliation of a means investigation. In view of this, the *Gazette* concluded, 'It is not surprising that the Government has been so kind to National Health Insurance in its economy requirements.'[1]

The apprehensions of the approved societies about the gravity of their own position were soon confirmed. At the end of 1931 appeared the third official valuation of approved societies. Because it covered only the years 1927, 1928, and 1929, it did not include the worst period of unemployment, but it showed clearly enough that the administrative institutions of national health insurance, particularly the smaller societies, were headed toward the sort of financial catastrophe that had overtaken unemployment insurance.[2] Disposable surplus had fallen by about £7 million since the previous valuation and although the aggregate surplus of all societies with an income larger than expenditure was still £36 million, those societies in deficiency showed a total deficiency of nearly £1 million. Worse, of the major part of the income of the societies which had made a profit, £6½ million had come from interest on the surplus itself and would hence disappear as the surplus was used up. Only £5 million profit was earned on contribution income which through the period had been only 88 per cent of expectation. For the first time the government actually found it necessary to order wholesale reductions in extra benefits. In 15 per cent of the societies all extra benefits were cut out, leaving only the statutory minimums outlined in the act of 1920, and in another 26 per cent some economies in coverage were required: 2,700,000 women and 950,000 men lost dental benefits; 1,300,000 women were deprived of ophthalmic benefits.[3]

The fact that these grim statistics covered years which, in terms of the interwar period, had been relatively prosperous was not lost upon the approved societies. In the spring of 1932 began a series of private and public demands generally emanating from the Consultative

[1] *National Insurance Gazette*, 19, 26 September 1931.
[2] *Cmd. 3978*, 'Third Valuation of Assets and Liabilities of Approved Societies', 1931–32.
[3] For a discussion and justification of these changes see the address by Walter Kinnear to the Insurance Institute of London, 7 March 1932, in *National Insurance Gazette*, 12, 19 March 1932.

U

Council, for legislation permitting the reduction of minimum statutory benefits. With unemployment approaching a quarter of the insured work force the Government could not avoid action. On 8 April the Cabinet privately promised a bill which received its second reading 11 May 1932.[1] The National Health Insurance and Contributory Pensions Act of 1932 was frankly, as the new Minister of Health Hilton Young admitted in the House of Commons, a result of approved society pressure and of the Government's unwillingness either to allow health insurance to fall into the chaos which had overtaken unemployment insurance or to produce the necessary funds to keep the scheme solvent at the present level of benefits.[2] Henceforth, a man unemployed on half benefit would be required to make up half his arrears of contribution, less the excusal of two payments, if he wished to be restored to full benefit when he found work. More important, statutory benefits for women were to be drastically reduced. The sickness benefit for married women was to fall from 12s. to 10s. and the disability benefit from 7s. 6d. to 5s., which was in fact the amount provided under the original act of 1911. Further disability benefit for unmarried women was reduced from 7s. 6d. to 6s. Approved societies, it was pointed out in the explanatory memorandum on the bill, had lost in the period 1928–30—no more recent statistics were available—an average of 2s. per year for each unmarried woman member and 7s. 6d. per year for each married woman member. These losses had been rising steadily and were estimated now to be more than £4 million above expectation.[3] Before the third valuation, Young noted, 95 per cent of the societies gave some extra benefits. Since then, extra benefits had been halted altogether for 4,250,000 of 17,000,000 insured and reduced for 6,250,000 more.[4] Two further provisions prolonged health insurance benefits until the end of 1933 for about 80,000 workers who had been continuously unemployed more than 33 months and continued eligibility for old age pensions for all unemployed until the end of 1935, while stipulating that any man over age 58 would not lose eligibility for the contributory pension under any circumstances.

In explaining his bill during the second reading Young had dilated upon the help and support the ministry had received from the approved societies in the preparation of the measure. Nevertheless, even on the first day of debate, it became clear that the societies were not altogether satisfied with the bill. In the second reading R. J. Meller, Chairman of the Consultative Council, a former executive of the

[1] See: 'A Bill at an Early Date', leading article, *National Insurance Gazette*, 16 April 1932.
[2] *H of C Deb.*, CCLXV (11 May 1932), cols, 1927–39, 1943.
[3] *Cmd. 4072*, 'Memorandum Explanatory of Bill', 1932.
[4] *H of C Deb.*, CCLXV (11 May 1932), cols., 1927–35.

Prudential and Conservative Member of Parliament for Mitcham since 1923, announced, apparently with complete confidence, that he hoped the Government would create an entirely new class of insurance for married women.

Upon marriage, the approved societies hoped, women would be required to requalify for national health insurance as if they were new entrants paying 26 weekly contributions and being excluded from the maternity benefit for a year and from the disability benefit for two years.[1] The chief argument for the approved society amendment lay in an anomaly that appeared to have escaped notice until the debates of 1932: that as trade grew worse through the 1920s and early '30s, and, as presumably more people were unemployed, the numbers leaving health insurance grew smaller. In the fiscal year of 1925–26 11·6 per cent of insured women had left health insurance for one reason or another. In each succeeding year this figure had grown smaller so that in 1930–31 only 6·6 per cent of the number of women previously insured had left the programme.[2]

The approved society amendment quickly became the focus of debate. Around it developed violent controversy in which the question of the financial stability of national health insurance was lost and the point at issue became the selfishness or usefulness of the approved societies' system. The societies in this case came under sustained attack by an unusual group made up not only of their normal opponents in the Labour movement but a group of women Members of Parliament headed by Viscountess Astor. Eventually, on 21 June, during the report stage, after an announcement by Hilton Young that the Government could not support it, the approved society amendment was negatived without a division.

The Government's action caused anger and surprise from approved society spokesmen both in the House of Commons and out of it. Meller's speech immediately before the vote charging the Government with bad faith was echoed in far stronger terms by the *National Insurance Gazette* which accused the Cabinet of buying votes at the cost of the solvency of the national insurance programme.[3] Generally, the insurance world tended to blame women Members of Parliament for the defeat of their proposal although in retrospect the Government clearly feared more the newly enfranchised woman voter under 30 who would make up most of the class at whom the amendment was directed.

While the approved societies had not received all they demanded in the National Health Insurance and Contributory Pensions Act of 1932, which was to be their last important legislative accomplishment, the

[1] *H of C Deb.*, CCLXV (11 May 1932) cols. 1971–2. The Chairman of the Consultative Council was almost invariably an MP of the majority party.

[2] *H of C Deb.*, CCLXVII (21 June 1932), cols. 933–6.

[3] *National Insurance Gazette*, 2, 9 July 1932.

reductions in benefit effected by the measure and the gradual reduction of unemployment from nearly three million in that year to the customary 1,200,000 by the end of 1936 allowed the national health insurance programme to proceed within actuarial limits. The fourth valuation published in 1937 and covering the assets and liabilities of approved societies on the last day of the years between 1931-34 showed that while the programme was no longer enjoying the prosperity of the 1920s it had at least reached a kind of equilibrium. Total accrued surpluses in societies that did show surpluses amounted to £37 million and deficits were only about £650,000.[1] Not surprisingly, societies whose membership included women only were still in the weakest financial position. Nearly one society out of five in this category showed a deficit although these altogether included only 6 per cent of the total number of female contributors. Compared with this, only 72 men's societies or branches out of a total of 2,622 were in deficit. As had been the rule throughout the entire life of national health insurance, the old friendly societies possessed the largest surpluses per member partly because they had a more prosperous and stable membership than the industrial insurance societies, but also because as a rule they had fewer women contributors.[2]

The enemy of progress

By the late 1930s, one can argue that the structure of national health insurance had nearly reached the practicable limits of beneficial and progressive evolution. Certainly this is not to say that the scheme was ideal, or that it was worth expanding into a comprehensive health service, or indeed that it would have been capable of such extensions. There were anomalies and paradoxes in coverage. Administration, because of the duplication in each locality of offices of scores of national societies, was uselessly expensive. It may be noted that the Irish Free State abolished approved societies in 1933, combining them all into a single national society. Competition among societies for contributors, a point upon which Lloyd George had laid so much stress when defending this form of administration, did not bring economy.

[1] *Cmd. 5496*, 'Report by the Government Actuary on the Fourth Valuation of the Assets and Liabilities of Approved Societies', 1937, 23.
[2] *Cmd. 5496*, 58–9, 108–9. Manchester Unity of Odd Fellows, for instance, one of the largest and oldest of the traditional friendly societies, had only 197,000 women among its 881,000 members and possessed a total surplus of £3,346,000. This may be compared with the Liverpool Victoria Approved Society, one of the leading collecting insurance organizations, which included 328,000 women in a total membership of 746,000 but which enjoyed a surplus of only £916,000. In effect the Manchester Unity had a surplus of nearly £4 per member as opposed to slightly more than £1 per member for the Liverpool Victoria.

But, on the other hand, the ever-present challenge for increased membership caused societies to offer extra and wider benefits and to tailor their programmes to the apparent demand of their clientele in a way that nationally operated social security programmes seldom do. By 1939, 91 per cent of the total insured of England received some extra treatment benefits and 72 per cent received extra cash benefits. By far the most popular was the dental benefit, usually half the cost of dental treatment, and frequently for men only, for which more than three-quarters of the English contributors were eligible.[1] Almost as popular was the ophthalmic benefit and the provision of convalescent homes for chronic illness. Suprisingly, the hospital benefit, the absence of which caused so much criticism of the health insurance programme, appears to have been little in demand. Although it was offered by societies totalling together 1,600,000 contributors, only £91,000 was spent upon it in 1938 out of a total of nearly £3,500,000 spent altogether on extra benefits.[2]

Typical extra cash benefits varied from between one and three shillings added to the sickness benefit—although some small homogeneous societies, the Warehousemen's and Clerks' Association for example, paid as much as nine—with similar increases in the disablement benefit. Almost invariably extra benefits were lower for unmarried women than for men and frequently did not exist at all for married women except in the case of the maternity benefit. Uniformly the societies required four years of membership and continuous contribution before the insured individual became eligible for extra benefits thus increasing again the cost of administration.[3]

In a way the competition to pay extra benefits represented a major weakness, rather than a strength, of the approved society system. The problem was not, primarily, as later critics had it, that the benefits were unequal and that the system therefore was unfair to many people who paid the same contributions as the others but somehow received smaller benefits. Invariably it is forgotten that, although there were nearly 2,000 separate approved societies and branches, more than nine-tenths of the insured population were members of fewer than a dozen huge societies. In fact a small society, if restricted geographically and containing, as many did, only members of a single trade, frequently would have far lower expenses and hence pay higher benefits than a national society. Rather the difficulty was that extra benefits were expensive to administer particularly as they included a

---

[1] Cmd. 6089, 'Twentieth Annual Report of the Ministry of Health', 1939, 149.
[2] Cmd. 6089, 149.
[3] For a survey see the Charity Organisation Society pamphlet, Additional Benefits Payable by Certain Approved Societies—Fourth Valuation, quoted in PEP, Report on the British Health Services, London, 1937, 204.

second set of membership requirements, that they penalized contributors moving from one society to another for a matter of personal con-
venience and, worst of all, that they added element of competition to
the health service which was far from healthy. Extra benefits were in a
way a form of advertising. Although the average man, remarked the
PEP in its survey of the health services in 1937, was 'in complete
ignorance' of the extra benefits of the various societies, nearly all
societies used them to promote membership. The fact remained that a
society which did not offer extra benefits was not able to gain, and
usually lost, members. As a result, despite the supervision of the
Government Actuary, the pressure to provide extra benefits frequently
led societies into financial difficulties as the wholesale reductions in
benefits showed in 1931.

The character of the benefits themselves, while in some cases generous and perhaps in no cases useless, probably did not represent the
most thoughtful means of distribution of the approved societies' resources. For instance, by far the most popular benefit was the dental
benefit which was enjoyed in some measure by about two-thirds of all
contributors to national health insurance and which absorbed about the
same proportion of the total amount spent on extra benefits. However
one cannot help wondering whether the dental benefit, desirable as it
was, was a more useful addition to the ordinary coverage of national
health insurance than, say, hospital and consultant care, and whether
the popularity of the dental benefit therefore may not have reflected
considerations other than those of public health. It may be noted, for
instance, that one of the most powerful figures in the industrial insurance world, Percy Rockliff, who was a member of the Consultative
Council from 1920 until 1948 as well as a member of the Dental
Benefit Council through which the Ministry of Health supervised the
administration of the dental benefit, also operated as a private venture
a dental service which for a fee offered to handle dental care for those
societies wishing to provide this benefit for their members.

It should be repeated in conclusion that the difficulties with national
health insurance which arguably made much further progress impossible were structural ones. It was not that approved societies were
ungenerous or badly administered; some were but many were not. A
few societies indeed were paying, in the last years before the war, a
24s. sickness benefit, which was the amount recommended in the
Beveridge report as the basic benefit for unemployment, disability or
training, based on 1938 prices. Rather the problem was that no one
in a position to make changes in national health insurance thought of
modifications in any other terms than of the effect it would have upon
the contributors in a single society. Even the Government, with the
possible exception of Neville Chamberlain's tenure at the Ministry of

Health, seldom approached the programme with any other goal than that of saving money. The civil servants within the ministry of health, although not exactly prisoners of the approved societies, reflected their point of view in public utterances. The societies themselves were always able to show that health insurance among all the social welfare programmes was both solvent and economical. When compared with housing, old age pension, or above all unemployment insurance, their smoothly running, self-contained apparatus was almost invulnerable to assaults by politicians.

Only twice were they seriously threatened: once by the Royal Commission when the minority report recommended the abolition of the approved society system and the majority urged a partial pooling of society supluses to provide uniform extended benefits, and second during the crisis of 1931-32 when unemployment seemed briefly about to threaten the solvency of the programme. On each occasion approved society political expertise had prevailed. At the time of the Royal Commission report the Government was far more interested in economy than in extending health insurance. They could not at once reduce the government contribution to the programme as envisioned in the National Economy Act and require the societies to broaden minimum benefits even though the funds for the latter course were already in existence. To do both was politically, albeit not economically, impossible. The choice in any event was to reduce the government contribution from two-ninths of the cost of benefit to one-seventh and to drop the recommendation of the majority report of the Royal Commission which had urged the pooling of surpluses. In 1932, under the National Health Insurance Act of that year, the Government again chose, with the societies' full concurrence, to secure solvency through economy. The alternatives on this occasion were an increase in the government contribution or a reduction in women's benefits, virtually a parallel of the situation in the previous decade.

Perhaps the lesson in all this was that national health insurance from its inception violated the basic principle of social welfare: that the public good must be regarded as an end in itself. In establishing health insurance Lloyd George had argued that the interest of the approved societies and of the contributors would be identical. The societies, he insisted, were run by and for their members. They had no other existence. There could be no competition for advantage. In fact, well before the National Insurance Bill became law, the Chancellor of the Exchequer and many of his advisers knew that this would not be the case. The initial assumption that national health insurance would become simply universal membership, with government encouragement, in friendly societies was destroyed by the demand from the industrial insurance industry that it too enter the programme. Furthermore, as it turned out, even the old fraternal orders, the true friendly societies, changed their character as membership became compulsory. As the years passed the administration of government benefits for all types of societies became simply a profitable sideline business and the friendly societies themselves, not to mention the industrial insurance approved societies, made a sharp distinction between government members and others. The running of national health insurance was for all of them simply a money making proposition which by 1939 earned for the societies, according to William Beveridge's calculation, 14·3 per cent of the amount of benefits paid.[1]

There existed then a vested interest that was by no means identical with the welfare of the people whom national health insurance was supposed to protect. The approved societies regarded national health insurance as their own. It was not in the ordinary sense a government programme and the societies found it both easy and advantageous to protect the government from the ordinary political skirmishing that so afflicted housing and unemployment insurance. Among themselves they competed for clients in an ordinary commercial way. When threats appeared they banded together to intercept the pressures of political democracy. To be sure the government often found the societies an annoyance particularly when, as has been discussed in other chapters of this study, the societies attempted to intervene in other social programmes. But usually, except when the matter was a question of saving government money, the societies were allowed to have their way. In the formation of the Ministry of Health, in the establishment of unemployment insurance, and in the disregard of both the minority and majority reports of the Royal Commission on National Health Insurance, it was easier to accommodate the societies than to fight them. Hence national health insurance never realized its potential. Although the scheme was by no means bad or useless, the conclusion upon it must be that the paramount welfare was that of its administrators and that the benefits to the British people, for whom the programme was designed, were residual.

[1] As part of his attack on the approved society system Beveridge included a long appendix in his report on the administrative ineptitude of approved societies. See: *Cmd. 6404*, 'Social Insurance and Allied Services', 277–86.

Conclusion

In a sense this book is about social politics rather than social policy. The two are not really the same thing. A nation may have a long-established social policy—the doctrine of less eligibility, for instance—and virtually no social politics. Social policy may refer to attitudes so well understood by the effective governing class that they scarcely need discussion. A compromise by politicians for the neglect of popular domestic social issues can itself be a social policy. Social politics on the other hand usually emerge when the consensus on social policy breaks down.

For most of the two decades between the wars Britain had no coherent social policy and was in search of agreement on the degree of State responsibility toward individual citizens. What, it was asked repeatedly in a thousand ways, does society owe its members: a bare maintenance, a decent minimum of existence, a standard of living approximating normal life, or above all, the right to work? In the search for answers, social politics became in the 1920s a first-rank matter of state, as important as the more traditional concerns of international diplomacy, the management of empire, or keeping the peace.

All of this no doubt was the inevitable result of substantial male franchise. One cannot help remembering Sidney Webb's warning to the Royal Commission on the Aged Poor only half a decade after the passing of the third Reform Act that the governing classes must be prepared for a new parliamentary climate. In words that might almost be the theme of this study, he observed that socialism was the 'economic obverse of democracy'. The dock labourer or the tram driver, he thought, would not regard their new voting privilege as a means of determining the party affiliation of the ambassador in Paris or even of deciding questions of war and peace. But surely, Webb asserted, they would see it as a way of altering 'the conditions under which they live and work'.

Socialism, it might be said in answer, did not become in fact the only issue in British parliamentary affairs in the 1920s and '30s, but the fear of it was the catalyst of social politics. Webb's phrase, 'the conditions under which they live and work', delineated the politics of the people as they appeared first in the New Liberalism before the war and as they became the chief continuing domestic problem at Westminster after the Armistice. The point of contention was not whether the government would assume the task of protecting popular welfare, but whether this would be done through socialism—either domestic

British or some ghastly foreign alternative—or some form of neo-liberal social reform.

Probably no one of first political rank understood better the new mood that David Lloyd George. Before the war he had attempted to rebuild the Liberal party and give it a new programme as Gladstone and Bright had done half a century before. The political liberties of the British subject, he argued, were as safe in Edwardian England as were the privileges of Parliament in the mid-nineteenth century. But political liberty without economic security meant little. The New Liberalism he proposed was therefore the logical successor of the old radicalism, while at the same time stealing votes from Labour party socialism.

After the war, the Prime Minister tried to institutionalize non-socialist social reform in a new party. He was sure that the remnants of Toryism with which he was identified damaged his Government and his programme. He assumed he was in a position after the Armistice to incorporate into a new organization built around himself those elements of the Conservatives he desired to keep and to discard the rest. As it turned out he was able to charm a few of the party leaders but the party machinery and the City of London remained hostile to his magnetism. Lloyd George thought he had captured the Conservatives with the device of the coupon. He found instead that he was the party's prisoner.

Although characteristically the Prime Minister held on even after the death of the fusion experiment, his failure marks the end not only of Liberalism and of the New Liberalism but the end of any coherent social policy in British politics for nearly two decades. There were to be sure men with elaborate and well-founded ideas about what the British people needed. Neville Chamberlain is the most obvious example and even Churchill in the late 1920s sought to regain a few of the radical credentials which had been so conspicuously his before the war. But neither party, Conservative nor Labour, had a programme which it was prepared to enact when in power, still less one upon which it agreed with the opposition. Social reform was simply a live grenade the front benches tossed back and forth in the hope that it would explode while in the opponent's possession.

This leads to a second fact about social politics of the late 1920s and '30s. It is that, while the nation's gravest concerns were social and economic, most politicians, always excepting Chamberlain, although admitting the gravity of these problems, were willing to leave them to experts while devoting themselves to traditional questions. In 1934, when there were still over 1,500,000 unemployed, the Government of India Bill consumed more days of parliamentary time, far more columns of newsprint, and above all caused far more turmoil and friction within the Conservative party, than did the complex and vital Unemployment Bill of the same year. Army and navy votes in the late '20s always evoked much greater public and legislative interest than did the Ministry of Health or Ministry of Labour estimates even though the latter two departments disbursed, or at least supervised the spending of, more money affecting many more people than did the fighting services in those peaceful years. Moreover the welfare ministries themselves had little status. They were regarded either as a transitional step to higher office or as a graveyard where a dying career could be quietly buried. Only a crisis such as the threat of national bankruptcy could make social policy a front bench matter.

The history of British social politics, as a result, was made not in parliamentary halls but in ministerial corridors. Social reform measures, which touched directly more citizens and excited more popular reaction than almost any other parliamentary matter, proved to be the least amenable to intelligent discussion in the ordinary forum of political democracy. Even royal commissions and select committees appeared to be more than usually ineffective. Except on the rare occasion when the issue was clear and simple, such as the rebellion over the Unemployment Assistance Board regulations, the ordinary gentleman Member of Parliament, after admitting that the subject was no doubt of great importance, found social reform debate squalid and boring. Many of those who attacked Oliver Stanley over the Standstill Act had failed to attend the debates the previous autumn when the regulations then being so severely criticized had been before Parliament for three days' consideration.

Of necessity, therefore, social politics were a matter for private adjustment, for conferences between low-level ministers, their civil servants and lobby delegations. The matters at issue were not less important or expensive on this account, nor were the results of mistakes less devastating. But somehow an increase in old age pension payments, although costing quite as much money and having far greater economic impact, never compared in glamour to the laying down of a new class of cruisers.

Hence social politics have to be recorded at a different level than other forms of public affairs. Of the nearly three score parliamentary enactments that come within the scope of this study, not half a dozen count as major pieces of legislation in political terms. Although each party used the plight of the unemployed as evidence of the incompetence and inactivity of the other, neither the Conservatives nor Labour had a solution for the problem. In some major areas, notably national health insurance, the administrators, the approved societies, deliberately kept themselves anonymous. The effect of all this was, of course, that the critical decisions, although frequently highly political in content, were made by administrators.

In Britain between 1919 and 1939, a public social policy did indeed evolve, but it was nearly unnoticed by Parliament, by the papers, or, in fact, by the men making the decisions. At the time of the Armistice, Britain had no social policy except for the discredited principles of 1834. But while all agreed that the Poor Law was detestable, there was no agreement about what to put in its place. Nevertheless, by the coming of the Second World War, a consensus on social responsibility had appeared. Out of hurried ministerial conferences, concessions gained by lobby organizations, through the fatigue of civil servants and the desperation of politicians, from whispered last-minute compromises in Parliamentary cloakrooms and hundreds and hundreds of minor relaxations of administrative rules, the British State had committed itself to the maintenance of all its citizens according to need as a matter of right without any concurrent political disability. This policy evolved, like the British empire, in a fit of absence of mind. But it was no less a policy. The administrative machinery was diffuse and archaic. The mode of finance—whether through insurance or tax support—was unsettled. All of these would have to wait upon the Beveridge Report. Still, after two decades of struggle, Britain had attained a *de facto* national minimum. An edifice had been built, shambling and rickety, without an architect. The only conceivable architect—the only man possessing at once the interest and the knowledge and the political power—had been sent packing with his plans in 1922. But the commitment was made.

Unlike 1918, when reconstruction had meant for many the reconstruction of Edwardian England, in 1945 no one was interested in reviving the 1930s. The thirties were not worth going back to. And so at the end of the Second World War, fair shares for all meant the distribution first of all to those who needed it whatever remained of the nation's wealth. Britain had moved from social welfare to social service.

Appendix I Select Tables

1 Expenditure on Housing 1920-39

Financial Year	Housing and Town Planning Act 1919	Housing (Additional Powers) Act 1919	Housing Act 1923	Housing (Financial Provisions) Act 1924	Housing (Rural Workers) Acts 1926-38	Housing Act 1930 (Later 1936)	Housing Act 1935 (Later 1936)	Housing (Financial Provisions) Act 1938	TOTALS
	£	£	£	£	£	£	£	£	£
1919-20	20,455								20,455
1920-21	568,749	2,528,552							3,097,301
1921-22	4,568,492	4,540,424							9,109,366
1922-23	7,227,911	2,427,847							9,655,398
1923-24	7,850,014	1,693	6,108						7,857,815
1924-25	7,951,582		96,665	1,885					8,050,132
1925-26	7,305,432		439,641	88,683					7,833,756
1926-27	6,953,157		948,459	474,428					8,376,044
1927-28	6,864,817		1,509,129	1,167,030					9,540,576
1928-29	6,827,364		1,976,897	1,865,713					10,669,974
1929-30	6,738,118		2,141,089	2,253,087	509				11,132,803
1930-31	6,723,699		2,621,250	2,528,263	2,594				11,875,806
1931-32	6,742,070		2,731,051	3,245,955	7,427	5,100			12,731,603
1932-33	6,781,395		2,633,567	3,873,297	11,369	50,130			13,349,758
1933-34	6,589,724		2,523,650	4,178,750	15,358	125,144			13,432,626
1934-35	6,671,006		2,499,822	4,264,145	19,819	303,464			13,758,256
1935-36	6,498,129		2,501,768	4,347,616	20,374	629,666			13,997,553
1936-37	6,275,321		2,533,171	4,286,967	27,603	1,203,229	4,603		14,330,894
1937-38	6,065,875		2,502,043	4,269,546	29,771	1,735,855	14,453		14,617,543
1938-39	6,018,330		2,477,731	4,242,748	28,879	2,154,314	49,268	14,854	14,986,124
TOTALS	121,242,090	9,498,156	30,142,041	41,088,133	163,703	6,206,902	68,324	14,854	208,424,183

Cmd. 6089, 'Twentieth Annual Report of the Ministry of Health, 1938-39', Appendix Table XVIII, 253

2 Poor Law Relief England and Wales 1919-39

	Total no. on relief and per cent of population	Total no. on Outdoor Relief	Total no. on Indoor Relief	Total no. on Medical Relief O.D.	I.D.	Total no. above age 70 on Relief	Total no. above age 70 on Medical Relief O.D.	I.D.
1919	554,600—1·5	287,250	267,350			43,200		
1920	576,418—1·54	305,849	270,569	116,420	82,666	46,846	8,008	18,476
1921	663,667—1·76	376,303	287,364	127,011	88,180	52,693	11,065	19,964
1922	1,493,066—3·94	1,183,516	309,550	163,990	93,958	63,970	19,300	20,510
1923	1,537,990—4·03	1,222,684	315,301	186,381	97,100	72,620	26,638	20,595
1924	1,372,098—3·57	1,051,376	320,722	201,777	101,363	80,404	32,957	21,075
1925	1,205,267—3·71	886,825	318,442	218,967	92,602	89,539	42,188	22,296
1926	1,439,810—3·70	1,113,078	326,732	252,373	95,141	101,538	52,424	23,440
1927	1,548,911—3·96	1,212,553	336,358	273,424	96,178	112,214	62,420	23,752
1928	1,364,691—3·47	1,026,678	338,013	276,287	94,551	116,316	67,612	24,312
1929	1,240,666—3·14	899,663	341,003	284,160	95,797	121,956	74,379	24,895
1930	1,204,417—3·04	867,066	338,351	297,422	94,746	125,474	79,227	24,401
1931	1,014,933—2·54	791,238	223,695	299,909	88,343	214,861	144,711	32,038
1932	1,143,025—2·86	932,695	210,327	314,907	75,278	224,676	155,656	30,850
1933	1,375,645—3·42	1,166,033	209,612	347,618	72,801	239,938	171,919	30,564
1934	1,402,725—3·47	1,202,912	199,813	362,023	68,126	246,631	178,971	29,953
1935	1,472,891—3·64	1,282,589	190,302	389,747	65,801	263,647	195,764	30,141
1936	1,387,720—3·41	1,207,425	180,295	420,540	61,400	287,401	219,589	28,305
1937	1,287,616—3·15	1,116,887	170,729	433,901	57,571	301,754	234,498	28,265
1938	1,089,557—2·66	925,294	164,263	442,447	56,290	317,030	247,893	27,803
1939	1,099,050	940,209	158,841	462,764	54,094	337,078	266,820	26,629

Abstracted from annual returns showing number of persons in receipt of relief on night of 1 January for year indicated

3 Insured Unemployment by Administrative Regions 1923–38

Average per Year per Thousand Insured

DISTRICT	1923	1924	1925	1926	1927	1928	1929	1930	1931	1932	1933	1934	1935	1936	1937	1938
London	101	90	78	69	58	56	56	81	122	135	118	92	85	72	63	80
South East	92	75	59	54	50	54	56	80	120	143	115	87	81	73	61	74
South West	106	91	85	84	72	81	81	104	145	171	157	131	116	94	73	76
Midlands	107	90	91	110	84	99	93	147	203	201	174	129	112	92	71	108
North East	122	109	150	172	137	151	137	202	274	285	260	221	207	168	107	132
Northern—carved out of North East and North West based on Newcastle															170	180
North West	145	129	114	147	107	124	133	238	282	258	235	208	197	171	139	177
Scotland	143	124	152	164	106	117	121	185	266	277	261	231	213	187	153	157
Wales	64	86	165	180	195	230	193	259	324	365	346	323	312	294	217	241
North Ireland	182	166	239	232	132	170	148	238	278	272	265	234	248	227		

Includes Agricultural Labourers after 1935

4 Insured Unemployment in Great Britain and Northern Ireland

DATE	Total in 1,000s	
	Number	Per Cent
1921		
December	2,038	17·9
1922		
January	2,015	17·7
February	1,948	17·1
March	1,827	16·0
April	1,811	15·9
May	1,667	14·6
June	1,563	13·7
July	1,502	13·1

DATE	Total in 1,000s Number	Per Cent	DATE	Total in 1,000s Number	Per Cent	DATE	Total in 1,000s Number	Per Cent
August	1,466	12·8	March	1,141	9·8	December	1,243	10·4
September	1,449	12·7	April	1,122	9·7			
October	1,443	12·6	May	1,091	9·4	1926		
November	1,485	13·0	June	1,087	9·3	January	1,318	11·0
December	1,464	12·8	July	1,138	9·8	February	1,248	10·4
			August	1,223	10·5	March	1,171	9·8
1923			September	1,242	10·6	April	1,094	9·1
January	1,525	13·3	October	1,281	10·9	May	1,719	14·3
February	1,421	12·4	November	1,274	10·8	June	1,751	14·6
March	1,336	11·7	December	1,263	10·7	July	1,737	14·4
April	1,316	11·5				August	1,685	14·0
May	1,291	11·2	1925			September	1,648	13·7
June	1,298	11·3	January	1,322	11·2	October	1,636	13·6
July	1,327	11·6	February	1,334	11·3	November	1,630	13·5
August	1,357	11·8	March	1,310	11·1	December	1,432	11·9
September	1,347	11·7	April	1,294	10·9			
October	1,350	11·7	May	1,297	10·9	1927		
November	1,327	11·5	June	1,409	11·9	January	1,451	12·0
December	1,229	10·6	July	1,329	11·2	February	1,315	10·9
			August	1,443	12·1	March	1,188	9·8
1924			September	1,426	12·0	April	1,133	9·4
January	1,374	11·9	October	1,354	11·4	May	1,059	8·7
February	1,229	10·6	November	1,314	11·0	June	1,069	8·8

DATE	Total in 1,000s		DATE	Total in 1,000s		DATE	Total in 1,000s	
	Number	Per Cent		Number	Per Cent		Number	Per Cent
July	1,114	9·2	February	1,454	12·1	November	2,369	18·9
August	1,130	9·3	March	1,204	10·0	December	2,500	19·9
September	1,126	9·3	April	1,181	9·8	1931		
October	1,156	9·5	May	1,177	9·7	January	2,663	21·1
November	1,210	9·9	June	1,164	9·6	February	2,697	21·3
December	1,194	9·8	July	1,178	9·7	March	2,666	21·0
			August	1,198	9·9	April	2,593	20·4
1928			September	1,204	9·9	May	2,578	20·3
January	1,261	10·7	October	1,254	10·3	June	2,707	21·2
February	1,228	10·4	November	1,326	10·9	July	2,806	21·9
March	1,127	9·5	December	1,344	11·0	August	2,813	21·9
April	1,128	9·5				September	2,880	22·4
May	1,168	9·8	1930			October	2,793	21·7
June	1,273	10·7	January	1,520	12·4	November	2,735	21·2
July	1,377	11·6	February	1,583	12·9	December	2,671	20·7
August	1,375	11·5	March	1,694	13·7			
September	1,355	11·3	April	1,761	14·2	1932		
October	1,403	11·7	May	1,856	15·0	January	2,855	22·2
November	1,453	12·1	June	1,911	15·4	February	2,809	21·9
December	1,334	11·1	July	2,070	16·7	March	2,660	20·8
			August	2,119	17·0	April	2,727	21·3
1929			September	2,188	17·5	May	2,822	22·0
January	1,466	12·2	October	2,319	18·5			

DATE	Total in 1,000s Number	Per Cent
June	2,843	22·2
July	2,921	22·8
August	2,947	23·0
September	2,925	22·8
October	2,810	21·9
November	2,849	22·2
December	2,776	21·6
1933		
January	2,955	23·0
February	2,915	22·7
March	2,821	21·9
April	2,737	21·3
May	2,626	20·4
June	2,498	19·4
July	2,508	19·5
August	2,459	19·1
September	2,375	18·4
October	2,335	18·1
November	2,309	17·9
December	2,263	17·5

DATE	Total in 1,000s Number	Per Cent
1934		
January	2,407	18·6
February	2,343	18·1
March	2,225	17·2
April	2,148	16·6
May	2,097	16·2
June	2,124	16·4
July	2,162	16·7
August	2,135	16·5
September	2,080	16·0
October	2,119	16·3
November	2,122	16·3
December	2,086	16·0
1935		
January	2,295	17·6
February	2,272	17·5
March	2,143	16·4
April	2,030	15·6
May	2,024	15·5
June	2,004	15·4
July	1,992	15·2
August	1,950	14·9

DATE	Total in 1,000s Number	Per Cent
September	1,953	14·9
October	1,902	14·5
November	1,906	14·5
December	1,858	14·1
1936		
January	2,131	16·2
February	2,017	15·3
March	1,879	14·2
April	1,807	13·6
May	1,697	12·8
June	1,708	12·8
July	1,660	12·4
August	1,612	12·0
September	1,620	12·1
October	1,614	12·0
November	1,621	12·0
December	1,622	12·0
1937		
January	1,677	12·4
February	1,625	12·0
March	1,576	11·6

DATE	Total in 1,000s		DATE	Total in 1,000s		DATE	Total in 1,000s	
	Number	Per Cent		Number	Per Cent		Number	Per Cent
April	1,436	10·5	1938			December	1,827	12·9
May	1,456	10·7	January	1,818	13·2	1939		
June	1,370	10·0	February	1,808	13·1	January	2,039	14·4
July	1,386	10·1	March	1,764	12·7	February	1,897	13·4
August	1,357	9·9	April	1,760	12·7	March	1,727	12·2
September	1,334	9·7	May	1,780	12·8	April	1,644	11·6
October	1,395	10·1	June	1,829	13·2	May	1,492	10·5
November	1,507	10·9	July	1,822	12·9	June	1,350	9·5
December	1,665	12·1	August	1,784	12·6	July	1,256	8·9
			September	1,811	12·8	August	1,232	
			October	1,799	12·7	September	1,331	
			November	1,839	13·0			

Appendix II Select Biographical Notes

ADDISON, Christopher, Viscount Stallingborough, 1869–1951. Born Hogs-thorpe, Lincolnshire; father a farmer; educated Trinity College, Harrogate, St Batholomew's Hospital; FRCS, Chairman, Medical Research Council, 1948; member of the faculty in medicine for Cambridge and London; editor, *Quarterly Medical Journal*. MP, Lib., Shoreditch, 1910–22, Lab., Swindon, 1929–31, 1934–35. Parliamentary Secretary to Board of Education, 1914–15; Parliamentary Secretary, Ministry of Munitions, 1915–16; Minister of Munitions, 1916–17; Minister of Reconstruction, 1917–18; President, Local Government Board, 1919; First Minister of Health, 1919–21; Minister without Portfolio, 1921; Parliamentary Secretary, Ministry of Agriculture, 1929–30; Minister of Agriculture and Fisheries, 1930, 1931; Secretary of State, Commonwealth Relations, 1945–49; Leader of House of Lords, 1945–51; Lord Privy Seal, 1947–51; Lord President of Council, 1951. Baron, 1937; Viscount, 1945.

ANDERSON, John, first Viscount Waverly of Westdean, 1882–1958. Born Midlothian, Scotland; educated George Watson's College, Edinburgh, and Leipzig University; entered civil service at Colonial Office, 1905; transferred to work for Morant in National Health Insurance, 1912; Ministry of Shipping, 1917–19, returned briefly to Local Government Board and Ministry of Health, 1919; Chairman of Board of Inland Revenue, 1919–22, although in fact spent most of time on Irish affairs; Permanent Under-secretary, Home Office, 1922–32, Governor of Bengal, 1932–37. MP, Nat. (i.e., Cons.), Scottish Universities, 1938–50; Lord Privy Seal, 1938–39; Home Secretary, 1939–40; Lord President of Council, 1940–43; Chancellor of the Exchequer, 1943–45; Chairman, Port of London Authority, 1946–58. Served on many advisory and investigative bodies, became increasingly conservative as political career continued and was bitterly opposed by Labour, making more and more difficult Anderson's use in non-political matters. CB, 1918; KCB, 1919; PC, Ire., 1920; GCB, 1923; GCIE, 1932; GCSI, 1937; OM, 1957; Viscount, 1952.

BARRAND, Authur Rhys, 1861–1941. Born Stoke Newington; educated Birbeck, Kingsland and Finsbury Technical College; actuary, 1895; called to the bar, 1906; MP, C. Lib., Pudsey and Otley Division, Yorkshire, 1918–22; joint editor, *Bunyan's Law of Life Assurance*. Joined Prudential Assurance Co., 1876; as assistant manager; leading figure in lobby effort that brought industrial insurance into health scheme; Secretary, Deputy Chairman and Chairman of Prudential Approved Societies; retired from Prudential Assurance Co. as Deputy General Manager, 1923; Director, Prudential Assurance Co., 1931–41.

BETTERTON, Henry Bucknall, Baron Rushcliffe, 1872–1949. Born Blackfordby, Leicestershire; father a brewer and JP; educated Rugby and Oxford; called to the bar, 1896. MP, Cons., Rushcliffe Division, Nottinghamshire, 1918–34; Parliamentary Secretary, Ministry of Labour, 1923–24; 1924–29; Minister of Labour, 1931–34; Chairman, Unemployment Assistance Board, 1934–41. Bart., 1929; Baron, 1935.

CHAMBERLAIN, (Jos.) Austen, 1863–1937. Born Birmingham; father Joseph Chamberlain; educated Rugby and Cambridge, Ecole des Sciences Politiques, Paris, and Berlin University. MP, Lib. U., Border Burghs, 1888–92; East Worcestershire, 1892–1914; Birmingham West, 1914–37. Civil Lord of the Admiralty, 1895–1900; Financial Secretary, Treasury, 1900–02; Postmaster-General, 1902–03; Chancellor of the Exchequer, 1903–06. Candidate with Walter Long for Leader of Conservative Party, 1911. War Cabinet, 1918; Chancellor of the Exchequer, 1919–21; Lord Privy Seal, 1921; Leader of the Conservative Party and Leader of the House of Commons, 1921–22; Foreign Secretary, 1924–29; First Lord of the Admiralty, August–October, 1931. Resigned under cloud of Invergordon mutiny. KG, 1925.

CORNWALL, Edwin, 1863–1953. Born Lapford, Devon; left school at 13 to enter office of a coal merchant in Hammersmith, at 17 became manager of a coal depot in Kensington. Went into Fulham Vestry; became first Mayor of Metropolitan Borough of Fulham, 1900. Entered LCC, 1892–1910, Vice-Chairman, 1903–05, Chairman 1905–06; chief whip Progressive Party, LCC, MP, Lib., Bethnal Green, 1906–22; Controller of Household, and Chairman, Joint Insurance Committee, 1916–19; Deputy Speaker, House of Commons, 1919–22. KB, 1905; Bart., 1918; PC, 1921.

DAWSON, Bertrand Edward, Viscount of Penn, 1864–1945. Born Croydon; father an architect; educated St Paul's School, University College, London and London Hospital. Member, Faculty in Medicine, London Hospital, 1906; diagnostician. Chairman, Consultative Council on Medical and Allied Services, 1919; member, Medical Research Council, 1931–35; organized Emergency Medical Services, 1939; member, Medical Planning Commission, British Medical Association, 1944. Baron, 1920; PC, 1929; Viscount, 1936.

FISHER, William Hayes, Baron Downham of Fulham, 1853–1920. Born Downham; father, Rector of Downham, Isle of Ely; educated, Haileybury School, Oxford; called to the Bar, 1879. MP, Cons., Fulham, 1885–1906, 1910–18. Junior Lord, Treasury and Ministerial Whip, 1895–1902; Financial Secretary, Treasury, 1902–03. Alderman, London County Council, 1907–13. Parliamentary Secretary, Local Government Board, 1915–17; President Local Government Board, 1917–18. Chancellor, Duchy of Lancaster, November, 1918–January, 1919. Director, Suez Canal Company, 1919–20. PC, 1911; Baron, 1918.

GEDDES, Auckland Campbell, Baron Rolvenden, 1879–1954. Born India, younger brother of Sir Eric Campbell Geddes, father a civil engineer from Edinburgh; educated George Watson's College, Edinburgh, Edinburgh

University, London Hospital, and University of Freiburg. Member, Faculty in Medicine, Edinburgh; Professor, McGill University Medical School and Principle, McGill University, Montreal. Served World War, 1914–16; Director, Recruiting, War Office, 1916–17; Minister, National Service, 1917–19. MP, Cons., Basingstoke, 1917–20; President, Local Government Board, 1918; Minister, Reconstruction, 1919; President, Board of Trade, 1919–20; Ambassador, USA, 1920–24; Regional Commissioner for Southeast and Northwest Regions, 1939–42. KCB, 1917; Baron, 1942.

HARVEY, Ernest Musgrave, 1867–1955. Father, Rector of Acton; educated Marlborough; entered Bank of England, 1885; Cashier, 1918; Comptroller, 1925–28; Deputy Governor, 1929–36. CBE, 1917; KBE, 1920; Bart., 1933.

HENDERSON, Arthur, 1863–1935. Born Glasgow; father a textile worker; early childhood in Newcastle-upon-Tyne; left school, 1875 for apprenticeship as foundry worker. Secretary, Newcastle Lodge, Ironfounders Union; entered trade union work, 1894; member, Newcastle City Council, 1892; Mayor, Newcastle. 1903; founding member, Labour Representation Committee, 1899. MP, Lab., Barnard Castle, 1903–18; Widnes, 1919–22; Newcastle, 1923; Burnley, 1924–31; Clay Cross, 1933–35. Chairman, Parliamentary Labour Party, 1908–10, 1914–17, 1931. President, Board of Education, 1915–16; Paymaster General, 1916; member, War Cabinet, 1917; Home Secretary, 1924; Foreign Secretary, 1929–31. President, World Disarmament Conference, 1932–33. Awarded Nobel Peace Prize, 1934.

HESSELTINE, Michael, 1886–1952. Son of a clergyman; educated Winchester, New College, Oxford; Assistant Secretary; Ministry of Health, 1928–33, Registrar, Dental Board, 1933–46; Registrar, General Medical Council, 1933–52. CB, 1919.

HICKS, William Joynson, first Viscount Brentford, 1865–1932. Born Canonbury; father, a merchant; educated Merchant Tailors' School; admitted as solicitor, 1887; MP, Cons., NW Manchester, 1908–10; Brentford, 1911–18; Twickenham, 1918–29. Postmaster and Paymaster General and Financial Secretary to Treasury, all with Cabinet seat, 1923; Minister of Health, 1923–24; Home Secretary, 1924–29. An evangelical churchman, highly conservative. Bart., 1919; Viscount, 1929.

HORNE, Robert Stevenson, Viscount Slamannan, 1871–1940. Born Slamannan, Stirlingshire; father a minister; educated George Watson's College, Edinburgh and University of Glasgow; admitted to Scottish Bar, 1896. Defeated, Stirlingshire, 1910; MP, Cons., Glasgow, 1918–37. Assistant Inspector-General, Transportation, 1917; Director, Department of Materials and Priority, Admiralty, 1917; Director, Admiralty Labour, 1918; Third Civil Lord, Admiralty, 1918; Minister of Labour, 1919; President, Board of Trade, 1920–21; Chancellor of the Exchequer, 1921–22. Director, Suez Canal Company, KC, 1910; Viscount, 1937.

JONES, Thomas, 1870–1955. Born Rhymney, Monmouthshire; educated, Pengam County School, University College, Aberystwyth, Glasgow University; held various university appointments in economics, investigator for Poor Law Commission, 1906–09; Secretary, Welsh Insurance Commission, 1912–16; Deputy Secretary, Cabinet, 1916–30; Secretary, Pilgrim Trust, 1930–45, later Director; Member, Unemployment Assistance Board, 1934–40.

KINNEAR, Walter Samuel, 1872–1953. Born Ireland; educated, University College, Dublin; entered commercial insurance, became Irish manager for Royal Exchange; appointed to Irish Insurance Commission, 1912; Deputy Chairman, 1912–19; Controller, Insurance Deparment, Ministry of Health, 1919–36; Deputy Chairman, National Health Insurance Joint Committee, 1919–38. KBE, 1918.

MACLEAN, Donald, 1864–1932. Born Farnworth, Lancashire; father a master cordwainer; educated Haverford and Carmarthen Grammar Schools; began practice as a solicitor, 1887; practised in Cardiff and London. Three times defeated for Parliament; MP, Lib., Bath, 1906 until defeat January, 1910, re-elected Peebles and Selkirk, December, 1910–18; Peebles and South Midlothian, 1918–22. Leader of 'Wee Frees' in House of Commons, 1919–22. Chairman, 'the Maclean Committee', Local Government Committee, Ministry of Reconstruction, 1917. Again three times defeated for Parliament in 1922, 1923, and 1924. Re-elected for North Camberwell, 1929–32. Threatened resignation from shadow cabinet over adoption of 1931 tariff. President, Board of Education, 1931. PC, 1916; KBE, 1917. Son, Donald Maclean, foreign service officer, defected to Russia.

MACNAMARA, Thomas James, 1861–1931. Born in the barracks, Montreal, Canada; father, non-commissioned officer, British Army; educated St Thomas's School, Exeter and Borough Road Training College for Teachers; taught elementary school, 1876–92; entered Labour movement as editor, *The School Master*, 1892–1907; elected President National Union of Teachers, 1892; member, London School Board, 1894–1902. Defeated Liberal candidate for Deptford, 1895; MP, Lib., North Camberwell, 1900–24; defeated as National Liberal 1924 and 1929. Parliamentary Secretary, Local Government Board, 1907–08; Parliamentary and Financial Secretary, Admiralty, 1908; Minister of Labour, 1920–22. Participated in driving Robert Morant from Board of Education over Holmes Circular. PC, 1911.

MASTERMAN, Charles Frederick Gurney, 1873–1927. Born Wimbledon; father a landowner; educated Weymouth and Cambridge; fellow, Christ's College, 1900. Wrote widely on social conditions for the *Daily News*, *The Speaker* (under J. L. Hammond), the *Nation* (under H. W. Massingham), and the *Athenaeum*. Poor Law Guardian for Camberwell, 1901–04. Defeated for Dulwich, 1903. MP, Lib., West Ham, 1906–10. Unseated by petition, for shady election practices. Elected for Bethnal Green, 1910–14. Brought into Cabinet as Chancellor of the Duchy of Lancaster, 1914–15; resigned after several election defeats, 1915. Elected for Rusholme Division, Manchester, 1923–24; defeated, 1924. Under-Secretary, Local Government Board, 1908; Under-Secretary, Home Office, 1909–12; Financial Secretary Treasury, 1912, First Chairman, National Insurance Commission, 1911.

Director, Wellington House (propaganda department), 1914–18; Director, literary department, Ministry of Information. PC, 1912.

MOND, Alfred Moritz, Baron Melchett of Landford, 1868–1930. Born Farnsworth near Widnes; father eminent chemist and industrialist; educated Cheltenham, Cambridge and Edinburgh; called to the Bar, 1894; entered family chemical business. MP, Lib., Chester, 1906–10; Swansea, 1910–23, Carmarthen, 1924–28. Changed parties in 1926 and was requested by his constituency to continue in office as a Conservative. Commissioner of Works, 1916–21; Minister of Health, 1921–22. Chairman, ICI Ltd, director, International Nickel Ltd, Mond Nickel Ltd and Westminster Bank. Considered himself an 'industrial statesman' and instituted Mond-Turner conference to discuss problems of employment. Broke with Liberals over increasing socialist policies and Lloyd George's land policy in particular. After World War I supported protectionist policies. Strong supporter of Zionism. Chairman Economic Board for Palestine. Bart., 1910, 1913; baron, 1928.

MONTAGUE–BARLOW, (Clement) Anderson, 1868–1951. Born Peterborough; father, Dean of Peterborough; educated Repton, King's College, Cambridge; Bar, 1895; Examiner in law, London University; LCC, Mod. East Islington, 1907–10. MP, Cons., Salford, 1910–23; Parliamentary Secretary to Ministry of Labour, 1920–22; Minister of Labour 1922–24, with seat in Cabinet. Director and then Chairman of Sotheby's, 1909–28; an ardent tariff reformer. KBE, 1918; Bart., 1924.

MORANT, Robert Laurie, 1863–1920. Born Hampstead; father, Robert Morant, artist; educated Winchester and Oxford; tutor to royal family of Siam and established public education there, 1886–94; upon return to England engaged in social and educational work in East London; resident, Toynbee Hall, 1895–96; joined Civil Service, 1895; Assistant Director, Department of Education, 1895–99; Private Secretary, Sir John Eldon Gorst, 1899–1902; Assistant Private Secretary, Duke of Devonshire during tenure as Lord President of Council, 1902–03; Permanent Secretary, Board of Education, 1903–11; Chairman, National Health Insurance Commission, 1911–19; first Permanent Secretary, Ministry of Health, 1919–20. KCB, 1907.

NEWMAN, George, 1870–1948. Born Leominster, Herefordshire; Quaker background; educated King's College, London, and University of Edinburgh; lecturer at King's College, 1896–1900; Medical Officer of Health, Finsbury in Bedfordshire; Chief Medical Officer, Board of Education, 1907–35; succeeded Arthur Newsholme, Chief Medical Officer to the Local Government Board in 1919, and continued as Chief Medical Officer to Ministry of Health with rank of Permanent Secretary in 1920 when the LGB was absorbed into the Ministry of Health; held post of CMO at both Ministries until retirement in 1935. Had greatest influence as a publicist in the cause of preventative medicine. Kt., 1911; KCB, 1918. Was refused peerage by Ramsay MacDonald.

NEWSHOLME, Arthur, 1857–1943. MD, London, 1881; Medical Officer of Health, Brighton, 1888–1908; Editor of *Journal of Hygiene*; prolific writer on public health, Chief Medical Officer, Local Government Board, 1908–19; lectured at the Johns Hopkins University, 1920–21. Editor, *Public Health* until February, 1908; CB, 1912; KCB, 1917.

ROBERTS, Charles Henry, 1865–1959. Born Sussex; father, Vicar of Tide-brook; educated Marlborough, Balliol, Oxford. MP, Lib., City of Lincoln, 1906–18; Borough of Derby, 1922–23; unable to win any seat thereafter. Undersecretary of State for India, 1914–15; Chairman, National Health Insurance Joint Committee, 1915–16; supported Asquith in 1916; devoted self to Cumberland County affairs after 1923, Chairman, Cumberland County Council, 1935–58; JP, 1900–50; wife a daughter of the Earl of Carlisle.

RIDDELL, George Allardice, Baron of Walton Heath, 1965–1934. Born London; father a photographer; educated privately, articled to a solicitor, admitted to practice, 1888; firm represented several leading newspapers and periodicals. Chairman, *News of the World*, 1903; served in official capacity in publishing trade associations; director various publishing and newspaper companies. Came to prominence during coal strike labour negotiations, 1912; personal friend and companion of Lloyd George. Kt., 1909; Bart., 1918; Baron, 1920.

ROBINSON, (William) Arthur, 1874–1950. Born Longmarton, Westmoreland; educated Appleby School and Queen's College, Oxford; entered Colonial Office, 1897. Assistant Secretary, Office of Works, 1912–18; Permanent Secretary, Air Ministry, 1918–20; Permanent Secretary, Ministry of Health, 1920–35; Supply Board, Committee of Imperial Defence, 1935–39; Permanent Secretary, Ministry of Supply, 1939–40. Held several important company directorships. Much less outspoken than Newman, but fully reciprocated the other's dislike. CB, 1915; CBE, 1918; KCB, 1919; GCB, 1929.

ROCKLIFF, Percy, 1869–1958. Born Boston Spa, Yorkshire; educated Buxton College. Professional administrator and lobbyist for industrial insurance companies; member, Consultative Council and Dental Benefit (Statutory) Council of the national health insurance administration; operated also Dental Services Ltd, and Opthalmic Services Ltd, contractual agencies for administration of extra benefits under NHI; Parliamentary Agent, National Union of Holloway Friendly Societies, 1920–56; Editor, *Thrift*. OBE, 1954.

SHAW, Thomas, 1872–1938. Born Colne, Lancashire; father, miner; elementary education; entered textile mill, aged 10. Secretary, International Federation of Textile workers, 1911–29, 1931–38; MP, Lab., Preston, 1918–31; Minister of Labour, 1924; Secretary of State for War, 1929–31.

SNOWDEN, Philip, first Viscount Snowden of Ickornshaw, 1864–1937. Born Irkcornshaw, West Riding, Yorks; father, weaver; educated board school; clerked in insurance office, entered Inland Revenue, 1886; retired, 1893, because of health (deterioration of muscles of legs); became writer and propagandist for newly-formed Independent Labour Party. MP, Lab., Blackburn, 1906–18; Colne Valley, Yorks., 1922–31; Chancellor of Exchequer, 1924, 1929–31; Lord Privy Seal, 1931–32. Viscount, 1931.

STANLEY, Oliver Frederick George, 1896–1950. Born London; younger son, 17th Earl of Derby; educated Eton, commissioned 1914 and served in France; called to the Bar, 1919; joined family stockbroking firm. Defeated Cons. for Edge Hill, Liverpool, 1923; MP, Cons., Westmoreland, 1924–45; Bristol West, 1945–50. Parliamentary Private Secretary, President Board of Education, 1924–29; Parliamentary Under-Secretary, Home Office, 1931–33; Minister of Transport, 1933–34; Minister of Labour, 1934–35; President, Board of Education, 1935–37; President, Board of Trade, 1937–40; Secretary of State for War, 1940; Secretary of State for the Colonies, 1942–45; Chairman, Conservative Party Finance Committee, 1945; Chairman, Conservative Party Imperial Affairs Committee, 1945.

STEEL-MAITLAND, Arthur Herbert Rummond Ramsay, 1876–1935. Born in India; educated Rugby, Balliol, Oxford; fellow of All Souls, 1900; contested Rugby as Cons., 1906; Special Commissioner to Royal Commission on Poor Laws, 1906–07; MP, Cons., East Birmingham, 1910–18; Erdington, 1918–29; Tamworth Division, Warwickshire, 1929–35; held a number of junior secretaryships, 1915–19; Minister of Labour, 1924–29.

THOMAS, David Alfred, Viscount Rhondda, 1856–1918. Born Ysgyborwen, Wales; father retail grocer and colliery speculator; educated privately at Clifton and Cambridge; entered colliery business. MP, Lib., Merthyr Tydfil, 1888–1910, unnoticed and received no committee appointments; returned to business, 1910; successfully represented Lloyd George for Munitions Ministry in North America, 1915 to expedite arms from US and Canada, having survived sinking of 'Lusitania'. President, Local Government Board, 1916; accepted office of Food Controller against medical advice, 1917–18. Baron, 1916; Viscount, 1918. Career in many ways resembles that of Arnold Bennett's Lord Raingo.

THOMSON, Basil Home, 1861–1939. Born Queen's College, Oxford; father Provost of Queen's, later Archbishop of York; educated Eton and Oxford. Colonial Service, 1886–96; called to the Bar, 1896. Entered prison administration, 1906–13; Assistant Commissioner, Metropolitan Police, 1913–19; active in gathering information to discredit Sir Roger Casement, 1916; Director of Intelligence, Home Office, 1919–21; Forced to retire under threat of loss of pension, 1921. Arrested in Hyde Park, 12 December 1925, consorting with a prostitute and convicted for violation of public decency. Kt., 1919.

WARREN, Alfred Haman, 1856–1924. Born Poplar; educated Wesleyan School, Poplar. Entered insurance work with Manchester Unity of Odd Fellows; Grand Master, Manchester Unity of Odd Fellows; President, National Conference of Friendly Societies; Parliamentary Agent, National Conference of Friendly Societies. MP, Cons., Edmonton, 1918–22. Mayor, Poplar, 1913–18. Kt., 1918.

WHEATLEY, John, 1869–1930. Born Waterford, Ireland; father, labourer, became coal miner when family moved to Lanarkshire; educated Roman Catholic schools and night school; shop assistant, 1893–1902; reporter, *Glasgow Observer* and *Catholic Herald*, 1902–12. Established small publishing business, 1912, in Glasgow and became prosperous; member United Irish League and an enthusiastic supporter of radical Irish nationalism but joined ILP, 1908, after deciding that Home Rule was no use to the Irish labourer in Scotland. Lanarkshire County Council, 1909–11; Member Glasgow Corporation, 1910–20; MP, Lab., Shettleston Division of Glasgow. 1922–30; Minister of Health, 1924. A leading member of the 'Clydesiders', whose militant radicalism embarrassed Labour administrations far more than it frightened the Conservative opposition.

WILSON, Horace John, 1882–   . Born Bournemouth; educated Kurnella School, Bournemouth, London School of Economics; entered civil service, 1900. Assistant Secretary, Ministry of Labour, 1919–21; Permanent Secretary, Ministry of Labour, 1921–30; 'Chief Industrial Adviser to Government', 1930–39 (in effect, economic adviser to Neville Chamberlain; accompanied Chamberlain to Ottawa, 1932, for talks to work out Empire Tariff Agreement); became confidential adviser to Chamberlain on a variety of topics not connected with economics after Chamberlain succeeded to Prime Ministership; accompanied Chamberlain to Munich; Permanent Secretary, Treasury, and head of the Civil Service, 1939–42. CBE, 1918; CB, 1920; KCB, 1924; GCMG, 1933; GCB, 1937.

WOOD, Howard Kingsley, 1881–1943. Born West Sculcoates, Hull; father, Wesleyan minister; educated Central Foundation Boys' School, London; articled to a solicitor; admitted to practice, 1903. Member, LCC, 1911–19. Retained by major industrial insurance companies to arrange for their inclusion in the National Health Insurance Act, 1911. MP, Cons., West Woolwich, 1918–43. Parliamentary Secretary to Christopher Addison, first Minister of Health, 1919–22; Parliamentary Secretary to Neville Chamberlain, 1924–29; Parliamentary Secretary, Board of Education, 1931; Postmaster-General, 1931–35; Minister of Health, 1935–38; Secretary of State for Air, 1938–40; Lord Privy Seal, 1940; Chancellor of the Exchequer, 1940–43; introduced PAYE plan. Civil Commissioner, Northern Division, General Strike, 1926. Chairman, Executive Committee, National Conservative and Unionist Association, 1930–32; succeeded Baldwin as Grand Master of Primrose League; immensely popular as a Conservative politician; during term as Chancellor relied heavily upon views of J. M. Keynes. Kt, 1918; PC, 1928.

YOUNG, Edward Hilton, first Baron Kennet of the Dene, 1879–1960. Born Cookham; educated Eton, Trinity College, Cambridge; Bar, 1904; MP, Lib., Norwich, 1915–23, 1924–29; and Cons., Sevenoaks, 1929–35; served in World War I with Navy; Financial Secretary to Treasury, 1921–22; Minister of Health, 1931–35. Served on many financial and economic missions during interwar period. CBE, 1927; Baron, 1935.

Bibliography

This bibliography includes the most important sources used in this study and a few others that would be best avoided. It does not list a number of well-known general histories of the interwar period nor any standard statistical or enclyclopedia references.

CONTEMPORARY MATERIALS

UNPUBLISHED SOURCES

A. Letter Collections

1 Beveridge Papers — London School of Economics Library
   Useful in this period mainly for Beveridge's comments upon social planning
2 Bonar Law Papers — Beaverbrook Library
   Bonar Law did not spend much time thinking about social reform but he thought about politics constantly
3 Lloyd George Papers — Beaverbrook Library
   At last available, and well indexed
4 Newman Diaries — Library of the Ministry of Health
   I   September 1907–31 December 1912
   II   1 January 1913–31 December 1915
   III 1 January 1916–31 December 1920
   IV   1 January 1921–31 December 1925
   V   1 January 1926–28 February 1935
   VI   1 March 1935–28 August 1946
   These six volumes covering most of Newman's adult life are of the greatest importance. The diaries contain also a number of letters
5 Newman Papers — Wellcome Historical Medical Library
   A very small collection dealing mostly with the later part of Newman's life

B. Unpublished Government Documents

1 Public Record Office, Cabinet Papers, down to 1938
   (a) Cabinet 21 — Health Insurance Committee
   (b) Cabinet 23 — War Cabinet Decisions, became Cabinet Minutes in 1920
   (c) Cabinet 24 — Cabinet Papers, GT Series, CP Series
   (d) Cabinet 26 — Home Affairs Committee
   (e) Cabinet 27 — Ad Hoc Committees

2 Public Record Office, Bill Papers
   (a) Pin 3/19, Bill File: 'Widows', Orphans' and Old Age Contributory
   Pensions Bill, 1925', Part I

PUBLISHED SOURCES

A. *Periodicals and Newspapers*

 1 *British Medical Journal*
 2 *Charity Organisation Review*
    (Edited in 1918, maybe later, by Mrs Bernard Bosanquet)
 3 *Contemporary Review*
 4 *Daily Herald*
 5 *Economist*
 6 *Evening Standard*
 7 *Fortnightly Review*
 8 *Institute of Actuaries, Journal*
 9 *Insurance Mail*
    Published by Stone and Cox from same address as *National Insurance
    Gazette.* Carried much of same material
10 *Lancet*
11 *Manchester Guardian*
12 *National and Athaeneum*
13 *National Insurance Gazette*
14 *New Statesman*
15 *Nineteenth Century*
16 *Poor-Law Officers' Journal*
17 *Public Administration*
18 *Public Health*
19 *Royal Statistical Society, Journal*
20 *Spectator*
21 *The Times*

B. *Government Documents*

 1 Official Report, House of Commons Debates
 2 Parliamentary Papers
    (a) Papers by Command
    (b) Other Parliamentary Papers and Ministerial Publications.
        i 'Persons in Receipt of Poor-Law Relief on Jan. 1'
          (Various years 1921–38)
        ii *Royal Commission on National Health Insurance, Minutes of
        Evidence,* 2 Vols., 1925. I Oral Evidence, II Appendix, 1925
        iii *Report of the Unemployment Insurance Committee,* 1927. 'The
        Blanesburgh Committee'
        iv *Minutes of Evidence Taken Before the Royal Commission on
        Unemployment Insurance,* 1931

v 'Housing: House Production and Slum Clearance in England and Wales', 1934

vi 'Widows' Orphans' and Old Age Contributory Pensions Acts, 1925–32, Report by the Government Actuary', 1935

vii *Report on the Overcrowding Survey in England and Wales*, 1936. Survey carried out by Ministry of Health
Compilation of 1,472 forms returned by LAs out of 1,536 sent out

viii 'Report of the Unemployment Insurance Statutory Committee on the Financial Condition of the Unemployment Insurance Fund on the 31st December, 1939', *Accounts and Papers*, 1930–40, No. 81

3 London County Council, *London Statistics*. Biennial publication.

C. Contemporary Books or Pamphlets of a Polemical, Didactic, or Partisan Nature

1 'AGP', *This Panel Business*, London, 1933
Very useful

2 Addison, Christopher, *The Betrayal of the Slums*, London, 1922

3 Beveridge, William Henry, *Full Employment in a Free Society*, London, 1944
Supposed to be a sequel to Social Insurance and Allied Services

5 ——. *Insurance For All and Everything*. January, 1924 (pamphlet 40 pp. published by *Daily News* 'under the auspices' of the Council of Liberal Summer Schools)

6 ——. *Voluntary Action, A Report on the Methods of Social Advance*. New York, 1948
Some statistics on approved societies 1911–46

7 Campbell, Dame Janet M. and Vernon, H. M. *National Health Services*, no date or place of publication (apparently London, clearly early in World War II)
Janet M. Campbell was a good friend of George Newman and an old employee of the Ministry of Health. Well thought out plan for comprehensive medical care and public health service along early Webbian lines

8 Clarke, Joan Simeon. *The Assistance Board*. Fabian Research Series, No. 57, London, July, 1941

9 *Daily Herald. Why Labour Left the Coalition*. London, November, 1918. (Paperback pamphlet, 8 pp.)
Labour's 1918 programme

10 Davis, Emil. *Our Ageing Population*. Fabian Tract No. 246. London, October, 1938. (Paperback pamphlet, 14 pp.)

11 Hannington, Wal. *Ten Lean Years, An Examination of the Record of the National Government in the Field of Unemployment*. London, 1940. (Left Book Club)
Useful on the Unemployment Assistance Board

12 Industrial Life Offices' Association. *The Beveridge Report, Preliminary*

Observations of the Industrial Life Offices. London, December, 1942.
(Paperback pamphlet, 16 pp.)
A defence of industrial insurance by its chief lobbying organization

13   Labour Party. *Reports on Maternal Mortality and the Maternity Services
and Women in Industry.* London, 1935
To be presented by the Standing Joint Committee of Industrial
Women's Organizations to the National Conference of Labour Women,
Sheffield, 15, 16 and 17 May 1935. (Paperback pamphlet, 43 pp.)

14   Macnamara, Thomas James. *If Only We Would: Some Reflections on
our Social Shortcomings, with Some Suggestions for Their Revival.*
London, 1926. Introduction by Lloyd George. (Some are articles from
the *Daily Chronicle*)

15   ——. *Success in Industry.* London, 1920. (Paperback pamphlet, 16 pp.)

16   National Conference of Industrial Assurance Approved Societies.
Beveridge Report: Case for the Retention of Approved Societies. London,
February, 1943
One of many pamphlets put out after the Beveridge Report by the
approved societies defending their place in national health insurance
and explaining their work in the interwar period

17   National Deposit Friendly Society. *Social Security, A Voluntary
Friendly Society's Comments on the Beveridge Report.* London, February,
1944

18   National Federation of Employees' Approved Societies. *The Beveridge
Report on Social Insurance and Allied Services.* London, February, 1943.
(Apparently written by Henry Lesser)

19   National Union of Holloway Benefit Societies. *Some Comments and
Criticisms on Certain Proposals in the Beveridge Report on Social Security.*
London, February, 1943. (Signed by C. H. Griggs, President, Cameron
Dix, Secretary, Percy Rockliff, Parliamentary Agent)

20   Newman, Tom Seth. *The Story of Friendly Societies and Social Security.*
London, June, 1945. (Published by Hearts of Oak.)
Electioneering pamphlet

21   Newman, Tom Seth and Townley, H. W. *Scheme for Utilization of
Approved Society Administration.* London, June, 1943. (Includes
printed letter by Newman and Townley to MPs dated 30 June 1943)

22   Nuffield Foundation. *Old People, Report of a Survey Committee on the
Problems of Ageing and the Care of Old People Under the Chairmanship
of B. Seebohm Rowntree.* London, 1947. Report made October 1946.
Apparently appointed in 1944

23   Ormerod, J. Redman. *National Insurance: Its Inherent Defects.* London,
1930. (Paperback pamphlet published by Stone and Cox.) Ormerod
was Vice-Chairman of Lancaster Insurance Committee until 1919, an
official of National Amalgamated Approved Society

24   Orr, John Boyd. *Food Health and Income.* London, 1936. (Pamphlet,
76 pp.) Widely reviewed, very influential, appeared in March 1936

25   Orwell, George. *The Road to Wigan Pier.* Penguin Books. London,
1962. (First published 1937)

26 Political and Economic Planning, PEP. *Housing, England*. London, 1934. PEP Report No. 3. (Dated December 1934)
27 ——. *Report on the British Health Services*. London, 1937
28 ——. *Report on the British Social Services*. London, 1937. Report begun 1935
29 Ridley, George, MP. *The Social Services, Yesterday, Today, and Tomorrow*. London, August, 1941. (Paperback pamphlet, 12 pp., published by Labour Party)
30 Silkin, Lewis. *The New Public Health Organization of the London County Council*. London, 1930. (Paperback pamphlet, 15 pp., published by London Labour publications)
31 Simon, E. D. *The Anti-Slum Campaign*. London, 1933
32 Tory Reform Committee. *Report on Industrial Assurance, Approved Societies, and Death Grant*. London, January, 1944. (Paperback pamphlet, 16 pp.)
33 The Trades Union Congress and the Labour Party. *Social Insurance and Trade Union Membership*. London, n.d. (apparently 1924), paperback pamphlet, 28 pp
34 Wilkie, G. B. *Nationalization of Insurance*. London, 1931. Pamphlet opposing nationalization of insurance

SECONDARY MATERIAL

SCHOLARLY OR TECHNICAL MATERIAL ON SPECIALIZED TOPICS

A. Periodicals

1 *American Economic Review*
2 *International Labour Review*
3 *Past and Present*
4 *Planning*, PEP Broadsheets
    PEP (Political and Economic Planning) is an independent privately financed research organization similar to the Brookings Institution in the United States. In the thirties William Beveridge and Arthur Salter were active in its affairs. Its opinions on social and economic legislation were of great influence
5 *Proceedings of the British Academy*
6 *Social Security Bulletin*

B. Books or Pamphlets

1 Abel-Smith, Brian. *The Hospitals 1800–1848*. London, 1964
2 Armstrong, Barbara N. *The Health Insurance Doctor, His Role in Great Britain, Denmark and France*. Princeton, 1939
    A doctoral dissertation. Useful
3 Bakke, E. Wight. *Insurance or Dole? The Adjustment of Unemployment*

   Insurance to Economic and Social Facts in Great Britain. New Haven,
   1935
      Useful, sociological
4 Beveridge, William H. *Unemployment, A Problem of Industry.* Rev. ed.
   London, 1931
5 Bowley, Marian. *Housing and the State, 1919–1944. London,* 1945
      Good book, many statistics
6 Bruce, Maurice. *The Coming of the Welfare State.* Rev. ed. London,
   1966
      A good survey of legislation. Of continuing popularity
7 Burns, Eveline M. *British Unemployment Programs, 1920–1938.*
   Washington, 1941 (SSRC Publication)
      Full of statistics
8 Cohen, Wilbur J. *Unemployment Insurance and Agricultural Labor in
   Great Britain.* Washington, DC, February 1940. (Paperback pamphlet
   published by SSRC, 32 pp.)
9 Cole, Margaret I. *The Story of Fabian Socialism.* London, 1966
10 Daalder, Hans. *Cabinet Reform in Great Britain, 1914–1963.* Stanford,
   1963
11 Davison, Ronald C. *British Unemployment Policy: The Modern Phase
   Since 1930.* London, 1938
      Very useful
12 Farley, Desmond. *Social Insurance and Social Assistance in Ireland.*
   Dublin, 1964
      Thin, but not bad
13 Ferguson, Sheila and Fitzgerald, Hilde. *Studies in the Social Services.*
   London, 1954. (United Kingdom Civil Histories)
14 Gibbon, Sir Gwilym and Bell, Reginald. *History of the London County
   Council.* London, 1939
15 Gilbert, Bentley B. *The Evolution of National Insurance in Great
   Britain: The Origins of the Welfare State.* London, 1966
16 Ginsberg, Morris, ed. *Law and Opinion in England in the 20th Century*
   London, 1959
17 Grant, A. T. K. *A Study of the Capital Market in Britain from 1919–
   1936.* 2nd ed. London, 1967. (First edition published 1937)
      Called a revised edition but shows age
18 Hammond, M. B. *British Labor Conditions and Legislation during the
   War.* New York, 1919
      Economic Studies No. 14 Carnegie Endowment Series
19 Harris, Richard W. *National Health Insurance, 1911–1946.* London,
   1946
      A disappointment, badly organized, really unfinished
20 Hurwitz, Samuel J. *State Intervention in Great Britain, A Study of
   Economic Control and Social Response, 1914–1919.* New York, 1949
21 Johnson, Paul Barton, 'Post-War Planning in Britain, 1916–1919, The
   Committees and Ministry of Reconstruction', University of Chicago,
   August, 1954. (Unpublished Ph.D. dissertation, 510 pp.)

    Has some cabinet papers that were not legally available in 1954. Very comprehensive, has been recently published

22   Kulp, C. A. *Social Insurance Coordination, An Analysis of German and British Organization.* Washington, 1938. (SSRC Report)

23   Matscheck, Walter. 'Administration of Unemployment Insurance and the Public Employment Service in Great Britain'. (Reproduced typescript. No date or place of publication. Sponsored by SSRC. Investigation done in 1936)

24   Millett, John D. *The British Unemployment Assistance Board, A Case Study in Administrative Autonomy.* New York, 1940

25   Morrah, Dermot. *A History of Industrial Life Assurance.* London, 1955
    Best left alone, hack work

26   Newman, Sir George. *The Building of a Nation's Health.* London, 1939
    Useful, but written by a master of discretion

27   ——. *Health and Social Evolution.* London, 1931. (Halley Stewart Lectures, 1930)

28   Newman, Tom Seth. *History of the Hearts of Oak Benefit Society.* London, 1942. (Centennial History)

29   Newsholme, Sir Arthur. *The Ministry of Health.* London, 1925

30   Pigou, Arthur C. *Aspects of British Economic History, 1918–1925.* London, 1948
    Useful

31   ——. *The Economics of Welfare.* 4th ed. London, 1932
    Primitive

32   Pimlott, J. A. R. *Toynbee Hall, Fifty Years of Social Progress, 1884–1934.* London, 1935

33   Pinker, Robert. *English Hospital Statistics, 1861–1938.* London, 1966
    A useful appendix to Brian Abel-Smith's *Hospitals*

34   Pipkin, Charles W. *Social Politics and Modern Democracies·* I (New York, 1931
    Thorough survey of legislation to 1929, but entirely descriptive. Not an analysis of social politics, but a list of acts

35   Shotwell, James T., ed. *War and Insurance.* London, 1927. (Introduction by W. H. Beveridge. Probably editor, but does not say so. Carnegie Endowment Series)
    Contains:
    (a) Beveridge, W. H. 'Unemployment Insurance in the War and After'. (Outspoken, useful)
    (b) Watson, Alfred W. 'National Health Insurance and Friendly Societies during the War'. (Written as a true civil servant. Most of the material to be found in the first approved society valuation)

36   Spann, R. N. 'The Use of Advisory Bodies by the Ministry of Health' in Vernon, Roland V. and Mansurgh, N., eds. *Advisory Bodies, A Study of Their Uses In Relation to Central Government, 1919–1939.* London, 1940.

37   Stevens, Rosemary. *Medical Practice in Modern England, The Impact of Specialization and State Medicine.* New Haven, 1966
    Contains some historical material

38   Titmuss, Richard M. *Problems of Social Policy.* London, 1950. (United Kingdom Civil Histories)

39 Vaughan, Paul. *Doctors' Commons: A Short History of the British Medical Association.* London, 1959

40 Webb, Sidney and Beatrice. *English Poor Law History: Part II: The Last Hundred Years.* II, London, 1929

41 Williams, Whiting. *Full Up and Fed Up. The Worker's Mind in Crowded Britain.* New York, 1921
    An important, unnoticed book by an American industrialist. Without apparent political bias except sympathy for the working man

GENERAL SECONDARY SOURCES

A. Biographies, Memoirs, Edited Diaries, Biographical Sketches, and Autobiographies

1 Addison, Christopher. *Politics From Within, 1911–1918.* 2 Vols. London, 1924
    Very useful. Contains material not found in the published portion of Addison's diaries. But Addison, like most politicians, tended to overestimate his own importance. An authorized autobiography

2 ——. *Four and a Half Years.* 2 Vols. London, 1934
    Addison diaries from June 1914 to January 1919. Very important but hard to assess. They contain perhaps the best existing published account of Lloyd George's activities during the critical first week of December 1916. Yet they were clearly written for publication and show many unacknowledged signs of editing

3 Allen, Bernard M. *Sir Robert Morant.* London, 1934
    A bad book, full of careless mistakes, compressions of time, sliding over dates. Nothing is ever clear, sharp, or precise, except how great were all of Morant's problems and how well he handled them

4 Amery, Leopold S. *My Political Life,* II, London, 1953

5 Attlee, Clement R. *As it Happened: The Autobiography of Clement R. Attlee.* London, 1954
    Slightly useful. Apparently Attlee never came in contact with anyone during his life who was not 'very able', 'very helpful', or 'very kind'

6 Bennett, Arnold. *The Journal of Arnold Bennett.* II, III, London, 1932–33

7 Beveridge, William H. *Power and Influence.* London, 1953

8 Blake, Robert. *The Unknown Prime Minister.* London, 1965
    Bonar Law is the only prime minister since Asquith to enjoy a respectable biography

9 Blaxland, Gregory. *J. H. Thomas, A Life for Unity.* London, 1964

10 Bolitho, Hector. *Alfred Mond, First Lord Melchett.* London, 1933
    A hack job

11 Boyd-Orr, John, Baron. *As I Recall.* London, 1966
    A better book than many of its kind, most outspoken

12 Boyle, Andrew. *Montague Norman.* London, 1967
    Clay understood finance better and is much fuller on Bank operations. Not really worth bothering with

13 Bullock, Alan. *The Life and Times of Ernest Bevin.* I, London, 1960.
   Depends too much on Feiling for the 1931 crisis
14 Bunbury, Henry N., ed. *Lloyd George's Ambulance Wagon: Being the Memoirs of William J. Braithwaite, 1911–1912.* London, 1957
15 Chamberlain, Austen. *Down the Years.* London, 1935
   Not very helpful
16 Churchill, Randolph S. *Winston S. Churchill.* II. *1901–1914 Young Statesman.* London, 1967
17 Citrine, Walter. *Men at Work.* London, 1964
18 Clay, Sir Henry. *Lord Norman.* London, 1957
   Discreet but revealing. Unfinished. Hard to read. Packed with information. Had full use of Bank sources and papers of Benjamin Strong
19 Cole, Margaret I., ed. *Beatrice Webb's Diaries, 1912–1924.* London, 1952
20 ——. *Beatrice Webb's Diaries, 1924–1932.* London, 1956
   These are less satisfying than the earlier volumes. The Webbs had more national influence when Sydney was in private life than when he was a cabinet minister
21 Cooper, Duff, Viscount Norwich. *Old Men Forget: The Autobiography of Duff Cooper.* London, 1953
22 Cox, Alfred. *Among the Doctors.* London, 1950
   Chatty, occasionally useful
23 Cross, Colin. *Philip Snowden.* London, 1966
   A disappointment
24 Davies, Sir Joseph. *The Prime Minister's Secretariat, 1916–20.* Newport, Monmouthshire, 1951
25 Feiling, Keith. *The Life of Neville Chamberlain.* London, 1947
   Written with great elegance, much insight into politics, and with access to Chamberlain's papers, yet frequently it misses the point
26 Fisher, H. A. L. *An Unfinished Autobiography.* London, 1940
   Not one of Fisher's major works
27 Fitzroy, Almeric. *Memoirs,* II. London, n.d. (1925)
28 Gollin, Alfred M. *Proconsul in Politics, A Study of Lord Milner in Opposition and in Power.* London, 1964
29 Grigg, P. J. *Prejudice and Judgment.* London, 1948
   Quotes too much textbook history
30 Hamilton, Mary Agnes. *Arthur Henderson.* London, 1938
   Suffers, like many other biographies of period, from a detestation of Lloyd George. All questions are easy to answer. He can be blamed for everything. But nevertheless a more than adequate book
31 Hill of Luton, Charles, Baron. *Both Sides of the Hill, the Memoirs of Charles Hill.* London, 1964
32 Jenkins, Roy. *Asquith.* London, 1964
   Clear and readable
33 Jerrold, Douglas. *Georgian Adventure, The Autobiography of Douglas Jerrold.* London, 1937.
   (Special Edition for the 'Right Book Club')

Jerrold was a civil servant in Treasury after the war. This is a charming and informative memoir if one can ignore quaint political presuppositions

34 Jones, Thomas. *Lloyd George*. London, 1951
The only Lloyd George biography worth bothering about

35 ——. *A Diary with Letters, 1931–1950*. London, 1954.
A useful book, although it could be more so. But Jones never gave secret information away

36 Lansbury, George. *My Life*. London, 1928
Enjoyable

37 Mackworth, Margaret Haig, Viscountess Rhondda. *D. A. Thomas, Viscount Rhondda*. London, 1921
Slightly useful

38 Macleod, Iain. *Neville Chamberlain*. London, 1961
Feiling is to be preferred

39 Markham, Violet R. *Return Passage, The Autobiography of Violet R. Markham*. London, 1953
Some information on the standstill

40 Middlemas, Robert Keith, ed. *Thomas Jones, Whitehall Diary, 1916–1925*. London, 1969
Volume I of series. Not so useful as one might have hoped. Either the diary is heavily edited or Jones was not so near the centre of events as he was reputed to be

41 Minney, R. J. *Viscount Addison: Leader of the Lords*. London, 1958
Addison's final tragedy

42 Newsholme, Arthur. *Fifty Years in Public Health, A Personal Narrative with Comments*. London, 1935
Mentions Newman and Morant once only, noting that the two had been important in founding the school medical service

43 ——. *The Last Thirty Years in Public Health: Recollections on my Official and Post-Official Life*. London, 1936
Does not mention Morant or Newman. Badly organized

44 Nicolson, Harold. *King George the Fifth*. London, 1952

45 Ogg, David. *Herbert Fisher, 1865–1940*. London, 1947
Pretty thin and unscholarly

46 Petrie, Charles. *Walter Long and His Times*. London, 1936

47 ——. *The Life and Letters of the Rt. Hon. Sir Austen Chamberlain*. II (London, 1940)

48 Postgate, Raymond. *The Life of George Lansbury*. London, 1951
Sloppy, small inaccuracies

49 Pound, Reginald and Harmsworth, Geoffrey. *Northcliffe*. London

50 Riddell, George, Baron. *Lord Riddell's War Diary*. London, 1933
These diaries are an indispensable source for Lloyd George

51 ——. *Lord Riddell's Intimate Diary of the Peace Conference and After, 1918–1923*. London, 1933

52 Samuel, Herbert, Viscount. *Memoirs*. London, 1954

53 Stocks, Mary D. *Eleanor Rathbone*. London, 1949

54 Swinton, Earl of. *Sixty Years of Power*. London, 1966

55 Sylvester, J. *The Real Lloyd George*. London, 1947
Sylvester was Lloyd George's secretary in 20s and 30s
56 Thomson, Basil H. *The Scene Changes*. New York, 1937
Thomson's public counter-attack upon Lloyd George. Of about the same reliability as Lloyd George's own memoirs.
57 Wheeler-Bennett, John W. *John Anderson, Viscount Waverley*. London, 1962
Good workman-like biography
58 Woolf, Leonard, *Downhill All the Way*. London, 1967
Some useful discussion of personalities and politics in the early twenties
59 Young, Kenneth. *Churchill and Beaverbrook, A Study in Friendship and Politics*. London, 1966
A book that could be very useful

B. *General Histories, Economic, Political, Social; and Political and Social Philosophy*

1 Attlee, Clement R. *The Labour Party in Perspective*. London, 1937. (Left Book Club)
Desiccated
2 Bassett, R. *Nineteen Thirty One, Political Crisis*. London, 1958
3 Beaverbrook, Lord. *The Decline and Fall of Lloyd George*. London, 1963
4 ——. *Men and Power*. London, 1956
5 ——. *Politicians and the War, 1914–16*. London, 1928
6 Brand, Carl F. *The British Labour Party*. Stanford, 1964
7 Churchill, Winston S. *The World Crisis, 1916–18*. II (London, 1927)
8 Cole, G. D. H. *A History of the Labour Party From 1914*. London, 1948
9 ——. *A Short History of the British Working-Class Movement, 1789–1947*. Rev. ed. London, 1948
10 Graubard, Stephen R. *British Labour and the Russian Revolution*. Cambridge, 1956
11 Gretton, R. H. *A Modern History of English People, 1880–1922*. London, 1930
A good description of social conditions during the war
12 Hirst, Francis W. *The Consequences of the War to Great Britain*. London, 1934. (Carnegie Endowment Series)
13 Hutt, Allen. *The Post-War History of the British Working Class* London, 1937. Introduction by Harold Laski
14 Lyman, Richard W. *The First Labour Government, 1924*. London, n.d. (1957).
Pretty good book
15 Marsh, David C. *The Changing Social Structure of England and Wales, 1871–1961*. Rev. ed. London, 1965.
16 Marwick, Arthur. *Britain in a Century of Total War*. London, 1968
An odd book. Padded bibliography
17 ——. *The Deluge, British Society and the First World War*. London, 1965
An attempt to measure the infinite

18 Masterman, C. F. G. *England After War*. London, 1922
19 Middlemas, Robert K. *The Clydesiders, A Left Wing Struggle for Parliamentary Power*. London, 1965
    Good book
20 Pelling, Henry. *The British Communist Party, A Historical Profile*. London, 1958
    Pretty thin
21 ——. *A Short History of the Labour Party*. London, 1961
22 Playne, Caroline E. *Britain Holds On, 1917, 1918*. London, 1933
    A useful assessment of public opinion drawn from newspapers
23 Richardson, H. W. *Economic Recovery in Britain 1932–39*. London, 1967
    Useful
24 Taylor, A. J. P. *English History, 1914–1945*. Oxford, 1965
25 Skidelsky, Robert. *Politicians and the Slump, the Labour Government of 1929–1931*. London, 1967
    First-class scholarship
26 Wilson, Trevor. *The Downfall of the Liberal Party, 1914–1935*. London, 1966
    Good analysis

Index